'THE NEW POET'
Novelty and Tradition
in Spenser's *Complaints*

LIVERPOOL ENGLISH TEXTS AND STUDIES

General editors: JONATHAN BATE and BERNARD BEATTY

This long-established series has a primary emphasis on close reading, critical exegesis and textual scholarship. Studies of a wide range of works are included, although the list has particular strengths in the Renaissance, and in Romanticism and its continuations.

Byron and the Limits of Fiction edited by Bernard Beatty and Vincent Newey. Volume 22. 1988. 304pp. ISBN 0-85323-026-9

Literature and Nationalism edited by Vincent Newey and Ann Thompson. Volume 23. 1991. 296pp. ISBN 0-85323-057-9

Reading Rochester edited by Edward Burns. Volume 24. 1995. 240pp. ISBN 0-85323-038-2 (cased) 0-85323-309-8 (paper)

Thomas Gray: Contemporary Essays edited by W. B. Hutchings and William Ruddick. Volume 25. 1993. 287pp. ISBN 0-85323-268-7

Nearly Too Much: The Poetry of J. H. Prynne by N. H. Reeve and Richard Kerridge. Volume 26. 1995. 224pp. ISBN 0-85323-840-5 (cased) 0-85323-850-2 (paper)

A Quest for Home: Reading Robert Southey by Christopher J. P. Smith. Volume 27. 1997. 256pp. ISBN 0-85323-511-2 (cased) 0-85323-521-X (paper)

Outcasts from Eden: Ideas of Landscape in British Poetry since 1945 by Edward Picot. Volume 28. 1997. 344pp. 0-85323-531-7 (cased) 0-85323-541-4 (paper)

The Plays of Lord Byron edited by Robert F. Gleckner and Bernard Beatty. Volume 29. 1997. 400pp. 0-85323-881-2 (cased) 0-85323-891-X (paper)

Sea-Mark: The Metaphorical Voyage, Spenser to Milton by Philip Edwards. Volume 30. 1997. 227pp. 0-85323-512-0 (cased) 0-85323-522-8 (paper)

'THE NEW POET'

Novelty and Tradition in Spenser's *Complaints*

RICHARD DANSON BROWN

LIVERPOOL UNIVERSITY PRESS

First published 1999 by
LIVERPOOL UNIVERSITY PRESS
Senate House, Abercromby Square, Liverpool L69 3BX

British Library Cataloguing-in-Publication Data
A British Library CIP Record is available for this book

ISBN 0-85323-803-0 cased
    0-85323-813-8 paper

Typeset by Northern Phototypesetting Co. Ltd, Bolton
Printed in Great Britain by
Bell and Bain Ltd, Glasgow

Contents

Acknowledgements   vii
Preface   viii
Abbreviations   x

Introduction   'Subject unto chaunge': Spenser's   1
Complaints and the New Poetry

PART ONE: THE TRANSLATIONS

Chapter One   'Clowdie teares':
Poetic and Doctrinal Tensions in *Virgils Gnat*   39

Chapter Two   Forming the 'first garland
of free Poësie' in France and England, 1558–91   63

PART TWO: THE MAJOR COMPLAINTS

Chapter Three   A 'goodlie bridge'
between the Old and the New: the Transformation
of Complaint in *The Ruines of Time*   99

Chapter Four   Poetry's 'liuing tongue'
in *The Teares of the Muses*   133

Chapter Five   Cracking the Nut?
Mother Hubberds Tale's Attack on Traditional Notions
of Poetic Value   169

Chapter Six   'Excellent device and wondrous slight':
Muiopotmos and Complaints' Poetics   213

Chapter Seven   'And leave this lamentable
plaint behinde': the New Poetry beyond the *Complaints*   255

Appendix   Urania-Astraea and '*Divine Elisa*' in
The Teares of the Muses (ll. 527–88)   271

Bibliography   275
Index   289

For Andrea Lyons

ACKNOWLEDGEMENTS

This book has been made possible through the support of Jacques Berthoud, Jean and Jonathan Brown and Andrea Lyons 'to whome', in Spenser's words, 'I acknowledge my selfe bounden, by manie singular favours and great graces'.

I would also like to thank other colleagues and students at the University of York: Graham Parry, John Roe, Mike Cordner, Geoff Wall, Jessica Aldis and Zoë Anderson for their enthusiasm and encouragement at various times in the process of this undertaking. At Oxford, Elizabeth Mackenzie and Nicholas Shrimpton first encouraged me as an undergraduate and have continued their support; Emrys Jones from the same university was courteous and informative in his reading of the work at an earlier stage.

I would like to acknowledge the vital moral and financial support given to me by other friends and family members: Barbara and David Jupe, Phil Barclay and Emma Robinson, Oliver Bond, Clare Jackson and Barney and Louise Quinn. Finally, I must thank the University Libraries of York and Newcastle upon Tyne.

PREFACE

This book is a modest monument to my ten year long enthusiasm for the poetry of Edmund Spenser. Though strictly a work of literary history, it necessarily embodies my sense of Spenser's aesthetic excellence; I hope that at the very least, these 'vaine labours of terrestriall wit' may encourage others to explore the diversity of Spenser's artistic achievements.

This study argues that Spenser's relationship to literary tradition is more complex than is usually thought. Through a detailed reading of the *Complaints*, I suggest that Spenser was a self-conscious innovator, whose gradual move away from traditional poetics is exhibited by these different texts. I suggest that the *Complaints* are a 'poetics in practice', which progress from traditional ideas of poetry to a new poetry which emerges through Spenser's transformation of traditional complaint.

The Introduction reviews scholarly reconstructions of the first publication of the *Complaints* volume in 1591, and investigates the traditional poetics and forms of complaint poetry available to Spenser. The study is then divided into two parts. Part One considers the translations included in *Complaints* as traditional texts which demonstrate Spenser's ability to replicate conventional complaint and his understanding of received notions of poetic meaning. In the Chapter 1 I read *Virgils Gnat* as at once a faithful translation of the pseudo-Virgilian *Culex*, and an autobiographical appropriation of its primary allegory, retaining a basic confidence in traditional theories of allegory. In Chapter 2, I argue that *Ruines of Rome* exhibits both Spenser's desire to emulate the achievements of Du Bellay in English, and his concern to differentiate his own poetry doctrinally from Du Bellay's troubling precedent.

Part Two explores the major, or Spenserian, *Complaints* as a development from these traditional positions to the innovative practice of *Mother Hubberds Tale* and *Muiopotmos*. In Chapter 3 I argue that *The Ruines of Time* is a self-consciously transitional text, which voices the tension between the humanist notion of literary immortality and Christian world-contempt, and transforms complaint into an interrogation of poetry itself. In Chapter 4 I see *The Teares of the Muses* as continuing *The Ruines of Time*'s debate between humanism and Christianity, but in a context of cultural change which puts both humanist and Christian ideas under pressure and envisages that the poetry represented by the complaining Muses may not recover its diminished prestige. In Chapter 5 I argue that *Mother Hubberds Tale* represents a radical break with the traditional fable form, articulating through complaint the narrator's social and poetic anxieties about the moral implications of the tale he rewrites: the poem no longer being tied to a didactic aesthetic, it achieves novelty through its troubled vision of a disunified world. In Chapter 6, I present *Muiopotmos* as an elegant demonstration of the ambiguity of the worlds of both artifice and mortality: like *Mother Hubberds Tale*, its fable self-consciously repudiates conventional didacticism in favour of a recognition of the arbitrariness of the mortal life.

Finally, Chapter 7 suggests that the process I have investigated in *Complaints* – in which a new poetry is created out of the perceived failure of traditional forms – can also be seen in the wider English poetry of the 1580s and 1590s.

ABBREVIATIONS

FQ   *The Faerie Queene* (Longmans Annotated English Poets), ed A. C. Hamilton (London: Longmans, 1977).

OED   *Oxford English Dictionary*

Var.   *The Works of Edmund Spenser: A Variorum Edition,* 10 vols, ed. E. A. Greenlaw *et al.* (Baltimore and London: Johns Hopkins University Press and the Oxford University Press, 1932-49).

YESP   *The Yale Edition of the Shorter Poems of Edmund Spenser,*ed. William A. Oram *et al.* (New Haven and London: Yale University Press, 1989).

All quotations from the Shorter Poems are from *YESP* unless otherwise indicated.

INTRODUCTION
'Subject unto chaunge':
Spenser's *Complaints* and the New Poetry

Poetic texts, like the human beings that make them, are themselves 'Subject unto chaunge'. Textual change can take many forms: from the rediscovery and re-evaluation of previously marginalized texts (and conversely the displacement and marginalization of previously classic texts), to the loss of distant classics or unpublished manuscripts. A static text – secure either in unexamined prestige or oblivion – is necessarily a dead one. Spenser's *Complaints*, though not as widely read as they deserve, have been generally overlooked since their first appearance in 1591 to the detriment of the understanding of Spenser's achievement. In recent years critical re-evaluation of *Complaints* has been evident both in numerous articles and books and in at least one new edition.[1] This edition signals one kind of change in the scholarly appreciation of the Spenser canon: where the *Variorum* edition (1947) calls the non-epic poetry *The Minor Poems*, the Yale edition (1989) uses the title *The Shorter Poems of Edmund Spenser*. Such editorial change aptly registers the more general change in the critical perception of the *Complaints* volume. In characterizing texts like *Complaints* and *Daphnaïda* as 'minor poems', earlier editors imply that they are a side show to the main attraction

---

1 See Bibliography for full details. For recent studies of Spenser which make use of the *Complaints*, see, for example, John D. Bernard, *Ceremonies of Innocence: Pastoralism in the Poetry of Edmund Spenser* (Cambridge: Cambridge University Press, 1989), pp. 106–22, and Richard Rambuss, *Spenser's Secret Career* (Cambridge: Cambridge University Press, 1993), pp.78–95. But also note Patrick Cheney, *Spenser's Famous Flight: A Renaissance Idea of a Literary Career* (Toronto: University of Toronto Press, 1993), who excludes the *Complaints* from his generic map of Spenser's career, and Douglas Brooks-Davies (ed.), *Selected Shorter Poems of Edmund Spenser* (London: Longmans, 1995), who, amazingly, excludes the *Complaints* altogether from his selection.

1

of *The Faerie Queene*.[2] Modern scholars no longer feel that a hierarchical categorization is appropriate: the *Complaints* are shorter than, not inferior to, Spenser's epic.[3] This is not to dispute the primacy of *The Faerie Queene* for the understanding of Spenser; but it does allow texts like *Complaints* to be read as serious (rather than 'minor') embodiments of his thinking.

This study argues that the *Complaints* volume is an important part of Spenser's oeuvre which has a vital bearing on both his conception of poetry and his innovation of traditional poetic modes. I begin by explaining the traditional contexts for this new poetry. The Introduction gives an overview of the bibliographical research into the *Complaints* volume, exploring the circumstances surrounding its first publication in 1591 and the extent of Spenser's involvement in its production. Then I outline my central argument: that the *Complaints* constitute a novel poetry, manifested both in the practical exploration of poetics and the transformation of traditional complaint. To contextualize the literary culture of the 1580s and 1590s, I discuss the poetics which were available to Spenser and the traditional forms of complaint poetry he would have been familiar with. In addition, I consider the mode of reading which I have used in this study to give a framework for the contemporary interpretation of the *Complaints*.

The *Complaints* volume

Although critical attitudes towards the *Complaints* poems have evolved, bibliographical understanding of the volume's first publication has remained relatively fixed. The prevailing view is represented

---

2 W. L. Renwick (ed.), *Complaints* (London: The Scholartis Press, 1928), p. 179, typifies this approach: 'It is not on these *Complaints* that Spenser's poetic reputation rests. None of his greatest things are here.'

3 Compare *YESP* Preface, p. xi: 'Nearly half a century of intensive Renaissance scholarship has had its effect, and we see the poems in a different light than did the editors of the *Variorum*'. YESP's editors do not, however, comment directly on the change of title.

by Harold Stein's *Studies in Spenser's Complaints* (1934). His research
indicates that the 1591 Quarto, *Complaints. Containing sundrie small
Poemes of the Worlds Vanitie.*, is an 'official' publication rather than a
printer's collation. Since *The Teares of the Muses, Mother Hubberds
Tale* and *Muiopotmos* have their own title pages, it can seem that the
1591 volume is simply 'a collection of pamphlets'.[4] Stein argues,
however, that the continuity of the volume's signatures and the fact
that its four title pages 'were set up one after another' from the same
type militates against this view.[5] The 1591 Quarto was printed as a
single collection, though its three texts with title pages could, in the-
ory at least, be separated from the rest of the volume. Such a proce-
dure would enable Spenser to give presentation copies of specific
texts to their respective dedicatees; while in the case of *Mother Hub-
berds Tale*, it would facilitate the poem's circulation after its official
suppression.[6]

Stein dates the volume's publication at some point between its
entry on the Stationer's Register on 29 December 1590, and H.
Cocke's purchase of a copy on 19 March 1590/91.[7] From this dating,
Stein argues that Ponsonby's preface, 'The Printer to the *Gentle
Reader*', is a protective blind for both the publisher and the poet.
Ponsonby makes clear the commercial motives which prompt the
publication, and the generic connections which unite its contents:

> Since my late setting foorth of the *Faerie Queene*, finding that
> it hath found a favorable passage amongst you; I have sithence
> endeavoured by all good meanes (for the better encrease of your
> delights,) to get into my handes suche smale Poemes of the

---

4 Harold Stein, *Studies in Spenser's Complaints* (New York: Oxford University
Press, 1934), p. 5.

5 *Ibid.*, pp. 6–8.

6 See Josephine Waters Bennett, 'A Bibliographical Note on *Mother Hubberds
Tale*', ELH, 4 (1937), pp. 60–61. This article shows from a 1596 account book that
despite its apparent suppression, the *Tale* was obtainable separately at an inflated
price.

7 Stein, *Studies in Spenser's Complaints*, pp. 10–12. The title page of H. Cocke's
copy is Stein's frontispiece.

same Authors; as I heard were disperst abroad in sundrie hands, and not easie to bee come by, by himselfe; some of them having bene diverslie imbeziled and purloyned from him, since his departure over Sea. Of the which I have by good meanes gathered togeather these fewe parcels present, which I have caused to be imprinted altogeather, for that they al seeme to containe like matter of argument in them: being all complaints and meditations of the worlds vanitie; verie grave and profitable. To which effect I understand that he besides wrote sundrie others … which when I can either by himselfe, or otherwise attaine too, I meane likewise for your favour sake to set foorth. In the meane time praying you gentlie to accept of these, and graciouslie to entertaine the new Poet. *I take leave.*

In Stein's view, the preface is firstly a disclaimer, a conventional formulation of the gentlemanly protocol: Ponsonby acts on Spenser's behalf as his literary agent, allowing 'the new Poet' to avoid explicit involvement in the commercial transaction of publication. The preface is also as a piece of disingenuousness through which Ponsonby and Spenser conceal their awareness of the political danger inherent in the attacks on Burghley made in *Mother Hubberds Tale* and *The Ruines of Time*. This political motive explains what Stein calls the 'striking inadequacy' of 'the description of the contents of the volume, a description which certainly does not cover *Mother Hubberds Tale*'.[8] So Spenser and Ponsonby are not being entirely honest about the volume they are 'setting foorth'. As we shall see, Ponsonby's remarks about the generic connections between the *Complaints* are not as inadequate as Stein believed they were.

Finally, Stein justifies the view that Spenser was involved in the publication of *Complaints* by proving firstly that he was in London at the beginning of 1591, and that he corrected copies of the volume as it was printed.[9] Though Ponsonby's preface suggests that at the time of publication, Spenser had departed 'over Sea', the dedication of *Daphnaïda* suggests otherwise. It is ambiguously dated 'London *this*

8 *Ibid.*, pp. 12–14.
9 *Ibid.*, pp. 16–24.

first of January. 1591'. Most authorities agree that this should be understood as a new-style dating: the *Daphnaïda* dedication places Spenser in London on 1 January 1590/91, and not on 1 January 1591/92.[10] If Spenser was in London in January 1590/91, he could have supervised the printing of *Complaints*. Confirmation of this conjecture is found in the variants in the 1591 Quarto. Stein distinguishes between variants produced by the mechanical working of Elizabethan presses (which produce minor changes in punctuation) and those which are literary emendations to the type.[11] It was the common practice of Elizabethan printers to allow writers to correct their texts as they were being printed. So in an uncorrected copy *Muiopotmos* l. 370 reads 'The which the *Lemnian* God did slily frame,'; a corrected copy has 'The which the *Lemnian* God framde craftilie,'.[12] The change is wholly literary: 'craftilie' satisfies the stanza's ottava rima scheme, while 'frame' does not.[13] As Stein observes, 'one cannot credit the printer with either the realization that corrections were desirable, or with the literary taste for making the corrections in a considerable number of variants where the original readings contain no positive errors'.[14] The examination of the text of 1591 leads to the inevitable conclusion that (Ponsonby notwithstanding) Spenser was centrally involved in the publication of *Complaints*.

Stein's view (or at least its representation in the *Variorum* edition) has recently come under attack from Jean R. Brink, who suggests that Ponsonby's preface should be taken at face value: *Complaints* is an

10 See Oram in *YESP*, p. 487; W. L. Renwick (ed.), *Daphnaïda and Other Poems* (London: The Scholartis Press, 1929), p. 175; and Helen Estabrook Sandison, 'Arthur Gorges, Spenser's Alcyon and Ralegh's Friend', *PMLA*, 43 (1928), pp. 645–74.

11 Stein, *Studies in Spenser's Complaints*, pp. 17–18.

12 *Ibid.*, pp. 18–20. See *Var.* VIII, p. 696, for a full collation of variants.

13 For a different kind of literary correction, see *The Teares of the Muses*, 1.549. The uncorrected quarto has 'And make a fruitfull Diapase of pleasures,'. In corrected copies, 'fruitfull' is changed to 'tunefull', which continues the musical metaphor of the stanza as a whole as well as giving a more plausible adjective for 'Diapase'. See *Var.* VIII, p. 692.

14 Stein, *Studies in Spenser's Complaints*, pp. 18–20.

unofficial publication because Spenser would not have sanctioned the publication of such politically dangerous pieces as *The Ruines of Time* and *Mother Hubberds Tale*.[15] Brink suggests that scholars have been wrong to argue that Spenser had any involvement in the publication of *Complaints*, and that the ordering of its contents is arbitrary. Though Brink's article is an energetic attack on Stein's hypothesis, as Rambuss notes, it throws up as many problems as it solves.[16] Notably, if Ponsonby was not acting for Spenser, the question must arise why Spenser continued to use him for his remaining publications?[17]

Stein's older though more plausible account of the 1591 Quarto has vital implications for the critical reading of the *Complaints* volume. Spenser's probable involvement in the publication suggests that its constituent texts should be approached, in Bond's words, as 'an integrated whole'.[18] This has not been the practice of modern scholars. Generally, subsequent writers have followed Stein in seeing the *Complaints* as 'a number of diverse and unrelated poems'[19] while acknowledging their common genres and themes.[20] Yet Ponsonby's preface states directly that the contents are unified by their 'like matter of argument' – they are 'all complaints and meditations of the worlds vanitie; verie grave and profitable'. If, as Stein argues,

15 Jean R. Brink, 'Who Fashioned Edmund Spenser? The Textual History of *Complaints*', *SP*, 83 (1991), pp. 153–68.

16 See Rambuss, *Spenser's Secret Career*, pp. 144–45.

17 After *The Shepheardes Calendar* (printed by Hugh Singleton), Spenser's poetry was published only by Ponsonby; after *Complaints*, this means *Daphnaïda* (1591), *Colin Clouts Come Home Againe* (1595), *Amoretti* (1595), the 1596 *Faerie Queene*, *Fowre Hymnes* (1596) and finally *Prothalamion* (1596). This is an impressive catalogue for a publisher who, if Brink is correct, must have earned Spenser's displeasure by his 'unofficial' publication of *Complaints*!

18 In *YESP*, p. 222.

19 Stein, *Studies in Spenser's Complaints*, p. 3.

20 The general trend in studies of the *Complaints* has been to approach the contents individually rather than as a group. See the Bibliography for details, and the footnotes in the ensuing chapters. Compare Renwick, *Complaints*, pp. 183–84; and Bond in *YESP*, pp. 217–22, for the suggestion that the volume is best approached as more than a collection of diverse poems.

Ponsonby was working under Spenser's direction,[21] this remark retains some authority as a reflection of authorial design, despite its perceived inadequacy as a description of *Mother Hubberds Tale*. Taken as a whole, Ponsonby's preface usefully signals a tension which I argue is present throughout the *Complaints*. On the one hand, he conceives of complaint as a traditional genre which is didactically 'profitable' to its readers. But on the other, the preface is a sales pitch which is predicated on the notion of Spenser as an innovator: the writer of *The Faerie Queene* is financially 'profitable' to Ponsonby in 1591 because he is 'the new Poet'. The tension between tradition and novelty, revealed both in the complaint genre and ideas of poetry, is visible in different ways throughout the *Complaints*. Though scholars have recognized that the volume's contents are related generically and thematically, this perception has not until now been adequately formulated. It is vital to the understanding of Spenser and the literary changes of the 1590s that it should be.

Complaints as a 'poetics in practice'

My central argument is that *Complaints* is a self-conscious collection of poems linked formally by their evocation (and eventual transformation) of traditional literary forms, and thematically by their concern with poetry and the rôle of the poet. The literary traditions evoked by the volume indicate the survival of the medieval poetic tradition in Spenser's work, the viability of which, as a Renaissance intel-

---

21 Stein, *Studies in Spenser's Complaints*, p. 4: 'it is highly probable that Ponsonby felt obligated to publish what Spenser wanted in the way Spenser wanted it. And it can be assumed that Spenser would have turned to another publisher if he had felt that Ponsonby was bringing out works that should not of have seen the light.' It is worth remembering in this context that Ponsonby was the 'official' (that is, approved by the Countess of Pembroke) publisher of Sidney's works; compare John Buxton, *Sir Philip Sidney and the English Renaissance* (London: Macmillan, 3rd ed., 1987), pp. 179–83.

lectual, he becomes forced to problematize. The *Complaints'* self-conscious 'like matter of argument' leads me to the formulation that the volume constitutes a 'poetics in practice'. This formula offers a new way of thinking about the connections between the *Complaints*. It is clear that the texts were written at different times in Spenser's life, and that there are significant differences between sonnet sequences of apocalyptic visions and complex beast fables. Yet as Ponsonby was the first to note, there is a basic congruence of perspective among these poems. Calling the *Complaints* a 'poetics in practice' is not meant to suggest that they constitute a unified exposition of a fixed aesthetic in the manner of Scaliger's *Poetics*, but rather, that they are a group of texts connected by their emerging, practical concern with issues of poetics. Read as a whole, the *Complaints* progress from traditional (or medieval) complaint to a more transitional (or unstable) form of complaint. This transformation of the complaint mode is mirrored by a thematic development from traditional notions of poetics to an innovative aesthetic which questions the truisms of conventional critical discourse. Describing *Complaints* as a 'poetics in practice' indicates that the volume is an organic unity in the sense that it is a collection unified by its designedly disparate elements.

In the main chapters I approach the poems both through their manipulation of the complaint mode and their preoccupation with the literary issues of poetry's cultural status and the poet's social rôle. The different *Complaints* present contrasting models of poetry and the poet. Poetry appears as a form of transcendent memorialization and as an inspired guarantor of social order. Yet its capacity to civilize its readers is fundamentally questioned, as is the virtue of its previously idealized practitioners. These conflicting yet co-existing accounts of poetry embody a tension within the volume (and hence within Spenser's thinking) between conventional and more radical ideas of poetry. The novelty and modernity of the *Complaints* volume stems from its self-conscious awareness that, to maintain its cultural pre-eminence, poetry can no longer rely on medieval and humanist traditions to sanction its worth.

In the process of making this break with the past, Spenser's 'poetics in practice' constitutes a new kind of poetry. In my reading, the

Complaints develop chronologically from juvenilia heavily steeped in the moralistic proscriptions of conventional aesthetics, to the poetry of the mature Spenser, which abandons these assumptions. The new poetry of *Complaints* replaces a mimesis which represents externally determined moral goals with a mimesis which represents the complexity of lived experience. In *Mother Hubberds Tale* and *Muiopotmos*, Spenser moves away from the abstract nouns which characterize conventional poetics towards the active verbs of experience. Within the *Complaints* volume, there's a progress from *The Visions of Petrarch*'s secure repudiation of the 'base world' to the *Tale*'s presentation of an ambivalent world in which the Fox is ultimately at liberty to 'flie' wherever he wants. The new poetry embodied by the *Complaints* volume constitutes a new way of thinking about how poetry relates to the external world. If Spenser's work is no longer determined by moralistic agendas, his poetry must increase in complexity to represent a world which it finds to be profoundly ambivalent.

But there is an important caveat that needs to be made at the outset. I am not claiming that Spenser is the first English poet to realize that there is a shortfall between the moral imperatives literary texts are supposed to inculcate and the reality those texts attempt to represent. Chaucer and Langland had made analogous discoveries two hundred years earlier. Chaucer in particular was highly alert to the discrepancies which necessarily exist between tale and moral. To cite but one example, *The Nun's Priest's Tale*'s apparent moral – 'Lo, swich it is for to be reccheles / And negligent, and truste on flatterye' – is immediately qualified by a further paragraph, which recycles Saint Paul's claim that 'al that writen is / To oure doctrine it is ywrite'. By intellectualizing the connection between tale and moral, the Nun's Priest archly raises the question of what is 'fruyt' and what 'chaf' in this particular tale. Is it simply 'a folye, / As of a fox, or of a cok and hen', a warning against flattery, a serious disquisition on dreams and predestination, or perhaps a comic amalgam of all these, and more?[22]

---

22 *The Nun's Priest's Tale*, ll. 3436–43. In *The Works of Geoffrey Chaucer*, ed. F. N. Robinson (London: Oxford University Press, 2nd ed., 1957), p. 205.

Chaucer refuses to say; the reader must make up his or her own mind.

Yet Chaucer's precedent, however powerful, does not foster any widespread discomfort with the notion of poetry as a moral medium in the fifteenth and early sixteenth centuries. As we shall see in Chapter 5, Chaucer's great Scottish disciple Robert Henryson is, despite his poetic subtlety, untroubled by the connection between tale and moral. Moreover, I am arguing that there is a specific, late-sixteenth-century English quality to Spenser's problematizing of didactic referral, substantively different from the analogous manoeuvres of his fourteenth-century predecessors. Spenser doesn't simply recover Chaucer's ironic sense of the distance between tale and moral; more tensely – more painfully indeed – he realizes through poetic practice the full implications of the Reformed understanding of original sin. In the words of the Thirty-Nine Articles of Religion (1571), original sin is 'the fault and corruption of every man' which 'in every person born into this world ... deserveth God's wrath and damnation':[23] it underlies all human experience, and combined with the Calvinist doctrine of Predestination (also central to the Articles) ultimately suggests the impossibility of making any meaningful temporal judgement. Only God has that power. This is a point to which I return throughout this book because it is pivotal to the understanding of *Complaints'* poetics. In sum, the growing power of the sixteenth-century conception of original sin changes the conceptual shape of human life – how actions are construed and how they can be represented artistically. Spenser's amoral 'poetics in practice' paradoxically enact the impact of this profoundly moral interpretation of human experience.

As a 'poetics in practice', *Complaints* stands on a cultural fault line between traditional poetics and a new, innovative mode of literary representation. This study casts a critical light on the conventional literary historical understanding of both the 'new' Elizabethan poetry and Spenser himself. The notion that a (or the) 'New Poetry' emerged in England during the 1580s and 1590s is a critical com-

---

23 Article IX, *The Book of Common Prayer*, p. 696. See also pp. 122–23 below.

monplace. Hallett Smith uses the phrase promiscuously to describe *The Shepheardes Calender*, the Ovidian poetry and the satire of the 1590s.[24] I use the idea of a 'new poetry' more specifically to describe the poetry which Spenser creates through his renovation of traditional complaint. I argue that he transforms the moralistic forms of traditional poetry into the self-conscious forms which support his 'new poetry' and raise questions of poetics. Spenser creates his 'new poetry' through his critical response to traditional poetry. In Chapter 7 I suggest, through the example of *Shakespeare's Sonnets*, that the wider Renaissance in English poetry in the 1590s should also be understood as a transformation of traditional poetic materials in a new cultural context. Instead of just stating that a new poetry emerged in the 1580s and 1590s, I attempt to explain how it emerged through the work of Spenser and Shakespeare.

Despite the vast growth in Spenser studies during the twentieth century, the outline view of his work has remained fairly clear: Spenser is an antiquarian nostalgist, hooked on reveries of an idealized golden age only recoverable in poetry. This view is repeated in many different guises. De Selincourt discerns in Spenser an urge to escape from the phenomenal world 'into the delightful land of his dream';[25] Judson similarly remarks, 'The past ... [Spenser] was prone to gild: he cherished the myth of Ovid's golden age, and liked to dwell on the bright and noble side of chivalry'.[26] This same conception can also be found in more recent work: Maclure bases his reading of *The Ruines of Time* on his perception of Spenser's 'centre of constitutional melancholy';[27] while in a more sophisticated context,

24 Hallett Smith, *Elizabethan Poetry: A Study in Conventions, Meaning and Expression* (Cambridge, Mass.: Harvard University Press, 1952), pp. 33, 103, 229–30.
25 In *The Poetical Works of Edmund Spenser*, ed. J. C. Smith and E. De Selincourt (London: Oxford University Press and Humphrey Milford, 1932), p. lxvii.
26 Alexander C. Judson, *The Life of Edmund Spenser* (Baltimore and London: The Johns Hopkins University Press, 1945), p. 211.
27 Millar Maclure, 'Spenser and the ruins of time', in *A Theatre for Spenserians*, ed. J. M. Kennedy and J. A. Reither (Toronto: University of Toronto Press, 1973), p. 11.

Bender argues that what he describes as Spenser's 'Neo-Gothic' treat-
ment of visual space is the result of the 'considerable vogue of Neo-
Medievalism at Elizabeth's court'.[28] Though used in different
contexts to support different kinds of study, the critical counter of
the 'nostalgic Spenser' has enjoyed a wide currency. Indeed, there is a
sense in which it has become an unexamined critical truism which
underlies Spenser studies.

This consensus leads to misconceptions of both Spenser himself
and the new English poetry of the 1580s and 1590s. In the case of
Spenser external indications have been taken as tokens of allegiance.
Spenser's interest in antiquarianism does not inevitably make him into
a nostalgist. Antiquarianism was becoming a prevailing intellectual
concern during Elizabeth's reign, and is symptomatic more of a grow-
ing consciousness of the English state and its antecedents than of a
commitment to the values of the past. Stow declares that writing *The
Survey of London* (1598) 'is a duty that I willingly owe to my native
mother and country, and an office that of right I hold myself bound in
love to bestow upon the politic body and members of the same'.[29] This
is not the language of nostalgia but of civic responsibility.[30] Similarly,
as I make clear in Part One, Spenser's archaic diction is paradoxically
a function of his readiness to make stylistic innovations rather than a
symptom of chronic conservatism. No new poetry can emerge outside
the context of traditional forms of writing. The fascination of the
Complaints volume is precisely that it shows Spenser in the process of
transforming the traditional poetic vocabulary he had inherited. So
the 'nostalgic Spenser' formula, and its allied conception of his poetry

28 John B. Bender, *Spenser and Literary Pictorialism* (Princeton: Princeton Uni-
versity Press, 1972), pp. 146–47.

29 John Stow, *The Survey of London*, ed. H.B. Wheatley; Introduction by Valerie
Pearl (London and Melbourne: Dent. Everyman's Library, 1912; rev. ed. 1987), p. xxv.

30 Compare the interchange between Eudoxus and Irenius in *A View of the Pre-
sent State of Ireland* preceding the discussion of Irish antiquities: 'all the Customes of
the Irishe which I haue often noted and Compared with that I haue redd woulde
minister occasion of a moste ample discourse of the firste originall of them and the
Antiquitye of that people … so as if it weare in the handlinge of some man of sounde
iudgement and plentifull readinge it woulde be moste pleasante and profitable',
1125–37. In *Var.* X, pp. 81–82.

as essentially backward-looking, are erroneous. The tag used by Ponsonby and E. K. – the mysterious annotator of *The Shepheardes Calender* – of 'the new Poet' is a more accurate description, validated by the *Complaints* volume's critical engagement with tradition.[31]

This approach to *Complaints* has implications for the understanding of the English poetry of the 1590s. There is no single explanation for the lateness of the Renaissance in England. *Complaints* demonstrates some of the reasons why it was hard for English intellectuals to embrace the new learning wholeheartedly much before the last quarter of the sixteenth century. The prestige and the influence of Middle English texts and forms lasted much longer in England than was the case in France, where the writers of the Pléiade defined their innovations against an avowed (if not actual) rejection of native traditions. Indeed, as we have seen, Chaucer – the 'Tityrus' of *The Shepheardes Calender* – partly anticipates Spenser's concern with the problems of poetic representation. Though as Colin Clout laments in the 'June' eclogue, 'The God of shepheardes *Tityrus* is dead' (line 81), Chaucer's poetic precedent is never 'dead' to Spenser.[32] Yet Chaucer remains culturally anomalous: his own innovative poetic does not wholly inform the work of his immediate successors. So the outward form of *Complaints* seems to be comprehensively traditional, indicating that a self-conscious rejection of tradition was not possible within English culture. The volume exemplifies the lengthy survival of the medieval tradition in English writing of the sixteenth century. The tension between traditional and innovatory impulses in *Complaints* shows in miniature the dependence of English Renaissance poetry on a medieval inheritance. The new poetry of the 1580s and 1590s can be seen as sharing in (and benefiting from) Spenser's predicament. The poet must 'make it new', but is only able to do so with the intellectual materials he has inherited. I suggest that the poetic innovations of the 1580s and 1590s emerge, like *Complaints*,

---

31 See E. K.'s 'Epistle' to *The Shepheardes Calender* for the first introduction of Spenser as 'the new Poete'. Patrick Cheney (*Spenser's Famous Flight*) also restores this title to Spenser.

32 Compare Alice S. Miskimin, *The Renaissance Chaucer* (New Haven: Yale University Press, 1975).

through the creative recycling and reinterpretation of the medieval tradition.

Finally, the *Complaints* volume's enactment of the tension between tradition and novelty can be seen as a reflection of wider social and intellectual changes in sixteenth-century England. In *Christianity in the West 1400–1700*, Bossy describes the Reformation as a translation from the stable text of traditional Christianity to the unstable (because of its plurality of doctrines and reinterpretations) texts of reformed Christianity.[33] The change in Western thinking between 1400 and 1700 can be seen as a 'transition from an ethics of solidarity to one of civility'.[34] The translation of Christianity encompasses a shift from a communal model of society and the relationship between God and His flock to what is eventually a more 'objective' or 'civil' model. In the process of this change, the reformers self-consciously attempted to reconstruct their different ideals of what Christianity should be. In England, this process was particularly protracted.[35] I argue that *Complaints* reflects this social and theological transition in two different ways: firstly, the traditional cast of the volume and its rendering of the tension between the old and the new effectively dramatizes wider intellectual debates. Like the English Church, *Complaints* is struggling towards modernity while retaining an ambivalent relationship with the forms and structures of the past. Secondly, and most importantly, the *Complaints* volume itself mirrors the shift away from the shared values characteristic of traditional Christianity towards the more uncertain values of the reformed Churches. Spenser's problematizing of traditional notions of didacticism in the major *Complaints*[36] is symptomatic of the reinterpretation of religious and social convention in

33 John Bossy, *Christianity in the West 1400–1700* (Oxford: Oxford University Press, 1985), p. 91.

34 *Ibid.*, p. 169.

35 See Patrick Collinson, *The Elizabethan Puritan Movement* (London: Jonathan Cape, 1967; rpt. Oxford: Clarendon, 1990).

36 This formula is used throughout the book to designate the volume's four major original poems: *The Ruines of Time*, *The Teares of the Muses*, *Mother Hubberds Tale*, and *Muiopotmos*.

sixteenth-century England. In the formation of its new poetics, *Complaints* reflects the wider transformation of contemporaneous European thought.

Complaints and Traditional Poetics

To understand the innovative poetics and poetry of the *Complaints*, we need to understand the kinds of theoretical poetics and models of complaint which were available to Spenser. Most sixteenth-century treatises on poetry were the product either of layman's enthusiasm or the initiative of individual poets.[37] As there were no professional writers in England much before the 1590s, so there were no professional critics until much later. The university syllabus was largely 'based on the learning of antiquity' in the form of rhetoric, logic and philosophy.[38] Though these disciplines were directly pertinent to the vernacular poetry of the sixteenth century, the point is that there was no institutional recognition of the subject we now call literature. 'Poetics' meaning 'That part of literary criticism that treats of poetry' is not recorded in English until 1727.[39] Sixteenth-century awareness of Aristotle's *Poetics* does not immediately anglicize this term – so Sidney states that 'Aristotle writes the Art of Poesy'.[40] Contemporaneous 'poetics' did not spring from either a philosophical interest in aesthetics or indeed academic requirements, but from such agendas as

37 See G. Gregory Smith (ed.), *Elizabethan Critical Essays*, 2 vols (Oxford: Oxford University Press, 1904).

38 Judson, *Life of Edmund Spenser*, p. 27.

39 *OED*, 'poetic' B.2.

40 In *Miscellaneous Prose of Sir Philip Sidney*, ed. Katherine Duncan-Jones and Jan Van Dorsten (Oxford: Clarendon, 1973), p. 109. Compare S. K. Heninger, Jr, *Sidney and Spenser: The Poet as Maker* (University Park and London: Pennsylvania State University Press, 1989), p. 60, for a discussion of the difference between the words 'poesy' and 'poetry' and their relation to the title of Sidney's treatise.

41 See the treatises of Gascoigne, Stanyhurst, Webbe in Smith, *Elizabethan Critical Essays*; and Derek Attridge, *Well-Weighed Syllables: Elizabethan Verse in Classical Metrics* (Cambridge: Cambridge University Press, 1974).

the perceived poverty of English metrics,[41] or the need to defend poetry from its detractors. In consequence, they vary in terms of outlook, approach, and profundity. In 1595 it would have been possible to read a great variety of printed texts that possessed some bearing on poetry. Within this group, the interested reader would have had to negotiate a course between such disparate works as Scaliger's encyclopaedic *Poetices libri septem* (1561), Webbe's impressionistic *Discourse of English Poetrie* (1586), Gentili's legal gloss, *Commentatio at L[egem] III C[odicis] de prof[essoribus] et med[icis]* (1593), and Sidney's concisely brilliant *Defence of Poetry* (1595). Despite their eclectic origins, these texts were unified by their view of the function poetry should perform.

The classic formulation of this view occurs in Horace's *Ars Poetica*:

> Poets would either profit, or delight,
> Or mixing sweet, and fit, teach life the right.[42]

For Horace and his numerous successors, poetry is a didactic art form which amalgamates aesthetic pleasure with moral precepts. In Horace's *exempla*, the mythical poets Orpheus and Amphion convey through their art a civilizing programme 'to abate / Wild ranging lusts; prescribe the marriage good; / Build towns, and carve the laws in leaves of wood'.[43] The Horatian model of the didactic poet underpins most subsequent poetics. So both Scaliger and Sidney structure their theories of imitation (or mimesis) around the truism that the end of poetry is 'to teach and delight'. Though Shepherd notes that the respective merits of profit and delight are alternately canvassed throughout medieval and Renaissance criticism 'in an interminable see-saw',[44] for both Scaliger and Sidney, there is no profound tension

---

42 Ben Jonson's translation, *Horace, of the Art of Poetry*, ll.477–78. In *The Complete Poems*, ed. George Parfitt (Harmondsworth: Penguin, 1975), p. 366. Compare Geoffrey Shepherd's introduction to his edition of Sidney's *Defence: An Apology for Poetry* pp. 66–69 (Manchester: Manchester University Press, 1965/1973), pp. 66–69.

43 Jonson, *Horace*, ll. 488–90.

44 Shepherd in Sidney, *Defence: An Apology for Poetry* pp. 66–69.

between the two categories. Aesthetic pleasure is essential, but sub-ordinate to the didactic demands of the poet's imitation.[45]

In sixteenth-century criticism, the Horatian dictum is linked with complex theories of literary representation. For Sidney, the defence of poetry as a didactic art form is rooted in the conception that it is 'an art of imitation, for so Aristotle termeth it in the word μίμσις – that is to say, a representing, counterfeiting, or figuring forth – to speak metaphorically, a speaking picture – with this end, to teach and delight'.[46] Sidney's definition is at once rhetorically magisterial and philosophically questionable. The Aristotelian conception of mime-sis is yoked to the Horatian dictum in an attempt to specify the lim-its of poetry's 'representing' and 'counterfeiting'. If poetry is a representation of either external reality,[47] or in Sidney's case the poet's idealized 'fore-conceit', it is not necessarily clear in what terms the

45 Compare Scaliger, 'Imitation is not the end of poetry, but is intermediate to the end. The end is the giving of instruction in pleasurable form, for poetry teaches, and does not simply amuse, as some used to think.' In *Select Translations from Scaliger's Poetics*, trans. F. M. Padelford (Yale Studies in English XXVI. New York: Henry Holt, 1905), p. 2; with Sidney, 'no learning is so good as that which teacheth and moveth to virtue ... none can both teach and move thereto so much as poetry'. In Sidney, *Defence* (1973), p. 102.

46 Sidney, *Miscellaneous Prose*, pp. 79–80. The punctuation and consequent interpretation of this paragraph has caused considerable controversy in recent years. A. Leigh DeNeef and S. K. Heninger Jr have argued that a full stop should be placed after 'metaphorically'. Such a reading furthers the claim that there is a fundamental relationship between mimesis and metaphor: DeNeef, for example, argues that this text means that 'Mimesis and metaphor thus imply and implicate each other', in *Spenser and the Motives of Metaphor* (Durham, NC: Duke University Press, 1982), p. 8 and n.6, p. 179. Similarly, Heninger (*Sidney and Spenser*, p. 287) argues that 'metaphor is a prominent means by which the poet may achieve the requisite mime-sis'. This has the effect of making a difficult text almost impossible. Van Dorsten, however, offers a comprehensive rejection of the textual speculation on which DeNeef and Heninger base their emendation. See Van Dorsten, 'How Not To Open the Sid-neian Text', Sidney Newsletter, 2.2. (1982), pp. 4–7. See also DeNeef, 'Opening and Closing the Sidneian Text', *Sidney Newsletter*, 2.1 (1981), pp. 3–6 and Heninger, *Touches of Sweet Harmony* (San Marino: Huntingdon Library, 1974), pp. 307ff.

47 See Erich Auerbach's seminal study, *Mimesis: The Representation of Reality in Western Literature*, trans. Willard R. Trask (Princeton: Princeton University Press, 1953).

poet's text will represent its substance. As we shall see in *Mother Hubberds Tale*, the poet's ability to represent and counterfeit can be turned to the 'end' of self-interest. Sidney's poetic is a strenuous attempt to reconcile the normative didactic goal of poetry with its ambiguous capacity for representation. In justifying the notion of the 'poet as maker', Sidney proclaims the power of the poet's 'invention'.

> Only the poet ... lifted up with the vigour of his own invention, doth grow in effect another nature, in making things either better than nature bringeth forth, or, quite anew, forms such as never were in nature, as the Heroes, Demigods, Cyclops, Chimeras, Furies, and such like: so as he goeth hand in hand with nature, not enclosed within the narrow warrant of her gifts, but freely ranging only within the zodiac of his own wit.[48]

Sidney magnificently achieves his goal of distinguishing the power and scope of poetry from that of those 'other sciences' which are 'subjected' to nature.[49] Yet he is treading on dangerous ground precisely because he is effectively endowing his poet with autonomous power 'within the zodiac of his own wit' and making him into something of a humanist 'Demigod'. Sidney aims to delimit the apparently excessive power he attributes to the poet's invention by making it clear firstly that external nature is fallen: it is a 'brazen' world in contrast with the 'golden' world 'deliver[ed]' by poets.[50] The poet's representation of another *idealized* nature is ultimately a means of reconciling man's 'infected will', which caused the fall, with his 'erected wit', which 'maketh us know what perfection is'.[51] The 'zodiac' of the poet's 'own wit' has clear Christian parameters. Secondly, Sidney argues that the poet's representation of ideal figures like Cyrus and Aeneas has the didactic goal of making the attentive reader imitate their behaviour:

---

48 Sidney, *Miscellaneous Prose*, p. 78.
49 *Ibid.*, pp. 77, 78.
50 *Ibid.* Compare Heninger, *Sidney and Spenser*, p. 298, for a similar reading of this passage.
51 Sidney, *Miscellaneous Prose*, p. 79.

Which delivering forth is not wholly imaginative ... but so far substantially it worketh, not only to make a Cyrus, which had been but a particular excellency as nature might have done, but to bestow a Cyrus on the world to make many Cyruses, if they will learn aright why and how that maker made him.[52]

Sidney controls the ambivalent notion of mimesis through a didactic psychology of reading. The poet's invention is pre-eminent because it constitutes the ideal mode of instruction. Literary texts (imitations) beget, or 'bestow', further patterns of virtue through the reader's secondary imitation of the poet's virtuous 'fore-conceit'. Sidney explains his theory more directly with the rhetorical question 'Who readeth Aeneas carrying old Anchises on his back, that wisheth not it were his fortune to perform so excellent an act?'[53] It does not seem to cross his mind that if this holds, a reader could theoretically be inspired by Sinon's 'False creeping craft and perjury' to attempt a similar deception.[54]

Yet as most readers discover, the *Defence* is the most attractive, intelligent and representative of the Elizabethan treatises on poetry. Nevertheless, it does not acknowledge either any uncertainties about literary mimesis, or any sense that it would be possible to conceive of a poetry other than one validated by its performance as a didactic vehicle. This is partly because it is constructed as an oration in defence of poetry. Since its critics allege that it is an immoral waste of time, Sidney counters with the view that poetry is a profitable and homogeneous art form. Yet the limitations of Sidney's didactic aesthetic are characteristic of most sixteenth-century poetics. At the furthest extreme from Sidney (and indeed his own earlier work) Sir John

---

52 *Ibid.*
53 *Ibid.*, p. 92.
54 Shakespeare, *The Rape of Lucrece*, l. 1517. In *The Poems*, ed. John Roe (Cambridge: Cambridge University Press, 1992), p. 215. Lucrece is a fascinating example of a fictional Elizabethan reader. Her tapestry is a visual representation of *Aeneid* II, in which she sees – rather than edifying images of virtue and heroism – an image of human dubiety in Sinon which reflects directly on her own tragic experience with Tarquin.

Harington's commentary on his translation of *Aeneid* VI (1604)[55] reveals the strong connections between humanist aesthetics and the medieval tradition of moralistic exegesis. Though he repeats the Horatian dictums that poetry is 'a speking picture' and a combination 'of proffyt as well as plesure',[56] Harington speaks of poetry as a reformed prodigal:

> ... they yt wold take away poetry are to be reprehended, and only to bee tawght how they may vse poetry to theyr benefyt and enstruccion.
>
> Allthowgh to speak trewly poetry ys no substanciall study, and geves but a weake nowryshment to vertuows desyres and ys rather a sawce to breed appetyte and take away loathsomnes, then a sownd food of ye mynde. and for my selfe that have spent to moche tyme in yt, I cowld lyken yt to a concubyn that a man in his fancy, in wyne and myrth, and wanton company, embraces and calls the Ioy of his lyfe, but retyred in his sober thowghts, and with his trew frends cold wysh they had been lesse acquaynted wth her and sooner left her ...[57]

Harington has practically become one of Sidney's 'poet-haters'.[58] Yet the interest of Harington's comments lies in his attempt to reconcile his repentant moral sense that 'poetry ys no substanciall study' with his latent humanism. He achieves this by invoking Augustine and the patristic tradition of allegorical reading. The 'concubyn' poetry can be put to 'vertuows accion' if the reader can 'winnow (as yt wear the chaffe from the Corne, the truth from the fable the veryty from the vanytye, and to lay vp in memory the good, and to let passe the yll matter'.[59] Both the conception and the metaphor can be traced back

---

55 Sir John Harington, *The Sixth Book of Virgil's Aeneid Translated and Commented on by Sir John Harington (1604)*, ed. Simon Cauchi (Oxford: Clarendon, 1991). This is the first edition of what had been thought to be a lost work; see pp. ix–xviii.

56 *Ibid.*, pp. 96, 98.

57 *Ibid.*, p. 96.

58 Sidney, *Miscellaneous Prose*, p. 99.

59 Harington, *Sixth Book of Virgil's Aeneid*, p. 98.

to Basil the Great and Augustine.[60] The latter's *De doctrina Christiana* argues in the context of the reading of the Bible that 'things which seem almost shameful to the inexperienced, whether simply spoken or actually performed either by the person of God or by men whose sanctity is commended to us, are all figurative, and their secrets are to be removed as kernels from the husk, as nourishment for charity'.[61] Harington follows the Augustinian method in arguing that, if approached allegorically, poetry will yield (in another metaphor) 'the pure nectar and honny' of moral instruction.[62] Harington's reassessment of poetry in fact repeats the allegorical exegesis he used in his earlier translation of *Orlando Furioso* (1591) which discerns five different levels of meaning in Ariosto's text.[63] Now it is clear that Sidneian mimesis and this allegorical poetics derive from different strands of traditional literary thought. Hume in particular has argued that Harington represents 'the "secret wisdom" tradition' in contrast to the Aristotelian–Horatian tradition represented by Sidney.[64] Yet the influences of Augustine and Horace are not mutually exclusive. Indeed, the value of Harington's crude volte-face is that it reveals baldly the moralizing foundations of sixteenth-century poetics. Though Sidney constructs a careful model of mimesis which avoids Haringtonian anxiety about poetic

60 *Ibid.*, p. 165.

61 *De doctrina Christiana* III,12. Quoted from *Chaucer: Sources and Backgrounds*, ed. Robert P. Miller (New York: Oxford University Press, 1977), p. 55. Compare Ernst R. Curtius, *European Literature and the Latin Middle Ages*, trans. Willard R. Trask (Bollingen Series XXVI. Princeton: Princeton University Press, 1953, new ed., 1990), p. 74. Curtius links Augustine's theory of reading with 'late antique Homeric and Virgilian allegoresis' and 'the Biblical allegoresis which had been accepted since Origen', and concludes that for Augustine 'an effort to unravel the hidden meaning is a wholesome and enjoyable intellectual activity.' Elsewhere (p. 136) he cites Alan of Lille's related 'alimentary metaphor', in which the Bible's different meanings are compared with the water, cheese and butter in milk. See also Russell Fraser, *The War Against Poetry* (Princeton: Princeton University Press, 1970), Chapter I, which discusses 'The Husk and the Kernel'.

62 Harington, *Sixth Book of Virgil's Aeneid*, p. 101. Cauchi traces this metaphor to Plutarch, p. 166.

63 *Ibid.*, pp. xliii–l for details.

64 Anthea Hume, *Edmund Spenser: Protestant Poet* (Cambridge: Cambridge University Press, 1984), p. 165.

meaning,[65] his case for the value of poetry remains – like Harington's – predicated on the notion of its didactic goal.

Spenser's most significant piece of surviving prose criticism,[66] the 'Letter to Ralegh' appended to the 1590 edition of *The Faerie Queene*, loosely describes his poem as an amalgam of Sidneian mimesis and allegorical method. Spenser explains that his poem is 'a continued Allegory, or darke conceit' in which 'The generall end ... is to fashion a gentleman or noble person in vertuous and gentle discipline'.[67] This 'end' is obtained through an 'historicall fiction', based around Prince Arthur in the manner of 'all the antique Poets historicall'.[68] Spenser advertises that his poem is grounded on a moralistic design and is executed both through an allegorical 'conceit' and the representation of ideal figures.[69] There is no more convincing demonstration of the coexistence of the Aristotelian and allegorical traditions in Elizabethan thought. The 'Letter' also shows that in prose, Spenser, like his contemporaries, conveys the prevailing conception of poetry as a didactic art form. Irrespective of their intellectual origins and conceptions of mimesis, Elizabethan poetics reinforce

65 Compare the first sentence of Harington's commentary: '*Yf I wear* to delyver my opinion *sencearly* whether more good or hurt come to the myndes and manners of yowng men by reeding Poets *I thinke I showld not dowbt* to say that *generally* the hurt wear greater then the good', in Harington, *Sixth Book of Virgil's Aeneid*, p. 95 (my italics). Harington's anxiety and ambivalence are graphically illustrated by the tentative and evasive means by which he articulates his negative judgement through the italicized phrases.

66 In the Argument to the 'October' eclogue, E. K. tantalizingly refers to Spenser's 'booke called the English Poete', which (despite E. K.'s promises) never saw the light of day. Though it is pointless to speculate what this text (if it existed) contained, I think it unlikely that Spenser (any more than Sidney or Harington) would have felt able to 'discourse' 'at large' of a poetics of instability.

67 *FQ*, p. 737.

68 *Ibid.*

69 *Ibid.* Spenser specifies that 'in the person of Prince Arthure I sette forth magnificence in particular, which vertue for that (according to Aristotle and the rest) it is the perfection of all the rest, and conteineth in it them all, therefore in the whole course I mention the deedes of Arthure applyable to that vertue, which I write of in that booke. But of the xii. other vertues, I make xii. other knightes the patrones, for the more variety of the history.'

Horace's dictum that poetry combines the pleasurable with the profitable.

But in the practice of writing less conspicuously public poems than *The Faerie Queene*, Spenser can articulate his uncertainties about traditional conceptions of poetry. The *Complaints* explore in practice anxieties which could not have been expressed in critical prose. The notion of a 'poetics in practice' helps to define the exploratory character of the volume's constituent poems, which is in sharp contrast to the more fixed ideas of Elizabethan treatises on poetry. In this view, the self-conscious practice of an innovative poet is in advance of its ancillary theoretical codification. Though Spenser undoubtedly drew on Sidney's aesthetic (as the 'Letter' demonstrates) he moves beyond the didactic territory mapped out in the *Defence* to a poetry which reflexively applies the complaint mode's traditional perception of the instability of the world to the status of poetry itself.

Spenser and the Tradition of Complaint

The second preliminary requirement for the study of the *Complaints* volume is an understanding of its relationship with the traditional poetry of complaint. As I have just indicated, complaint is crucial to Spenser's innovative poetics because of its central perception of the instability of the world and human accomplishments. Spenser suggests that if the world is unstable, then so is the means by which we make this perception intelligible. There are two kinds of instability which are pertinent to the study of *Complaints*. The first is the traditional matter of complaint poetry: the instability of the external world. The writer of complaint records his perception that the world 'fals is and vein, / Sithen that hise welthes ben uncertain' as an indisputable intuition into the 'way things are'.[70] As the same poem aptly puts it, 'It is rather to beleve the waveringe wind / Than the chaunge-

---

70 R. T. Davies (ed.), *Medieval English Lyrics: A Critical Anthology* (London: Faber and Faber, 1963; new edn, 1966), poem 83, pp. 173–75.

able world, that maketh men so blind'.[71] To 'trust in the world' is (in traditional complaint) to be subject to a species of intellectual blindness. The second kind of instability is Spenser's reflexive application of this view to poetry itself in the major *Complaints*. So *The Teares of the Muses* is based on the conceit that society has abandoned poetry, leaving the Muses to lament its death. In Spenser, complaint's traditional concern with the instability of the external world is transformed into a concern with the instability of poetry itself.

Traditional complaint has some claim to being an almost universal literary mode.[72] As such, it is unlikely to be the subject of a comprehensive analysis since stylized lament is a prominent feature of most European poetry. The medieval tradition of complaint is particularly complex. As Bond notes, Spenser could have been aware of Chaucer's experiments, love complaints, religious lyrics, as well as what Curtius calls the 'censure of the times'.[73] In this passage, Curtius describes the topic of inversion, in which the poet '"string[s] together impossibilities"' to highlight contemporary abuses.[74] For Bond, this kind of complaint is particularly close to the predominant mood of Spenser's *Complaints*. That is, the volume takes its initial stimulus from a literary mode which laments the fragility and inadequacy of

71 *Ibid.*

72 Because of its occurrence in such a wide range of texts and guises, I prefer to describe complaint as a mode rather than a genre. Compare Hugh Maclean's usefully flexible definition: '… in this essay the term "complaint" refers not merely to "a subcategory of reprobative literature during the Middle Ages and the Renaissance," but generally to plaintive poems, or plaintive passages within larger poems, expressing grief or lamentation for any variety of causes: unrequited love, the speaker's affairs, or the sorrows of the human condition.' Maclean, '"Restlesse anguish and unquiet paine": Spenser and the Complaint, 1579–1590', in *The Practical Vision: Essays in English Literature in Honour of Flora Roy*, ed. Jane Campbell and James Doyle (Waterloo, Canada: Wilfred Laurier University Press, 1978), p. 30. See also Rambuss, *Spenser's Secret Career*, pp. 85–87, for a valuable discussion of the complaint mode. Patrick Cheney *Spenser's Famous Flight*, pp. 3–4), suggestively describes complaint as 'a metagenre: a genre about genre'. My analysis of the *Complaints* volume will argue that for Spenser it becomes a genre instinctively preoccupied with the status and value of poetry.

73 Bond in *YESP*, p. 218.

74 Curtius, *European Literature*, pp. 94–98.

the sublunary world. I will argue, moreover, that there is a progression within the *Complaints* from this kind of traditional lament to the more complex representation of a problematic world.

Peter describes this basic form of 'censorious' complaint in *Complaint and Satire in Early English Literature*, advancing a plausible if idiosyncratic view of the mode's development.[75] Complaint emerges as a Christian compromise of Roman satire, eventually rendered obsolete by the creation of a new vernacular verse satire by writers like Donne, Marston and Hall in the 1590s.[76] This view depends on the questionable judgement that complaint is a second-rate form of satire: for Peter, complaint is a moralistic sub-art purveying Christian 'propaganda'.[77] Despite its exaggerations, Peter's work provides a workable definition of traditional complaint as a didactic mode which maintains a 'nostalgic' attitude to the past it laments in the face of a corrupt present.[78]

This potent combination of lament, nostalgia and instruction is well illustrated by the lyric quoted from above, 'Why is the world beloved, that fals is and vein'. This fifteenth-century poem is a loose translation of the eleventh- or twelfth-century Latin, 'Cur mundus militat', itself 'a classic expression of the theme of contempt for the world'.[79] It develops from a generalizing account of the world's instability (ll. 1–10) through an *ubi sunt* lament (ll. 13–24) into an admonitory warning that the values (and sins) of the world may prevent human beings from attaining 'Hevenriche blis' (ll. 27–40).[80] The text succinctly embodies Peter's description of traditional complaint as a moralizing and conservative literary mode. And yet, despite its transparency as a didactic vehicle, this poem (like many

75 John Peter, *Complaint and Satire in Early English Literature* (Oxford: Clarendon, 1956).

76 *Ibid.*, pp. 3–23, 125–26.

77 *Ibid.*, p. 55.

78 *Ibid.*, p. 68: 'The attitude to the past found in complaint is ... nostalgic. Just as the contemporary world is always represented as wicked the past is seen in terms of a lost felicity.'

79 Davies, *Medieval English Lyrics*, p. 339.

80 *Ibid.*

traditional complaints) remains a powerful and compact expression of the instability of human life. This is arguably why 'censorious' complaint remained such a popular literary mode. It articulates the basic truths of mortal instability in a memorable form.

It should not be surprising then that the complaint mode was extensively used in sixteenth-century English poetry. In addition to the Petrarchan love complaints of court poets like Wyatt and Surrey, complaint poetry of all kinds continued to flourish in English. Sidney, for example, focuses on 'censorious' complaint to the virtual exclusion of love complaint in his description of 'the lamenting Elegiac':

> which in a kind heart would move rather pity than blame; who bewails with the great philosopher Heraclitus, the weakness of mankind and the wretchedness of the world; who surely is to be praised, either for compassionate accompanying just causes of lamentations, or for rightly painting out how weak be the passions of woefulness.[81]

As Shepherd observes, Sidney's primary interest here is in 'reflective, moralizing verse', which we can gloss as traditional complaint.[82] For Sidney, complaint is justified by its moralizing reflections on 'the weakness of mankind and the wretchedness of the world', as well as its capacity 'for rightly painting out how weak be the passions of woefulness'. Shepherd plausibly takes this phrase as a glance at love poetry;[83] it also suggests in its painting metaphor that complaint can be seen as a form of mimetic representation. Nonetheless, Sidney's comment illustrates Peter's argument that the complaint tradition persists almost unchanged in sixteenth-century writing. Sidney expresses with a tinsel of neo-classicism the complaint mode's basic perception of the world's instability. Complaint is didactically effective because it excites both the reader's 'pity' and consciousness of the 'weakness' of human beings and their 'passions'.

Hence Sidney praises the *Mirror for Magistrates*, the most important Elizabethan complaint poetry before Spenser, as 'meetly furnished of

---

81 Sidney, *Miscellaneous Prose*, p. 95.
82 In Sidney, *An Apology for Poetry*, p. 187.
83 *Ibid.*

beautiful parts'.[84] Modern readers find it difficult to concur with this judgement. Yet as a collection of poems which combines the medieval 'fall of the princes' motif with political and moral advice, the *Mirror* can be seen as a realization of Sidney's didactic aesthetic. Its fluid text is formed as a sequence of monologues by historical figures which are linked by their writers' prose reflections.[85] As such, the *Mirror* continuously signposts its didactic intentions in prose and verse: in the link between the complaints of Lord Mowbray and Richard II a parenthesis reminds the reader of the writers' aim, 'to diswade from vice and exalte vertue'.[86] The poems themselves are structured around the conceit that the lives, and most importantly, the deaths of historical figures are exemplary demonstrations of the instability of human life and power. The 'mangled' figure of Richard II makes 'his mone' to a 'sely route' of onlookers, who see in him that 'the power, the pride, and riche aray / Of mighty rulers lightly fade away'.[87] Richard himself links this commonplace with the claim that his 'vicious story' can be used 'to make the living wise': although he was a bad ruler, current 'magistrates' can learn from his precedent not to despise 'Good counsayle, lawe, or vertue'.[88]

The *Mirror* shows that throughout the period of its revision and republication between 1559 and 1610, the complaint mode was being used traditionally in a popular and influential text sanctioned by no less an authority than Sidney. Spenser's transformation of complaint emerges out of a culture profoundly influenced by and receptive to the mode. Hallett Smith argues that there was 'a revival of the complaint form' during the 1590s,[89] beginning with Daniel's *The Complaint of Rosamond* (1592) and including Shakespeare's *The Rape of Lucrece*

84 Sidney, *Miscellaneous Prose*, p. 112.

85 See E. M. W. Tillyard, *Shakespeare's History Plays* (London: Chatto and Windus, 1944; rpt. Harmondsworth: Penguin, 1962), pp. 71–90, for a classic and highly sympathetic description of the *Mirror*. Roe in Shakespeare (*The Poems*, pp. 38–39) discusses the *Mirror* in relation to later Elizabethan complaint.

86 Geoffrey Bullough (ed.), *Narrative and Dramatic Sources of Shakespeare*, III (London and New York: Routledge and Kegan Paul and Columbia University Press, 1975), p. 419.

87 *Ibid.*, pp. 419–20.

88 *Ibid.*

89 Hallett Smith, *Elizabethan Poetry*, p. 103.

(1594). This was a specialized adaptation of the *Mirror* tradition, which records the complaints of seduced, raped and chaste women.[90]

I argue, however, that Spenser's *Complaints* are a more extensive renovation of the complaint mode. The contents progress from the exemplary complaint of the *Mirror* to the innovative explorations of the possibilities of complaint in texts like *The Teares of the Muses and Mother Hubberds Tale*. My work is therefore divided into two parts. Part One discusses *Virgils Gnat* and *Ruines of Rome* (which were in all probability early works) as transitional complaints in which Spenser adopts the mode as a means of articulating his own autobiographical grievances and literary ambitions through the translation of classic texts.[91] Part Two approaches the major *Complaints* as mature texts in which he uses complaint to explore specific problems in poetics.

Spenser's replication of traditional complaint is most clearly visible in the sonnet sequences he initially translated for Jan van der Noot's *A Theatre for Worldlings* (1569) as an adolescent and revised to include in the *Complaints* volume as *The Visions of Bellay* and *The Visions of Petrarch*. Though these poems are metrically subtler than much of the

90 *Ibid.*, pp. 104–26. Other 1590s complaints include Giles Fletcher the Elder's *Licia* (1593?); Drayton's *Piers Gaveston* (1593) and *Matilda* (1594) and *Willobie His Avisa* (1594). Smith's account of the complaint revival is notable for the fact that it makes no mention of Spenser's *Complaints*. Although only *The Ruines of Time* has any substantial connections with the form of the female complaint, it is to say the least likely that Spenser's innovative precedent had an influence on the practice of Daniel, Drayton and Shakespeare. The influence of *The Ruines of Time* on Shakespeare's *A Lover's Complaint* (1609) is at least well documented; see *The Sonnets and A Lover's Complaint*, ed. John Kerrigan (Harmondsworth: Viking, 1986), pp. 390–92; and Shakespeare, *The Poems*, pp. 64–65; and Kerrigan's useful critical anthology, *Motives of Woe: Shakespeare and 'Female Complaint'* (Oxford: Clarendon, 1991), which reprints *The Ruines of Time* alongside a broad range of 'Female Complaint' texts.

91 It will be noted that I do not directly discuss the various *Visions* which close the *Complaints* volume. These texts do however provide an important context for Spenser's work in the complaint mode which I examine here and in Chapter 2. The *Visions*, and significantly van der Noot's *Theatre*, have been more comprehensively examined by Jonathan Crewe, *Hidden Designs: The Critical Profession and Renaissance Literature* (New York and London: Methuen, 1986), pp. 94–116; and Carl J. Rasmussen, '"Quietnes of Minde": *A Theatre for Worldlings*', *SSt*, 1 (1980), pp. 3–27.

Mirror, their preoccupation with 'this tickle trustles state / Of vaine worlds glorie'[92] remains congruent with traditional complaint. In the *Theatre* van der Noot offers a didactic reading of the 'Epigrams', a version of Petrarch's visionary *Rime* 323, as an enactment of 'the poet's conversion from the world's vanities "to Godwarde"'.[93] Without the help of this commentary in the *Complaints* volume, Spenser changes his original twelve-line translations into full-scale sonnets with moralizing couplets.[94] The closing lines of the final vision, which in the *Theatre* read 'Alas in earth so nothing doth endure / But bitter grief that doth our hearts anoy',[95] in *Complaints* become:

> Alas, on earth so nothing doth endure,
> But bitter griefe and sorrowfull annoy:
>> Which make this life wretched and miserable,
>> Tossed with stormes of fortune variable.[96]

The additional couplet bears witness to Spenser's receptivity to traditional complaint. Mortal instability leads to the 'sorrowfull annoy' (a powerful improvement on the original phrasing) which comprehends that 'this life' is 'wretched and miserable' because of its dependence on 'fortune variable'. In *The Visions of Petrarch*'s final sonnet (original to Spenser) the complainant states his didactic conviction as earnestly as the writer of 'Cur mundus militat': we should 'Loath this base world, and thinke of heavens blis' in response to the poem's images of the world's instability.[97]

After the juvenilia of the *Visions*, Spenser subjects the complaint mode to more critical scrutiny. To recapitulate, I view the major

---

92 *The Visions of Petrarch*, ll. 85–86.

93 *Var.* VIII, p. 274.

94 'Epigrams' [1] and [3] were already fourteen-line poems; the impact of the revision is most apparent in *The Visions of Petrarch*, ll. 55–56, 69–70, 83–84.

95 'Epigrams' [6], ll. 11–12.

96 *The Visions of Petrarch*, ll. 81–84.

97 *The Visions of Petrarch*, l. 96. Compare Spenser's own Visions of the Worlds vanitie, ll. 163–68: 'ye, that read these ruines tragicall / Learne by their losse to love the low degree … For he that of himselfe is most secure, / Shall finde his state most fickle and unsure.'

Complaints as transformations of the complaint mode from a means of depicting the instability of the external world into a means of exploring the instability of poetry itself. *The Ruines of Time* begins as a lament for the Dudley-Sidney family and hence as a meditation on the evanescence of mortal endeavour, yet becomes a theological debate about poetry. Verlame's complaint urges that an 'eternizing' poetry can surmount death, whereas the 'tragicke Pageants' critically suggest that poetry is another instance of human 'vanitie and griefe of minde'. For Spenser, the writing of an elegy for Sidney becomes a wider debate about the function of poetry. Similarly, in *Mother Hubberds Tale* complaint highlights both the poetic capacities of the Fox and the Ape, and the instability of the narrator's humanist ideal of what poetry should be. In my reading, the *Complaints* volume is revealed as a progression from the traditional complaint of the *Visions* to the innovative use of complaint in the major poems.

A New Reading of the *Complaints*

This is a new approach both to Spenserian complaint and to the *Complaints* volume. Other writers have tended to pursue the idea of complaint in relation to the larger structures of *The Faerie Queene* and *The Shepheardes Calender*. Maclean draws a distinction between what he calls complaint 'as Christmas-tree ornament', or as a decorative end in itself, and the 'more challenging ... incorporation of complaint within larger structures'.[98] According to this view, Spenser progresses from 'early'[99] texts like *The Teares of the Muses* of free-standing[100] complaint, to more demanding texts like *Mother Hubberds Tale* and *The Shepheardes Calender* where the mode is used 'to illuminate character'; Maclean's real interest is in texts where 'the

98 Maclean, '"Restlesse anguish and unquiet paine"', p. 36.

99 Unlike Maclean, I date *The Teares* as a mature work. See Chapter 4, below.

100 This paraphrase reveals the inadequacy of Maclean's ornament metaphor. A real Christmas-tree ornament is a decorative addition to the larger whole of the tree; in texts like *The Teares* and the *Visions*, there is no larger structure (or tree) for the 'decoration' of complaint to adorn. Complaint is free-standing.

combination of complaint with other elements may properly be described as a concern for structural *articulation*'.[101]

I do not dispute the value of such an inquiry. Yet an exclusive concern with the aesthetic 'articulation' of complaint-within-narrative can obscure the connections between texts like *The Teares* and the *Tale* and the underlying issues at stake in the *Complaints* volume. I argue that the 1591 volume is a deliberate grouping of poems related through their shared employment of the complaint mode. This takes different forms – from 'free-standing' complaint in *Ruines of Rome* and *The Teares of the Muses*, to the inset complaints of *Virgils Gnat*, *Mother Hubberds Tale* and *Muiopotmos*. In all these cases, my primary concern is what Spenser is lamenting rather than how complaint is integrated within larger narrative structures. Read in this way, both *The Teares* and the *Tale* use complaint to articulate a loss of intellectual faith in poetry. Spenser's rerouting of traditional complaint to explore problems in poetics transforms complaint, creating a new, self-conscious form of poetry. My approach surveys Spenser's development from traditional to innovative complaint, seeking to align this change with his wider questioning of traditional ideas of poetic meaning in the major *Complaints*.

The idea that there is a development within the *Complaints* impacts on how the 1591 volume should be approached. I discuss the texts in a different sequence from that of the volume.[102] This sequence is not intended to be a reordering of the original Quarto: Spenser's involvement in this publication gives it primary authority. Yet its arrangement of contents was not necessarily designed to facilitate the understanding of Spenser's transformation of complaint, or his creation of a new poetry. The attraction of presenting the poems in a different sequence is twofold. Firstly, it enables us to divide the translations (in Part One) from the original poems (in Part Two). This means that the study progresses from texts which are exercises within traditional forms to new poems which creatively extend the boundaries of these forms – from a classical

---

101 *Ibid.*, p. 37; Maclean's italics.

102 For the original sequence, see below, p. 33. My sequence is: (Part One) *Virgils Gnat*, *Ruines of Rome*; (Part Two) *The Ruines of Time*, *The Teares of the Muses*, *Mother Hubberds Tale*, *Muiopotmos*.

miniature epic in *Virgils Gnat* to a Spenserian miniature in *Muiopotmos*. Though these poems are superficially alike, a large conceptual and practical distance separates them. Secondly, my sequence represents a speculative reconstruction of the poems' chronology.[103] Though specific evidence is necessarily scarce, the translations seem to be earlier work than the original poems. The division into two groups of poems reflects a biographical development which the 1591 sequence does not.

Yet my sequence is not a complete rearrangement of the 1591 text. After dividing translations and originals, each Part discusses the poems in the sequence in which they appear in the Quarto.[104] Given that the chronology of texts like *The Teares of the Muses* and *Mother Hubberds Tale* is difficult to establish with certainty, the outline sequence of the original volume is the best guide we have. In Part Two, a development from *The Ruines of Time* to *Muiopotmos* is both conceptually satisfying and biographically plausible.

The original sequence cannot simply be dismissed.[105] Though it clearly does not represent a chronological arrangement of texts, it can be seen as a characteristically artful piece of Spenserian design. In the original order, the poems are sequenced according to their dedicatees. By placing *Virgils Gnat* third in the volume, Spenser avoids having two consecutive poems dedicated to the Spencer sisters. *Virgils Gnat* separates *The Teares* (dedicated to Alice Spencer, Lady Strange) from the *Tale* (to Anne Spencer, Lady Compton and Mounteagle), just as the undedicated *Ruines of Rome* separates the *Tale* from *Muiopotmos* (to Elizabeth Spencer, Lady Carey). Similarly, *The Ruines of Time* (dedicated to Mary Sidney, Countess of Pembroke) is divided from *Virgils Gnat* (to the Earl of Leicester) by *The Teares*. Such a pattern would give the contents an interwoven effect, almost of a kind of sequenced rhyme between the Spencer and Dudley families as Spenser's patrons. Since these dedicated texts become interspersed

103 For detail, see the individual chapters.
104 So, for example, *The Ruines of Time* (first in the original sequence) is discussed before *The Teares* (second) in Part Two. Similarly in Part One, *Virgils Gnat* (third) is discussed before *Ruines of Rome* (fifth).
105 Compare Brink, 'Who Fashion Edmund Spenser?', pp. 165–68.

with the undedicated sequence of *Visions*, the contents of the 1591 volume can be diagrammatized as a rhymed stanza:

1 *The Ruines of Time.* (Dudley)
2 *The Teares of the Muses.* (Spencer)
3 *Virgils Gnat.* (Dudley)
4 *Mother Hubberds Tale.* (Spencer)
5 *Ruines of Rome.* (Undedicated)
6 *Muiopotmos.* (Spencer)
7 *Visions of the Worlds vanitie.* (Undedicated)
8 *The Visions of Bellay.* (Undedicated)
9 *The Visions of Petrarch.* (Undedicated)

I am nearly tempted to suggest that this 'stanza' arrangement is not far from the interweaving of actual rhymes in the Spenserian stanza. In the light of the priority given to patrons in the volume – and the Spencer sisters in particular, since it is their three texts which are dignified with separate title pages[106] – this decorous external arrangement may be the key to the organization of the 1591 *Complaints*.

A principle of interspersion also seems operative if we look at the sequence on purely literary grounds. *Ruines of Rome* is divided from its tailpiece, *The Visions of Bellay*, by *Muiopotmos* and *Visions of the Worlds vanitie*, disrupting the original integrity of *Les Antiquitez de Rome* and the 'Songe'. Similarly, *Ruines of Rome* separates the two beast fables, *Mother Hubberds Tale* and *Muiopotmos*. Only in the case of the first two poems, and the visionary coda of lament, does the volume place similar poems in sequence. This apparently perverse ordering can suggest valuable parallels. The appearance of *Virgils Gnat* between *The Teares* and the *Tale* can seem purely arbitrary: for this study, the connection between the crisis in poetry revealed by the usurped Muses and the *Tale*'s anxious narrator is a powerful one. Yet *Virgils Gnat*, despite its

---

106 These title pages are reprinted in both *YESP* and *Var*. VIII. Only the title page for *The Teares* omits prominent reference to its patron. Compare *Colin Clouts Come Home Againe*, ll. 485–583, where Colin praises the ladies Cynthia's court. Notably, Urania (the Countess of Pembroke) comes first as 'the highest'; while the Spencer sisters (under the names '*Phyllis, Charillis,* and sweet *Amaryllis*') receive the lengthiest panegyric (ll. 536–71).

own profound tensions, is nonetheless a pastoral narrative. As such, it is a change in tempo from the elegiac concerns of both *The Ruines of Time* and *The Teares*. As well as giving the reader a respite from the intense crises of the first two poems, *Virgils Gnat* widens the generic possibilities within the volume. By its incorporation of formal complaint into a pastoral and a narrative context, it initiates a more fluid idea of complaint. Though *Virgils Gnat* lacks the shared approach to the problem of traditional poetry of the *Tale* and *The Teares*, its casting of complaint into narrative is an important generic precedent for the *Tale*. The *Complaints* volume's interweaving of its contents can be seen both as an attractive aid to the reader's enjoyment, and as a way of suggesting correspondences between its different texts.

The final issue which I want to raise in this Introduction is the method of reading I employ. This is essentially a form of close reading: I attempt to present the separate poems as coherent wholes, which illuminate one another as components of a larger structure. As we have seen, this has not been the practice of previous critics. From the nineteenth century onwards, *Complaints* criticism has rested on the premise that these are 'inferior' poems, and has gone on to question their structural integrity.[107] Since the *Complaints* lack either the epic scale of *The Faerie Queene*, or the homogeneous design of *The Shepheardes Calender*, critics have complained of their flawed structure and posited hiatuses in their composition. Though some of this work has had the positive effect of stimulating critical interest in these texts, the bias in previous criticism has been towards using individual *Complaints* in the service of wider arguments about *The Faerie Queene*,[108] or indeed Spenser's biography.[109]

107 For older views of the *Complaints*, see *Var.* VIII, Appendices I, II, III, IV and V and also Renwick, *Complaints*, pp. 179–87.

108 Compare DeNeef, *Spencer and the Motives of Metaphor*, pp. 28–40, for this approach in relation to *The Ruines of Time*; and Harry Berger, Jr, 'The Prospect of Imagination: Spenser and the Limits of Poetry', *SEL*, I (1961), pp. 104–07, where the 'illustrative' text is *Mother Hubberds Tale*.

109 The classic instance of this approach is Edwin Greenlaw's *Studies in Spenser's Historical Allegory* (Baltimore: Johns Hopkins University Press, 1932; rpt. London: Frank Cass, 1967), pp. 104–32, which uses *Virgils Gnat* and *Mother Hubberds Tale* to reconstruct Spenser's diplomatic career.

It was as a means of counteracting these views that I approached the *Complaints* with the different premise that we should seek to understand them as they were published – as discrete units within a larger whole. My reading was initially an attempt to restore a sense of the *Complaints'* aesthetic value in their own terms, rather than as anticipations of *The Faerie Queene*. This became an important part of my argument. To transform traditional complaint is necessarily to heighten it aesthetically; similarly, a 'new poetry' based on this transformation must be demonstrably different from its forebears. So I suggest that Spenser's precise innovations – the specific ways in which he transformed English poetry – are best understood through this form of close reading.

But my close reading does not replicate the practice of the New Critics. The main reason why I use close reading is that Spenser's critical anxiety about poetry produces poetry: to understand his poetics (and his novelty) we must carefully explore these self-conscious poetic texts. If this 'poetics in practice' is now to achieve full transparency, the language acts of the individual poems must be read in detail. Secondly, close reading enables us to understand Spenser's transformation of the complaint mode. Language acts are made intelligible not only through grammatical rules, but also through their use and purpose; the purpose of these poems can only be recovered through close analysis of their handling of traditional genres. Finally, close reading reveals the poems' cultural context in the more general social and political life of Elizabethan England. This summary should not imply that the poems are approached schematically; these contexts enter the study variously and at various points. In brief, my close reading presents the *Complaints* as evolving parts of a complex whole, and not as socially and culturally insulated artefacts.

Close reading also enabled me to explore the conceptual (as opposed to the structural) fissures in Spenser's writing. As I have already argued, the questions Spenser poses about didactic art within the major *Complaints* were probably not ones which he could have formulated freely in prose discourse because of their subversion of conventional poetic preconceptions. A close reading of these poems must expose those moments when traditional ideas of poetry are evoked, and observe how they are treated. So *The Ruines of Time* ll. 344–455 and *Mother Hubberds Tale* ll. 760–70 are often cited as illustrations of Spenser's artistic credo. Contextualized reading of these passages indicates that they are conventional postures within larger units; these units in turn modify Spenser's assertions. It is possible to formulate the principles which govern my close reading of the *Complaints*. Firstly, the poems are approached as coherent wholes, themselves parts of a greater whole. Secondly, such close reading reveals that all the major poems are concerned with aesthetic issues in the shape of either poetry itself or the poet's social rôle. This developing intertextual concern is revealed in the 'fissures' (or tensions) both within the individual poems, and in the cumulative reading of the *Complaints* as a whole.

PART ONE
The Translations

CHAPTER ONE

'Clowdie teares':
Poetic and Doctrinal Tensions in *Virgil's Gnat*

This study explores 'the new Poet's' novelty: how his achievement is the result of his predicament. I argue that Spenser's work develops from traditional poetics to newer ideas of writing that reflect the uncertainties of a society in the process of rapid change. In my view, the *Complaints* reveal the tensions between literary tradition and novelty which eventually produce an innovative conception of poetry. Spenser's achievement in *Complaints* is to register his critical concern with poetry in such a way as to let the reader appreciate the conceptual change it was undergoing.

I begin with *Virgils Gnat* because it is probably the earliest of the *Complaints* (with the exception of the *Visions*), and because of the tensions it exhibits in the purpose and process of its translation of the pseudo-Virgilian *Culex*.[1] Spenser's purpose is avowedly more

---

1 The main evidence for the date of *Virgils Gnat*'s composition is the Dedicatory sonnet's heading. This states that the poem was 'Long since dedicated / *To the most noble and excellent Lord,* / the Earle of Leicester, late / deceased'. This statement seems to link the poem with the period 1579–80 when Spenser was employed by Leicester in some capacity before his departure for Ireland in the summer of 1580. Though Edwin Greenlaw (*Studies in Spenser's Historical Allegory* [Baltimore: The Johns Hopkins University Press, 1932; rpt. London: Frank Cass, 1967], pp. 104–32) uses the poem's probable composition at this time in his reconstruction of Spenser's rôle in the Alençon affair, there is no convincing reason to gloss the riddle of the sonnet through this event. Nonetheless, dating *Virgils Gnat* at some time in the late 1570s makes good stylistic and conceptual sense. There is some incidental support for this date in the fact that *The Faerie Queene* III.II.30–51 imitates the pseudo-Virgilian *Ciris*. If Bennett was right about the composition of the epic, Spenser may have been at work on two different pieces from the Virgilian appendix during the late 1570s and early 1580s. See Alexander Judson, *The Life of Edmund Spenser* (Baltimore and London: The Johns Hopkins University Press, 1945), pp. 54–72; *Var.* VIII, pp. 543–44, 571–80; and Josephine Waters Bennett, *The Evolution of* The Faerie Queene (Chicago: Chicago University Press, 1942).

than just to make an accurate translation. In the Dedicatory sonnet, he appropriates *Culex*'s primary allegory, claiming that 'this Gnatts complaint' is a 'clowdie' representation of his 'case' to the Earl of Leicester. But the sonnet is caught between Spenser's desire to disclose the general idea that his poem is a personal allegory, and his concern to withhold any particularized key to the meaning of that allegory. There is a tension in *Virgils Gnat*'s purpose between Spenser's political caution and his desire to proclaim his innocence. The sonnet also displays Spenser's initial understanding of traditional allegorical poetics, and his expectation that his reader will share such hermeneutic strategies. This traditional aesthetic is in turn in tension with the poem's innovatory translation of Latin hexameters in ottava rima stanzas.

In the process of translation, Spenser is involved in other agendas which are not raised in the Dedicatory sonnet. Though *Culex*'s allegorical defence of the court poet was directly congruent with Spenser's experience and ambitions in the late 1570s and early 1580s, its affirmation of the Roman state as the embodiment of civilization through a pagan theology is in direct conflict with the world view of an Elizabethan Protestant. This conflict leads to Spenser's partial medievalizing of the gnat's complaint. Spenser's manipulation of the complaint mode is already critical to his transformation of traditional poetry.

Culex in the Sixteenth Century

Despite modern scholars' rejection of its authenticity, during the Renaissance *Culex* was viewed as Virgil's first poem.[2] Its prestige is indicated by Bembo's edition of 1530, reprinted (with alterations) by

2 For the sixteenth-century view of *Culex*, see Bond in *YESP*, pp. 293–96. For the modern rejection of the poem's authenticity, see Virgil, *Works*, The Loeb Classical Library, 2 vols ed. and trans. H. R. Fairclough (Cambridge, Mass. and London: Harvard University Press and Heinemann, 1918; revised edn 1934), II, pp. 526–27; and W. F. Jackson Knight, *Roman Virgil* (revised edn Harmondsworth: Penguin, 1966), pp. 84–85.

Dumaeus in 1542. This was the text probably used by Spenser.[3] The English title unambiguously identifies *Culex* as Virgil's; for Spenser as for his contemporaries, the poem anticipates the themes of the *Aeneid* and supports the notion that Virgil's career develops from the 'juvenile' genre of pastoral (in the *Eclogues*) to the 'mature' genre of epic (in the *Aeneid*).[4] Suetonius asserted that Virgil was sixteen when he wrote *Culex*.[5] For sixteenth-century readers, then, the poet's promise to write an epic 'when the seasons yield' him 'their fruits in peace' (ll. 9–10),[6] underlines Virgil's precocious consciousness of the shape of his literary career.

As an unchallenged part of the Virgilian canon, *Culex* was a legitimate area for scholarly and poetic interest. William Lisle, writing in 1628, describes it as 'a little fragment of Virgil's excellence'; Spenser's translation creates an intimidating precedent for would-be translators of Virgil:

> it is not improbable that this very cause was it [the publication of *Virgils Gnat*], that made every man els very nice to meddle with any part of the Building which [Spenser] had begun, for feare to come short with disgrace of the pattern which hee had set before them.[7]

For Lisle the leap from *Culex* to the *Aeneid* is a logical development both for Virgil and his English translator. The problem he envisages is that later translators will not attain the standard set by Spenser.

---

3 See O. F. Emerson, 'Spenser's *Virgils Gnat*', *JEGP*, 17 (1918), pp. 94–118 and H. G. Lotspeich, 'Spenser's *Virgils Gnat* and its Latin Original', *ELH*, 2 (1935), pp. 235–41. *Var.* VIII, pp. 550–58, reprints the Dumaeus text.

4 See Helen Cooper, *Pastoral: Mediaeval into Renaissance* (Totawa, NJ: Rowman and Littlefield, 1977), pp. 130–31. Compare Spenser's direct use of these ideas in the 'October' eclogue in *The Shepheardes Calendar*.

5 See *YESP*, *loc. cit.*

6 Virgil, *Works*, II, pp. 370–403. All translations (other than Spenser's) are H. R. Fairclough's from this edition. But I have consulted the Dumaeus text when explicit comparison is needed between *Culex* and *Virgils Gnat*.

7 R. M. Cummings (ed.), *Spenser: The Critical Heritage* (London: Routledge and Kegan Paul, 1971), pp. 146–47. See also *YESP*, *loc. cit.* and *Var.* VIII, p. 545.

Contemporaneous readers must have been sensitive to *Culex* as a strange concoction of contrasting devices. The poem showcases a number of familiar pastoral topoi (praise of the shepherd's life; catalogues of trees and flowers) alongside miniature epic tropes (the combat with the serpent; the gnat's descent into the underworld and the description of the shipwrecked Greek navy). The first word of the Latin text, 'Lusimus', gives one kind of explanation: *Culex* is a piece of literary 'play', yoking unusual topoi together into a 'little fragment' which is apparently no more than a trifle designed to divert the young Augustus. Yet beneath its unorthodox appearance, the poem advances two serious allegories. Spenser's Dedicatory sonnet displays his sympathy with the first, while the tensions within his translation exhibit his familiarity with the second.

Reading *Culex*: Two Allegories

The primary, or Spenserian, allegory uses the narrative of the gnat and the shepherd to defend the rôle of the court poet. The preliminary address establishes a client relationship between 'Virgil'[8] and Octavius: 'Virgil's' poetry will glorify Octavius, and the Emperor will – implicitly at least – support his poet. The pastoral narrative of *Culex* indicates that the relationship between poets and patrons is not necessarily so ideal. Through the tale of the gnat rescuing the shepherd, 'Virgil' suggests a correspondence between the gnat and the shepherd and himself and the Emperor. Like the gnat, the court poet appears to be an insignificance, an irritant. But also like the gnat, the poet's interventions may safeguard the Emperor's best interests. The gnat's complaint is a miniature epic poem which both reminds the shepherd of the debt he owes the gnat, and demonstrates with impressive concision the literary powers of the poet. The implication of this allegory is that Octavius should pay attention to (and remunerate) his own insignificant poet.

---

8 I have used this typographical device to distinguish between the writer of *Culex* and Virgil himself. It is both useful and appropriate, since the *Culex* poet poses as the real Virgil.

For 'Virgil' the secondary allegory is a logical development on the first. Through his carefully modulated criticism of the shepherd the poet suggests that the cultivated Roman way of life is the ideal form of civilization. The shepherd initially inhabits a Golden Age (ll. 79–97). As the poem progresses, its fictional locus becomes more complex; in the catalogue of trees (ll. 109–47), 'Virgil' retells tragic myths and makes an important allusion to Ceres. Recalling that acorns were 'once given for man's sustenance before the grains of Ceres' (ll. 134–35), the text locates the Golden Age as an event which occurred in the distant past. The allusion indicates that despite his idyllic existence, the shepherd is (like the reader) a product of the iron age. Ovid's account in *Metamorphoses* V further explains that Ceres was the goddess who introduced agriculture: she was 'the first to turn the glebe with the hooked plowshare; she first gave corn and kindly sustenance to the world'.[9] For Ovid, agricultural labour, sponsored by Ceres, enables humanity to survive through its own efforts.

So the shepherd's idleness is suspect as well as idyllic. 'Virgil's' criticism of the shepherd accumulates through his encounter with the serpent (when he is almost killed through his 'care-free slumber')[10] and the gnat's complaint. This is effectively a poem within the larger structure of *Culex*. It aims to rouse the shepherd from inactivity through the reproach of the gnat's accusations (ll. 210–31; 372–84), and the warning that in the underworld vice is punished (ll. 231–58) and virtue rewarded (ll. 258–371).

This exemplary text also contains a political dimension. The gnat's catalogue of heroes in Elysium (ll. 295–371) is a contrastive presentation of Greek and Roman imperial power, implying the moral and military superiority of Rome. While Greek power reaches its apogee at Troy (ll. 304–10), from the Roman perspective of *Culex*, the sack of Troy can be seen as an act of piracy against Rome's ancestor. The gnat juxtaposes the wreckage of the Greek navy in the Hellespont after Troy (an illustration of 'human vicissitudes') with the Scipios'

9 Ovid, *Metamorphoses*, The Loeb Classical Library, 2 vols, ed. and trans. Frank Justus Miller (Cambridge, Mass. and London: Harvard University Press and Heinemann, 1916), I, pp. 262–63. Book V, ll. 341–42.

10 *Culex*, ll. 161–62.

'desolation' of Cartharge (the summit of 'Roman triumphs').[11] The
message is clear: while the Greek heroes were glorious, their heroism
was not underpinned by the civic idealism which characterizes the
Roman heroes (ll. 358–71).

The gnat's complaint offers a complex critique of the shepherd.
Not only is he oblivious to the gnat, he is unaware of the ethical
context of his own behaviour. When he makes a pastoral monu-
ment (ll. 385–414), the shepherd demonstrates his understanding
both of the gnat's rôle in his survival, and that cultivation is the
moral and religious basis of Roman civilization. His 'toil' mirrors
the heroic will of the Roman heroes which makes Rome into the
'glory of the mighty world' (l. 360). Through the gnat's suasive ora-
tory, the shepherd has become a Roman, whose subsequent behav-
iour typifies that of the virtuous pagan. He has begun to sow the
grains of Ceres. The image of the shepherd constructing the memo-
rial for the gnat draws together the two strands of allegory.
Through the monument, the patron recognizes his poet, and the
shepherd understands the virtues of Roman civilization. It is a
visual emblem of the resolution of both allegories.

Beyond its canonical prestige as 'a little fragment of Virgil's excel-
lence', *Culex* advances a Roman conception of human conduct sup-
ported by a pagan theology. Spenser's response to the poem is initially
conditioned by his sense that he can appropriate its primary allegory
for his own purposes. From this angle, *Virgils Gnat* is an important
stage in *Complaints'* poetics, exhibiting both Spenser's self-confi-
dence and his traditional conception of poetic meaning and com-
plaint. Yet his translation also displays an awareness of *Culex's*
secondary allegory. This presents him with political and technical
problems, especially in the second half of the poem. How should an
English Protestant translate the text of a Roman pagan? *Virgils Gnat*
is Spenser's attempt to resolve the tensions between his own world
and that of *Culex*.

11 *Culex*, ll. 339–40, 370–71.

Virgils Gnat: Spenser as a translator

Earlier commentators on *Virgils Gnat* dismissed it as 'a vague and
arbitrary paraphrase' of *Culex*.[12] Assuming that Spenser's text of *Culex*
(as well as the formal principles of his translation) were identical to
their own, they asserted that Spenser's 'version is in many places
wrong'.[13] Twentieth-century consideration of the text used by
Spenser has led to the conclusion that *Virgils Gnat* is a 'poetical para-
phrase' which accurately reports much of the Dumaeus text, while
embellishing the original to create 'a poem in its own right'.[14] Emer-
son and Lotspeich's primary concern was to identify Spenser's text
and show how far he diverged from the original. Their work inci-
dentally raises the question of what theoretical principles of transla-
tion Spenser used in *Virgils Gnat*.

At one level, Spenser's practice is congruent with that of Gavin
Douglas, who claimed of his *Eneados* (1513):

> For quha lyst note my versys, one by one,
> Sall fynd tharin hys [Virgil's] sentens euery deill,
> And al maste word by word, that wait I weill.[15]

As Bawcutt notes, Douglas alludes to the traditional dictum 'that one
should translate not word for word, but sense for sense ... As a trans-
lator, [Douglas] rejected the extremes of literalism yet tried to stay
close to his text.'[16] Similarly, the reader of *Virgils Gnat* will find much
of *Culex*'s 'word by word' meaning alongside a wealth of embellish-
ments that transform the poem into a typically Spenserian text.
However, *Virgils Gnat* is a very different kind of translation from

---

12 Warton in W. L. Renwick (ed.), *Complaints* (London: The Scholartis Press,
1928), p. 219.

13 Jortin in *Var.* VIII, p. 545.

14 See Emerson, 'Spenser's *Virgils* Gnat' and Lotspeich, 'Spenser's *Virgils*
Gnat'. Renwick, *Complaints*, pp. 220–25 and *Var.* VIII, pp. 334–49 also provide
detailed comparison between the two poems.

15 'Directioun', ll. 44–46. In Priscilla Bawcutt, *Gavin Douglas: A Critical Study*
(Edinburgh: Edinburgh University Press 1976), pp. 110–11.

16 *Ibid.*

Eneados chiefly because of the professed attitudes of the writers towards their work. Douglas tries to make a version of the *Aeneid* which will give his readers a full picture of the poem's literal meaning and the wider allegorical 'sentens' he believes it to be imbued with. He sees himself as primarily the vernacular servant of Virgil.[17] Spenser by contrast makes use of *Culex* to represent a private incident in literary code; he appropriates his original for his own purposes. Clearly there is a great conceptual distance between the translation of *Culex* and of the *Aeneid*; yet bearing in mind *Culex*'s then-authoritative status, the difference between Spenser and Douglas as translators is also one of self-image and cultural perception. Spenser is able to add to the medieval theory of translating sense rather than word the self-aware profile of an independent poet with the confidence to appropriate 'Virgil' for his own ends;[18] the sonnet to Leicester implicitly reveals the self-consciousness of a fully-fledged Renaissance poet.

As the example of Douglas demonstrates, the medieval academic tradition allowed a certain amount of deviation from the literal meaning of a text to provide a more expository, or 'sententious', translation. This tradition did not permit the fundamental reshaping of a text, or the altering of its meaning to suit the prejudices of its translator.[19] It is this freedom which Dryden claims in the Preface to *Sylvae* (1685). He argues that enlargements in his translations are justified on the principle of congruity between his thought and that of the original writer: 'if he were living, and an *Englishman*', Dryden's translations are texts 'such, as he wou'd probably have written'.[20] This

17 *Ibid.*, pp. 81–82.

18 Compare Jacques Peletier du Mans's analogous use of the French verb 'appropier' in describing his translation of Horace's *Ars Poetica* (1544) as an appropriation for the concerns of the emerging vernacular poetry: 'j'ai translaté cetui livre intitulé l'Art Poetique, et l'ai voulu approprier a icelle notre Poesie Francoise'. In Terence Cave, *The Cornucopian Text: Problems of Writing in the French Renaissance* (Oxford: Clarendon, 1979), p. 56. See also pp. 65–69 below.

19 See Bawcutt, *Gavin Douglas* pp. 81–82, for Douglas's objections to Caxton's loose translation of the *Aeneid*.

20 John Dryden, *Sylvae* (Menston and London: The Scolar Press, facsimile edn, 1973), sig. A 3. See also James Anderson Winn, *John Dryden and his World* (New Haven and London: Yale University Press, 1987), pp. 396–97.

psychological approach to translation simultaneously raises the status of the translator and allows him to repoint his original as he sees fit. *Virgils Gnat* stands squarely between the practice of *Eneados* and *Sylvae*. Spenser deviates from and embellishes *Culex*, but he cannot change it to suit his own prejudices. His appropriation of the primary Roman allegory does not involve any substantial alteration to *Culex*; rather, Spenser grafts his personal disclosure on top of an allegory already present in the original. The careful reader of *Virgils Gnat* must assess how Spenser appropriates *Culex*, and how it deals with the tensions of ideology between Imperial Rome and Elizabethan England.

Appropriating *Culex*: the sonnet to Leicester

Spenser's appropriation of *Culex* occurs in the sonnet of dedication to Leicester:

> Wrong'd, yet not daring to expresse my paine,
> To you (great Lord) the causer of my care,
> In clowdie teares my case I thus complaine
> Unto your selfe, that onely privie are:
> But if that any *Oedipus* unware
> Shall chaunce, through power of some divining spright,
> To reade the secrete of this riddle rare,
> And know the purporte of my evill plight,
> Let him rest pleased with his owne insight,
> Ne further seeke to glose upon the text:
> For griefe enough it is to grieved wight
> To feele his fault, and not be further vext.
> But what so by my selfe may not be showen,
> May by this Gnatts complaint be easily knowen. (ll. 1–14)

The power and fascination of the sonnet emerges partly out of its unusual structure – a strophic interlocking of the twin argumentative motifs of disclosure and withholding. Lines 1–4 and 13–14 *disclose* that *Virgils Gnat* is a representation of a quarrel between Spenser and

Leicester; while lines 5–12 warn the reader from prying too closely, and *withhold* 'the secrete of this riddle rare'.²¹ Disclosure and withholding are the formal pivot of the sonnet's meaning; the reader is simultaneously told the sonnet is an allegorical representation of the quarrel, and warned not 'to glose upon the text'. The sonnet is deliberately paradoxical: the reader must struggle to make sense of its contradictions, then read *Virgils Gnat* in the light of this perplexity. The problems posed by the sonnet only begin with the recognition of its paradoxical structure. Because of its content, the sonnet raises issues of critical and biographical interest which are habitually discussed separately.²² Yet its powerful gnomic utterance makes distinctions between autobiographical and intellectual content at best artificial. The sonnet's critical concerns are coeval with its articulation of 'secrete' grievances. Since a historically nuanced (and accurate) solution to the 'riddle' is now extremely unlikely, response to the sonnet must focus primarily on its articulation of critical ideas against the prominent background of its biographical context. And because the sonnet invites the reader to see the narrative as an allegorical representation of the poet/patron relationship, *Virgils Gnat* raises the issue of allegory in a way which the Latin text does not.

The sonnet firstly shows how Spenser deals with the primary allegory of *Culex*. By disclosing that the translation is a 'clowdie' representation of his 'case' to Leicester, and the identification of 'this Gnatts complaint' as the site of this expression, Spenser shows his awareness of the primary Roman allegory and presents himself as the typological descendant of the 'Virgil' of *Culex* in his relation to

21 Compare A. Leigh DeNeef, *Spenser and the Motives of Metaphor* (Durham, NC: Duke University Press, 1982), pp. 145, 152, who cites the sonnet in his discussion of the 'wise' or correct reading of *The Faerie Queene* envisaged by Spenser. See also Chapter 4 below, pp. 150–51.

22 See Greenlaw, *Studies in Spenser's Historical Allegory*, pp. 128–30, who discusses the sonnet's biographical content without reference to its critical concerns. For more discussion of the relationship between Spenser and Leicester, see Eleanor Rosenberg, *Leicester, Patron of Letters* (New York: Columbia University Press, 1955), pp. 338–48. Richard Rambuss, *Spenser's Secret Career* (Cambridge: Cambridge University Press, 1993), pp. 19–21, provides fresh conjecture about the riddle in the context of his analysis of Spenser's secretarial career.

Leicester.[23] This awareness reinvests the ancient text with potency by suggesting its contemporary relevance: 'insignificant' poets like 'Virgil' and now Spenser still need a means of communicating their value to their powerful patrons. This appropriation is symptomatic of Spenser's self-consciousness as a 'newe' poet, a poet of the Renaissance, sufficiently confident in his relation to the classics to present his own concerns as being on a par with 'Virgil's'.[24]

Yet the sonnet's autobiographical disclosure paradoxically transmits an intense idea of the anxiety attendant on such self-consciousness. While Spenser's recognition of 'this Gnatts complaint' as an independent rhetorical unit is important, the sonnet's overall tone gives no sense that he believed his poem could reconcile the quarrel between this poet and patron as it does fictionally in *Culex*. The sonnet is dominated by the heavy sense of the poet's grievance (ll. 1–4) combined with his consciousness of the hazards of direct disclosure of what is 'privie' between Leicester and himself. The sonnet makes the reader aware of the mournful irreducibility of Spenser's grievance. The impact of this self-presentation is to make *Virgils Gnat* a tensely self-conscious artefact invested not just with 'Virgil's' ideas about the status of the poet, but Spenser's reflexive anxieties. The sonnet internalizes the primary Roman allegory in such a way as to make the reader conscious of the social and political hazards at stake for Spenser. He is worried about disclosure since remonstrating with powerful patrons is necessarily fraught with difficulty;[25] yet because

23 This typology recalls the evocation of the *Aeneid* at the beginning of *The Faerie Queene* (Book 1, Proem) where Elizabeth and England stand for Spenser as Augustus and Rome stood for Virgil as the inspirations for, and objects of, his panegyric.

24 Compare David L. Miller, 'Spenser's Vocation, Spenser's Career', *ELH*, 50 (1983), pp. 210–12. Miller sees the sonnet as a revelation of 'the dynamics of textual and authorial self-presentation'. However, he views the primary allegory as a Spenserian creation and not as something already present in *Culex*.

25 Compare Spenser's first Letter to Harvey (published in 1580 and therefore possibly contemporaneous with *Virgils Gnat*) in which he displays a profound anxiety about his social relationship to 'his excellent Lordship' (Leicester) and the danger of 'ouer-much cloying their noble eares' with dedications and, implicitly, pleas for support. In *Var.* X, p. 5.

of the nature of the poem and its primary allegorical meaning – and possibly the circumstances of its original composition – he cannot simply relinquish its autobiographical encoding. Printing the sonnet along with *Virgils Gnat* indicates Spenser's sense of the poem's value as an appropriation, not merely as a 'safe' translation.

As a result of this self-conscious revelation, the sonnet clarifies Spenser's understanding of poetic meaning in *Virgils Gnat*. It expresses a traditional conception of allegorical interpretation; as the couplet puts it, 'what so by my self may not be showen, / May by this Gnatts complaint be easily known' – what Spenser cannot say directly about his relationship with Leicester can be garnered 'easily' from an allegorical reading of the complaint. Decoding the gnat's complaint is a simple task: Spenser assumes his readers are adept allegorizers who can 'easily' apply the hint about Leicester to their reading of the poem. Paradoxically for a text so anxious about the pitfalls of interpretation, Spenser's idea of reading strongly evokes medieval allegoresis. While traditional notions of allegory are present in *Virgils Gnat*, the tense self-conscious voicing of the disclosure indicates that these traditions do not facilitate a correspondingly 'easy' resolution to Spenser's perplexity. Although few readers have had much trouble seeing the general applicability of *Culex*'s allegory of 'Virgil' and Octavius to Spenser and Leicester, no historicized reading of the poem has solved the sonnet's 'riddle rare'.[26]

The sonnet establishes that *Virgils Gnat* is to be read as an allegory of a quarrel between Spenser and Leicester. To understand this typology, readers of *Culex* do not need to make any radical reinterpretations of the original since Spenser's allegory is a logical extension of what was always present in *Culex*. Spenser's appropriation is also a valuable indication of his approach to the translation. Firstly, it shows his self-consciousness, manifested simultaneously in the confident adaptation of a classic to his own purposes and his concomitant anxiety about how his disclosure will be read. Secondly, by directly rais-

---

26 Compare Greenlaw, *Studies in Spenser's Historical Allegory*, pp. 124–32, with Harold Stein, *Studies in Spenser's Complaints* (New York: Oxford University Press, 1934), pp. 75–77. See also *Var.* VIII, pp. 543–44.

ing the idea of allegory, the sonnet reveals the traditional nature of
Spenser's conception of allegory at this point in *Complaints*. Yet there
is already a discernible tension within Spenser's thinking about
poetry. He presents himself as a self-conscious poet aware of the
ambiguities of his rôle and his work, indicating a novelty of
approach; yet he relies on traditional modes of reading familiar to less
assuming 'clerks' like Douglas.

The sonnet makes no reference to the secondary Roman allegory.
In the context of the sonnet, this is no surprise: it stands in place of
a prose dedication to 'the most noble and excellent lord' and informs
the reader of the poem's covert meanings. However, the paradise of
reconciliation in the original poem is the result of a subtle combina-
tion of two allegories: the affirmation of the Roman Empire is a prod-
uct of 'Virgil's' plea for recognition. How then does Spenser deal with
the affirmation of the Roman Empire in his translation?

Spenser and the secondary allegory of *Culex*

As will be seen in the next chapter, Spenser's conception of Rome was
ambiguous and problematic. As a protestant intellectual, his political
attitude was conditioned by the polemical view of Rome as the
Whore of Babylon; the Visions from Revelation he translated for van
der Noot's *A Theatre for Worldlings* (1569) equate the 'Woman sitting
on a beast' with the political and administrative centre of Catholi-
cism.[27] As Hume argues, Spenser's anti-Catholicism (and hence anti-
Romanism) is constant throughout his work,[28] as long as Rome is
identified with Catholicism. *Culex* provokes other responses to the

---

27 *Sonets* [13] ('Visions from Revelation' [2] in *Var.* VIII). As Schell notes, in
YESP, p. 482, 'Babylon is code for Rome (in Revelation) and the Roman church (in
sixteenth-century English protestant polemic)'.

28 Anthea Hume, *Edmund Spenser: Protestant Poet* (Cambridge: Cambridge
University Press, 1984), pp. 1, 93. See Christopher Hill, *The English Bible and the
Seventeenth Century Revolution* (Harmondsworth: Allen Lane, 1993), p. 317, for the
anti-Catholicism of Spenser and other poets.

idea of Rome. Spenser's problem is that in addition to the polemical view of Catholic Rome, he must recognize that Imperial Rome nurtured humane culture. In this context, Sir John Harington's commentary to his translation of *Aeneid* VI (1604) is pertinent.[29] Harington's remarks illustrate that, in spite of humanist admiration for Virgil, political and theological hostility to Catholic Rome could easily be transferred to the Empire. Harington views Rome's rise and fall as a compelling instance of lapsarian 'pryde and presumption'.[30] In translating *Culex*, Spenser is confronted by a poem which embodies a view of Rome that is antithetical to his own.

Spenser did not fundamentally re-jig *Culex* to make *Virgils Gnat* more distinctively his own poem, or a poem embodying English protestant values. The differences between the two poems are largely unconscious testimonies to the cultural distance which separates Spenser from 'Virgil'. As such, the tension between the two poets' conceptions of Rome emerges in the minutiae of the translation. Many of the differences between the two texts consist of Spenserian embellishment and clarification of obscure or ambiguous passages in the Latin. In lines 137–40, Spenser inserts a singular 'God': while the Latin shepherd is 'victu contentus abundet' ('content with any fare'), his English counterpart is 'Content with any food that God doth send'. The singular deity slips easily into *Virgils Gnat* and equips Spenser's shepherd with an instinctive Christian piety. This detail is illustrative of Spenser's general procedure: he makes unconscious emendations which register his different systems of belief.[31]

So *Virgils Gnat* adjusts the secondary Roman allegory mainly through minor emendations and embellishments. But these fall short of a complete Christianization of *Culex*. In its final third, Spenser's version incorporates a medieval style of complaint which both indi-

29 Sir John Harington, *The Sixth Book of Virgil's Aeneid Translated and Commented on by Sir John Harington (1604)*, ed. Simon Cauchi (Oxford: Clarendon, 1991), pp. 90–95.

30 *Ibid.*, p. 95.

31 Compare also *Culex*, ll. 193–94 (Dumaeus text) with *Virgils Gnat*, ll. 300–04 for an example of Spenser shifting gears from the neutral 'What God' (i.e. 'what god among many') to the emphatic singular 'God' in the next line.

cates his reservations about the pagan heroism praised in *Culex*, and diminishes its closing image of reconciliation. 'Virgil's' description of the wreckage of the Greek is followed by a brief, moralizing comment, which Spenser expands into a whole stanza:

> Illa uices hominum testata est copia quondam,
> Ne quisquam propriae fortunae munere diues
> Iret ineuectus coelum super. omne propinquo
> Frangitur inuidiae telo decus, ... [32]

> Well may appeare by proofe of their mischaunce,
> The chaungefull turning of mens slipperie state,
> That none, whom fortune freely doth advaunce,
> Himselfe therefore to heaven should elevate:
> For loftie type of honour through the glaunce
> Of envies dart, is downe in dust prostrate;
> And all that vaunts in worldly vanitie,
> Shall fall through fortunes mutabilitie. (ll.553–60)

The English not only amplifies the Latin, but transforms its tone. In *Culex*, the 'force' of the destruction of the Greek navy is a 'witness' ('testata') to 'human vicissitudes' and a warning against presumption. For 'Virgil', the comment is a bridge between the heroic but flawed Greeks and their ideal successors: the Romans. In *Virgils Gnat* the comment has much greater prominence, initiating a full-scale attack on hubris. The perspective is reminiscent of the didactic strategy of *The Mirror for Magistrates*, in which pride is the basis of moral and political misjudgement. The 'mischaunce' of the storm on the Hellespont is illustrative, in a wonderfully orotund Spenserian line, of 'The chaungefull turning of mens slipperie state'. The rest of the stanza develops this line of thought with comparable gusto, concluding with the emphatic statement typical of traditional moralistic literature that 'all that vaunts in worldly vanitie, / Shall fall through fortunes mutabilitie'. This moralizing style recalls the vocabulary of

---

32 *Culex*, ll. 339–42: 'That force bore witness in its time to human vicissitudes, lest anyone, enriched by his own Fortune's bounty, should mount exalted above the heavens: all glory is shattered by Envy's nigh-awaiting dart'.

traditional complaint; in Churchyard's 'The Two Mortimers' from *The Mirror for Magistrates*, the final stanza instructs the reader to:

> Se here the staye of fortunate estate,
> The vayne assurance of this britell lyfe,
> For I but yong, proclaymed prince of late,
> Right fortunate in children and in wife,
> Lost all at once by stroke of bloody knife:
> Wherby assurde let men them selues assure,
> That welth and lyfe are doubtfull to endure.[33]

The connections between these stanzas are clear enough. In each case, disaster demonstrates the 'mutabilitie' of human life. But Spenser's employment of this tradition is different from Churchyard's: he neither reproduces the dispassionate tone of the comment in *Culex*, nor fully adopts Mortimer's world-weariness. His stanza communicates an energetic enjoyment of the spectacle it moralizes.[34] The passage in *Culex* gives Spenser the opportunity to develop a traditional topos, which in turn enables him to expatiate (before the catalogue of Roman heroes four stanzas later) on the universality of hubris. By making this emphatic statement at this point in the gnat's complaint, Spenser undercuts *Culex*'s affirmation of the Roman ideal by linking pre-Christian heroism to the medieval interpretation of pride.[35] This embellishment of the original makes *Virgils Gnat* more equivocal in its approach to the affirmation of Rome; Spenser problematizes the secondary allegory through his assimilation of the tropes and values of medieval complaint into the gnat's text.

So while the ending of *Virgils Gnat* is consistent with the rest of the translation, it lacks the harmonization of the close of *Culex*.

---

33 'Howe the two Rogers, surnamed Mortimers, for theyr sundry vices ended theyr lyues vnfortunatelye', ll. 141–47. In *The Mirror for Magistrates*, ed. Lily B. Campbell (Cambridge: Cambridge University Press, 1938, rpt. 1960), p. 89.

34 The same effect is evident in lines 577–84, which are largely improvised from the original.

35 Elsewhere in *Complaints*, Spenser uses similar materials to suggest a different outcome, as in the description of the importunate humanist in *The Ruines of Time*, ll. 421–27. See Chapter 3 below, pp. 122–23.

There, the shepherd's construction of the pastoral monument unites the two allegories: the patron recognizes his poet, while the shepherd himself becomes a true Roman. Since Spenser does not engage the secondary allegory, the closure in *Virgils Gnat* remains incomplete, overshadowed by the Dedicatory sonnet.

Virgils Gnat translates the close of *Culex* with the same degree of accuracy and embellishment as the rest of the poem; apart from the passage on hubris, it is not a psychological paraphrase.[36] Since Spenser was not able to justify theoretically a wholesale rewrite of *Culex*, his poem must follow the lead of its model. Because he cannot substitute a Protestant allegory in place of 'Virgil's' Augustan panegyric,[37] the close of *Virgils Gnat* refocuses attention on the sonnet's intimation of the incompletion of the relationship between Spenser and Leicester. The poem's publication two-and-a-half years after Leicester's death impoverishes the reconciliation explicit in the original text.[38] This is especially clear when *Virgils Gnat* is read in conjunction with *The Ruines of Time*, ll. 184–238, where Verlame attacks Spenser (in his pastoral persona, Colin Clout) for his neglect of Leicester's posthumous fame. That *Virgils Gnat* was 'long since dedicated' to the 'late deceased' Leicester intensifies the sense of an irretrievable breakdown of the relationship between poet and patron.

To summarize, *Virgils Gnat* exhibits tensions between Spenser's perception of Rome and 'Virgil's'. Though Spenser provides a recognizable version of the Dumaeus *Culex*, his poem shows his cautious response to a pagan text. *Virgils Gnat* falls between autobiographical appropriation and ideological uncertainty.

---

36 See Emerson, 'Spenser's *Virgils Gnat*' pp. 114–18.

37 Compare with *The Ruines of Time*, ll. 680–86, where Spenser consoles Leicester's niece, the Countess of Pembroke, with the anti-materialism of radical Protestantism.

38 Leicester died on 4 September 1588, while *Complaints* appeared between 29 December 1590 and 19 March 1590/91. See Introduction above, pp. 3–5; Stein, *Studies in Spenser's Complaints*, pp. 10–11; and Milton Waldman, *Elizabeth and Leicester* (London: Collins, rpt. The Reprint Society, 1946), p. 215.

Technical innovation: the form of *Virgils Gnat*

But *Virgils Gnat* is not just a troubled encounter between Eliza-
bethan England and Augustan Rome. As a translation of a Latin
classic, the poem enacts Spenser's ambition to create a new vernac-
ular literature in English which can equal the achievements of
Greece and Rome.[39] Though the Dedicatory sonnet displays
Spenser's confidence in traditional allegorical poetics, the stanzaic
form of his translation constitutes a technical innovation, angliciz-
ing *Culex* by means of a fashionable verse form imported from the
Italian Renaissance.

Ottava rima had been used previously in English by Sir Thomas
Wyatt, but not at such length and not to translate hexameters. Its
appearance here and in *Muiopotmos* indicates Spenser's absorption of
a modish continental form previously used by Ariosto, Tasso and
Camões; it can be seen as either a preliminary to his development of
The Faerie Queene stanza with its greater intricacy of rhyme, or as a
by-product of this technical achievement. Spenser's poetry is essen-
tially stanzaic, building up a cumulative impact of shaped semantic
units. Latin poetry has little in common with this kind of writing: the
verse paragraph of Virgil uses longer syntactic units, the sense of
which is not ideally translated through the predetermined semantic
'room' of a rhyming stanza. Spenser's decision to use stanzaic verse to
render *Culex* may appear eccentric. His alternatives were limited to
the heroic couplet – which the example of *Mother Hubberds Tale* sug-
gests he strongly associated with the style of Chaucer – and non-dra-
matic blank verse, which had been used by Surrey a generation
earlier, but does not seem to have engaged Spenser's attention.[40] It is
also significant that Spenser did not choose an English quantitative
metre despite his enthusiasm for the project in his published *Letters*
to Harvey of 1580 which may be contemporaneous with *Virgils
Gnat*.[41] Possibly the example of Stanyhurst's quantitative version of
the first four books of the *Aeneid* (1582) was enough to convince him

39 See Chapter 2 below.
40 Compare Renwick, *Complaints*, p. 219.
41 *Var.* X, pp. 6–7.

that this new scansion of English was not supported by sufficient artistic success or conceptual agreement.[42]

There were Italian precedents for Spenser's innovation in the ottava rima translations of Virgil by, amongst others, Lodovico Dolce (1568) and Vincentio Menni (1567). Yet as Cauchi notes, *Virgils Gnat* is the only English example of this kind of translation before Harington's version of *Aeneid* VI.[43] Retrospectively, the decision to translate *Culex* into ottava rima seems to have been carefully considered. By doing so, Spenser displays his confidence in stanzaic poetry. Though Gascoigne and Sidney felt that native English verse forms could not parallel the intellectual complexity of Latin scansion, the intricate rhyming stanzas of *Virgils Gnat* and *The Faerie Queene* constitute, if not equivalents to the hexameter and the verse paragraph, successful and technically challenging English forms.[44]

Harington's poem is an excellent yardstick by which to gauge the technical achievement of *Virgils Gnat*. For him, the difference between the *Aeneid* and his chosen stanza was an insoluble problem. In spite of his familiarity with the stanza after translating *Orlando Furioso* (1591), Harington could not fit Virgil comfortably within his stanzas. The translation habitually joins the matter from separate Latin verse paragraphs in the same stanza; there are few rhetorical reasons why Harington's stanzas begin and end where they do:

> Yowr fyrst good hap which yow wold least suspect
> shall from a town of greece to yow bee wrowght.
> this Sibill spake, and words to lyke effect,
> fortelling things to come, to soche as sowght

---

42 See *Var.* X, *loc. cit.* for Spenser's uncertainty about which 'Rules' he and Harvey were using. See Derek Attridge, *Well-weighted Syllables: Elizabethan Verse in Classical Metrics* (Cambridge: Cambridge University Press, 1974) for a full discussion of the English quantitative project and its problems.

43 Harington, *The Sixth Book of Virgil's Aeneid*, p. xviii.

44 Sir Philip Sidney, *Miscellaneous Prose of Sir Philip Sidney*, ed. Katherine Duncan-Jones and Jan Van Dorsten (Oxford: Clarendon, 1973), pp. 119–20; Gascoigne, *Certayne Notes of Instruction* (1575), in G. Gregory Smith (ed.), *Elizabethan Critical Essays* (Oxford: Oxford University Press, 1904), I, 50.

> with hideows noyse, and with a feerce aspect,
> Obskuring truthe with clowds as Phebus towght.
>   Now when shee ceast and all her fury stayd,
>   the Prince replyde agayn and thus hee sayd.[45]

The stanza begins awkwardly with the close of the Sibyl's prophecy and compounds this by climaxing with the introduction to Aeneas's reply in the couplet.[46] There is little sense that Harington has made the best use of the stanza form to convey the drama of the Sibyl's prophecy. He not only lames the impact of its ending, but also hurries too briskly to the next speech: Virgil's paragraphs have not become coherent units of stanzaic verse. In Harington's hands, ottava rima cripples the narrative movement from the Sibyl to Aeneas; it neither gives an adequate idea of the original nor replaces it with a rhetorically balanced stanza. By contrast, Spenser is much better at sequencing paragraph transitions in the Latin with new English stanzas. Major changes in the narrative of *Culex* at lines 43, 203 and 385 correspond with new stanzas in *Virgils Gnat* at lines 65, 313 and 641. Unlike Harington, the matter of discrete Latin paragraphs is not spliced across stanzas. Spenser also shows how self-contained stanzas can parallel the fluidity of the Latin verse paragraph:

> Them therefore as bequeathing to the winde,
> I now depart, returning to thee never,
> And leave this lamentable plaint behinde.
> But doo thou haunt the soft downe rolling river,
> And wilde greene woods, and fruitful pastures minde,
> And let the flitting aire my vaine words sever.
>   Thus having said, he heavily departed
>   With piteous crie, that anie would have smarted.

45 Harington, *The Sixth Book of Virgil's Aeneid*, p. 12.

46 Compare Harington's stanza with Dryden's version of the same passage. The Sibyl's speech ends a paragraph (Dryden, ll. 146–47); the description of her inspiration takes up a paragraph of eight lines (ll. 147–54); while the introduction to Aeneas's speech takes up four words at the start of the new paragraph: 'Then thus the chief' (ll. 155). In *The Works of Virgil*, trans. John Dryden (London and New York: Frederick Warne, no date), p. 141.

Now, when the sloathfull fit of lifes sweete rest
Had left the heavie Shepheard, wondrous cares
His inly grieved minde full sore opprest;
That baleful sorrow he no longer beares,
For that Gnats death, which deeply was imprest:
But bends what ever power his aged yeares
Him lent, yet being such, as through their might
He lately slue his dreadfull foe in fight. (ll. 633–48)

Both stanzas have semantic links with their neighbours: the gnat's final lament continues the sense if not the syntax of lines 631–32; while lines 646–48 prepare for the construction of the memorial. Yet they are not semantically determined by the need to accommodate the surrounding narrative, as with Harington. In each stanza, syntax modifies and makes full use of the possibilities of ottava rima. Lines 633–40 divide formally into three sentences: 633–35, 636–38 and 639–40, which are, with the exception of line 639, firmly end-stopped. Through this arrangement, Spenser focuses attention on to the rhyme scheme and allies the sense with one possible syntactic permutation of that scheme. The gnat's final sentences (lines 633–35 and 636–38) are balanced by their interlocking rhyme words, which in turn – by being given their full value through endstopping – contribute to the elegiac lament of this final statement. Interplay of strong and weak rhymes highlights the emotive force of these key words: the gnat will 'never' return to the Shepherd; all he can leave 'behinde' is the words of his complaint which the 'winde' will finally 'sever'. The symmetrical shaping of these 'vaine words' through rhyme elegantly reveals their pathos, while the couplet acts as a concluding summary of the gnat's complaint as a whole, marked out from the rest of the stanza by its separate rhymes and its choric character as narrated comment.

The second stanza narrates instead of lamenting, so its syntax and deployment of rhyme are less elaborate. It is a clausal sentence with major pauses at the end of lines 643 and 645, with smaller pauses in lines 642, 645 and 647 which all vary the placement of caesura. The couplet closes the sentence, but unlike in the previous stanza it is not an independent unit of sense. This more fluid syntax (not always allowing the reader to pause over rhyme words) suits the stanza's purpose of introducing the Shepherd's act of energetic reparation, and incidentally shows Spenser's easy movement from formal lament in one stanza to busy narrative in the next. The variety of syntactic units Spenser showcases in the formal confines of ottava rima illustrates the flexibility of his stanzaic writing and his ability to naturalize *Culex* through his own emerging poetic style.

Hence *Virgils Gnat* exhibits a technical novelty that anticipates the greater achievement of *The Faerie Queene*. Spenser demonstrates that English stanzaic poetry need not be as rhythmically and syntactically predictable as it is, say, in the bulk of *The Mirror for Magistrates*. Though he could use the heavy endstopping typical of *Mirror* poets, this was one style among a broad range, rather than an habitual mode of expression.[47]

Moreover, although *Virgils Gnat* reproduces traditional complaint, the technical subtlety of the English poem anticipates the transformations the complaint mode undergoes in the major poems. In addition to its appropriation of 'this Gnatts complaint' to express personal grievances, *Virgils Gnat* demonstrates that traditional complaint can be used inventively. This inventiveness is visible both in Spenser's medievalizing version of the wreckage of the Greek navy, and in his handling of the complaint mode through ottava rima. Though at this stage in the volume Spenser is content to mimic traditional complaint and exploit its moralistic expectations, *Virgils Gnat*'s approach to the complaint mode is analogous to that of *The Ruines of Time* or *Mother Hubberds Tale*. In this text, complaint articulates the instability of the poet's rôle, and only intermittently the instability of the external world. Though the sonnet presumes an historical dialogue between Spenser and Leicester which may have resolved their differences, by publishing the poem with the rest of the

---

47 The possible influence of Spenser's ottava rima is indicated by the ambitious use of the form by other poets in the 1590s. See for example Daniel's *Civil Wars* (1595) and the Countess of Pembroke's translation of Psalm 78 (c.1599) as well as Harington's *Orlando Furioso* (1591) and Edward Fairfax's *Jerusalem Delivered* (1600).

Complaints, Spenser implies that it is only a short step from his early anxiety about the instability of the court poet to his mature perception of the instability of the poetic text.

Beyond the Monument?

I have begun this study with *Virgils Gnat* because it is concerned with how Spenser made use and made sense of a literary past he admired artistically and disparaged doctrinally. In this case, he makes a partial accommodation with the values of *Culex*, through his appropriation of the primary allegory in the Dedicatory sonnet. But in the translation itself, he is forced to negotiate the political and theological hazards raised for him by *Culex*'s secondary allegory. It is a text which articulates the tensions between Elizabethan writers and their classical models. The Dedicatory sonnet gives an initial context for the consideration of Spenserian allegory and of his relationship with traditional poetics. While Spenser displays a traditional understanding of allegorical interpretation, the sonnet's self-conscious voicing is indicative of a poet with a distinctive agenda. *Virgils Gnat* reveals the fault line between literary tradition and novelty on which the *Complaints* are uneasily balanced. The poem holds its conflicting concerns in an uneasy equilibrium.

Finally, *Virgils Gnat* records the court poet's desire for recognition, and if possible, an enduring monument to match the literary immortality he or she confers on their patrons. William Browne's *Britannia's Pastorals* (1616) contains an ironic footnote to this central poetic fantasy. Book II Song 1 relates the story that after Spenser's death, Thetis commissioned a memorial for him 'whose head like winged Fame / Should pierce the clouds'; however, her 'factor' is intercepted by 'curs'd Avarice' who robs 'our Colin of his monument'.[48] Judson notes that this may be a poetic account of Elizabeth I's failure to memorialize Spenser.[49] What impresses the reader of *Virgils Gnat* is that the

48 *Poems of William Browne of Tavistock*, 2 vols, ed. Gordon Goodwin (London and New York: George Routledge and E. P. Dutton, no date), I, pp. 225–27.

49 Judson, *The Life of Edmund Spenser*, pp. 206–07.

reticence of its version of the shepherd and gnat's reconciliation, cou-
pled with the darker tone given to the narrative by the sonnet, is
apparently supported by Browne's account of Spenser's memorial.
The modern self-conscious poet can evoke an ancient image of
mutual understanding between poets and patrons, but the fact that
'gold is a taking bait' scuppers the Mausolean good intentions of a
Leicester or an Elizabeth.[50] The tone of *Virgils Gnat* (and especially
its Dedicatory sonnet) anticipates that the poet will finally have to
construct his own memorial in 'vaine words'.

---

50 William Browne, *Poems of William Browne of Tavistock*, pp. 225–27.

CHAPTER TWO
Forming the 'first garland of free Poësie'
in France and England, 1558–91

The self-conscious appropriation of *Culex* by *Virgils Gnat* invites the consideration of Spenser's practice as a translator elsewhere in *Complaints*. I have argued that he stands between the medieval tradition of faithful 'sententious' translation and later conceptions of translation as psychological paraphrase. In *Virgils Gnat*, Spenser adapts the original to voice his own social and literary anxieties: the English poem both translates *Culex* and discloses aspects of Spenser's relationship with Leicester. In the light of this practice, we must ask if *Ruines of Rome*, Spenser's translation of Du Bellay's *Les Antiquitez de Rome*, exhibits the same kind of appropriation. *Les Antiquitez* presents Spenser with different technical problems from *Culex*: a modern language rather than an ancient, and a verse form he must negotiate and cannot ignore. Moreover, in translating the poetry of a near-contemporary, he is more explicitly occupied with his ambitions as a vernacular poet than he was in *Virgils Gnat*, since for Spenser, Du Bellay's achievement manifests the successful raising of a vernacular literature by a self-consciously innovative poet. *Ruines of Rome* is both an act of homage to Du Bellay and an expression of Spenser's own poetic ambitions: he adapts the French poem ideally to inaugurate a new English form of poetry.

While it is clear that *Ruines of Rome* provides a direct link between Spenser and the continental Renaissance, the belief that the translation is Spenserian juvenilia has undermined its status.[1] But the fact

1 The links between Spenser and the Pléiade were initially explored by W. L. Renwick, 'The Critical Origins of Spenser's Diction', *MLR*, 17 (1922), pp. 1–16; more recent interest is exemplified by Margaret W. Ferguson, '"The Afflatus of Ruin": Meditations on Rome by Du Bellay, Spenser, and Stevens', in *Roman Images: Selected Papers from the English Institute*, New Series, No. 8, ed. Annabel Patterson (Baltimore: The Johns Hopkins University Press, 1982); and Lawrence Manley, 'Spenser and the City: The Minor Poems', *MLQ*, 43 (1982), 203–27.

that the sequence is usually and plausibly dated as early work (late 1560s or early 1570s) does not prevent it from having a bearing on Spenser's growing conception of poetry.[2] Rather, the date of writing indicates the formative quality of Du Bellay's influence on Spenser; the date of publication in *Complaints* (1591) suggests how long he continued to regard it as an important work. I argue that this importance lies in Spenser's recognition that Du Bellay creates in *Les Antiquitez* a new kind of vernacular writing that is concerned with the reappraisal of the European classical inheritance. Read in this way, even the relatively modest achievement of *Ruines of Rome* as translation or as poetry in its own right, is charged with Spenser's central concern with poetic innovation.[3] *Ruines of Rome* shows Spenser paying homage to Du Bellay's novel handling of the most basic fact of the European intellectual tradition – the Roman Empire.

Les Antiquitez de Rome (1558) innovates through its application of the Petrarchan love sonnet to a meditation on Rome,[4] and its attempt to dignify the French language by associating it with the lament over the evanescence of Roman grandeur. Yet as Allen points

2 For the date of the translation, see the *Var.* VIII, pp. 378–80; Alexander C. Judson, *The Life of Edmund Spenser* (Baltimore and London: The Johns Hopkins University Press, 1945), p. 150; and Schell in *YESP*, pp. 383–84. *Ruines of Rome* is conventionally dated in the late 1560s or early 1570s. This rests on the idea that Spenser would have moved from his work on the 'Songe' for van der Noot's *Theatre* (1569) to *Les Antiquitez*. Internal evidence equally suggests an early date because of the relative unsubtlety of the translation. Nonetheless, there is force in the comment of the *Var.* editor that 'It is more likely than not that Spenser, on the eve of publication, here and there tuned up these earlier efforts to his later pitch'. Similarly, Schell remarks that 'Spenser's version is undatable, apart from the reference to Du Bartas's *Uranie* of 1579 in the Envoy which, as Spenser's own addition to the sequence … could be of later date'.

3 Compare M. J. Stapleton, 'Spenser, the *Antiquitez de Rome*, and the Development of the English Sonnet Form.' *CLS*, 27 (1990), pp. 259–74, who provides a formalist defence of *Ruines of Rome* as poetry in its own right. Though this is an interesting approach, Stapleton's claims for the superiority of Spenser's translation over Du Bellay's original are, at best, patchily convincing.

4 See Wayne A. Rebhorn, 'Du Bellay's Imperial Mistress: *Les Antiquitez de Rome* as Petrarchist Sonnet Sequence', *RenQ*, 33 (1980), pp. 609–22, for the view that Du Bellay treats Rome as Petrarch treats Laura: as the object of his erotic melancholy.

out, poetry lamenting the ruins of Rome was not original: neo-Latin and vernacular Italian poets had covered similar ground.[5] But Du Bellay's fusing of the poetic trope of ruined Rome with an innovatory and experimental technique, and his highly ambiguous attitude towards that city as an outsider and champion of French culture, creates a text which explores and questions the political and literary tradition embodied in Rome. So *Les Antiquitez* challenges Spenser on three related levels: as an enactment of Du Bellay's critical ideas about vernacular poetry; as a technical experiment with the sonnet form and the complaint mode; and as a critical reassessment of Rome. In this perspective, *Ruines of Rome* is a work that brings to fuller consciousness the unresolved tensions in *Virgils Gnat* between the Latin poet's idea of Rome and Spenser's. His uneasiness about the Roman panegyric of *Culex* makes him specially responsive to Du Bellay's melancholy scepticism when confronting the greatness that was Rome.

Du Bellay's influence on Spenser

If *Ruines of Rome* is an act of homage to an early master,[6] the question arises of how precisely Du Bellay influenced Spenser. I suggest, following Prescott's comments on the influence of Du Bellay's *La Deffence et Illustration de la Langue Francoyse* (1549) on English Renaissance writing, that his primary impact on Spenser was as an

---

5 Don C. Allen, *Image and Meaning: Metamorphic Traditions in Renaissance Poetry* (Baltimore: The Johns Hopkins University Press, 1960), pp. 63–65.

6 I have borrowed the idea of a poetic 'master' from W. H. Auden's essay, 'Making, Knowing and Judging', in which he describes the would-be poet's 'apprenticeship' to 'any Master he likes, living or dead'. Auden keenly describes his own early imitation of Hardy, and how 'apprentice' poets can learn 'how a poem is written' from their chosen master. Auden usefully stresses both the process of emulative imitation he underwent and how this process may (and possibly should) reveal to the novice the limitations of his Master. In *The Dyer's Hand* (London: Faber and Faber, 1963), pp. 37–38.

idealist of vernacular literature.[7] The *Deffence* is a powerful polemic against post-medieval French poetry and the Ciceronian neo-Latin of continental humanism; it also embodies a programme for a new vernacular literature based on a neo-classicizing model.[8] Greene aptly characterizes the Du Bellay of the *Deffence* as 'consciously iconoclastic, consciously the spokesman of a movement taking shape, inspirational and disheveled, withering and buoyant'.[9] It is these qualities which give Du Bellay's precedent such force for the young Spenser.

In Book I of the *Deffence* Du Bellay argues that all languages are created of equal capacity for the communication of ideas. Therefore all languages (including 'notre vulgaire') are capable of sophisticated usage. This argument for the basic equality of languages justifies Du Bellay's principal claim: that with the cooperation of the learned, French could become as prized a literary language as Greek and Latin. Though Du Bellay's linguistic ideas are not original,[10] his forceful presentation of this case was vindicated by the growth of European vernacular literature during the sixteenth century, which in turn led to the dwindling in the power and prestige of neo-Latin.[11] Du Bellay argues against the retention of 'an art-language (neo-Latin)

7 Anne Lake Prescott, *French Poets and the English Renaissance: Studies in Fame and Transformation* (New Haven: Yale University Press, 1978), p. 65: 'One is apt to find traces of the *Deffence* not in passages justifying the enterprise of feigning or those exploring the relation of mimesis to philosophy but rather in books or chapters explaining how to write poetry, celebrating the vernacular, or discussing the nature of language itself'.

8 For detailed discussions of Du Bellay's theoretical framework, see Terence Cave, *The Cornucopian Text: Problems of Writing in the French Renaissance* Oxford: Clarendon, 1979), pp. 60–77; and Thomas M. Greene, *The Light in Troy: Imitation and Discovery in Renaissance Poetry* (New Haven: Yale University Press, 1982), pp. 189–96.

9 Greene, *The Light in Troy*, p. 190.

10 *Ibid.*, p. 192. Du Bellay derived much of his theory of language from Speroni's *Dialogo delle lingue* (1542).

11 J. W. Binns, *Intellectual Culture in Elizabethan and Jacobean England: The Latin Writings of the Age* (Leeds: Francis Cairns, 1990) provides a catalogue – and something of a defence – of neo-Latin publications in Elizabethan and Jacobean England. The fact that such a work is necessary indicates the eventual outcome of the battle between the Ancients and the Moderns.

wholly dissociated from nature' in favour of the living – or natural – vernacular.[12] This language must demonstrate its potential by the creative absorption of classical precedents. French must be enriched as Latin had been – by the imitation of its illustrious forebears. Imitation becomes a key concept for Du Bellay, encompassing the means of producing a new French literature to the privileging of original texts over translations. Translations cannot 'donner perfection à la langue française' because they are unable to render the rhetorical 'élocution' of a foreign text, or in the case of poetry, its irreducible 'genius'.[13] Creative imitation of the classics alone is the 'oeuvre digne de prix en son vulgaire'.[14]

Yet what concerns us here, rather than the wider philosophical and critical issues raised by Du Bellay's theory of imitation,[15] is his polemical presentation of the vernacular poet as a revitalizer of humane culture. Du Bellay's 'poète futur' is a recluse whose monastic dedication to his task of endowing his vernacular with a new literature is the price that must be paid for ultimate success.[16]

12 Cave, *The Cornucopain Text*, p. 74. Cave explores Du Bellay's cyclic conception of linguistic history with acuity.

13 Joachim Du Bellay, *Les Regrets, Les Antiquités de Rome et La Défense et Illustration de la Langue française*, ed. S. De Sacy (Paris: Gallimard, 1967), pp. 210–14. The '*genius*' of poetry includes 'divinité d'invention … grandeur de style, magnificence des mots, gravité desentences, audace et variété de figures'.

14 *Ibid.*

15 Du Bellay's formulation of the concept of imitation of models has come under close scrutiny in recent years from both Cave and Greene. Their work valuably contextualizes Du Bellay's discussion of imitation in the wider rhetorical debate between Ciceronian humanists like Bembo and non-Ciceronians like Erasmus. Essentially, their arguments centre on how Du Bellay conceives of imitation as a means of new creation. Both writers agree that Du Bellay's conception of imitation as consubstantiation leads to internal contradictions and fissures in his wider linguistic arguments (Cave, *The Cornucopian Text*, pp. 67ff; Greene, *The Light in Troy*, p. 194). However, as Prescott's remarks (note 6 above) about the influence of the *Deffence* in England suggest, such texts were not necessarily received in this linguistically specialized way by contemporary readers.

16 *La Deffence* II.IV in Du Bellay, *Les Regrets* …, p. 238; compare Cave, *The Cornucopian Text*, p. 71, on the death of the poet to the world.

Donc, ô toi, qui, doué d'une excellente félicité de nature,
instruit de tous bons arts et sciences … versé en tous genres de
bons auteurs grecs et latins, non ignorant des parties et offices
de la vie humaine, non de trop haute condition, ou appelé au
régime public, non aussi abject et pauvre, non troublé d'affaires
domestiques, mais en repos et tranquillité d'esprit, acquise pre-
mièrement par la magnanimité de ton courage, puis entretenue
par ta prudence et sage gouvernment, ô toi (dis-je), orné de tant
de graces et perfections, si tu as quelque-fois pitié de ton pau-
vre langage, si tu daignes l'enricher de tes trésors, ce sera toi
véritablement qui lui feras hausser la tête, et d'un brave sourcil
s'égaler aux superbes langues grecque et latine, comme a fait de
notre temps en son vulgaire un Arioste italien … (II.V)[17]

Such sentences typify the inspirational and hortatory character of the
Deffence as a whole, and of Book II in particular with its focus on how
patriotic French poets should proceed. Du Bellay wants to persuade
his readers into aspiring to be the 'poète futur' of the French nation,
which he does by simultaneously insisting on the selfless dedication
needed to be such a writer, while also holding out the lustre of the
prize to be striven for: 'la gloire, seule échelle par les degrés de laque-
lle les mortels d'un pied léger montent au ciel et se font compagnons
des dieux'.[18] Such poetic patriotism will raise the timeless reputation
of the individual poet, but most importantly, will defend and illus-
trate the virtues of the vernacular.

The *Deffence* is not just an affirmation of the capacity of French to
communicate as effectively as Latin, but an assertion of the central-
ity of the work of the poet in 'raising' any vernacular to the canoni-
cal level of Latin and Greek. Du Bellay sees the poet as the vital
benefactor of the vernacular: without the corpus of classic texts he
alone can provide, no language can compete with the established
humanist status of the 'superbes langues grecque et latine'. As
Prescott argues, ideas like these were of intrinsic interest to English
writers concerned with increasing the prestige of the vernacular:

17 Du Bellay, *Les Regrets* …, pp. 240–41.
18 *Ibid.*, p. 243.

Richard Mulcaster, the headmaster of Spenser's school, probably drew on the *Deffence* in the course of his preference for English over other languages in his *Elementarie* (1582).[19] Spenser's own work shows evidence of his wider absorption of ideas from the *Deffence*. His archaic diction, or 'old rustic language',[20] takes its cue from Du Bellay's argument that 'le modéré usage de tels vocables … donne grande majesté tant aux vers comme à la prose'.[21] Du Bellay's theoretical support for a diction ornamented with 'quelques mots antiques … ainsi qu'une pierre précieuse et rare' accords well with Spenser's practice throughout his career. Archaic diction is paradoxically a tool in the creation of a new vernacular poetry. Far from illustrating his stylistic conservatism, Spenser's diction shows – as Sidney recognized – a commitment to innovative poetic practice.

The influence of the *Deffence*, combined with his translation of *Les Antiquitez*, suggests that Spenser saw Du Bellay as a writer who prac-

---

19 Prescott, *French Poets and the English Renaissance*, pp. 64–68.

20 Sir Philip Sidney, *Miscellaneous Prose of Sir Philip Sidney*, ed. Katherine Duncan-Jones and Jan Van Dorsten (Oxford: Clarendon, 1973), p. 112. Sidney and Du Bellay are directly at odds on this point. Du Bellay claims that the use of 'quelques mots antiques en ton poème' is justified by 'l'exemple de Virgile' (II.VI); while Sidney argues that he 'dare not allow' such innovation 'since neither Theocritus in Greek, Virgil in Latin, nor Sannazzaro in Italian did affect it'.

21 Du Bellay, *Les Regrets …*, pp. 245–46. See Renwick, 'The Critical Origins of Spenser's Diction', for a more detailed discussion of these ideas and compare E. K.'s claim that the usage of 'olde and obsolete wordes … bring[s] great grace and … auctoritie to the verse' of *The Shepheardes Calender* (Epistle to Harvey, ll.43–46). E. K.'s point is chiefly a stylistic one, like Du Bellay's, and should not be confused with the kind of absolutist position taken by Sir John Cheke on the writing of English. Cheke argued that written English should be 'cleane and pure', employing 'old denisoned' English words in preference to 'borowing' vocabulary 'of other tunges'. While Spenser's usage of 'obsolete' English (or pseudo-English) words appears to parallel Cheke's programme, it is misleading to lump this stylistic approach with Cheke's linguistic moralism. The two positions are related in practice, but are dissimilar in intent. Cheke wants to hark back to a notional golden age of English linguistic virginity, while Spenser wants to raise a vernacular literature. See Baldasare Castiglione, *The Courtier* (1561), trans. Sir Thomas Hoby (London: Everyman's Library, Dent, 1928), pp. 7–8, 'A Letter of Syr J. Cheke To his loving frind Mayster Thomas Hoby'.

tised what he preached.[22] His 'Envoy' to *Ruines of Rome* reduplicates Du Bellay's own promise of 'gloire' to the 'poète futur' in the *Deffence*: 'Needs must he all eternitie survive, / That can to other give eternall dayes' (ll. 455–56). Spenser's Du Bellay is the triumphant champion of the vernacular whose poetry – freshly imported into English – confirms the programme for vernacular writing envisaged in the *Deffence*. Yet Du Bellay himself is unlikely to have seen such a clear enactment of the theory of the *Deffence* in the practice of *Les Antiquitez*. When the *Deffence* was published in 1549, Du Bellay had been part of a Parisian intellectual coterie, yet from 1553 to 1557 his position changed because of his 'malheureux voyage'[23] to Rome as a member of Cardinal Jean Du Bellay's household. While the stay in Rome provoked Du Bellay's best work in *Les Antiquitez* and *Les Regrets*, it was, as the latter sequence records, a time of personal unhappiness and artistic compromise. With his neo-Latin *Poemata* (1558), Du Bellay went back on his earlier rejection of such writing because, as he explains in a superb sonnet to Ronsard, 'le français, / ... Au rivage latin ne se peut faire entendre'.[24] *Les Antiquitez* emerge out of a biographical context of disillusionment with sixteenth-century Rome and, latently, with his earlier poetic idealism. Since the model for imitation urged in the *Deffence* is the classical Roman adoption of 'the best Greek writers',[25] and the literature resulting from this emulative imitation, Du Bellay's own experience of Rome arguably revises his attitude to the city and the empire.

---

22 This view is partly modified by the fact that in the *Deffence*, Du Bellay attacks translation as a vehicle for new literature; see Stapleton, 'Spenser ...', pp. 259–60.

23 Du Bellay, *Les Regrets* ..., p. 90.

24 *Ibid.*, p. 75; *Les Regrets* sonnet 10. This sonnet replies to one by Ronsard which remarks that 'l'air des Latins te fait parler latin, / Changeant à l'étranger ton naturel langage'; in *Poésies Choisies* (ed. Pierre de Nolhac (Paris: Éditions Garnier Frères, 1959), p. 147. Du Bellay's sonnet eloquently rebuts Ronsard's mild imputation that Du Bellay has been wilfully unfaithful to French firstly by a rephrasing of Ronsard's opening quatrain and secondly by the comparison of his predicament with that of the exiled Ovid, who also had to write in a foreign language 'Afin d'être entendu'. Du Bellay's 'exile' in Rome thus wittily inverts that of the Roman poet.

25 Translated from Du Bellay, *Les Regrets* ..., p. 214.

Recent analysis of *Les Antiquitez* has approached the sequence from this biographical perspective.[26] The advantage of this approach is that, as in Greene's reading, the sequence can be seen as a reassessment of the humanist project to revive the culture and physical setting of Classical Rome. Greene argues that Du Bellay is obliged to concede that the rebuilding of Rome (whether through architectural recovery or poetic magic) is, for all its initial confidence, doomed to failure. In making this discovery, Du Bellay enacts the 'central humanist drama' of the tension between the influence of the past and the predicament of the present moment. The modern poet must interpret the classical legacy, but is unable fully to evoke or recreate its glories.[27] Greene's argument has the appeal of dramatizing *Les Antiquitez* as Du Bellay's dialogue with the past, with the result that the sequence is read as a largely negative reinterpretation of the concept of emulative imitation outlined in Book I of the *Deffence*. If Greene is correct in characterizing the sequence as an account of the failure of Renaissance idealism, then Spenser's 'L'Envoy' reveals a naïvely optimistic attitude towards the text of his master.[28] Before turning to *Ruines of Rome*, it is important to recognize that there are alternative approaches to *Les Antiquitez*.

The Structure of *Les Antiquitez*

Greene's account of *Les Antiquitez* sees it as a developing argument, a 'Dialectical imitation', which begins confident in the artistic ability to revive the past. But through the course of the sonnets this confidence is overturned: no resuscitation of the past is possible.[29] There

---

26 *Ibid.*, pp. 271–73, for an outline chronology of Du Bellay's life. See Yvonne Bellenger, *Du Bellay, ses Regrets qu'il fit dans Rome: Étude et Documentation* (Paris: A.-G. Nizet, 1975) and Greene, *The Light in Troy*, pp. 220–41 (especially pp. 220–21), for readings of Du Bellay's later poetry through his experience.

27 Greene, *The Light in Troy*, p. 221.

28 Compare Deborah Cartmell, *Edmund Spenser and the Literary Uses of Architecture in the English Renaissance* (unpublished doctoral dissertation, University of York, 1986/87), p. 39.

29 Greene, *The Ligh in Troy*, p. 228.

are problems with this account of *Les Antiquitez*'s structure. The sequence does not progress from a position of confidence to one of disillusionment: the first sonnet invokes the 'antique fureur' of the classical Roman poets, while the last (sonnet 32) states Du Bellay's claim to be an innovator in the steps of these writers through direct allusions to Horace and Virgil.[30] Though Greene recognizes the eccentricity of sonnet 32 as a conclusion for his argument, a paradoxical structuring of ideas is evident throughout the sequence. Though recurring images and mythical exempla are deployed in widely dispersed sonnets, they do not organize the discrete sonnets into a homogeneous argument. So the Titan myth is employed in sonnets 4, 11, 12 and 17 almost promiscuously. These texts offer contrasting interpretations of Rome through contradictory treatments of the myth. In sonnet 4 Jupiter imprisons the spirit of Rome under the seven hills in order to avoid a repetition of the Titans' insurrection:

> Jupiter ayant peur, si plus elle croissait,
> Que l'orgueil des Géants se relevât encore,
> L'accabla sous ces monts, ces sept monts qui sont ore
> Tombeaux de la grandeur qui le ciel menaçait.[31]

whereas in sonnet 12, the same hills are a platform for the Roman assault on heaven:

> ... on a vu par-dessus les humains
> Le front audacieux des sept coteaux romains
> Lever contre le ciel son orgueilleuse face:[32]

Sonnet 4 explains Roman topography by juxtaposing Jupiter's anxiety with the litany of the hills in the sestet. The rest of the sonnet confirms the extent of Roman power even as Jupiter seeks to confine it under the hills. By contrast, sonnet 12 uses the Titan myth as a typo-

---

30 The poem as a whole follows Horace's 'Exegi monumentum' (*Odes* III.30), while the phrase 'peuple à longue robe' translates Virgil's 'gentem ... togatam' (*Aeneid* I.282). See Schell's note in *YESP*, p. 404.

31 Du Bellay, *Les Regrets* ..., p. 29.

32 *Ibid.*, p. 34.

logical explanation of the fall of Rome: as the war in heaven resulted in the Titans' fall to Earth, so Roman audacity meets with comparable ruin. But sonnet 12 does not supersede 4 – it rather suggests that the Titan material is being used eclectically in each separate sonnet. Du Bellay does not resolve whether the reader should view the seven hills as either 'Tombeaux de la grandeur qui le ciel menaçait', or as Rome's climbing-frame towards Olympus. Equally, while these two poems show that Rome's 'orgueil' and failure can parallel that of the Titans, sonnet 11 reapplies the myth by casting the Goths as the new Titans. This inconsistency looks deliberate: the image is neither developed or brought into a hierarchy of significance. The Titans function according to the independent requirements of each sonnet; competing interpretations of Rome are juxtaposed rather than subjected to dialectical development.

Such usage of imagery is characteristic of *Les Antiquitez*. This shifting exploration of parallel ideas and images underlies the sequence, which Du Bellay uses to structure his central perception of Rome as inherently paradoxical. This idea is never far from the surface of the text. For all its quondam glory and current dilapidation, Rome remains a central embodiment of human contradictions that cannot adequately be reduced to a simple formulation. Rome can only be compared with Rome (sonnet 6); it must be recognized as 'la carte du monde' (sonnet 26). At the clearest moment of intuition into the paradox, Du Bellay exclaims, 'O merveille profonde! / Rome vivant fut l'ornement du monde, / Et morte elle est du monde le tombeau' (sonnet 29).[33] This point underlies the structure of *Les Antiquitez*. Because Rome is an historical paradox, all Du Bellay can do is bear witness to its cultural centrality and recognize it as a 'merveille profonde'. The sequence illustrates the miracle by offering a series of fluctuating accounts of the Roman paradox. As in the case of sonnets 14 and 15 – a pair that form a diptych of opposed viewpoints – positive and negative judgements of Rome alternate throughout the sequence, forcing the reader to reinterpret Roman history and make sense of the city's singularity. In this light, Greene's reading of *Les*

33 *Ibid.*, p. 46.

Antiquitez as a dialectical structure becomes unconvincing. Du Bellay's sequence uses contrast and re-evaluation to present a Rome which is simultaneously the most powerful of cities and the greatest monument to human self-destructiveness.

But although *Les Antiquitez* centres on this paradox, some sonnets look towards a divine transcendence of time and the paradoxical cycle of Roman history.[34] In these apocalyptic sonnets Du Bellay looks forward to the 'Songe', the first sonnet of which asserts 'Dieu seul au temps fait résistance' – a direct rebuttal of the paradox of the Tiber resisting time in sonnet 3. The presence of pointers towards the 'Songe' in *Les Antiquitez* implies that a self-conscious distinction is being made between the two sequences. *Les Antiquitez* is a meditation on Rome as a temporal phenomenon, whereas the 'Songe' aims at a visionary revelation of the divine perspective on human works. This change from earthly poetry to divine is critical to Spenser, whose work on the 'Songe' through van der Noot's *Theatre* almost certainly precedes his work on *Les Antiquitez*. Spenser preserves the value judgements implicit in this move in his 'L'Envoy' to *Ruines of Rome*.

This reading upsets Greene's account of the structure of *Les Antiquitez*. The major sequence illustrates Du Bellay's perception of Rome as a paradox, while the dream visions of the 'Songe' provide an eschatological solution to the Roman paradox. Such a description is also responsive to *Les Antiquitez*'s generic novelty. The classic sonnet sequences available to Du Bellay, *La Vita Nuova* and the *Rime Sparse*, organize their contents on essentially narrative principles.[35] For Dante, this takes the form of a prose narrative that connects the poems with the incidents which prompted them; in Petrarch the individual poems are carefully sequenced to give an analogous impression of the progressive development of the speaker's interior life. Du Bellay innovates both in his abandonment of such sequential

34 See particularly sonnets 7, 9, 20 and 22.

35 See Petrarch, *Petrarch's Lyric Poems: The 'Rime Sparse' and Other Lyrics*, ed. and trans. Robert M. Durling (Cambridge, Mass. and London: Harvard University Press, 1976), p. 10, where Durling compares the narrative structure of *La Vita Nuova* and the *Rime Sparse*.

organization, and most visibly, in his transformation of the sonnet sequence from a vehicle for love complaint into a critical lament for Rome.[36] By associating complaint with Rome and utilizing the high-prestige sonnet form, Du Bellay extends the traditional range of complaint to encompass his meditation on the paradox of a decayed civilization. Spenser in turn, by including this text alongside the more traditional usage of the complaint mode in the gnat's petition to the shepherd, advertises his awareness that Du Bellay had revolutionized complaint from its classical and medieval antecedents.

How does such a reading of the sequence approach individual sonnets? Since *Les Antiquitez* is governed by the elucidation of a paradox, the sonnets are discrete explorations of Rome which have a cumulative impact on our understanding of that paradox. This approach can best be seen in contrast with Greene's. Sonnet 6, for example, Greene reads as a plangent evocation of *Aeneid* VI.785–91, which reveals the defeat of Du Bellay as Virgil's 'latter-day emulator'.[37] This reading foregrounds the imitation of Virgil to further Greene's general point that *Les Antiquitez* reveals the impossibility of any kind of reconstructive imitation of the classical past. However, it is possible to read the sonnet as a less directly 'aporetic' text than Greene does. Imitation of Virgil frames Du Bellay's exploration of Roman history, and gives him a context for his perspective on the Empire.

> Telle que dans son char la Bérécynthienne
> Couronnée de tours, et joyeuse d'avoir
> Enfanté tant de dieux, telle se faisait voir
> En ses jours plus heureux cette ville ancienne:
>
> Cette ville, qui fut plus que la Phrygienne
> Foisonnante en enfants, et de qui le pouvoir
> Fut le pouvoir du monde, et ne se peut revoir
> Pareille à sa grandeur, grandeur sinon la sienne.
>
> Rome seule pouvait à Rome ressembler,

---

36 Rebhorn, 'Du Bellay's Imperial Mistress', takes the contrary view: Du Bellay's Rome is his Laura. See also Schell in *YESP*, pp. 382–83.

37 Greene, *The Light in Troy*, pp. 224–25.

Rome seule pouvait Rome faire trembler:
Aussi n'avait permis l'ordonnance fatale

Qu'autre pouvoir humain, tant fût audacieux,
Se vantât d'égaler celle qui fit égale
Sa puissance à la terre et son courage aux cieux.[38]

Du Bellay imitates Virgil in order to outdo his formulation of Roman power and draw attention to the *Aeneid*'s wider failure to predict accurately the course of Roman history. The original image occurs during Anchises's forecast to Aeneas of the extent of Roman rule; Rome's incipient power and dominance of the world is connected with Cybele's reproductive virtue as the Great Mother of gods:

> ... great Rome
> Shall rule to the ends of the earth, shall aspire to the
>   highest achievement,
> Shall ring the seven hills with a wall to make one city,
> Blessed in her breed of men: as Cybele, wearing her
>   turreted
> Crown, is charioted round the Phrygian cities, proud of
> Her brood of gods, a hundred of her children's children –
> Heaven-dwellers all, all tenants of the realm above.[39]

In this passage, the stream of Roman heroes waiting to be born (presented by Anchises to Aeneas as the ultimate justification for his wanderings) mirrors Cybele's divine progeny. This is a straightforward comparison between Rome's 'blessed ... breed of men', and Cybele's 'brood of gods'. Du Bellay adapts this image to make a historical assessment of Roman power which counters Virgil's prediction. In the sonnet's first quatrain, the terms of Virgil's simile remain intact: the turreted goddess parallels the fecund Rome 'En ses jours plus heureux'. But in the second quatrain, Du Bellay distances Rome from 'La Phrygienne': Rome was '*plus* ... Foisonnante en enfants'[40] and could not see

---

38 Du Bellay, *Les Regrets* ..., pp. 30–31.
39 Virgil, *The Aeneid*, trans. C. Day Lewis, (Oxford: Oxford University Press, 1956; rpt. 1986), p. 183.
40 My italic.

any other power on a comparable scale to her own. Rome's universal singularity threatens to erase the simple structure of Virgil's simile. The sestet completes Du Bellay's rewriting firstly through its stark assertion of Rome's ontological dissimilarity from 'autre pouvoir humain'. Du Bellay outdoes his model by showing that the simile will not work as a description of Roman history. The prophetic linkage of the joyful goddess and the flourishing city takes no account of Rome's mortality. Yet the sonnet is constantly aware of time and its own status as a retrospect on Rome through the lamenting undertone of its insistent past tenses: the city was more fecund than Cybele; Rome *could* only be *compared* with Rome. This implies that Rome's period of dominance is over: 'cette ville … de qui le pouvoir / *Fut* le pouvoir du monde'.[41] And because of its singularity, 'Rome seule pouvait Rome faire trembler': the city's pre-eminence, signalled by Virgil, becomes the means of its eventual defeat in civil wars.

Sonnet 6 structures Du Bellay's idea of Rome as a paradox through its imitation of Virgil. Far from testifying to the defeat of humanist idealism, the sonnet illuminates Du Bellay's position as a sixteenth-century observer of Roman history through its critical allusion to Anchises's prophecy. As Du Bellay sees the imperial project as a completed process, so the sestet concentrates on Rome's singularity, stressing its temporal bounds in a way Virgil could not have done. These lines indicate that Rome is a unique manifestation in human history, which for all its power was not able to escape its temporal confinement and become the everlasting empire envisaged by Virgil. Imitation of *Aeneid* VI has given Du Bellay a context through which to explain both Rome's singularity and its decline.

The poem can stand as a test case for the interpretation of *Les Antiquitez* as an innovative text. In Greene's view the sonnet is a moment of aporia in which Du Bellay is forced to realize that Rome's singularity precludes it from being a tenable model for sixteenth-century imitators. Because of 'l'ordonnance fatale', Rome is unrepeatable, either in itself or as a model for others. This strong reading of the poem meshes with Greene's argument that *Les Antiquitez* is concerned with the failure of humanist idealism to effect a physical restoration of 'la gloire

41 My italic.

ausonienne'. Greene offers what is in essence a sophisticated literalist
reading of the sequence – when Du Bellay writes in his dedicatory son-
net of inspiring King Henri II to 'rebâtir en France une telle
grandeur',[42] this is seen as an attempt at a literal reduplication of the
humanist architectural recovery of ancient Rome. For Greene, Du Bel-
lay's belief in the mythic power of poetry to reawaken the dead and
rebuild cities only reinforces his own sense of incapacity. His experi-
ence of Rome means that the 'ardeur' which inflames him is not ulti-
mately sufficient to rebuild Rome 'au compas de la plume'.[43]

My reading of sonnet 6 suggests a different approach to the
sequence. If imitation is a technique employed in the sonnet rather
than the dominating philosophical problem of the whole sequence,
texts like sonnets 25 and 32 cease to sound like examinations of imita-
tion or embodiments of a forlorn poetic idealism. Instead, these poems
should be read as more direct indications of Du Bellay's self-conscious
awareness of the novelty of his presentation of Rome. Sonnet 25 is a
sustained usage of the modesty topos through which Du Bellay defines
the parameters of his poetic achievement. Though Rome cannot be
rebuilt by human hands, poetry can at least act as an agent for the
preservation of the faded 'gloire ausonienne'.[44] The poem juxtaposes
the skills of the ideal poetic forerunners – Orpheus, Amphion and Vir-
gil – against Du Bellay's 'plume'. Though these images seem to count
against Du Bellay, his 'plume' retains the capacity to create a literary
image of ancient Rome. It is too easy to take the poem's disclaimers at
face value: Du Bellay would have been unlikely to claim artistic parity
with any of these poets. But by including his lesser undertaking along-

---

42 Du Bellay, *Les Regrets* ..., p. 25. The line 'De rebâtir en France une telle
grandeur' may be worth pausing over. I suggest that there is a balance here between
the forceful activity of 'rebuilding' and the less specific image suggested by 'une telle
grandeur' – which we could paraphrase as 'a similar grandeur, a grandeur in the same
style as that of ancient Rome'. Such a formulation suggests the kind of 'rebuilding'
undertaken by neo-classical architects outside Rome. The classical past is not liter-
ally raised 'hors du tombeau', but 'une telle grandeur' is painstakingly evoked
through the imitation of classical models. Sonnet 27 does, however, describe an
actual 'resuscitation' of ancient Rome by the 'ouvriers les plus industrieux'.
43 *Ibid.*, p. 43.
44 *Ibid.*

side the idealized achievements of the past, Du Bellay indicates that poetry, including his own, can recapture in print 'Ce que les mains ne peuvent maçonner'. Reflection on the glory that was Rome naturally evokes a pessimistic tone in *Les Antiquitez*, but in sonnet 25 at least, it is a self-conscious blind to Du Bellay's conviction – unaffected by experience – that vernacular poetry can express 'en papier' 'les monuments que je vous ai fait dire'.[45]

Du Bellay's confidence in poetry as a preserver of the past recalls Spenser's 'L'Envoy'. Though this original sonnet takes the form of an unclouded panegyric to two of Spenser's favourite French poets, it none the less covertly indicates the kind of dialogue which explicitly takes place within the translation. Its poetic hierarchy has important implications for the reading not just of *Ruines of Rome* but of the conception of poetry in *Complaints* as a whole:

> *Bellay*, first garland of free Poësie
> That *France* brought forth, though fruitfull of brave
>   wits,
> Well worthie thou of immortalitie,
> That long hast traveld by thy learned writs,
>   Olde *Rome* out of her ashes to revive,
> And give a second life to dead decayes:
> Needes must he all eternitie survive,
> That can to other give eternall dayes.
>   Thy dayes therefore are endles, and thy prayse
> Excelling all, that ever went before;
> And after thee, gins *Bartas* hie to rayse
> His heavenly Muse, th'Almightie to adore.
>   Live happie spirits, th'honour of your name,
>   And fill the world with never dying fame. (ll. 449–62)

Though the sonnet is readily comprehensible as a tribute to Du Bellay and then Du Bartas as representative French poets of the new school, its terminology of praise and structuring of ideas repay close study. The first two lines define Du Bellay's novelty in terms of traditional French poetry. Though previously 'fruitful' of 'brave wits',

45 *Ibid.*, pp. 47–48.

France's first flowering of 'free Poësie' is Du Bellay. This juxtaposition indicates that traditional French poetry is not as 'free' as Du Bellay's: his work inaugurates a 'freer' practice of the art. In this reading 'free' functions as a distinction rather than a definition, meaning 'unrestricted'.[46] Yet the prominent position of the phrase suggests that it is a defining characterization of Du Bellay's novelty. The adjective would then take on its older meaning of 'noble' or 'honourable'.[47] Du Bellay's 'free Poësie' is related to the 'noble Poësie' lamented by Polyhymnia in *The Teares of the Muses*: a 'sacred skill' for the artful ordering of language – the opposite of unstructured poetic 'libertie'.[48] This parallel can be extended to encompass the wider depiction of the decay of learning in *The Teares of the Muses*. The poem presents the decline of the Muses' authority as an imprisonment of poetry by Ignorance which restricts the human spirit and ultimately the capacity for heroic action.[49] Du Bellay's 'free Poësie' is implicitly a high-status poetics – both in terms of social origins and intellectual breadth – which recaptures some of the ground already ceded to barbarity. Spenser's tribute to Du Bellay paradoxically regards his originality as a reassertion of poetry's ancient authority.

The rest of the octave confirms this impression by arguing that Du Bellay merits 'immortalitie' because of his quasi-antiquarian recovery of ancient Rome. Spenser's point in these lines is easy to misread. In praising Du Bellay for reviving 'Old *Rome* out of her ashes' and giving 'a second life to dead decayes', Spenser apparently asserts in direct contradiction to sonnets 25 and 32 that *Les Antiquitez* effects a literal resurrection of the past. Yet such a reading lacks contextual nuance. Since Spenser is engaged in literary panegyric, he is able to state hyperbolically the implicit assertions of sonnets 25 and 32, where Du Bellay's 'plume' can 'acquérir telle immortalité' through its literate preservation of Rome for its readers.[50] Here, Spenser indicates that

46 *OED* II.4.
47 *OED* I.4.
48 *The Teares of the Muses*, ll. 541–94.
49 See in particular lines 73–78; 187–92; 307–18 and 487–92, and Chapter 4 below, pp. 152–57.
50 Du Bellay, *Les Regrets* ...., pp. 47–48.

Du Bellay deserves a secular immortality as a reward for his innova-
tive poetry: as he revived Rome, so the 'never dying fame' of his text
will ensure the continuing 'honour of [his] name' among subsequent
generations of readers. The octave locates the originality of Du Bel-
lay's poetry in its recovery of the past, and through its reassertion of
the authority of 'free Poësie'.

In the sestet Spenser broadens both his reading and his concep-
tion of 'immortalitie'. Du Bartas's *Uranie* is seen as a smooth devel-
opment   from   Du   Bellay's   path-finding   innovation.   The
grammatical ease with which Du Bartas emerges from Du Bellay's
shadow partly belies the importance of the change these lines signal
in Spenser's approach to poetry. Since Du Bartas was a devotional
poet, the allusion to him establishes a hierarchy of poetic genres
based on the work of the two poets. In contrast with Du Bellay's ter-
restrial and historical concerns, Du Bartas aims solely at the adora-
tion of 'th'Almightie'. Spenser's simple wording suggests that Du
Bartas may qualify as a modern equivalent to the ancient divine
poets Sidney describes as 'The chief, both in antiquity and excel-
lency, were they that did imitate the unconceivable excellencies of
God'.[51] Like Sidney, Spenser believes the 'heavenly Muse' takes
precedence over the terrestrial. The sestet further clarifies Du Bel-
lay's 'immortalitie' by its evocation of Du Bartas's praise of God. As
there are two kinds of poetry – the human and the divine – so there
are two kinds of immortality. Du Bellay has access like Shakespeare's
young man in sonnet 55 to 'praise … in the eyes of all posterity'
through his poetry; but also like the young man, his fame is tempo-
rally limited until 'the ending doom' of apocalyptic judgement.[52] Du
Bellay's renown will last as long as his text finds readers. Du Bartas
on the other hand opens the way towards the adoration of God, and
by implication the immortality He confers on the faithful. As in *The*

51 Sidney, *Miscellaneous Prose*, p. 80.
52 Shakespeare, *The Sonnets and A Lovers Complaint*, ed. John Kerrigan (Har-
mondsworth: Viking Penguin, 1986), p. 104.

Teares of the Muses, Uranian poetry privileges its readers with a 'viewe' of 'Th'eternall Makers majestie'.[53]

Through this hierarchy of poets, 'L'Envoy' draws a distinction between the 'immortalitie' endowed by terrestrial poetry, and the transcendence of God. While the basic move from a human to a divine perspective is common in *Complaints*, 'L'Envoy' contrasts with *The Ruines of Time* where, as we shall see, divine transcendence seeks to replace the claims of 'eternizing' poetry. But in *Ruines of Rome*, Spenser characterizes Du Bellay as a new poet whose novelty is partly contingent on his ability to immortalize. As Spenser's retrospective comment on his translation, 'L'Envoy' makes clear that this kind of writing is valid. Moreover, the sonnet highlights Spenser's self-conscious involvement at one level with Du Bellay's literary reviving of Rome. But 'L'Envoy' also guides our reading of *Ruines of Rome* through its praise of Du Bartas's 'heavenly Muse'. The hierarchy of genres indicates that *Ruines of Rome* only represents one – earthly – form of poetic expression. Ultimately, the progress from Du Bellay to Du Bartas implies the eschatological replacement of the finite city, Rome, by its timeless counterpart, the New Jerusalem, in the manner of Augustine's *City of God*. Such a movement of ideas conveys a sense of Du Bellay's time-bound lament being answered by Du Bartas's transcendent contemplation of 'th'Almightie'. The sonnet's structure of ideas parallels the theological hierarchy of palaces and cities in *The Faerie Queene* 1, which culminates in the Red Cross Knight's 'vew' of 'The New *Hierusalem*'.[54]

The allusion to Du Bartas also recalls him as a specifically Protestant poet, an active Huguenot, and indicates Spenser's residual ideological unease with *Les Antiquitez* as the poetry of a Catholic. Though 'L'Envoy' makes no criticism of the project of reviving Rome 'out of her ashes' – rather the reverse – Du Bartas's prominent posi-

---

53 *The Teares of the Muses*, l. 512. S. K. Heninger, Jr, *Sidney and Spenser: The Poet as Maker* (University Park and London: University of Chicago Press, 1989) uses the phrase 'Uranian poetry' to describe a numerological aesthetic; however, I feel the term can be legitimately used to evoke a divine poetry of the kind Spenser ascribes to Du Bartas.

54 *FQ* I.X.55–57, p. 140.

tion in the sonnet shows Spenser's consciousness of the potential risks he was taking in the translation. I suggest that the hierarchical structure of ideas about poetry also serves the purpose of stressing Spenser's orthodoxy. By showing terrestrial poetry as a 'worthie' endeavour ultimately superseded by the 'heavenly' goal of divine poetry, Spenser incidentally – and advantageously – ranks the Protestant writer higher than the Catholic. The smooth panegyric of 'L'Envoy' should not obscure its pertinence to greater issues. It sharpens our approach to the translation through its linkage of ideological affiliations to devotional ideals. As in *Virgils Gnat*, a novel poet is also a doctrinally self-conscious one.

Spenser's version of 'Olde *Rome*'

'L'Envoy' provides an agenda for the reading of *Ruines of Rome*. By its focus on Du Bellay as an innovative poet and its insinuation of a hierarchy of genres underpinned by theological affiliations, the poem suggests that the translation should be approached both through its presentation of Du Bellay's new poetry, and in terms of its negotiation of the doctrinal problems *Les Antiquitez* posed for Spenser. This analysis will show that Spenser's practice as a translator is consistent with that already displayed in *Virgils Gnat*. The anglicizing of Du Bellay's sequence produces a text charged with poetic and national self-consciousness.

The first issue to be addressed, then, is the kind of poetic presentation Spenser makes of Du Bellay. Because *Ruines of Rome* is an essentially faithful version of *Les Antiquitez* within the constraints of rhyme and metre, it is vital to distinguish between accidental slips of translation and deliberate revisions. Renwick thoroughly catalogues Spenser's deviations from the French text, but makes small allowance for the possibility that apparent errors can be embellishments or forced alterations.[55] For example, there is a major disjunction

---

55 W. L.Renwick (ed.), *Complaints* (London: The Scholartis Press, 1928), pp. 244–48.

between the Petrarchan form of Du Bellay's sonnets and Spenser's translations, which are in the standard English form of three quatrains and a couplet. This variation in form has a significant impact on how *Ruines of Rome* renders *Les Antiquitez*; Du Bellay's text is transformed into an alien poetic syntax. Thus Spenser's poetic presentation of *Les Antiquitez* is best examined in the translation's diction and precise choice of words. The transposition of French poems into Spenser's idiom is well illustrated by the octaves of sonnet 9:

> Astres cruels, et vous dieux inhumains,
> Ciel envieux, et marâtre nature,
> Soit que par ordre ou soit qu'à l'aventure
> Voise le cours des affaires humains,
>
> Pourquoi jadis ont travaillé vos mains
> A façonner ce monde qui tant dure?
> Ou que ne fut de matière aussi dure
> Le front brave de ces palais romains?[56]

>   Ye cruell starres, and eke ye Gods unkinde,
> Heaven envious, and bitter stepdame Nature,
> Be it by fortune, or by course of kinde
> That ye doo weld th'affaires of earthlie creature;
>   Why have your hands long sithence traveiled
> To frame this world that does endure so long?
> Or why were not these Romane palaces
> Made of some matter no lesse firme and strong? (ll. 113–20)

Though Spenser stays close to Du Bellay's wording, the English diction does not reproduce that of the French poem. Despite his advice in the *Deffence*, Du Bellay's style is unarchaic. The exceptions in this sonnet, 'Voise' and 'corrompable' (older forms of 'aller' and 'corruptible') were in common usage in sixteenth-century French; Du Bellay's sonnet displays a poetic heightening of conventional language. By contrast, Spenser eschews the normal usage of sixteenth-century English. Archaic connectives like 'eke' and 'sithence' predominate,

---

56 Du Bellay, *Les Regrets* ..., p. 32.

with the result that the translation has the timbre of the authentic Spenser. For example, in lines 115–16, Spenser transposes the plain French into a quasi-middle English idiom: 'ordre' becomes 'course of kinde' and 'des affaires humains', 'th'affaires of earthlie creature'. This shift in diction and vocabulary implies a neo-medieval conception of 'bitter stepdame Nature' underlying the English text which is absent from the original. The phrase 'course of kinde' is suggestive of the medieval nature lore Spenser later used in *The Mutabilitie Cantos*, and would indicate his translation of Du Bellay into his own poetic nomenclature.[57] Yet Spenser's more portentous vocabulary does not disclose revised conceptions of either 'ordre' or 'les affaires humains'. Rather, these formulations show Spenser seeking to heighten the rhetorical texture of his poem: as in *Virgils Gnat*, the archaic, medievalizing idiom is an integral part of the translation's ornamentation.

Despite its basic fidelity, *Ruines of Rome*, like *Virgils Gnat*, makes no sustained attempt to parallel the syntactic structure of its original. This means that the reader of the English sequence must take Du Bellay's stylistic innovations either on trust or through the filter of Spenser's already innovative diction. Yet paradoxically, Spenser's commitment to novelty manifests itself through archaism. The diction of the English text apparently contradicts Spenser's self-presentation as a poetic modernizer. However, it is important to remember the revolutionary origins of this diction in the *Deffence*. Furthermore, a 'free Poësie' does not imply the desire to effect a rupture with an undifferentiated past; rather, as the parallel with *The Teares of the Muses* indicates, it signals the wish to restore poetry's ancient authority. Spenser's diction embodies this idealism. E. K.'s 'Epistle' to *The Shepheardes Calender* is helpful here: 'in my opinion it is one special prayse, of many whych are dew to this Poete, that he hath laboured to restore, as to theyr rightfull heritage such good and naturall English words, as have ben long time out of use and almost cleare disherited'.[58] The 'new Poet' achieves distinction through his recovery of a

57 Compare *Var.* VIII, p. 383.
58 'Epistle' to *The Shepheardes Calender*, ll.83–87.

pure English in his verse. His poetry is new in turn by its self-conscious desire to renovate the 'heritage' of English words. Poetry therefore possesses an implicit heritage of aristocratic prestige, which is revealed through Spenser's apparently retrogressive archaism.

This analysis points to Spenser's self-conscious awareness of how *Les Antiquitez* could illuminate his own poetic ambitions. In addition to the rhetorical framework provided by his distinctive idiom, at critical points in the sequence Spenser highlights this self-consciousness by his deviations from the French text. The most relevant of these occur in the poetically significant sonnets 25 and 32. In the sestet of sonnet 25, Spenser disrupts Du Bellay's concluding articulation to the modesty topos:

> Pussé-je au moins d'un pinceau plus agile
> Sur le patron de quelque grand Virgile
> De ces palais les portraits façonner:
>
> J'entreprendrais, vu l'ardeur qui m'allume,
> De rebâtir au compas de la plume
> Ce que les mains ne peuvent maçonner.[59]

> Or that at least I could with pencill fine,
> Fashion the pourtraicts of these Palacis.
> By paterne of great Virgils spirit divine;
> I would assay with that which in me is,
>   To builde with levell of my loftie style,
>   That which no hands can evermore compyle. (ll. 345–50)

Renwick observes that line 348 'scarcely translates' the French, while the Variorum editor rejoins that 'with its echo of Psalm 103.1, and with the two following lines, it far surpasses Du Bellay'.[60] Both are in their different ways correct. 'I would assay with that which in me is' not only does not translate 'J'entreprendrais, vu l'ardeur qui m'allume', it erases Du Bellay's image of his inspiration – an important idea carried through from the *Deffence*'s dis-

59 Du Bellay, *Les Regrets* ..., p. 43.
60 *Var.* VIII, p. 388.

cussion of the poet's need for natural inspiration, or 'ardeur', com-
bined with study. Furthermore, Spenser's echo of Psalm 103 has the
effect of undermining the poem's modesty topos. For the French
text, line 12 is the culmination of a litany of incapacity: if Du Bel-
lay had Orpheus's or Amphion's harp, or even Virgil's paint-brush,[61]
he *would undertake* the task of poetic rebuilding. The tone of this
conditional implies that such a project is beyond his skill. But the
final tercet allows the reader to draw the modest inference that *Les
Antiquitez* does rebuild Rome 'au compas de la plume' in the son-
nets themselves. The modesty topos explicitly discounts Du Bel-
lay's poetic ability while also implicitly affirming it. By contrast,
Spenser's line 348 transforms the final tercet into a direct affirma-
tion of the poet's skill. Psalm 103.1 reads, 'Praise the Lord, O my
soul: and all that is within me praise his holy Name' – the psalmist
begins with an internal command to raise his performance to the
height of God's 'holy Name'.[62] It is a pious instruction to poetic
excellence. In *Ruines of Rome*, 25, the phrase implies that the poet's
'assay' will have a positive outcome: he will rebuild Rome 'with lev-
ell of [his] loftie style'. This phrase in turn reads as a self-conscious
advertisement of poetic ability in a way that Du Bellay's original
does not. Thus, through his deviation from the French text,
Spenser advertises his ability and his awareness that his translation
can be a building block in his own poetic career. The 'assay' to build
a 'loftie style' takes its cue from Du Bellay's 'ardeur' and 'plume',
but also indicates Spenser's ambitions beyond the text in hand.

The translation of sonnet 32, on the other hand, is a self-authen-
ticating appropriation of Du Bellay's success.

> Vanter te peux, quelque bas que tu sois,
> D'avoir chanté, le premier des François,

---

61 Since modern English has lost the older meaning of 'pencil[l]' as 'paint-
brush', I use the modern term to translate 'pinceau'. I do not intend to correct
Spenser's word, however, which was the standard term in the sixteenth century; see
OED I.i.

62 Quoted from *The Book of Common Prayer*'s Psalter.

L'antique honneur du peuple à longue robe.[63]

Well maist thou boast, however base thou bee,
   That thou art first, which of thy Nation song
   Th'olde honour of the people gowned long. (ll. 446–48)

Spenser directly associates Du Bellay's achievement as the first Frenchman to have sung 'Th'olde honour of the people gowned long' with his own as the sequence's English translator. The 'premier des François' neatly becomes the 'first, which of thy Nation song' – a phrase which refers as much to Spenser as Du Bellay. This alteration witnesses both Spenser's self-conscious attitude towards *Ruines of Rome* as a part of his growing poetic output, and his enthusiastic recognition of *Les Antiquitez* as an innovative text. By allying his work with Du Bellay's, Spenser identifies himself as the first English garland of 'free Poësie'. Thus *Ruines of Rome* represents Spenser's conscious adoption of Du Bellay's mantle as a new poet who will recover poetry's ancient power. For the reader of *Complaints* in 1591, Spenser's poem is freighted with familiar Spenserian concerns – antiquarianism similar to that of *The Ruines of Time* and portions of *The Faerie Queene*; the development of a distinctive diction, and also a 'noble' conception of poetry like that lamented in *The Teares of the Muses*. The translation of sonnet 32 is a piece of sleight of hand that envisages *Les Antiquitez's* anglicization as a direct transference of poetic innovation from Du Bellay to Spenser, and temporarily blunts one's sense that *Ruines of Rome* is a translation. However, Du Bellay's innovations do not occur in a sequestered poetic world. As Spenser self-consciously adopts Du Bellay's claims to novelty, so he must wrestle with his ideologically loaded subject matter.

The distance between Du Bellay's perception of Rome and Spenser's can be gauged from small shifts like line 359, where 'Rome fut tout le monde, et tout le monde est Rome'[64] becomes '*Rome* was th'whole world, and al the world was *Rome*', through to the rendering of whole sonnets like 27 or 28. Line 359 is an interesting case

---

63 Du Bellay, *Les Regrets* …, p. 48.
64 *Ibid.*, p. 44.

because Spenser is under no pressure to mistranslate through the difficulty of the French, so that the change of tense must be a deliberate alteration. Spenser seems to want to temper Du Bellay's enthusiastic depiction of 'la romaine grandeur' as 'la carte du monde', and accomplishes this by fixing Rome in a continual past tense. The change is significant precisely because it is so unnecessary. The implication is that Spenser's Rome cannot be as ambiguous and as nuanced as Du Bellay's. This problem is illustrated well by sonnet 27. The octet apostrophizes an observer of Rome's ruins who is amazed at its 'antique orgueil'; it then instructs him to guess what time has obliterated by the fact that fragments of the ancient city still serve as patterns to contemporary architects. The sestet continues:

> Regarde après, comme de jour en jour
> Rome, fouillant son antique séjour,
> Se rebâtit de tant d'œuvres divines:
>
> Tu jugeras que le démon romain
> S'efforce encor d'une fatale main
> Ressusciter ces poudreuses ruines.[65]

Du Bellay witnesses the architectural recovery of ancient Rome as an incredible 'resuscitation' of its 'antique séjour' – 'ces poudreuses ruines' are almost magically reinvested with life by 'le démon romain'. The sonnet registers this reawakening with some shock. The figure of the observer of Rome ('Toi qui de Rome émerveillé contemples') allows Du Bellay to objectify his overt amazement and subdued horror at this rebuilding. Yet the horror remains carefully implicit – the 'démon' of Rome, though ambiguous, is no more diabolical than 'th'auncient *Genius* of that Citie brent' of *The Ruines of Time*. Spenser's sestet, however, is predominantly horrific:

> Then also marke, how Rome from day to day,
> Repayring her decayed fashion,
> Renewes herselfe with buildings rich and gay;
> That one would judge, that the *Romaine Dæmon*

---

65 *Ibid.*

> Doth yet himselfe with fatall hand enforce,
> Againe on foote to reare her pouldred corse. (ll. 373–78)

In the French, Rome's gender is neutral: the pronoun 'son' qualifies 'séjour', so the reader must supply the city's gender, and whether the city and the 'démon' are one and the same. By contrast, Spenser insists firstly that Rome is feminine (l. 374) and secondly that the '*Romaine Dæmon*' is a male demiurge bringing life back to the 'pouldred corse' of the Woman/City. Furthermore, in rendering 'fouillant son antique séjour' as 'Repayring her decayed fashion', Spenser replaces Du Bellay's factual image of archaeological excavation with a literary image of the female spirit restored to spectral existence and surface glamour. Spenser's self-conscious rewrite casts Rome as the Whore of Babylon.[66] His early adaptation of this image in the *Theatre for Worldlings* similarly uses the Whore and her seven-headed beast as a metaphor for Rome and its seven hills.[67] In this case, Spenser makes an apocalyptic emendation of Du Bellay's image of a magically renascent Rome. The implied reservation in the French poem about Rome's resuscitation becomes an explicit Protestant shudder of revulsion at the Whore's living 'pouldred corse' in the English translation. The essential ambiguity of Du Bellay's observation of contemporary Rome is subordinated by Spenser to the received political values of a literary image.

Ruines of Rome sonnet 27 registers the doctrinal and experiential gulf which divides Spenser from Du Bellay. Yet it is misleading to see these contrasting interpretations of Rome as simple disagreements between a Catholic writer and a Protestant. *Les Regrets* documents Du Bellay's contempt for the excesses of Papal Rome. Similarly, *Les Antiquitez* does not endorse the seat of Papal authority. Rather, as was argued above, it explores the paradox of the Roman Empire, and is more directly concerned with the classical past than sixteenth-century Rome. Within this framework, however, Du Bellay touches on Rome's subsequent history, as in sonnet 18, where the Papacy illustrates the circularity of Roman history. Yet such allusions do not

---

66 See Schell's notes in *YESP*, p. 401.
67 See *Sonets* [13], and Chapter 1 above, pp. 51–53.

result in any ideological commitment to the idea of the Papacy. *Les Antiquitez* remains consistent with its central perception of Rome as a paradox; sonnet 27 states that a dimension of this paradox is Rome's unfixed position between life and death. Hence sonnet 28 is an immediate reversal of the terms of 27. Where the latter witnesses Rome's upsurgence towards an improbable resuscitation, the former images Rome as 'un grand chêne asséché', more dead than alive. Sonnet 28 revises the optimism of 27 and makes the reader juxtapose two conflicting accounts of the city's vitality. In *Ruines of Rome*, however, sonnet 27 has already been made into an apocalyptic image of Roman corruption. Since the critical contrast between the poems is thus erased, Spenser's sonnet 28 magnificently misses the point of the original by over-embellishing its assault on the tottering Roman edifice. While this makes for a startling recasting of the octet, Spenser's version paradoxically dilutes the critical punch of Du Bellay's:

> Qui a vu quelquefois un grand chêne asséché,
> Qui pour son ornement quelque trophée porte,
> Lever encore au ciel sa vieille tête morte,
> Dont le pied fermement n'est en terre fiché,
>
> Mais qui dessus le champ plus qu'à demi penché
> Montre ses bras tout nus et sa racine torte,
> Et sans feuille ombrageux, de son poids se supporte
> Sur un tronc nouailleux en cent lieux ébranché:
>
> Et bien qu'au premier vent il doive sa ruine,
> Et maint jeune à l'entour ait ferme la racine,
> Du dévot populaire être seul révéré:
>
> Qui tel chêne a pu voir, qu'il imagine encore
> Comme entre les cités, qui plus florissent ore,
> Ce vieil honneur poudreux est le plus honoré.[68]

> He that hath seene a great Oke drie and dead,
> Yet clad with reliques of some Trophees olde,
> Lifting to heaven her aged hoarie head,

---

68 Du Bellay, *Les Regrets* ..., p. 45.

Whose foote in ground hath left but feeble holde;
    But halfe disbowel'd lies above the ground,
Shewing her wreathed rootes, and naked armes,
And on her trunke all rotten and unsound
Onely supports herselfe for meate of wormes;
    And though she owe her fall to the first winde,
Yet of the devout people is ador'd,
And manie yong plants spring out of her rinde;
Who such an Oke hath seene, let him record
    That such this Cities honour was of yore,
    And mongst all Cities florished much more. (ll. 379–92)

Spenser's octave is a critical adaptation of Du Bellay's. He intensifies the oak's corruption: where the French tree is dried out ('asséché') and more than half bent over ('plus qu'à demi penché'), its English counterpart is 'drie and dead' and 'halfe disbowel'd' respectively. This process culminates with Spenser's image of the tree holding itself up only as 'meate for wormes', which has no precedent in the original. Clearly Spenser wants the reader to be sure that the oak / Rome is thoroughly dead, and that any reverence 'the devout people' feel for it is misplaced. The result is a poetically pungent attack on Rome, which is reminiscent of the description of Error's carcass supplying her children with a poisonous dinner in *The Faerie Queene* I.I. That Spenser's use of the image suggests such a parallel indicates its lack of ambiguity; as with Error, the reader is to be left in no doubt of the corruption of the 'great Oke drie and dead'. Indeed, Spenser's oak is effectively a further portrait of the Whore of Babylon from sonnet 27. But rather than describing her 'decayed fashion', or her external appearance, in this text Spenser metaphorically displays the Whore's noxious pudenda: in the Protestant vision, 'her wreathed rootes' are literally 'meate for wormes'. Like Duessa in *The Faerie Queene* I, the oak is an image of the 'rotten' sexuality Protestants perceived in the Catholic Church.[69]

69 Compare Anthea Hume, *Edmund Spenser: Protestant Poet* (Cambridge: Cambridge University Press, 1984), pp. 74–75, 96.

By contrast, Du Bellay's description is much less definite.[70] In place
of the 'meate for wormes' image, for example, Du Bellay describes the
oak as 'without shady leaves, support[ing] its weight / On a knotty
trunk, stripped of its branches in a hundred places'. Yet this compar-
ative neutrality about the oak is a prelude to the sharply ironic tone
of the final tercet. These lines expose the tensions underlying the oak
simile by their revelation of Rome as an absurdly honoured geriatric
city: 'Ce vieil honneur poudreux' like the oak retains a prestige 'entre
les cités, qui plus florissent ore' which is out of proportion to its
actual condition and power. Like the oak, Rome has the appearance
of life but not the substance. Thus the poem calls into question son-
net 27's view of Rome as on the verge of resuscitation. But in *Ruines
of Rome*, because the octave has been rendered so unequivocally, the
sestet's force does not fully emerge. Spenser's closing lines read as a
wordy statement of the obvious rather than a critical presentation of
Rome's enduring authority. However, the importance of Spenser's
version lies not so much in its failure to render the subtleties of the
original, as in the reasons for its divergence.

This reading of sonnets 27 and 28 suggests that Spenser felt the
need to exercise an editorial control over aspects of *Les Antiquitez*. I
argue that the decision to change sonnet 27's sestet inevitably leads
to the rewriting of sonnet 28. Once Spenser colours Du Bellay's
observation of Rome with an apocalyptic typology, he alters the
French text's essential balance, enabling him to make explicit his own
criticisms of Rome. Like *Virgils Gnat*, *Ruines of Rome* displays
Spenser's concern with the political and religious values of the texts
he wishes to emulate. While he appropriates some of *Les Antiquitez*'s
formal novelty, Spenser is none the less compelled to provide through
translation English Protestant revisions of the French text.

It is in this spirit that 'L'Envoy' distinguishes Spenser's conception
of poetry from Du Bellay's. To recap, this text privileges devotional
poetry and its ascent from a terrestrial to a divine perspective.
Spenser's self-conscious rewriting of sonnets 27 and 28 is a move in

70 Du Bellay's image is an imitation of Lucan's simile for Pompey in *Pharsalia*
I.137–44; and as such sonnet 28 stays close to Lucan's wording. See the discussion
of this borrowing in Greene, *The Light in Troy*, pp. 225–26.

the direction of the hierarchy of genres in 'L'Envoy'. As the corrupt city is superseded by its divine counterpart in apocalyptic Christianity, so terrestrial poetry will be replaced by Uranian. By making a more explicit condemnation of Rome than Du Bellay, Spenser perhaps hoped to accelerate this apocalyptic process. Arguably, the 'Songe' represents Du Bellay's move towards this eschatological system of values. But for Spenser in 'L'Envoy', this shift is not enough to allow Du Bellay to stand as a representative of both secular and divine poetry: the Protestant Du Bartas is a safer, more doctrinally sound, model of the Uranian poet. The French poets' different beliefs underlie the generic hierarchy derived from their writings. Spenser's emendations to *Les Antiquitez* further differentiate his conception of 'free Poësie' from Du Bellay's. The translation and 'L'Envoy' suggest that a new English poetry will take its prompt from Du Bellay in its desire to recover the art's ancient authority, but will also endorse the idealism – and paranoia – of English Protestantism.

Ruines of Rome is, like *Virgils Gnat*, an act of creative appropriation. In this case, Spenser adopts a text which is an innovative complaint by a writer who was fundamentally concerned with the creation of a new poetry in the vernacular. So the translation of *Les Antiquitez* is firstly a platform for Spenser's own poetic ambitions: he wishes to emulate Du Bellay's achievement as a vernacular poet, whose novelty is witnessed in his renovation of traditional complaint. But *Ruines of Rome* also shows that the new English poetry could not simply be a replication of the French precedent. Though in the wider context of his career, Spenser realizes Du Bellay's aspiration for a vernacular epic through *The Faerie Queene*, in 'L'Envoy' he highlights his concern with a specifically Protestant devotional poetry. Hence the English sequence raises the issue of the political and religious basis of the new English poetry. For the Spenser of *Ruines of Rome*, poetry must be grounded on the 'prayse' of the Protestant 'Almightie'. In the first part of this book, I have progressed from *Virgils Gnat*, which ignores *Culex*'s affirmation of Imperial Rome, to *Ruines of Rome*, which foregrounds the conflicts between Spenser's view of Rome and Du Bellay's. The two poems indicate that while Spenser was able to appropriate the poetic achievements of 'Virgil' and Du Bellay for his own purposes, he was aware that his literary models served political and theological masters whose values he could not endorse.

But how does the appropriation of classic complaint texts in these translations anticipate the transformation of traditional complaint in the original poems still to be discussed? The translations embody Spenser's desire for literary innovation, as is shown in the explicit statement of 'L'Envoy' and the use of ottava rima to translate *Culex*. Yet this desire coexists with traditional ideas of poetic meaning and traditional forms of complaint. The translations are creative exercises in the poetic tradition through which Spenser exhibits his technical facility and his interest in complaint as a complex mode of poetic expression which can extend from classical oratory (in the Gnat's complaint) to the renovation of the love sonnet (in *Ruines of Rome*). In both these poems, the idea of complaint is closely associated with poetry either in the ancient poet's petition to his patron or the modern poet's literary recreation of ruined Rome. In anglicizing *Culex* and *Les Antiquitez*, Spenser displays an awareness of how other poets had made the complaint mode into a means of interpreting their cultural inheritance. It is in this way that the translations provide a precedent for the original *Complaints*: the renovation of the complaint mode enables 'the new Poet' to explore and transform the conceptions of poetry he inherited himself.

PART TWO
The Major *Complaints*

CHAPTER THREE

A 'goodlie bridge' between the Old and the New: the transformation of complaint in *The Ruines of Time*

To move from *Complaints'* translations to its original poems is to become more conscious of the differences between Spenser and his contemporaries. Though ostensibly an elegy for Leicester and Sidney, *The Ruines of Time* in fact uses their deaths much as Milton was to use the death of Edward King in *Lycidas* – as an opportunity to discuss poetry and the rôle of the poet. Though Spenser uses complaint to bewail the death of Sidney, his poem is not a conventional lament for great men, despite his claims in the Dedication to the Countess of Pembroke that it was 'speciallie intended to the renowming' of the Dudley family, 'and to the eternizing of some of the chiefe of them late deceased'. The differences between Spenser's treatment of Sidney's death and that of his contemporaries can be illustrated by 'The Funeral Songs of that honourable gentleman, Sir Philip Sidney, Knight' set by Byrd and published in his *Psalms, Sonnets, and Songs of Sadness and Piety* (1588). Though this poem's quantitative metre is unusual, its lament is stylized and relatively predictable. It aims to amplify our sense of the loss of Sidney by the staccato iteration of its lament: 'SID-NEY is dead!'; 'SIDNEY, the sprite heroic!'; 'Come to me grief, for ever!'[1] The poet's grief leads directly to the plaintive text whose goal is to move its listener to acknowledge the justice of its 'plaint'.

By contrast, *The Ruines of Time* uses the complaint mode in a much more complex way. I argue that it is a transitional blend of traditional genres and tropes, best understood as a meeting point between tradition and novelty. Spenser transforms traditional didactic and elegiac complaint by using them to discuss the philosophical implications of literary memorialization. Unlike the writer of 'The

---

1 In *Shorter Elizabethan Poems*, ed. A. H. Bullen (New York: E. P. Dutton, no date), pp. 22–23.

Funeral Songs', Spenser extends lament for Sidney into an explo-
ration of the literary immortality offered by humanist poetry and the
conflict which arises between this idea and the apocalyptic world-
contempt of Protestantism. *The Ruines of Time* is Spenser's attempt
to reconcile these oppositions through the mythologized figure of the
redeemed Sidney.

But the poem is more than a bridge between humanist ideas of lit-
erary 'eternizing' and Christian eschatology. Its transformation of
complaint bridges Spenser's practice as a translator and his practice as
a poet, for whom the values and forms of the past must be reinter-
preted and rewritten if they are to remain viable. In addition to being
the first poem in the 1591 volume,[2] *The Ruines of Time* is also the key
text for understanding the major *Complaints*. Its transitional form
reveals Spenser creating a new poetry in these poems: by self-con-
sciously revitalizing traditional complaint to explore problems in
poetics, he questions traditional poetry and makes innovative poetic
texts. *The Ruines of Time* prepares the way for the more radical trans-
formations of traditional complaint and poetics in *The Teares of the
Muses*, *Mother Hubberds Tale* and *Muiopotmos*.

A 'curious macedoine'?[3] The integrity of *The Ruines of Time*

Though in recent years *The Ruines of Time* has been recognized as an
important embodiment of Spenser's concern with poetry, critics have
generally followed Renwick's theory that the poem is a fragmentary
text, put together from disparate working poems to serve as a belated

---

2 See pp. 31–34 above for discussion of the ordering of the 1591 volume.
3 W. L. Renwick (ed.), *Complaints* (London: The Scholarbis Press, 1928), p.
204.

elegy for Sidney and Leicester.[4] Renwick argues that there are no proper transitions between the poem's different parts: Verlame has no connection with Leicester; the elegy for Sidney emerges abruptly from the lament for the Dudleys; the final 'Pageants' are 'a relic of the *Dreames* and *Pageants* mentioned by Spenser and Harvey in their letters'.[5] Because Renwick fails to see any organizing principle – beyond imitation of *Les Antiquitez* – the poem becomes a collage of frag-

4 *Ibid.*, pp. 189–90. Renwick's view of the text is supported by M. C. Bradbrook, 'No Room at the Top: Spenser's Pursuit of Fame' in *Elizabethan Poetry*, ed. J. R. Brown and Bernard Harris (Stratford-Upon-Avon Studies 2. London: Edmund Arnold, 1960), pp. 106–07; Alfred W. Satterthwaite, *Spenser, Ronsard and Du Bellay: A Renaissance Comparison* (Princeton: Princeton University Press, 1960), pp. 93–94; Millar MacLure, 'Spenser and the Ruins of Time', in *A Theatre for Spenserians*, ed. Judith M. Kennedy and James A. Reither (Toronto: University of Toronto Press, 1973), pp. 15–16; and, most thoughtfully, by DeNeef, '"The Ruines of Time": Spenser's Apology for Poetry', *SP*, 76 (1979), pp. 262–71, and *Spenser and the Motives of Metaphor* (Durham, NC: Duke University Press, 1982), pp. 28–40. Only Carl J. Rasmussen, '"How Weak Be the Passions of Woefulness": Spenser's *Ruines of Time*', *SSt*, 4 (1981), pp. 159–81, offers a significantly different view. He argues that Verlame's complaint is 'a perverse *consolatio*' (so that the poem is unified by its use of Boethius) and that Verlame is a type of the Whore of Babylon. See Margaret W. Ferguson, '"The Afflatus of Ruin": Meditations on Rome by Du Bellay, Spenser and Stevens, in *Roman Images*, Selected Papers from the English Institute, New Series No. 8, ed. Annabel Patterson (Baltimore: The Johns Hopkins University Press, 1982), pp. 33–39, for an analogous perspective, without structural analysis of the text. However, the most perceptive recent critic of the poem is J. A. Van Dorsten, 'Literary Patronage in Elizabethan England: The Early Phase', in *Patronage in the Renaissance*, ed. Guy F. Lytle and Stephen Orgel (Princeton: Princeton University Press, 1981), p. 205. He sees it as a record of Spenser's early emulation of Du Bellay; so the 'Pageants' are 'quaint, Anglo-Saxon ur-sonnets' (i.e. pairs of rhyme-royal stanzas linked by a shared rhyme). Van Dorsten's conclusion is that 'the 1591 *Ruines* recapture the earliest attempts to evolve, within an English tradition, a new, visionary poetry'. I share Van Dorsten's idea that *The Ruines of Time* represents a new poetry, but in my view he overstates both the datedness of the poem and its structural dependence on Du Bellay.

5 Renwick, *Complaints* pp. 189–90. For the Spenser-Harvey letters, see *Var.* X, pp. 18, 471–72.

ments written at different points in time.[6] This misleading image of
The Ruines of Time as a piece of 'ingenious carpentry'[7] has dominated
discussion ever since: few scholars have offered alternative accounts
of its structure. Renwick and his successors have not considered
whether the poem can be read as a coherent whole. That it uses a vari-
ety of genres and tropes does not preclude it from having an overall
coherence. To make the composition of this 'macedoine' less opaque,
I provide a systematic description – in the absence of an authorial
recipe – of the different ingredients Spenser blends into a unity.

Argument and Genre

As Spenser himself points out, the poem's central concern is to
memorialize the Dudley family, especially Leicester and Sidney. To
do this, Spenser uses the dream image of the '*Genius*' of Verulamium
who links her own ruin and the neglect of her history with the deci-
mation in the late 1580s of the Dudley family. By means of the *ubi
sunt* trope, Verlame illustrates the futility of the 'vaine worlds glorie'
(l. 43) through a catalogue of historical disasters culminating with
the deaths of Leicester and Sidney. But Verlame also recognizes that
literature can create an enduring record of the past: she functions as
a choric figure, whose protracted *ubi sunt* develops into an assertion
of the power of 'eternizing' poetry. Though cities and human beings
are transient, poetry can immortalize them.

Hence the lament for Sidney identifies him as the perfection of the
Dudley line both as man and poet. Having completed her lament for
the Dudleys, Verlame now comprehensively asserts the power of
poetry to preserve the glory of great men, and to transcend mortal-

6 All datings other than c.1590–91 depend on the kind of textual disintegration
practised by Renwick. Lines 435–39 unequivocally date the finished poem after the
death of Sir Francis Walsingham on 6 April 1590, while the rest of the poem (if
indeed it was composed in fragments) must be dated at least after the deaths of Sid-
ney (1586) and Leicester (1588). In addition to Renwick, *Complaints*, pp. 180,
188–90, see Schell in *YESP*, p. 225, and *Var.* VIII, pp. 526–29.

7 Renwick, *Complaints* pp. 189–90.

ity. The assertion of the benefits of literary 'eternizing' develops from
Verlame's earlier enthusiasm for Camden and commemoration of the
Dudleys into the radical claim that poetry can keep its patrons alive.
The immortality embodied in poetry becomes Verlame's panacea for
the tragic limitations of mortal life.

The poem concludes with two sets of visionary 'ur-sonnets',[8] or
'tragicke Pageants' (l. 490), which appear to the narrator after his
bewildered reaction to the main complaint (ll. 472–87). These
'Pageants' are emblematic glosses on the poem's first 490 lines. While
the first series validates Verlame's world-contempt but corrects her
interpretation of mortality, the second series accommodates the con-
flicting absolutes of Christian salvation and poetry through Sidney's
apotheosis.

So the poem can be read as a coherent argument. To memorialize
Sidney and Leicester, Spenser uses the figure of Verlame to initiate a
complex exploration of literary immortality and the conflict between
this humanist idea and the Christian notion of the ultimate 'vanitie'
of terrestrial comforts. Nevertheless the thematic and generic com-
plexity of the text can be confusing. It evokes a variety of traditional
tropes in unfamiliar contexts, while the speaker of the main com-
plaint can seem inconsistent. As well as understanding its argument,
we need to isolate the ingredients in its 'macedoine' of genres, since
generic diversity is the means by which Spenser makes *The Ruines of
Time* into a poem about poetry.

As the first poem in the *Complaints* volume, *The Ruines of Time*
appropriately makes extensive use of the complaint mode. But it is
not simply (in Ponsonby's words) a meditation 'of the worlds vanitie;
verie grave and profitable'.[9] In contrast with those critics who stress
the poem's dependence on *Les Antiquitez* (and hence its failure to
reproduce the lucid structure of the sonnet sequence),[10] I suggest that

---

8 Van Dorsten, 'Literary Patronage in Elizabethan England' p. 205.

9 See pp. 3–5 above.

10 See Renwick, *Complaints*, p. 189; Satterthwaite, *Ronsard and Du Bellay*, p.
93; Lawrence Manley, 'Spenser and the City: the Minor Poems', *MLQ*, 43 (1982),
pp. 213–14, sees the poem as Spenser's independent response to 'the Continental
mode of ruins poetry'.

the poem should primarily be viewed as a dream vision.[11] Within the overall form of a dream vision, however, Spenser self-consciously adapts the modes of didactic and elegiac complaint to discuss literary immortality.

Though dream vision does not receive separate classification in Sidney's *Defence of Poetry*,[12] Elizabethan readers would have been familiar with a wide range of such texts. Dream vision is a pervasive literary mode which encompasses a vast body of writings from the Bible and classical Rome, through to medieval Europe. A brief conspectus of dream vision literature readily available to Elizabethans would include Ezekiel, Daniel 7 and Revelation; *Aeneid* VI and Cicero's 'Somnium Scipionis'; the *Divinia Commedia*, the *Hous of Fame* and *Piers Plowman*. Spenser's familiarity with the medieval version of the genre is aptly demonstrated by his reworking of Chaucer's *Book of the Duchess* for *Daphnaïda* (1591).[13]

Spenser may also have drawn on Petrarch's *Trionfi*, which he would have known either through Lord Morley's Henrican translation,[14] or the Countess of Pembroke's version of the 'Triumph of Death', writ-

11 This approach has some affinities with that of Rasmussen, '"How Weak Be the Passions of Woefulness"', inasmuch as Boethius's *Consolation* is itself a dream-vision. However, Rasmussen's essay does not prove that the *Consolation* is the determining influence on *The Ruines of Time*.

12 Nonetheless, he mentions specific dream-visions with approval; see Sir Philip Sidney, *Miscellaneous Prose of Sir Philip Sidney*, ed. Katherine Duncan-Jones and Jan Van Dorsten (Oxford: Clarendon, 1973), pp. 81, 89.

13 Compare Duncan Harris and Nancy L. Steffen, 'The Other Side of the Garden: An Interpretive Comparison of Chaucer's *Book of the Duchess* and Spenser's *Daphnaïda*', *JMRS*, 8 (1978), pp. 17–36.

14 Petrarch, *Lord Morley's 'Tryumphes of Fraunces Petrarcke': The First English Translation of the 'Trionfi'*, ed. D. D. Carnicelli (Cambridge, Mass.: Harvard University Press, 1971).

ten between the mid-1580s and early 1590s.[15] Like the *Trionfi, The Ruines of Time* uses the dream device in its opening and to explain the procession of 'Pageants' witnessed by the dreamer.[16] Both poems contain a dialectical development from the terrestrial perspective of the poet-lover and Verlame to the divine perspective of the religious initiate and the redeemed Sidney. Finally, Petrarch's argument that the fame endowed by literature is itself at the mercy of time has a clear connection with *The Ruines of Time*'s critical presentation of 'eternizing' poetry. But Spenser concludes his poem with a synthesis of religious and poetic transcendence, whereas the *Trionfi* ostensibly purge poetry from Petrarch's vision of eternity.

But the most immediate source for the poem's use of dream vision is Du Bellay's *Les Antiquitez* and 'Songe'. Like the *Trionfi*, the French poems progress from a terrestrial perspective, contemplating the fall of Imperial Rome, to a divine perspective, demonstrating that 'onely God surmounts all times decay'.[17] Renwick argued that in *The Ruines of Time* Spenser adopts Du Bellay's 'device of a double structure, a series of direct assertions followed by a series of allegorical restatements of the same motives'.[18] Though the English poem contains 'a double structure', it is over-simplistic to equate the paradoxical structure of Du Bellay's sonnet sequences with Spenser's cumulative stanzas.[19] Spenser's debt to Du Bellay is more generic than structural: he uses the motif of

15 See Margaret P. Hannay, *Philip's Phoenix: Mary Sidney, Countess of Pembroke* (New York and Oxford: Oxford University Press, 1990), pp. 107–09; and Mary Sidney, Countess of Pembroke, *The Triumph of Death and Other Unpublished and Uncollected Poems*, ed. G. F. Waller (Salzburg Studies in English Literature. Salzburg: Universität Salzburg, 1977), pp. 11–18. The Countess's translation is more conveniently reprinted in *The Silver Poets of the Sixteenth Century*, ed. Douglas Brooks-Davies (Everyman's Library. London and Rutland, Vermont: J. M. Dent and Charles Tuttle, new edn 1992), pp. 291–99.

16 Carnicelli's claim that 'the *Complaints* volume … derived its Petrarchanism chiefly from Du Bellay' rests on the misconception that *The Ruines of Time* is simply a reduplication of *Ruines of Rome*. In Petrarch, *Lord Morley's 'Tryumphes of Fraunces Petrarcke'*, p. 63.

17 *The Visions of Bellay*, l. 13. Compare Chapter 2 above, pp. 74, 81–82.

18 Renwick, *Complaints* p. 189.

19 See Chapter 2 above, pp. 71–83.

the visionary 'Pageant' he had already translated in *The Visions of Bellay* as a symbolic gloss to the dream encounter between the narrator and Verlame. By incorporating this Du Bellayan device into his own poem, Spenser illustrates both his understanding of, and his desire to 'overgo', his model, itself a novel amalgam of the amatory sonnet with dream vision and innovatory complaint.[20]

The Ruines of Time should be read as a series of contrasting visions, progressively developing the narrator's understanding of mortality and the place of poetry in this world. Though Spenser does not explicitly state at the beginning of the poem that his 'travailer' is dreaming, the opening stanzas imply that he is experiencing a vision of some kind. He walks by the Thames, 'Nigh where the goodly *Verlame* stood of yore' (l. 3), although Camden's *Britannia*, which ironically Verlame will praise, demolishes this myth.[21] Verlame herself appears as an iconic embodiment of Verulamium: 'Rending her yeolow locks, like wyrie golde, / About her shoulders careleslie downe trailing … In her right hand a broken rod she held, / Which towards heaven she seemd on high to weld' (ll. 9–13). As most commentators have observed, Spenser here embellishes his version of 'Songe' X,[22] describing the Genius of Rome 'Hard by a rivers side' lamenting her 'great glorie' and 'auncient praise' (*The Visions of Bellay*, ll. 127, 132). He is rewriting a visionary image. So after seeing her rod, the narrator does not return to the idea that Verlame could be just 'A Woman' (l. 8). The 'broken rod' convinces him that he is seeing a symbolic image which he must interpret: in the next stanza he identifies her as 'th'auncient *Genius* of that Citie brent' (l. 19). Like a tableau-vivant, the visionary and symbolic origins of Verlame are highlighted before she even speaks.

20 Compare Van Dorsten, 'Literary Patronage in Elizabethan England', p. 205. See also Chapter 2 *loc. cit.*

21 Renwick, *Complaints*, p. 194, notes that Camden's account of Verulamium expressly corrects the idea '"that the river *Tamis* sometimes had his course and chanell this way"'.

22 John B. Bender, *Spenser and Litarary Pictorialism* (Princeton: Princeton University Press, 1972), pp. 156–57, contains the best literary comparison of the two texts; see also Ferguson, '"The Afflatus of Ruin"', p. 34.

The dream encounter with Verlame is supplemented by the 'Pageants' which close the poem. Spenser shows, in accordance with the traditional literary depiction of the psychological impact of visions, the bewilderment and spiritual anguish that Verlame's 'doubtfull speach' causes the narrator (l. 485). Like the seer in Daniel 7.15, the narrator is troubled by 'the visions of his head'; also like Daniel, the narrator is granted further visionary glosses which aim to explain his original vision. The 'Pageants' function as a necessary coda to the narrator's vision of Verlame, modifying her 'doubtfull' assertions and attempting to reconcile the reader to mortality. In this way, the overall form of *The Ruines of Time* can be seen as an internally congruent adaptation of the visionary tradition.

This account of the poem also clarifies the problems of its transitions. Following Renwick, scholars have tended to argue that after line 238, Spenser 'begins to lose sight of' Verlame,[23] betraying an 'inability to maintain a consistent speaking voice'.[24] Such objections may appear well-founded. Can Spenser simultaneously expect his readers to accept Verlame as the tutelary spirit of a ruined city and as a self-conscious poet who incidentally presents herself as a mortal being? Yet there are strong connections between the different stages of the main complaint. The *ubi sunt* unites Verlame's sense of civic loss with the deaths of Leicester and Sidney, while her panegyric of Camden anticipates the defence of 'eternizing' poetry. At one level the problem of the speaker is a red-herring: Spenser organizes *The Ruines of Time* through related ideas and rhetorical tropes. To be an effective lament for Sidney, the poem does not need to characterize Verlame consistently.

Moreover, since the poem is a dream vision, Verlame need not be a 'consistent speaking voice' for the text to be a valid expression of the psychology of dreams, as exhibited especially in Chaucerian dream visions. In these texts, linked ideas and images are of more importance than the exhaustive exploration of imagined characters and situations. *The Hous of Fame* relates three outwardly unconnected

---

23 Renwick, *Complaints*, p. 195.
24 DeNeef, *Spenser and the Motives of Metaphor*, p. 30.

segments of 'Geffrey"s dream,[25] ultimately linked by his intellectual and physical progress towards the Palace of Fame. Even though it is unfinished, therse is no sense that such abruptness is aesthetically clumsy. Rather, the best dream visions imitate the random shifts of voice and environment characteristic of actual dreams. Against such a template, *The Ruines of Time* is a coherent dream vision.

In traditional poetry, dream vision and complaint are frequently complementary: in the *Mirror for Magistrates* the complainants are ghosts whose narratives the text records. Similarly, the *Book of the Duchess* uses its dream scenario as a means of artfully contextualizing the Black Knight's elegiac lament for his lady. In *The Ruines of Time*, the relationship between dream vision and complaint is more problematic both because of the density of the poem's structure and because Spenser does not use traditional complaint passively. His manipulation of the different literary modes within the poem indicates that it will not be contained by the normative expectations of either dream vision or traditional complaint.

For example, the didactic complaints of the *Mirror* would seem to offer a compelling analogy to Verlame's.[26] Verlame twice alludes to this tradition – firstly in her view that Rome's fall is an image of her own 'fatall overthrowe' (ll. 78–79); secondly in her final adjuration to the wise to 'behold the piteous fall of mee: / And in my case their owne ensample see' (ll. 459–60). Spenser's phrasing recalls that of the *Mirror* poets. Churchyard's *Shores Wife* instructs other women to make 'A myrrour … of my great overthrowe' and hence to 'Defye this world, and all his wanton wayes'.[27] Such rhetorical continuity may

---

25 *The Hous of Fame*, l. 729. In Chaucer, *The Works*, ed. F. N. Robinson (London: Oxford University Press, 1957), p. 289.

26 See Roe's discussion of this genre in, William Shakespeare *The Poems*, ed. John Roe (Cambridge: Cambridge University Press, 1992), pp. 38–41, 64–65. Compare also Hallett Smith, *Elizabethan Poetry: A Study in Conventions, Meaning and Expression* (Cambridge, Mass.: Harvard University Press, 1952), pp. 102–26, for a discussion of the 1590s 'revival of the complaint form' in texts like Daniel's *The Complaint of Rosamond*. See pp. 27–28, n.90, above for the influence of *The Ruines of Time* on Shakespeare's *A Lover's Complaint*.

27 *The Mirror for Magistrates*, ed. Lily B. Campbell (Cambridge: Cambridge University Press, 1938; rpt. 1960), p. 386.

suggest that *The Ruines of Time* is merely a conventional recycling of
the tradition of didactic complaint. However, texts like *Shores Wife*
have few ambitions beyond the articulation of formulaic exemplars;[28]
The Ruines of Time uses didactic complaint to introduce its lament for
the Dudleys and its discussion of the motif of 'eternizing' poetry. So
Verlame's complaint only partly approximates to the paradigm of
didactic complaint as exhibited in the *Mirror*. The apparently tradi-
tional cast of her final recapitulation does not highlight the moral the
reader is to extract from the text as a whole. Though traditional, Ver-
lame's world-contempt (ll. 454–69) in fact bewilders the narrator: he
cannot understand such conventional moralism after the literary dis-
cussion of the previous 100 lines. Far from reduplicating the didactic
values of traditional complaint, Verlame's monologue problematizes
them by transforming complaint into a debate about poetry.

In sum, *The Ruines of Time* is a dream vision which incorporates
Spenser's transformation of traditional complaint into a medium for
the discussion of poetics. Though this description clarifies the poem's
genre and structure, enfranchising it as a serious embodiment of
Spenser's intellectual concerns rather than as insipid public verse,[29] it
should not erase the sense that the poem's form is unfixed. In its use
of traditional genres and tropes, *The Ruines of Time* is designedly het-
erodox. The reader is exposed in quick succession to a wide range of
contrasting poetic modes, sampling modified exemplary complaint,
pastoral elegy, an encomium of 'eternizing' poetry, and visionary
'Pageant' in just under 700 lines.

The remaining question is why Spenser evolved this unorthodox
form for the purpose of an apparently routine public poem. I suggest
that *The Ruines of Time*'s transitional form allows Spenser self-con-
sciously to raise the aesthetic problems which are the focal concern of
this text: the relationship between poets and their patrons, and from

28 See my article, '"A talkatiue wench (whose words a world hath delighted
in)": Mistress Shore and Elizabethan Complaint', *RES*, 49 (1998), pp. 395–415 for
a reconsideration of Churchyard's poem in the light of the wider Elizabethan Shore
literature.

29 Compare Dodge in *Var.* VIII, p.522: '*The Ruins* [sic] *of Time* is mainly offi-
cial verse, melodious and uninspired'.

this the relationship between poetry and mortality. The poem's formal ambiguities are necessitated by its dynamic progression of ideas. Spenser adopts this form because he is not writing a conventional public elegy: unlike *Astrophel*, *The Ruines of Time* is complicated by the aesthetic issues its lament for the Dudleys provokes. So we can suggest a reading of the poem in which its form fluctuates as its argument develops. Spenser begins with the dream image of Verlame, whose exemplary complaint of her 'fatall overthrowe' (l. 79) mirrors the ruin of the Dudley family in the late 1580s. As he makes this transition, Spenser modifies the conceit of the exemplary complaint by raising the notion of literary immortality. This idea conditions his pastoral elegies for Leicester and Sidney: as a poet, Spenser has a vocational responsibility to 'eternize' his patrons. These self-conscious elegies logically give way to a defence of 'eternizing' poetry as a humanist ideal which guarantees the fame of its subjects. But since this defence shades into the near-idolatry that poetry alone can 'mount' its subjects 'to heaven' (l. 426), Spenser returns to the dream-frame to introduce the corrective 'Pageants'. These aim to counter Verlame's argument by symbolically revealing that 'all is vanitie and griefe of minde' (l. 583). Yet even this moralizing form is forced to concede a place for poetry through the closing images of the redeemed Sidney.

The Ruines of Time is therefore written in a deliberately transitional form. While this 'macedoine' may seem to be a unique recipe, Spenser's procedure in making a text in which form and content interpenetrate to underline a central concern with the morality of art is repeated in *Mother Hubberds Tale* and *Muiopotmos*.

The Ruines of Time on Poetry

This discussion of the poem's argument and form suggests that it is both a coherent progression of ideas and a designedly novel cocktail of traditional genres and tropes. I will now argue that it can be read as a 'goodlie bridge' (l. 557) between the traditional poetry Spenser inherited and the new poetry he was in the process of creating.

1 Lament and 'eternizing'

The connection between literature and the survival of the ruined past – and so the case for literary 'eternizing' – arises when Verlame has reached complete despair. Since both her city and inhabitants no longer exist, as Verulamium's tutelary spirit[30] she has become useless. But she remembers the emotive truism that

> ... it is comfort in great languishment
> To be bemoned with compassion kinde,
> And mitigates the anguish of the minde. (ll. 159–61)

Verlame's 'comfort' is that her existence is confirmed through compassionate complaint: if she is mourned, her memory, and therefore her purpose as the spirit of Verulamium, is at least poetically maintained. Literature, specifically Camden's antiquarian 'record' of Verulamium in *Britannia*, performs this function for her:

> *Cambden* the nourice of antiquitie,
> And lanterne unto late succeeding age,
> To see the light of simple veritie,
> Buried in ruines, through the great outrage
> Of her owne people, led with warlike rage,
> *Cambden*, though time all moniments obscure,
> Yet thy just labours ever shall endure. (ll. 169–75)

Though Camden is an historian, the 'nourice of antiquitie', Verlame describes his 'just labours' in terms which anticipate her subsequent praise of poetry as a means of escape from mortality. Camden has seen 'the light of simple veritie, / Buried in ruines', and despite the destruction of the city by 'her owne people', his textual recovery of the past evades the decay of 'all moniments'. Figuratively Camden's work makes him into a modern counterpart of Amphion, the poet-

---

30 Compare *OED*'s first definition of 'genius'. Since Verlame is clearly related to the Virgilian *lares et penates*, it is surely somewhat perverse to gloss 'Genius' as demon or goblin, as in the strategy of Rasmussen, '"How Weak Be the Passions of Woefulness"', pp. 162–64.

builder of Thebes.[31] Though '*Amphions* instrument' has the power in
Ruines of Rome, 'To quicken with his vitall notes accord, / The stonie
joynts of these old walls now rent',[32] at this stage in *The Ruines of
Time*, the modern antiquarian-cum-poet simply produces a text in
which ruins are historically recreated. Camden does not rebuild
Verulamium, he catalogues it. Nonetheless, Verlame believes (how-
ever erroneously) that the *Britannia* confirms her historic importance
and the grounds of her complaint. Historical literature 'sees' beyond
the 'ruins' through to 'the simple veritie' of what once was. As in
Horace's 'Exegi monumentum' (*Odes* III.30), 'eternizing' literature
creates a textual monument more enduring than the physical 'moni-
ments' of the Pyramids or Roman Britain.

This confidence in the power of literature actuates the lament for
Leicester as another victim of human forgetfulness and hypocrisy.
But Spenser intensifies the 'eternizing' topos through Verlame's
attack on Colin Clout. As well as its lament for Leicester, this passage
prominently asserts the duties of poets to their patrons. Leicester was
one of England's 'greatest ones' (ll. 186–87), yet was cheated of
proper commemoration from his 'Poets' after his death. The poets
prove that in this world 'All is but fained, and with oaker dide' (l.
204) by their negligence of Leicester's reputation:

> He now is dead, and all his glorie gone,
> And all his greatnes vapoured to nought,
> That as a glasse upon the water shone,
> Which vanished quite, so soone as it was sought:
> His name is worne alreadie out of thought,
> Ne anie Poet seekes him to revive;
> Yet manie Poets honourd him alive. (ll. 218–24)

The hypocrisy of the poets not only symbolizes the duplicity of the
'courting masker' (l. 202); it exhibits – in the light of Camden's

31 See Deborah Cartmell, 'Edmund Spenser and the Literary Uses of Architec-
ture in the English Renaissance' (unpublished PhD thesis, University of York,
1986/87), pp. 39–43, for the view that Spenser uses Amphion as a symbol of poetic
rebuilding; and Chapter 2 above, pp. 86–87.

32 *Ruines of Rome*, ll. 341–43.

example – the neglect of a higher calling. Leicester's 'glorie' and 'greatnes' disappear because of the poets' neglect of his posthumous reputation. Again, the implication is that poetry has the power to preserve human life. The poet's urgent duty is 'to revive' Leicester to save his 'name' from oblivion:

> Ne doth his *Colin*, careless *Colin Cloute*,
> Care now his idle bagpipe up to raise,
> Ne tell his sorrow to the listning rout
> Of shepherd groomes, which wont his songs to praise:
> Praise who so list, yet will I him dispraise,
> Untill he quite him of this guiltie blame:
> Wake shepheards boy, at length awake for shame.

> And who so els did goodnes by him gaine,
> And who so els his bounteous minde did trie,
> Whether he shepheard be, or shepheards swaine,
> (For manie did, which doo it now denie)
> Awake, and to his Song a part applie:
> And I, the whilst you mourne for his decease,
> Will with my mourning plaints your plaint
>   increase. (ll. 225–38)

These stanzas evoke the troubled relationship between Spenser and Leicester underlined by the Dedicatory sonnet of *Virgils Gnat*.[33] The indictment of Colin Clout alone among Leicester's poets is an intensely self-conscious poetic artifice through which Spenser furthers the idea of literature as an enduring 'record' of the past. The first stanza denounces Colin Clout for having wilfully abandoned his duty to Leicester. The 'praise' Verlame has lavished on Camden is withheld from Colin: 'Untill he quite him of this guiltie blame', he does not properly function as the 'eternizing' poet Spenser claims to be in the dedication to the Countess of Pembroke. In the second stanza, Verlame provides a text for Colin's lament while also indicating the severity with which she views his 'guiltie blame'. Insistent parallelism and anaphora subtly convey the shift in emphasis from the

33 See pp. 47–51 above.

initial reproach of line 231 – '*Wake* … at length for shame' – to the
rallying cry of line 236 – '*Awake*, and to his Song a part applie' –
which has the force of a command that is being carried out by the text
itself.[34] Lines 236–38 constitute a 'part' song or elegy for Leicester,
through the mouthpiece of Verlame, to which the Earl's former pro-
tégés can 'a part applie'. The communal pressure to 'eternize' is given
further emphasis by the implication of line 235 that the poets' aban-
donment of Leicester mirrors Peter's denial of Christ: 'manie'
received patronage from Leicester 'which doo it now denie', as Peter
'denied' his association with Jesus after his arrest.[35] The human frailty
of Peter's betrayal is repeated in the poets' forsaking of Leicester when
he can no longer reward their labours. For Verlame, the writing of
'eternizing' poetry is a responsibility which cannot be shirked with-
out sin. The pious action of Colin, the poets and Verlame, atones for
the lapsarian sins of hypocrisy and neglect in a 'plaint' for the fallen
condition of the world imaged in the death of Leicester.

Verlame advances the case for 'eternizing' poetry through the self-
conscious introduction of Spenser's persona, and the consequent
implication – supported by the Dedication – that Spenser himself
shares Verlame's poetic idealism. But this dual self-consciousness is
also a prelude to Verlame's revealing presentation of her 'Song' as a
form of communal wish-fulfilment. Like the Dedicatory sonnet to
Virgils Gnat, this passage dramatizes Spenser's sense that his relation-
ship with Leicester was profoundly troubled.[36] Yet Verlame wants to
believe that Colin's 'guiltie blame' – in effect the Fall of man itself,
since Leicester's death is inextricably linked to the mutability of civi-
lizations occasioned by human cupidity – can be entirely wiped clean
by the harmonious unison of 'Song'. Poetry can transcend death and
thus ameliorate all wrongs. But Spenser's text leaves no doubt that

34 My italics.
35 See for example Matthew 26.69–75. The Synoptic Gospels all have the same
basic story, with its stress on Peter's verbal 'denials' of Christ.
36 See Edwin A. Greenlaw, *Studies in Spenser's Historical Allegory* (Baltimore:
The Johns Hopkins University Press, 1932; rpt. London: Frank Cass, 1967), pp.
104–32, and Eleanor Rosenberg, *Leicester, Patron of Letters* (New York: Columbia
University Press, 1955), pp. 336–48, for historical speculation on the quarrel, and
also Chapter 1 above, pp. 47–51.

this belief is a form of wish-fulfilment: ultimate amelioration is not within the gift of 'eternizing' poets or indeed their patrons. As the 'Pageants' will make clear, human vanity and incapacity undermine all our constructions, in spite of Verlame's fantasy.

The lament for Sidney is the first place where the tension between Christian and poetic transcendence is suggested. Unlike the majority of his family, Sidney was himself a poet. So in the lament, Spenser balances idealized images of Sidney as a perfect Christian soldier and as a perfect English poet. Though Spenser's lament has been dismissed as containing 'but one fit phrase',[37] it is a complex piece of writing in which Sidney is successively praised as a type of Christ and a type of Orpheus. The correlations between these two mythic archetypes anticipate the poem's final accommodation of poetry and Christianity.

Sidney's condensed biography follows that of Christ from conception onwards: Marie Dudley Sidney brings forth 'of her happie womb … The sacred brood of learning and all honour; / In whom the heavens powrde all their gifts upon her' (ll. 278–80). Sidney's birth mirrors Christ's in the text's perception of him as a nonpareil of human virtue: though not born of a virgin, Sidney is a 'sacred brood' blessed with heavenly gifts.[38] Thus the first image of Sidney as a soldier metaphorically presents him as an imitator of Christ, who becomes a national hero by virtue of his 'blessed spirite full of power divine' (l. 288):

> Yet ere his happie soule to heaven went
> Out of this fleshlie goale, he did devise
> Unto his heavenlie maker to present
> His bodie, as a spotles sacrifise;

37 Bradbrook, 'No Room at the Top', p. 106. Bradbrook's favoured phrase, 'Most gentle spirite breathed from above' (281) seems as perverse as her remark. The whole lament is a succession of 'fit phrases'!

38 This explains why Spenser omits any mention of Sir Henry Sidney, which puzzled Renwick (*Complaints*, p. 196) and possibly led him to overstate the 'clumsiness' of this passage. But see also Hannay, *Philip's Phoenix*, p. 79, who suggests that Sir Henry lacked his Dudley wife's financial power, and so was not a fruitful source of literary patronage.

> And chose, that guiltie hands of enemies
> Should powre forth th'offring of his guiltles blood:
> So life exchanging for his countries good. (ll. 295–301)

Sidney's deliberate 'devis[ing]' of his death marks it as peculiarly Christ-like. This typological connection between Christ and Sidney is reinforced by Verlame's mythologizing of the skirmishes in the Netherlands;[39] Sidney '*chooses*' 'that guiltie hands of enemies' should kill him in the same way that Christ foresees and sanctions the pattern of his death in the Gospels.[40] The symbolic function of Sidney's death is highlighted typologically: Spenser builds a dualistic image of Sidney/England being 'sacrificed' by 'enemies'/Spain, which is itself a development of Verlame's opposition of spirit and matter at lines 288–94. This metaphorical account of Sidney's death encourages emotional extremity and reinforces Verlame's awareness of the 'wretchedness' of the material world (l. 293) in comparison with the 'celestiall grace' (l. 289) enjoyed by Sidney's soul. His life is unequivocally that of a national hero and true Christian. The final couplet of this stanza presents his 'sacrifise' as a national sacrament: 'th'offring of his guiltles blood' is done in 'exchang[e] … for his countries good'. Yet while such patriotic heroism is analogous to Christ's crucifixion, it does not ransom the sins of the human race; Christ's 'deare blood clene washt [us] from sin';[41] Sidney's death, on the other hand, encourages only the emulation of his virtuous example.

39 *The Ruines of Time* is at the forefront of the Elizabethan mythologizing of Sidney's death. Katherine Duncan-Jones, *Sir Philip Sidney: Courtier Poet* (London: Hamish Hamilton, 1991), p. 296, makes it clear that the engagement at Zutphen which resulted in Sidney's mortal wound was a 'skirmish' and not a battle as has been argued from 1586 onwards; Spenser is of course not remotely concerned with giving a factual account of Sidney's death here or in *Astrophel*.

40 My italic; for Christ's anticipation of his death, see for example Matthew 20.17–19.

41 *Amoretti*, LXVIII, l. 7. Compare also *An Hymne of Heavenly Love*, ll. 166–68, which expresses the Pauline view that Christ's sacrifice cleanses original sin: 'To heale the sores of sinfull soules unsound / And cleanse the guilt of that infected cryme, / Which was enrooted in all fleshly slyme'.

The second half of the lament presents Sidney as the new Orpheus, who excels his mythic prototype. Sidney is appropriately described as a pastoralist:

> Yet will I sing, but who can better sing,
> Than thou thy selfe, thine owne selfes valiance,
> That whilest thou livedst, madest the forrests ring,
> And fields resownd, and flockes to leap and daunce,
> And shepheards leave their lambs unto mischaunce,
> To runne thy shrill *Arcadian* Pipe to heare. (ll. 323–28)

While this may appear an unremarkable assemblage of pastoral conventions, the accumulation of detail recalls the impact of Orpheus's music on the inanimate world of 'forrests' and 'fields'. Spenser's rendition of the myth in *Virgils Gnat* typifies classical descriptions of the impact of 'Orpheus musicke' on 'swift running rivers', 'wilde beasts', and especially 'the shrill woods'.[42] Texts like *Culex* evoke a half-magical poet, whose amazing skill is evidenced in the impact of his art on the natural world. Sidney's 'shrill *Arcadian* Pipe' has an analogous effect: the sheer delight his art has for its audience compels them to abandon their normal tasks almost against their will.[43]

But what is most intriguing about this allusion is its disregard of what Cain calls the 'Renaissance' interpretation of the Orpheus myth.[44] Following Horace's *Ars Poetica*,[45] humanists viewed Orpheus's mastery over the natural world as a metaphor for primitive poetry's suasive linguistic codification of laws and rules of conduct to control what Sidney wittily calls 'stony and beastly people'.[46] Yet neither at

42 *Virgils Gnat*, ll. 450–56.

43 One could argue that these two passages bear the relics of some influence on each other. For example, the adjective 'shrill' is appropriate for Sidney's '*Arcadian* Pipe', but seems rather strained for the 'shrill woods'. Perhaps Spenser had the word lodged in his mind in connection with Sidney and Orpheus.

44 Thomas H. Cain, 'Spenser and the Renaissance Orpheus', *UTQ*, 41 (1971), pp. 25–28.

45 See Shepherd's note in Sir Philip Sidney, *An Apology for Poetry*, ed. Geoffrey Shepherd (London: Thomas Nelson, 1965; rpt. Old and Middle English Texts. Manchester: Manchester University Press, 1973), p. 147.

46 Sidney, *Miscellaneous Prose*, p. 74.

this point, or in the direct allusion in line 332, is this humanist inter-
pretation invoked, despite its wide currency. So what does the align-
ment of Sidney and Orpheus signify in *The Ruines of Time*? On the
surface, the allusion functions as an encomiastic demonstration of
Sidney's poetic singularity:

> ... thou now in *Elisian* fields as free,
> With *Orpheus*, and with *Linus*, and the choice
> Of all that ever did in rhymes rejoyce,
> Conversest, and doost heare their heavenlie layes,
> And they heare thine, and thine do better
> > praise. (ll. 332–36)

Sidney has the virtue of not just being a poet: he is 'now mongst that
blessed throng / Of heavenlie Poets and Heroes strong' (ll. 340–41).
As such, he is both poet and hero. Orpheus and Linus implicitly con-
cede that Sidney's 'heavenlie layes' are 'better' than theirs because he
possesses an 'excellent' heroic 'desart' (ll. 343) which they do not. As
Sidney himself recognized that Orpheus, Amphion and 'Homer in
his Hymns' were vatic or religious poets (albeit in the service of 'a full
wrong divinity'),[47] so Spenser in his turn implies that Sidney betters
these mythic poets because he is also a Christian hero. *The Ruines of
Time* posthumously presents Sidney as both a national hero, living
and dying in imitation of Christ, and a poet of Orpheus-like abilities,
superior to his model because of his heroic virtue:

> So thou both here and there immortall art,
> And everie where through excellent desart. (ll. 342–43)

In this formulation, literary immortality and Christian transcen-
dence are neatly balanced. Sidney is 'immortall' both 'here' on earth
and 'there' in heaven as a result of his excellence as a man and a poet.

Yet the allusions to Orpheus can also be seen to exploit more
ancient associations, rather than distinctions, between Orpheus and
Christ. As the lament for Sidney typologically compares his heroism
with Christ's and his poetry with Orpheus's, it recalls the early Chris-

---

47 *Ibid.*, p. 80.

tian reading of the myth which persisted into the medieval period.[48] This equates Orpheus's rescue of Eurydice with Christ's harrowing of hell, allegorizing Orpheus as a type of Christ. Friedman cites Pierre Bersuire's allegorization of the *Metamorphoses* in his *Reductorium Morale* (c.1325–37), which reads Orpheus as 'Christ the son of God the Father, who from the beginning led Eurydice, that is the human soul [to himself?]'. While such allegories seem a long way from *The Ruines of Time*, it is intriguing that Bersuire goes on to argue that:

> Christ-Orpheus wished to descend to the lower world, and thus he retook his wife, that is, human nature, ripping her from the hands of the ruler of Hell himself; and he led her with him to the upper world, saying this verse from Canticles 2.10, 'Rise up, my love, my fair one, and come away.'[49]

This passage indicates Spenser's awareness of the traditional parallel between Orpheus and Christ.[50] Instead of repeating Bersuire's formulation, Spenser amalgamates aspects of both Christ and Orpheus in the figure of Sidney, 'spotles sacrifise' and Orphic poet. In the context of the wider debate in *The Ruines of Time* about the value of poetry, this is more than just an epideictic strategy. The notion that the mythic poet can be associated with Christ allows Spenser to present Sidney as a metaphorical bridge between poetry and Christianity. So in the second set of 'Pageants', which present Sidney as Orpheus, Spenser also includes the apocalyptic vision of the 'virgine' and 'her Bridegroome' (ll. 631–44), paraphrasing the same verse from the Song of Songs quoted by Bersuire. Though the lament for Sidney ignores the 'Renaissance' Orpheus, its adaptation of what might be called the 'medieval' Orpheus creates an initial rapprochement between Christian salvation and 'eternizing' poetry.

48 See John Block Friedman, *Orpheus in the Middle Ages* (Cambridge, Mass.: Harvard University Press, 1970).

49 *Ibid.*, pp. 126–28.

50 Bersuire's work was, as Friedman *Orpheus in the Middle Ages* notes, pp. 126–28, 'popular and influential'. Alistair Fowler assumes that Spenser was familiar with 'Bersuire's influential exegesis'; see *Spenser and the Numbers of Time* (London: Routledge and Kegan Paul, 1964), pp. 67, 85.

2 In defence of 'eternizing' poetry

However, the next section's praise of 'eternizing' poetry effectively abandons the possibility of a counterpoise between humanism and Christianity. Though Schell notes that 'The death of the poet-knight Sidney leads naturally into the third section of the poem, a defense of poetry and the secular immortality that poetry can give',[51] the transition is more complex than this suggests. Though the connection between Sidney and poetry is 'natural', we must ask whether the claims made for 'eternizing' poetry square with either the subsequent 'Pageants' or the image of Sidney as both a Christian hero and Orphic poet.

Reading the lament for Sidney as part of Verlame's continuous utterance establishes greater coherence between it and the praise of poetry. In the lament, Verlame insists on the 'wretchedness' of mortal life (ll. 290–305). This is not surprising, since Sidney's transcendence of 'this sinfull earth' (l. 290) intensifies Verlame's ongoing awareness of this 'cumbrous world anoy' (ll. 305; 43–56). Only the remembered aesthetic pleasure of Sidney's pastoral poetry affords her any respite from her sense that this world is tragically imperfect (ll. 323–28). In this context of world-contempt, poetry embodies an artistic order which is felt to be absent from 'this wretched world' (l. 294):

> For deeds doe die, how ever noblie donne,
> And thoughts of men do as themselves decay,
> But wise wordes taught in numbers for to runne,
> Recorded by the Muses, live for ay (ll. 400–03)

Poetry not only lasts longer than the 'thoughts of men';[52] these lines state that it lasts because it is 'wordes taught in numbers for to runne' – the metrical order of verse ensures that it can preserve 'deeds ... noblie done'. Where death is 'obscure oblivion' and 'rustie darknes' (ll. 346–49), poetry is an ordered form of remembrance. Like Polyhymnia's complaint in *The Teares of the Muses*, these lines assert the value of poetry as the intellectual arrangement of 'winged words' into

---

51 In *YESP*, p. 247.
52 Compare line 222.

a 'tunefull Diapase of pleasures'.[53] But Verlame pursues this idea into
an exaggeration of what poetry can 'eternize'.

At first, she seems to amplify the notion that poetry metaphori-
cally preserves the transient (ll. 365–71). But gradually, Verlame's
conception of how poetry achieves this preservation becomes less
metaphorical and more literal:

> The seven fold yron gates of grislie Hell
> And horrid house of sad *Proserpina,*
> They [the Muses] able are with power of mightie spell
> To breake, and thence the soules to bring awaie
> Out of dread darknesse, to eternall day,
> And them immortall make, which els would die
> In foule forgetfulnesse, and nameles lie. (ll. 372–78)

This passage is ambiguous about the nature of the resurrection
achieved by the Muses. While this stanza suggests a Christian resur-
rection in which 'soules' are brought 'Out of dread darknesse, to eter-
nall day', it also recalls the figurative immortality Verlame promised
Lord and Lady Warwick (ll. 253–59). The Muses make the dead
'immortall', 'which els would die/In foule forgetfulnesse'. In this
case, the 'death' referred to by the verb 'to die' seems metaphorical –
the death of the name, not the death of the body. Poetry ensures that
its subjects will not perish 'in obscure oblivion, as the thing / Which
never was' (ll. 346–47) through its record of the past. Like Verlame's
catalogue of the Dudleys (ll. 183–280), poetry preserves the reputa-
tions of the great and the good from historical anonymity.

Nonetheless, the stanza does not make clear whether the Muses
will literally 'breake' the 'yron gates of grislie Hell' and resurrect those
chosen 'soules', or whether this is an elaborate periphrasis for literary
immortality. As the praise of poetry develops, so the sense of ambi-
guity deepens. The humanist heaven progressively becomes, instead
of a metaphor for literary immortality, an actual place beyond the
grave which is accessible to those 'Whom the *Pierian* sacred sisters
love' (l. 394). In this idealized environment, the elect are 'freed from

---

53 *The Teares of the Muses,* ll. 548–49.

bands of impacable fate' and share their meals of 'Nectar and Ambrosia' with the Gods 'for former vertues meede' (ll. 395–99).[54]

This conception of a humanist transcendence, accessed by good deeds and wealth, is in tension with orthodox Protestant soteriology. Articles XI and XII of the Thirty-Nine Articles of Religion (1571) state that 'We are accounted righteous before God, only for the merit of our Lord and Saviour Jesus Christ by Faith, and not for our own works or deservings', and further that 'Good works … cannot put away our sins, and endure the severity of God's Judgement'.[55] As a representative statement of Protestant doctrinal orthodoxy,[56] the Articles allow that 'Good works' may be the fruits of Faith, but reject the idea that such works have a determining impact on the destiny of the human soul. The Elizabethan Protestant cannot presume on any investment of good deeds, relying wholly on Faith for his or her justification. The first 'voyce' of the 'Pageants' expresses the essence of this view: 'Ne other comfort in this world can be, / But hope of heaven, and heart to God inclinde' (ll. 584–85). Yet Verlame insists that heaven can be stormed by the importunate humanist on the strength of 'vertuous deeds':

> But fame with golden wings aloft doth flie
> Above the reach of ruinous decay,
> And with brave plumes doth beate the azure skie,
> Admir'd of base-borne men from farre away:
> Then who so will with vertuous deeds assay
> To mount to heaven, on *Pegasus* must ride,
> And with sweete Poets verse be glorifide. (ll. 421–27)

This stanza states that poetry can evade the universal impact of original sin, categorically described by the Articles as 'the fault and cor-

54 Spenser's humanist heaven derives from Du Bellay's image of the reward he imagines for the writer of a vernacular epic – see Chapter 2 above, p.68.

55 *The Book of Common Prayer*, p. 697.

56 Patrick Collinson *The Elizabethan Puritan Movement* (London: Jonathan Cape, 1967; rpt. Oxford: Clarendon, 1990), p. 117, notes that puritan radicals wanted to use 'the more strictly doctrinal of the Articles … as a searching test of lay as well as clerical orthodoxy', though they were less enthusiastic about the more political of the Articles.

ruption of every man ... and therefore in every person born into this world, it deserveth God's wrath and damnation'.[57] 'Ruinous decay' means the decay which is attendant on the fallen condition of the world, since 'ruinous' means 'falling', as in Donne's bitter pun, 'We are borne ruinous'.[58] Poetry is apparently able to avoid the taint of original sin: it will 'never tast deaths woe',[59] and neither will the subject of poetic 'fame'. 'Eternizing' poetry allows the virtuous (and wealthy) individual 'To mount to heaven' on '*Pegasus*' through 'sweete Poets verse'.[60] This is the poem's cumulative statement of the power of 'eternizing' and as such deliberately contradicts the corrective view asserted in the first 'Pageants'.[61]

However, *The Ruines of Time* is not a bland juxtaposition of simple choices: poetry doesn't cancel Christianity, or vice versa. As has been frequently recognized, this defence of 'eternizing' has substantial correlations with the rest of Spenser's oeuvre, and the humanist belief in the power of literature.[62] Verlame is not simply good or evil: as a poetic mouthpiece, she exaggerates, but this does not prevent her from 'speaking for' Spenser himself.

Her complaint reaches a climax with the satiric comparison of Walsingham and Burghley as patrons (ll. 435–55). In praising Walsingham at Burghley's expense, Verlame voices Spenser's grievance

57 Article IX, *The Book of Common Prayer*, p. 696.

58 See Schell's note in *YESP*, p. 232. See also Patrides's comment on this pun in John Donne, *The Complete English Poems*, ed. C. A. Patrides (Everyman's Library. London and Melbourne: Dent, 1985), p. 331.

59 *Holy Sonnets* VII, l. 8. In Donne, *Complete English Poems*, p. 439.

60 On the image of Pegasus in relation to poetry, see Mary Lascelles, 'The Rider on the Winged Horse' (1959), in *Notions and Facts: Collected Criticism and Research* (Oxford: Clarendon, 1972).

61 Compare Patrick Cheney, *Spenser's Famous Flight: A Renaissance Idea of a Literary Career* (Toronto: University of Toronto Press, 1993), pp. 14–15, who claims that this stanza should be read allegorically as a Christianization of poetic fame. Like his comparable argument about *The Teares of the Muses*, ll. 457–63, Cheney's reading is to me too schematic: because Spenser was a Christian does not mean that we should Christianize every ambiguous passage he wrote!

62 Compare Renwick, *Complaints*, pp. 196–98. See Rasmussen '"How Weak Be the Passions of Woefulness"', p. 170, for the contrary view of this passage as 'another manifestation of [Verlame's] insatiable egocentricity'.

that the Lord High Treasurer had a poor estimation of poetry.[63] As
the Proem to *The Faerie Queene* IV puts it, Burghley's 'rugged for-
head' sees no use for Spenser's superficially 'looser rimes'.[64] In *The
Ruines of Time*, Burghley's inhibition of literary and political patron-
age (ll. 449–53) demonstrates why poetry has needed defending.
Unlike the dead Leicester, whose 'bounteous minde' sustained 'manie
Poets' (ll. 224, 233), the aged, but still living, Burghley 'Scorns'
poetry 'in his deeper skill' (ll. 448). The hard-up poet has no option
but to return this scorn with interest: 'O let the man, of whom the
Muse is scorned, / Nor alive, nor dead be of the Muse adorned' (ll.
454–55).[65] The hyperbolical Verlame allows Spenser to make explicit
his criticism of Burghley.[66]

As a whole, Verlame's complaint maintains that 'eternizing' signif-
icantly ameliorates the tragedy of human mortality. As the poem
memorializes the Dudleys, it advances a progressive conception of
'eternizing' developed out of traditional defences of poetry.[67] This
conception defines 'eternizing' through the clarification of the recip-

63 See Alexander Judson, *The Life of Edmund Spenser* (Baltimore and London:
The Johns Hopkins University Press, 1945), pp. 153–55, for Spenser's belief that
Burghley directly obstructed his preferment.

64 *FQ*, p. 426.

65 DeNeef, *Spenser and the Motives of Metaphor*, p. 38, sees this couplet as a
humourless paraphrase of Sidney's closing peroration to the *Defence of Poetry*.
Though the parallel is undeniable, DeNeef's reading dilutes our sense of the satiri-
cal dimension of this passage.

66 Though like *Mother Hubberds Tale*, this passage was omitted from the 1611
Folio of Spenser's works. See *YESP*, p. 251; *Var*. VIII, pp. 685–86, 690; and Harold
Stein, *Stdies in Spenser's Complaints* (New York: Oxford University Press, 1934), p. 37.

67 Compare DeNeef, *Spenser and the Motives of Metaphor*, pp. 28–40, who views
the poem as an embodiment of Sidney's *Defence*. DeNeef sees Sidney's theory of imi-
tation in the main complaint's catalogue of social interrelationships, which 'define
the conceit "Sidney"' (p. 32). While DeNeef's approach is analogous to the one
adopted here, I am cautious of seeing *The Ruines of Time* as a poetic representation
of a critical theory. In other words, while Spenser undoubtedly makes use of broadly
Sidneyan ideas and images, his central concern with the morality of art is not best
understood as a practical demonstration of 'the principal theorems of the *Apology*'.
Rather, poetic practice *raises* theoretical issues which are in fact external to the con-
cerns of Sidney's *Defence*.

rocal duties of poets and patrons and the idealization of poetic tran-
scendence. Yet from a Christian perspective, the mortal artifice of
poetry cannot arrogate to itself the resurrection of the dead. So it is
unsurprising that this vision should bewilder the narrator: Verlame's
complaint cannot provide a single cogent *moralitas* both because of
its generic diversity and its central concern with poetry.

3 The 'Pageants': reconciling poetry with Christianity

Since Verlame's complaint does not resolve the philosophical issues it
raises, in the final 200 lines of the poem, Spenser adopts a different
strategy to conclude his meditation on poetry. The first series of
'Pageants' (ll. 491–588) is a suitably 'tragicke'[68] demonstration of the
frailty, and consequent futility, of every human construction, includ-
ing poetry. Wholly in the style of the 'Songe', or Spenser's own
Visions of the Worlds Vanitie,[69] these six texts symmetrically link
descriptions of 'greatest things' with their inherent propensity to
ruin. The first stanza of each 'ur-sonnet' describes the doomed object,
while the second (linked to its partner by a shared rhyme) moralizes
its fall. So the fourth vision describes the Colossus of Rhodes in its
first stanza as 'a Giaunt … Of wondrous power and of exceeding
stature' (ll. 533–39). In the second stanza, his fall 'into the deepe
Abisse' exhibits 'the end and pompe of fleshlie pride' (ll. 540–46). As
in the 'Songe', the symbolic image reveals 'this worlds inconstancies'
and allows the poet to advance a moralizing commentary.[70]

The third vision is most directly pertinent to *The Ruines of Time*'s
debate on poetry. It describes the destruction of 'a pleasant Paradize'

68 See 'tragic', *OED* 2: 'Resembling tragedy in respect of its matter; relating to
or expressing fatal or dreadful events'. The word indicates that the 'Pageants' are con-
cerned with the fall of man.

69 Hence the view of Van Dorsten ('Literary Patronage in Elizabethan Eng-
land'), p. 205, of the 'Pageants' as already 'quaint' for the reader of the 1590s, since
they embody Sidney and Spenser's 'earliest attempts to evolve, within an English tra-
dition, a new, visionary poetry'. This view will not do justice to the synthetic inno-
vation of the second series.

70 *The Visions of Bellay*, ll. 11–12.

(l. 519), and implies through contrast a connection between this gar-
den and Spenser's own poetry:

> Such as on earth man could not more devize,
> With pleasures choyce to feed his cheerefull sprights;
> Not that, which *Merlin* by his Magicke slights
> Made for the gentle squire, to entertaine
> His fayre *Belphoebe*, could this gardine staine. (ll. 521–25)

Renwick suggests that this simile derives from 'an episode apparently
designed for *The Faerie Queene*' – Spenser expected his readers to rec-
ognize Merlin, and especially Belphoebe and 'the gentle squire'
(Timias), as figures from the epic.[71] Yet the origins of the image are of
less interest than its function. I suggest that such off-cuts from *The
Faerie Queene* serve to inculpate poetry along the other 'vaine labours
of terrestrial wit'.[72] Lines 521–25 make clear that the 'Paradize' is an
artificial environment through the comparison of it with 'that, which
Merlin by his magicke slights / Made'. Like the poetry Spenser expects
his reader to recall, the garden is 'Made' through artifice, or more dis-
quietingly, 'magicke'. The vision implies that all such artifice is ulti-
mately pointless: the 'short pleasure' of aesthetic enjoyment is 'bought'
with the 'lasting paine' (l. 526) which attends the realization that art
also is transitory. The implication is that the dissolution of this poetic
garden undercuts Verlame's confidence in the power of poetry to tran-
scend death. Yet the second stanza of this vision is not a bald repudia-
tion of art. The narrator stresses his receptivity to aesthetic experience:
the fate of the garden brings home to him the frailty of his 'pleasure'
and 'delight / In earthlie blis', so that in the couplet he confesses 'That
I, which once that beautie did beholde, / Could not from teares my
melting eyes with-holde' (ll. 526–32). Though the moral of the vision
is clear, the narrator's response to it is not. The destruction of aesthetic
'beautie' prompts – in suitably beautiful poetry – the 'teares' of his
'melting eyes'. While the narrator understands intellectually that art is
transitory, emotionally he is still attached to its 'pleasures'.

71 Renwick, *Complaints*, p. 201.
72 Compare *The Teares of the Muses*, ll. 19–42, where the ruin of the Muses's
'desolate groves' symbolizes the death of recreative poetry. See pp. 147–49 below.

Nonetheless, the first set of visions ostensibly demonstrates that all mortal works of art, whether these take the form of poetic gardens or golden bridges, are 'brickle' (l. 499) and made in vain. This position is stated explicitly by the 'voyce' (l. 580) which calls to the narrator at the end of the first set of visions:

> Behold ... and by ensample see
> That all is vanitie and griefe of minde,
> Ne other comfort in this world can be,
> But hope of heaven, and heart to God inclinde;
> For all the rest must needs be left behinde ... (ll. 582–86)

The 'voyce' instructs the narrator in the lapsarian moral he should draw from the first 'Pageants'. In the face of the 'vanitie' of mortal endeavour, he should embrace the distant 'hope of heaven', as the Protestant is ultimately saved 'only for the merit of our Lord and Saviour Jesus Christ by Faith'. Despite the apparent authority of this instruction, the first 'Pageants' do not close *The Ruines of Time*. As throughout the poem, hyperbolical assertions are modified by what follows them. So the first set of visions, which problematizes Verlame's view of poetry, is in its turn adjusted by the second set.

The second series of visions (ll. 589–686) is both more formally and thematically complex than the first. Spenser is forced to alter the form because these 'Pageants' are all in different ways concerned with Sidney's death. Instead of presenting exemplary symbols of the frailty of mortal constructions, these visions symbolically convey an idea of Sidney's transcendence.[73] In contrast with the first series, this set of 'Pageants' does not use the double stanza form to moralize the visionary symbol, but rather to develop the image. For example, the second stanza of the first vision (ll. 596–602) completes the first stanza's narrative of the 'snowie Swan' prophesying its 'owne death in dolefull Elegie' (ll. 590–95) by describing its stellification. In transforming the didactic form of the vision into something more symbolic, Spenser effects an accommodation between Christian and humanist ideas of immortality through the transcendent Sidney. Arguably, the

73 See Renwick, *Complaints*, pp. 201–03, who traces the cosmological progression of the transcendent Sidney across the heavens.

second set of visions rescues poetry from the malediction pro-
nounced against it in the first set.

These visions intersperse eschatological images of the redemption
of the Christian soul with mythic images of Orpheus-Sidney's trans-
formation into 'an heavenly signe' (l. 601). Through manipulation of
the Orpheus myth, Spenser makes Sidney into a mediator between
the competing priorities of Christianity and poetry. So in the second
vision Spenser rephrases the earlier alignment of Orpheus with Sid-
ney. The narrator sees 'an Harpe' descending 'the *Lee*', which reminds
him inevitably of 'The harpe, on which *Dan Orpheus* was seene /
Wylde beasts and forrests after him to lead' (ll. 603–08). In this case,
Sidney replaces '*Dan Orpheus*':

> [It] was th'Harpe of *Philisides* now dead.

> At length out of the River it was reard
> And borne above the cloudes to be divin'd,
> Whilst all the way most heavenly noyse was heard
> Of the strings, stirred with the warbling wind,
> That wrought both joy and sorrow in my mind:
> So now in heaven a signe it doth appeare,
> The Harpe well knowne beside the Northerne
>   Beare. (ll. 609–16)

Spenser's focus on the harp draws on a mythographic tradition that
is not present in his main classical sources.[74] Boccaccio records this
aspect of the myth and initiates its 'Renaissance' interpretation: the
harp is the oratorical faculty through which 'Orpheus alone moved
the most fixed and firmly rooted trees, that is, men of obstinate
opinions, who cannot be moved from their obstinacy except
through men of eloquence'.[75] This would suggest that all roads lead

---

74 Compare Ovid, *Metamorphoses* XI.44–60; Virgil, *Georgics* IV.514–27.

75 In Friedman, *Orpheus in the Middle Ages*, p. 140. See also Giovanni Boc-
caccio, *Genealogie: Paris 1531*, rpt. of the 1531 edn published by P. Le Noir, ed.
Stephen Orgel (New York and London: Garland, 1976), Book V, Chapter VIII,
sheet lxxxix.

to Rome: Spenser's apparent omission of the 'Renaissance' Orpheus in the lament for Sidney conceals its presence in the image of 'The Harpe'. But Spenser's Orpheus is not a replica of Boccaccio's. Where Boccaccio interprets Orpheus as a symbol of eloquence, Spenser equates his 'Harpe' with the aesthetic value embodied in Sidney, the 'most heavenly noyse' which 'wrought both joy and sorrow' in the narrator's mind. This is a symbolic evocation of Sidney's poetry which balances a sense of the validity of aesthetic experience with a sober recognition of the poet's mortality. Such a Christian poetry suggests that the art over-endorsed by Verlame can be reconciled with an awareness of the limitations of mortal life. It recognizes with 'sorrow' the fact of Sidney's death, yet evokes the joys of redemption through the aesthetic experience it describes and creates. Sidney's transfiguration also ensures that even the two Dudley bears, destroyed in the first series (ll. 561–74), are amalgamated into the poetic image of 'The Harpe' resting 'beside the Northern Beare'. The conflict between 'eternizing' and Christianity has been over-come: the visionary symbol of Philisides's harp allows Spenser covertly to immortalize the Dudley family.

The remaining 'Pageants' further the accommodation this vision implies between Christianity and poetry. The fourth vision (ll. 631–44) presents, through recollections of the Song of Songs and Revelation,[76] an allegorical image of the soul's marriage with God:

> I heard a voyce that called farre away
> And her awaking bad her quickly dight,
> For lo her Bridegrome was in readie ray
> To come to her, and seeke her loves delight:
> With that she started up with cherefull sight,
> When suddeinly both bed and all was gone,
> And I in languor left there all alone. (ll. 638–44)

This passage also furthers the parallel between Sidney and Bersuire's 'Christ-Orpheus' through its paraphrase of the same scriptural pas-

76 See Renwick, *Complaints*, pp. 201–03.

sage.[77] Its intimation of the composite figure of 'Christ-Orpheus-Sidney' enables Spenser to write a poetry which is both mystic in aim (foreshadowing the apocalyptic marriage of the 'virgine' and 'the Bridegroome') and aesthetically sensuous in practice. The narrator anticipates the marriage as an erotic encounter, a 'joyous night' (l. 635) which will complete the 'loves delight' of both partners. In this 'Pageant', poetry furthers the eschatological vision which looks to complete the union between the individual soul and God.

The 'strife' between poetry and Christianity is finally 'appease[d]' in the sixth vision through the figure of Mercury (ll. 659–72). He acts as arbiter in the dispute between 'the heavens and the earth' about who should be 'keeper' of Sidney's 'ashes' (ll. 664–67). This conception of Mercury works on a number of levels.[78] Firstly, he performs his traditional pagan rôle as the 'Shepherd', or conductor, of souls into Elysium, in carrying Sidney's ashes to their 'second life' in heaven (ll. 668–70).[79]

The association of Mercury with Sidney also recalls the myth recorded by Boccaccio that Mercury originally gave Orpheus his lyre (or harp).[80] This detail is suggestive of the amazing syncretism of Spenser's thought in the second 'Pageants'. Sidney is firstly equated with Orpheus and Christ and then with other figures like Perseus (ll. 645–51) and Mercury. Through the by now thoroughly mythologized figure of Sidney, Spenser is able to appease the strife not only

77 This vision indicates Spenser's responsiveness to the orthodox reading of the Song of Songs as an allegory rather than an erotic poem; the lost 'Canticum canticorum translated' referred to by Ponsonby in 'The Printer to the Gentle Reader' would presumably have reiterated the conventional interpretation. See Christopher Hill, The English Bible and the Seventeenth-Century Revolution (Harmondsworth: Allen Lane, 1993), pp. 362–70, for an account of sixteenth- and seventeenth-century literary (ab)uses of the Song of Songs.

78 But compare his much more ambivalent rôle in Mother Hubberds Tale, discussed in Chapter 5 below, pp. 205–07.

79 See Horace, Odes I.X, ll. 17–20 in Odes, (trans. James Michie (London: Rupert Hart-Davis, 1966), p. 39. Mitchie uses the word 'Shepherd'. See also Robert Graves, The Greek Myths, 2 vols (Harmondsworth: Penguin, 1955) I, ll. 65–66.

80 See Boccaccio, Genealogie, and Friedman, Orpheus in the Middle Ages, pp. 126–28.

between 'eternizing' poetry and Christian transcendence, but also between pagan and Christian religious imagery. Though the association between Orpheus and Christ was traditional, Spenser stretches these mythographic associations by using Sidney as a mediating figure whose literary and military careers may be paralleled by an impressive array of divine figures, including the ambivalent Mercury. In short, *The Ruines of Time* synthesizes conflicting imagery and tropes into a heterodox, but brilliantly coherent, whole. Properly speaking, it is a humanist text.

A bridge from tradition to novelty

The poem is an intriguing amalgam of conflicting forms and ideas about poetry: a 'goodlie bridge' between a relatively uncritical confidence in 'eternizing', and the need to make a more intellectually strenuous defence of poetry in the light of the Protestant suspicion that art is a mortal 'vanitie'. This poetic self-consciousness is also evident in the form of the text. As a blend of dream vision and exemplary complaint, *The Ruines of Time* shows itself repeatedly as a text in which old formal priorities are transformed as a consequence of its self-conscious argument. Spenser does not end the poem with a conventional *moralitas*, but extends its debate on poetry through the densely compacted symbolism of the 'tragicke Pageants'. These mythic images replace the didactic strategies of traditional exemplary complaint. Unlike the *Mirror for Magistrates*, the poem's point cannot be made by the simple expedient of a generalizing summary; rather, as in *The Faerie Queene*, sense must be made of complex images by further complex images. The didactic tradition of the *Mirror* is strained to breaking point in *The Ruines of Time*.

So I argue that this poem is in itself a 'goodlie bridge' between the two major approaches to poetry which Spenser exhibits in the *Complaints* volume. On the one hand, in its concern to 'eternize' the Dudleys and its adaptation of Du Bellay's precedent, *The Ruines of Time* recalls the translations discussed in the first part of this book. In this view, poetry is a powerful medium which can imitate the achievements of the past and initiate a new kind of writing by its creative replication of those achievements in English. Such a neo-classical poetry can hope, like the 'Virgil' of *Culex* and the Du Bellay of *Les Antiquitez* sonnet 32, that 'l'oeuvre d'un lyre / Puisse acquérir telle immortalité'.[81] Verlame defends precisely this conception of poetry as an art of 'eternizing'. On the other hand, *The Ruines of Time* displays the problems which undermine this view of poetry for the Protestant writer. Though literature can momentarily raise the spirits of the past like Verlame, it must eventually concede defeat to the 'time' that 'doth greatest things to ruine bring' (l. 556). Hence the text tries to balance an exaggerated confidence in the power of poetry with a bleak awareness of the limitations of all works of art. Spenser manages to revalidate poetry in the second set of 'Pageants' through the figure of Sidney. But as the final vision makes clear, after Sidney's transcendence, the narrator can only offer a 'broken verse' (l. 678) to offset this loss. Despite its syncretic ending, *The Ruines of Time* initiates the ambivalent approach to poetry which characterizes the major *Complaints*. In these texts, Spenser progressively challenges traditional notions of the power and function of poetry through his transformation of complaint. This new poetry of complaint – a poetry of instability – responds to the complex stimuli of a 'sinfull world' (l. 686), ever more distant from the stellified Sidney. In brief, *The Ruines of Time* bridges the distance between the traditional poetry of the translations and innovatory poetry of the major *Complaints*.

81 Joachim Du Bellay, *Les Regrets, Les Antiquites de Rome et La Defense et Illustration de la Langue francaise*, edition etablie par S. De Sacy (Paris: Gallimard, 1967), p. 47.

CHAPTER FOUR

Poetry's 'liuing tongue' in *The Teares of the Muses*

The Ruines of Time reveals the tensions within Spenser's intellectual heritage and one way of resolving them. Through the figure of Sidney, the poem establishes an accommodation between the conflicting imperatives of poetic 'eternizing' and Christian world-contempt. Yet this accommodation is conditioned by the memorial context of *The Ruines of Time*, whose poetic concerns are a function of its wider purpose as a 'thankefull' elegiac 'remembrance' of Sidney and the Leicester circle.[1] As the text which immediately follows *The Ruines of Time* in the *Complaints* volume, *The Teares of the Muses* continues to explore the tension between Christian and humanist views of poetry, but without the mediation provided by the mythologized Sidney. *The Teares* shows the Muses in despair. Confronted by 'ugly Barbarisme, / And brutish Ignorance', they bear witness to the fragility of poetry's cultural prestige. The poem dramatizes the sense, which often accompanies accelerated historical change, that society has lost all respect for traditional artistic values.[2] Yet the Muses' complaints do not offer a unified response to a single threat; they continue the debate of *The Ruines of Time* by contrasting Christian and humanist poetics. Here the ongoing debate about the abstract value of poetry is given added resonance by the failure of all poetry – all the Muses – to revitalize a debased society. Spenser prophetically envisages the death of art in the Muses' closing silence: poetry's 'liuing tongue' can be silenced through social and intellectual atrophy.

The Teares is both a self-reflexive poem and a novel complaint. The unresolved debate between Christian and humanist Muses intimates that traditional poetics are breaking down because they are inadequate to the current crisis. Neither a Christian nor a humanist poetics will be

---

1 Dedication to *The Ruines of Time*.
2 For convenience I refer to this process as 'the crisis'.

sufficient to support Spenser's conception of a new English poetry. As a novel complaint, *The Teares* is itself an example of this new poetry. Spenser's use of the complaint mode for this self-conscious text furthers the transformation of complaint begun in *The Ruines of Time*. Instead of expressing political or amatory woes, complaint here exhibits Spenser's critical anxieties. The poem's central enigma is then the Muses' despair – why they complain, and what the implications of their complaints are for his new poetry. *The Teares* demonstrates the fragility of traditional poetics in the face of cultural change. The poetic options embodied by the Muses may not provide an adequate framework for Spenser's literary innovation. *The Teares* bridges the syncretic brinkmanship of *The Ruines of Time* and the innovative mimesis of *Mother Hubberds Tale*. Though both *The Teares* and the Tale ostensibly regard all change as a downward spiral towards 'fond newfanglenesse', on closer inspection these texts reveal that the old certainties have become outmoded. Spenser's new poetry of complaint emerges from this recognition of the limitations of the poetic tradition.

Previous criticism has not extensively studied *The Teares*. Despite controversy about its date,[3] there is a consensual view that the poem's form and purpose are straightforward: *The Teares* is a repetitive complaint which, though carefully structured, administers 'on Spenser's behalf ... a thoroughly damning diagnosis of contemporary literary illness'.[4] *The Teares* is seen as a second-rate poem, retaining historical

---

3 See *Var.* VIII, pp. 533–40; and Harold Stein, *Studies in Spenser's Complaints* (New York: Oxford University Press, 1934), pp. 42–53. The dating of the poem has been complicated by attempts to identify the 'pleasant *Willy*' lamented by Thalia (ll. 205–22). If Willy is Sidney, the date should be late (post-1586), but if he is Gascoigne, the poem may be earlier. Indeed, Shakespeare has been reinstated as a potential Willy by E. A. J. Honigmann, *Shakespeare: The 'Lost Years'* (Manchester: Manchester University Press, 1985), pp. 71–76; see also *Var.* VIII, pp. 317–21. At this distance, it is probably impossible to identify '*Willy*'. The broader discussion of the date ranges between the idea that *The Teares* must be an early work (circa 1580) because it is perceived to be poor, and therefore immature, and the late date favoured by Stein. In the light of the profundity of Spenser's cultural vision in the text, I favour Stein's dating.

4 Alfred W. Satterthwaite, *Spenser, Ronsard and Du Bellay: A Renaissance Comparison* (Princeton: Princeton University Press, 1960), p. 66.

interest as a Spenserian equivalent of Sidney's prose inquiry into 'why England ... should be grown so hard a stepmother to poets'.[5]

These views are hard to substantiate. *The Teares'* form is deliberately deceptive; the stylized cycle of the Muses' complaints outwardly forms a homogeneous lament, while individual complaints support contrasting poetics. In my view, the form is a complex component of the poem's meaning through which Spenser expands the register of traditional complaint. Like *The Ruines of Time*, *The Teares* is concerned with poetry in the abstract rather than with specific English verse of the 1580s and 1590s. Rather than a versified review, the poem articulates Spenser's anxieties about the survival of poetry in an ambiguous present. This chapter hopes to enfranchise the poem from its lowly position in the Spenser canon, and present it as a central constituent of the poetic innovation embodied in the *Complaints* volume.

'Ragged rimes'?: the Form and Argument of *The Teares*

The form of *The Teares* has appeared simple in comparison with that of *The Ruines of Time*.[6] Its use of complaint to structure the Muses' laments seems unsubtle: as the title suggests, the poem voices the tears of the Muses, which the narrative frame 'display[s]' (l. 50) in a roughly equal pageant of 'sorowfull sad tine' (l. 3). Paradoxically the clarity of the poem's design has obscured the complex relationship which exists between its form and its argument. Since the form structures the argument, it also determines – and therefore limits – what the text is able to say. To understand the poem's argument, the reader must evolve a nuanced view of its form.

The poem presents the set-piece laments of the Muses in a procession. The Muses' texts are framed both by a proem (ll. 1–54), and by choric link-stanzas which close and introduce each complaint. These framing devices both support and impair the thematic homogeneity

5 Sir Philip Sidney, *Miscellaneous Prose of Sir Philip Sidney*, ed. Katherine Duncan-Jones and Jan Van Dorsten (Oxford: Clarendon, 1973), p. 110.

6 See W. L. Renwick, *Complaints* (London: The Scholartis Press, 1928), p. 204.

among the Muses. The repetitive stylization of the link-stanzas implies that the Muses share a common view of poetry, yet the link-stanzas function as dividers between the Muses' complaints.

This tension is also apparent in the outwardly simple numerological scheme. Each complaint including the proem has nine stanzas, with the exception of Euterpe's which has ten.[7] At one level, this scheme again suggests the homogeneity of the Muses' complaints in their pursuit of a single argumentative goal. Yet the breach of this simple format may also indicate that the complaints will not coalesce into a single argument. So the external form of the text raises the issue of how the poem's content is organized. The structural tension between homogeneity and dissonance is the formal expression of the thematic enigma of the Muses' despair. Since *The Teares* takes the form of a procession, we need to ask how the Muses are sequenced, and whether this sequence constitutes an argumentative design.

Renwick noted that the Muses' procession follows the order of 'certain mnemonic verses, *de Musarum inventis*, printed in early editions of Virgil'.[8] The widespread currency of this text is shown by Nicholas Grimald's translation, 'The Muses', in *Tottel's Miscellany* (1557), and Harvey's use of the same order in *Smithus, vel Musarum Lachrymae* (1578).[9] Yet *de Musarum inventis* can only give *The Teares* the received order of an aide-memoire: its order facilitates memorization, but does not constitute a rationalized hierarchy of Muses.[10] Similarly, though Spenser begins the procession by instructing Clio to 'Begin thou eldest Sister of the crew, / And let the rest in order thee ensew' (ll.

7 The numerology of *The Teares* is noted by Oram in *YESP*, p. 267; Gerald Snare, 'The Muses on Poetry: Spenser's *The Teares of the Muses*', *Tulane University Studies in English*, 17, (1969), pp. 31–52; and Hugh Maclean's article on the poem in *The Spenser Encyclopedia*, ed. A. C. Hamilton *et al.* (Toronto, Buffalo and London: University of Toronto Press and Routledge, 1990), pp. 182–83.

8 Renwick, *Complaints*, p. 206.

9 For Grimald, see *Tottel's Miscellany*, 2 vols, ed. Edward Arber (English Reprints. London: Constable, 1921), Vol. I, 100–01. See *Var.* VIII, pp. 540, for Harvey's influence on *The Teares*.

10 Grimald, indeed, arbitrarily shuffles the Muses from the Latin text to produce the new order: Calliope, Clio, Thalia, Melpomene, Terpsichore, Erato, Polyhymnia, Urania, Euterpe. As with its original, there is no underlying principle in this rearrangement.

53–54), the remainder of the poem does not expand on the notion that its sequence is a hierarchy based on age. Yet the idea of hierarchy seems residually important, since the link-stanzas present each new complainant as 'the next in rew', though without any further explanation of the placement of particular Muses. *The Teares* uses a received and familiar sequence, implying an unspecified hierarchy.

So is this received sequence developed into an incremental argument? Not altogether. The Muses broadly divide between humanism and Christianity. Clio's modified 'eternizing' is followed by Melpomene's lapsarian view of Tragedy. The sequence is a procession of contrasting points of view, which lacks the promise of an argumentative conclusion. This processional structure recalls Petrarch's *Trionfi*. The individual *Trionfi* describe neo-classical pageants, in which symbolic figures represent each 'stage' in procession. In 'The Triumph of Death' Laura joins the 'never-numbered sum' of the dead who 'appear' to Petrarch.[11] The text as a whole is also a progressive movement from the Triumph of sexual love to the Triumph of eternity. Petrarch uses the classical idea of the Triumph both as a device within the individual poems, and as a unifying principle for the whole work. The motif of procession implies the incremental development from one state (earthly love) to another (divine love) through a series of intermediary stages (chastity, death, fame and time). Set against this precedent, the procession motif in *The Teares* is plainly less incremental. The procession from Clio to Polyhymnia presents itself as a series of related yet distinct complaints. It ends when Spenser runs out of Muses – and there is therefore nothing more to say – rather than by reaching a dialectical conclusion. The tensions between the Muses are, however, brought to full consciousness by the final pair in the sequence, Urania and Polyhymnia. Their complaints juxtapose a transcendent Christian poetics with a humanist aesthetic which aims to recover poetry's ancient status as a vessel of 'sacred lawes' to govern the polity.

Since the sequence of Muses does not fully explain the poem's argument, I suggest that it is structured on a principle of contrast

11 Mary Sidney's translation; in Douglas Brooks-Davies (ed.), *Silver Poets of the Sixteenth Century* (Everyman's Library. London and Vermont: Dent and Charles E. Tuttle, new edn 1992), p. 292. See pp. 104–05 above.

between humanist and Christian Muses; its argument is best seen in the tensions between the Muses, irrespective of sequence.

So if we juxtapose the complaints of Melpomene (Tragedy) and Calliope (Epic) we notice discordance between their Christian and humanist poetics. But these Muses do not follow each other: they are respectively the second and seventh complainants. This divide is intriguing because in both classical and contemporaneous criticism, Tragedy and Epic were seen as interrelated genres. Plato and Aristotle viewed Homeric epic as the direct ancestor of Athenian tragedy; Sidney connects them in terms of their didactic potential. Tragedy is 'so excellent a representation of whatsoever is most worthy to be learned', while Epic ('the Heroical') 'teacheth and moveth to the most high and excellent truth'.[12] In *The Teares* Calliope follows Verlame, defining herself as the:

> golden Trompet of eternitie,
> That lowly thoughts lift up to heavens hight,
> And mortall men have powre to deifie:
> *Bacchus* and *Hercules* I raisd to heaven,
> And *Charlemaine*, amongst the Starris seaven. (ll. 458–62)

Though Charlemagne is a token Christian in Calliope's heaven, her literary ideas evoke Verlame's humanist idealism. Epic has the 'powre to deifie' 'mortall men ... raisde to heaven' through their emulation of heroic accomplishments recorded in poetry. As the 'golden Trompet of eternitie', Calliope aligns herself with Homer, who appears in Petrarch's famous sonnet as the 'chiara tromba' of Achilles's fame.[13] Eternizing poetry finds its classic justification – for Petrarch, Verlame and now Calliope – in the idea of Alexander, 'the Easterne Conquerour', astonished by Achilles's good fortune in finding 'So brave a Trompe, thy noble acts to sound'.[14] Like Verlame's, Calliope's poetry is simultane-

12 Sidney, *Miscellaneous Prose*, pp. 97–98.

13 Petrarch, 'Giunto Alessandro a la famosa tomba', no. 187. In *Petrarch's Lyric Poems: The Rime Sparse and Other Lyrics*, trans. and ed. Robert M. Durling (Cambridge, Mass. and London: Harvard University Press, 1976), pp. 332–33. E. K. quotes from this poem in his commentary to the 'October' eclogue.

14 *The Ruines of Time*, ll. 432–34.

ously a recorder of and stimulus to 'famous acts' (l. 430). Her complaint embodies a humanism which defines poetry as the commemorator of the 'noble' human ambition for transcendent glory.[15]

Yet Melpomene recalls the apocalyptic view of the 'tragicke Pageants' in stressing human vanity and impotence.

> Ah wretched world the den of wickednesse,
> Deformd with filth and fowle iniquitie;
> Ah wretched world the house of heavinesse,
> Fild with the wreaks of mortall miserie;
> Ah wretched world, and all that is therein,
> The vassals of Gods wrath, and slaves of sin. (ll. 121–26)

Melpomene outlines a lapsarian view of this 'wretched world', flawed through the human 'wickednesse' of original sin. The stanza's cumulative repetitions point towards the orthodox Christian view that mortals are 'The vassals of Gods wrath, and slaves of sin'.[16] Where Calliope's poetics is predicated on the notion of human potential, Melpomene's emphasizes human powerlessness without the divine 'intendiment' (l. 144) of Christian revelation.

But this complaint constitutes a more complex Christian response to art than the world-contempt of *The Ruines of Time*. In this case, art is not simply another instance of 'vanitie and griefe of minde'. After her assertion of terrestrial 'wretchedness', Melpomene laments human ignorance through an allusion to the Hebrew Bible's Wisdom literature. Guided by 'rules of Sapience' and 'the staffe of Wisdome', the 'gentle mind' is 'wisely taught to beare' 'all this worlds affliction'. But in the current cultural crisis, 'Man' is the 'most miserable creature under sky' because he lives 'without understanding' (ll. 127–40).

---

15 Compare Patrick Cheney, *Spenser's Famour Flight: A Renaisance Idea of a Literary Career* (Toronto: University of Toronto Press, 1993), pp. 9–10, who argues that there is 'a Christianization of the idea of poetic fame' in this stanza. Yet as Cheney concedes, 'The thought is by no means explicit', and I suggest that the reading adopted here is the more natural one.

16 See pp. 122–23 above. This formulation is a possible anticipation of the extreme anxieties expressed in *Muiopotmos* about the divine governance of the mortal world. See pp. 236–39 below.

Hebrew Wisdom literature articulates what James G. Williams calls 'a sense of order': the Wisdom text 'depicts a vital order informed by retributive justice and given human expression in wise utterance'.[17] Similarly, for Melpomene, the crisis is a wilful derogation against intellectual order, through which the ignorant man has become:

> like a ship in midst of tempest left
> Withouten helme or Pilot her to sway,
> Full sad and dreadfull is that ships event:
> So is the man that wants intendiment. (ll. 141–44)

Retributive justice will ensure that 'that ships event' is 'dreadfull', just as in Biblical Wisdom it sees that 'Who so despiseth wisdome … is miserable, … and their woorkes unprofitable'.[18] By incorporating this tradition into her lament, Melpomene recalls Wisdom as a theologically powerful form,[19] purveying a core of 'wise utterance'. The 'man that wants intendiment' should be warned by 'that ships event' to learn the 'rules of Sapience'.

Biblical Wisdom is also related to Biblical lament: a proverbial text may include elements of complaint, and vice versa. The Book of Job 'is heavily stamped with traditional Wisdom poetics'[20] alongside its use of complaint in the guise of curses, impossible and 'existential' questions, and soliloquies.[21] Melpomene's evocation of Wisdom introduces another variety of traditional complaint to the surface of *The Teares*.

Melpomene then presents Tragedy as a form of neo-medieval complaint. Here literary mode and theological outlook become intertwined: Tragedy is the logical expression of lapsarian pessimism.

---

17 James G. Williams, 'Proverbs and Ecclesiastes', in *The Literary Guide to the Bible*, ed. Robert Alter and Frank Kermode (London: Fontana, 1987), pp. 263, 265

18 The Wisdom of Solomon, 3.11. In Renwick, *Complaints*, p. 208.

19 Compare Sidney's classification of 'Solomon in his Song of Songs, in his Ecclesiastes, and Proverbs; … and the writer of Job' among 'The chief' poets 'that did imitate the unconceivable excellencies of God'. In Sidney, *Miscellaneous Prose …*, p. 80.

20 Williams, 'Proverbs and Ecclesiastes', p. 266.

21 See J. Gerald Janzen, *Job*, Interpretation: A Bible Commentary for Teaching and Preaching (Atlanta: John Knox, 1985), pp. 18–22; 61–71; 187–201. Though Janzen does not mention complaint as such, his account of the literary features of the text effectively constitutes a reading of The Book of Job as an innovative complaint.

My part it is and my professed skill
The Stage with Tragick buskin to adorne,
And fill the Scene with plaint and outcries shrill
Of wretched persons, to misfortune borne:
But none more tragick matter I can finde
Then this, of men depriv'd of sense and minde.

For all mans life me seemes a Tragedy,
Full of sad sights and sore Catastrophees;
First comming to the world with weeping eye,
Where all his dayes like dolorous Trophees,
Are heapt with spoyles of fortune and of feare,
And he at last laid forth on balefull beare. (ll. 151–62)

Melpomene transforms tragedy from a purely literary or dramatic form into a metaphor for 'all mans life': the 'plaint and outcries shrill' of literature are realized by the 'tragick matter' of the crisis. Despite the image of 'The Stage', this 'Tragedy' resembles Chaucer's definition of a non-dramatic 'dite of a prosperite for a tyme, that endeth in wrecchidnesse',[22] rather than Sidney's neo-classical dramatic mode.[23] Melpomene's 'dolorous' Tragedy evokes the exemplary didacticism of the *Mirror for Magistrates*: the individual is an exemplum of authentic 'life' – a 'weeping' microcosm of the universal Tragedy. Melpomene's lapsarian view of 'mans life' predicates her conception of Tragedy. Since human life necessarily provokes lamentation, Tragedy offers a symbolic display of 'plaint and outcries shrill', whose exemplary 'Catastrophees' school 'foolish men' in the 'rules of Sapience'.

Melpomene's Christian poetics is a fusion of Biblical Wisdom and medieval complaint. Art has a necessary educative function: even in a world 'Deformd with filth and fowle iniquitie', poetry can voice the

22 *Boece* II, prose 2, line 70. See also the analogous definition in *The Monk's Prologue* ll. 1973–77. In Geoffrey Chaucer, *The Works*, ed. F. N. Robinson (London: Oxford University Press, 1957), pp. 331, 189. Compare the definition of 'ditee' in *A Chaucer Glossary*, comp. Norman Davis, Douglas Gray, Patricia Ingham and Anne Wallace-Hadrill (Oxford: Clarendon, 1979), p. 39, 'literary composition, poem or song'.

23 Sidney, *Miscellaneous Prose* ..., p. 115, 'tragedy should be still maintained in

pious conclusion of Job's Wisdom poem – 'Behold, the fear of the Lord, that is Wisdom, and to depart from evil, is understanding'.[24]

The initial conclusion to be drawn from these complaints is that they embody differing poetics. The humanist Calliope restates Verlame's poetics: poetry is a form of heroic memorialization through which 'the noble race' can be 'deifie[d]'. Melpomene in contrast stresses the 'miserie' of 'mortall' life; her poetry is a synthesis of Biblical Wisdom and medieval complaint with the goal of didactic instruction. Calliope and Melpomene continue the debate of *The Ruines of Time* between humanist and Christian imperatives. But where Calliope's complaint echoes Verlame's, Melpomene's constitutes a Christian poetics which avoids the rejection of all human art made in the first 'tragicke Pageants'. *The Teares* replaces *The Ruines of Time*'s questioning of the morality of art with the non-hierarchical contrast of humanist and Christian models of art.

So far I have stressed the conceptual differences between Melpomene and Calliope to illustrate the divisions between the Muses, and so to clarify *The Teares*' argumentative form. It is a procession of contrasting complaints and not an incremental movement privileging one meta-poetics above all others. But the Muses articulate their different aesthetics within the frame of the same text and against the same thematic background. The juxtaposition of Calliope and Melpomene can also show what the Muses collectively share.

Like their sisters, both these Muses lament the cultural crisis manifested in the human disregard for poetry. Despite their different poetics, Melpomene and Calliope use similar images to describe the prevailing insensibility. Melpomene aligns it with drowning:

> Most unhappie wretches,
> The which lie drowned in deep wretchednes,
> Yet doo not see their owne unhappines. (ll. 148–50)

Calliope presents it as a corrosive sloth:

> They all corrupted through the rust of time,
> That doth all fairest things on earth deface,

24 The Book of Job 28.28.

Or through unnoble sloth, or sinfull crime
That doth degenerate the noble race;
Have both desire of worthie deeds forlorne,
And name of learning utterly doo scorne. (ll. 433–38)

Images of mental paralysis and stagnation recur throughout the procession. Misled by Ignorance or paralysed by 'sloth', human beings have become 'Most unhappie wretches', oblivious to the benefits conferred on them by humanist and Christian poetry alike. In Calliope's brilliant metaphor, ignorance of poetry literally 'deface[s]' the 'fairest things' of the poetic tradition, leaving only a residue of 'rust' in place of the 'living praises' (l. 431) of former heroes. Melpomene's drowning 'wretches' and Calliope's 'degenerate' nobility suffer an identical cognitive delusion: by ignoring poetry they are unable to 'see their own unhappines'. In this case, the Muses' theoretical differences do not impinge on their shared perception that human culture is under threat. Because the cultural apocalypse is imminent, the Muses lament as a group. Their formation in a traditional procession re-emphasizes the value of the poetic traditions which the human community is senselessly abandoning.

This analysis of the form and argument of *The Teares* suggests that the view of the text as formally simple is inadequate. Both the external form and internal arrangement of ideas reveal an intricate structural tension between homogeneity and dissonance. I suggest that this tension serves the poem's central conceit (which is also the basis of its innovation of traditional critical and poetic discourse) of the Muses' despair. This is the enigmatic core of *The Teares* which demands analysis.

'Therefore I mourne': Presenting the Muses

Before exploring the Muses' despair, we need a fuller understanding of what the Muses represent. In brief, they embody Spenser's conception of the western poetic tradition. Yet Snare has argued that they symbolize a more universal repository of human knowledge. By tracing their profiles in contemporaneous mythographies, he maintains that 'The whole encyclopedia of knowledge ... is under the aegis of the Muses'.[25] *The Teares* displays an awareness of the Muses' complex identity in the mythographies as the purveyors of all knowledge and as embodiments of universal concord, whose gifts are only bestowed on an exclusive group of poets and initiates. The Muses 'represent in figure a profound conception of the nature and function of the sacred poet and his poetry. The Muses' votaries ... perceive the whole encyclopaedia of truth in a harmonious and unified whole.'[26] Snare's article provides an invaluable abstract of the mythographic associations which underpin *The Teares*. He seeks to expand understanding of the poetic tradition symbolized by the Muses by revealing its encyclopedic aspects. Yet this approach ignores the conceptual tensions between the Muses, and tends to regard the poem as the unified exposition of a homogeneous epistemology.

Snare's reading also accentuates the Muses' mythographic origins at the expense of their immediate literary sources. *The Teares* owes an extensive debt to Du Bellay's *La Musagnoeomachie* (1550) and Ronsard's *Ode à Michel de l'Hospital* (1552) in its presentation of the Muses and Ignorance. While Ronsard's Muses may have residual associations with encyclopaedic knowledge, their primary function in his Ode is as the divine sponsors of true poetry. In Ronsard's myth of poetic inspiration, the Muses conduct Jupiter's original afflatus to the ancient 'Poëtes divins' through a kind of spiritual magnetism.[27] This primary inspiration is symbolically linked with Ronsard's own both in the text's formal recreation of the Pindaric ode and its triumphal literary history, culminating with the revival of the Muses' cultural prestige in the work of the Pléiade poets and their patrons. Ronsard's poem provides a compelling image of the Muses as sponsors of the Pléiade's new poetry. Ronsard's poem specifically equates

25 Snare, 'The Muses on Poetry', pp. 34–35, 45. See also Ernest R. Curtius, *European Literature in the Latin Middle Ages*, trans. Willard R. Trask (Bollingen Series XXVI. Princeton: Princeton University Press, 1953; new edn 1990), pp. 228–46.

26 *Ibid*, p. 52.

27 *Ode à Michel de l'Hospital*, l. 548. In Pierre de Ronsard, *II Odes, Hymns and other poems*, ed. Grahame Castor and Terence Cave (Manchester: Manchester University Press, 1977), p. 48.

the Muses with his own poetic innovation. In *The Teares* as in the *Ode*, the Muses' representation of the 'whole encyclopaedia of knowledge' is secondary to their more familiar rôle as the inspirers of the poet – whether Ronsard or Spenser – in his self-appointed task of making a new poetry through the revivification of the poetic tradition. But Spenser cannot replicate Ronsard's optimism because he perceives the disintegration of that tradition. The Muses' despair articulates this perception.

The Teares presents these complex Muses chiefly through the link-stanzas and the proem (ll. 1–54). This provides the only detailed editorial contextualization of the Muses' laments. It invokes the Muses to 'Rehearse' (l. 1) their laments in Spenser's text. Spenser implicitly identifies himself as the narrator of this text by alluding to his own version of the Muses' parentage (ll. 2, 7–12)[28] and rewriting the myths of Phaeton and the Palici (ll. 13–17). He then describes the ruin of the Muses' locus amoenus 'Beside the silver Springs of *Helicone*' (l. 5); finally, he presents the Muses' 'griefe' as an enigma which will be 'display[ed]' by the ensuing text. So the proem contains two presentations of the Muses which further the understanding of the crisis and their despair.

Firstly, the proem inverts the normative relationship between the poet and his Muses, disturbing the traditional notion of the Muses' ecstatic self-sufficiency (ll. 19–20). According to traditional poetic discourse, the Muse enables the poet to write his poem. In *Epithalamion* the first stanza is an elaborate invocation of the Muses to engage themselves in Spenser's undertaking:

> Ye learned sisters which have oftentimes
> beene to me ayding, others to adorne:

28 Spenser's use of this myth was eclectic; compare Renwick, *Complaints*, p. 206, 'Why Spenser here (and at lines 57–58) makes the Muses daughters of Apollo instead of Jupiter is known to himself alone'. He may, however, have received some stimulus in this direction from texts like Ronsard's *Ode* and *de Musarum inventis*, which both present Apollo playing a key part in the Muses' ecstatic rapture. Apollo appears as the 'father of the Muse' also in *Epithalamion*, l. 121 and *The Faerie Queene*, I.XI.5, III.III.4 and VII.VII.1; however, Jove takes his traditional rôle in *The Ruines of Time*, l. 368 and *The Faerie Queene*, IV.XI.10.

Whom ye thought worthy of your graceful rymes,
That even the greatest did not greatly scorne
To heare theyr names sung in your simple layes,
But joyed in theyr prayse:
And when ye list your owne mishaps to mourne,
Which death, or love, or fortunes wreck did rayse,
Your string could soone to sadder tenor turne,
And teach the woods and waters to lament
Your dolefull dreriment:
Now lay those sorrowfull complaints aside,
And having all your heads with girland crownd,
Helpe me mine owne loves prayses to resound …,[29]

Spenser requests the Muses' assistance on the strength of their previous sponsorship of his work. The syntax is a verbal enactment of his homage to them. The active verb is delayed until line 12, so that the preceding lines interweave into a summational prayer, re-evoking their previous artistic accomplishments. Spenser lists the ways in which the 'learned Sisters' have 'beene to me ayding' as a preliminary to his request for help in the 'resound[ing]' of his 'owne loves prayse'. The verb in line 12 is itself a preliminary to the active plea for inspiration in line 14: the Muses must 'Now *lay* those sorrowfull complaints aside' so that they may then '*Helpe* me mine owne loves prayses to resound'.[30] After the intricate rehearsal of their deeds in the preceding lines, line 14 jumps the poem into action, while also stressing that the poet is dependent on their good will. The delay of his request skilfully heightens the power of the compliment and its value as an invocation: even in this most private of poetic tasks, the poet courteously requires the participation of the Muses.

By contrast the first stanza of *The Teares* inverts the classic relationship between the poet and the Muses:

Rehearse to me ye sacred Sisters nine:
The golden brood of great *Apolloes* wit,

---

29 *Epithalamion*, ll. 1–14.
30 My italics.

Those piteous plaints and sorowful sad tine,
Which late ye powred forth as ye did sit
Beside the silver Springs of *Helicone*,
Making your musick of hart-breaking mone. (ll. 1–6)

Where *Epithalamion* delays its verbs, *The Teares* begins with the active
'Rehearse', which dominates the stanza's syntax. The 'sacred Sisters
nine' must 'Rehearse to me', the poet, their 'piteous plaints'. The verb
is an imperative, not a request. As such, the stanza stands in place of
an invocation to indicate the self-conscious nature of the text in hand.
Spenser does not need to ask the Muses to inspire him, since his text
sets out to record the Muses' pre-existing laments. This stanza para-
doxically implies that the poet is now assisting the Muses by bringing
their laments into literary form. It has been argued that *The Teares* is
the literary favour which Spenser reminds the Muses of in *Epithala-
mion*.[31] The divine enablers of poetry have become its thematic focus.

The first stanza initiates the motif of inversion and change which
dominates the proem. The description of the spoliation of Helicon
overturns the traditional image (originally derived from Hesiod's
Theogony) of the Muses' 'great and holy' habitat.[32] Helicon, or Par-
nassus, is an idealized pastoral Mountain occupied by the Muses. In
Metamorphoses V Pallas visits Helicon and declares 'the daughters of
Mnemosyne to be happy alike in their favourite pursuits and in their
home'.[33] In *The Teares*, this environment has become a wilderness:

And all that els [1] ‖ was wont to worke delight [2] ‖
Through the divine infusion [3] ‖ of their skill, [4] ‖
And all that els [1] ‖ seemed faire and fresh in
    sight, [2] ‖
So made by nature [3] ‖ for to serve their will, [4] ‖

31 Compare *Var.* VIII, p. 459, for Grosart's view.

32 Hesiod, *Theogony* 1–9. In *Hesiod; The Homeric Hymns and Homerica*; The
Loeb Classical Library, ed. and trans. Hugh G. Evelyn-White (Cambridge, Mass.
and London: Harvard University Press and Heinemann, 1914), pp. 78–79.

33 Ovid, *Metamorphoses*, The Loeb Classical Library, 2 vols, ed. and trans. F. J.
Miller (Cambridge, Mass. and London: Harvard University Press and Heinemann,
1916), I, pp. 256–57.

Was turned now to dismall heavinesse,
Was turned now to dreadfull uglinesse. (ll. 37–42)

This stanza enacts Spenser's inversion of the Heliconian idyll. The quatrain is made up of two syntactically analogous clauses, lines 37–38 and 39–40. The first concentrates on the Muses' art, 'the divine infusion of their *skill*[34] and its capacity 'to worke delight'. The second presents Helicon as a product of 'nature' expressly 'made' 'to serve [the Muses'] will'. I have broken the clauses into matching numerical units to display their syntactic and rhythmic parallels.[35] Lines 37 and 39 share the same anaphoristic opening [1]. Similarly, the descriptive phrases [2] serve the same function: glossing of the next lines. These phrases are further linked through rhyme and their identical metrical pattern of three iambic feet in six syllables. Though lines 38 and 40 lack this intense symmetry, their images of art and nature are carefully balanced: in [3] 'the divine infusion' of the Muses' poetic gift mirrors terrestrial 'nature', while [4] juxtaposes the Muses' active artistic 'skill' with their passive reception of nature's service. As such, the two clauses are syntactically blended to produce a retrospective image of Helicon as a successful amalgam of Art and Nature. In other words, the Muses' poetry – witnessed in their chosen habitat – was a beneficial influence which harmonized the perennial conflict between Art and Nature. In the present tense, the intricate symmetry of the quatrain is resolved into the stark repetitions of the couplet; the idyll is converted into 'dismall heavinesse' and 'dreadfull uglinesse'.

What do these inversions communicate about *The Teares* as a whole? The crucial point is that despite Spenser's sympathy for the Muses' 'hart-breaking' predicament, his text has the effect of making the concept of 'the Muse[s]' problematic. If I write a poem and ask the Muses for inspiration, I implicitly position myself within the tradition of poetry which has previously been written under their authority. This is what Chaucer does in the Proem to Book II of *The Hous of Fame*:

34 My italic.
35 The symbol ‖ is primarily used the divide the different units of each clause. However, it also functions as a caesura marking; though it is not vital to give these lines such definite breathing spaces.

And ye, me to endite and ryme
Helpeth, that on Parnasso duelle,
Be Elicon, the clere welle.[36]

Chaucer's invocation is a knowing appeal to tradition, shown in the rhyming tag cum display of erudition – 'the clere welle'. But if I, like Spenser, transform my invocation into a command and describe 'Elicon' as the site of catastrophe, I turn the Muses from the enablers into the subject of my poem, and imply that the poetic tradition which they represent is under some sort of trial. It is the notion that their traditional prestige is under scrutiny that generates the Muses' complaints.

The proem's second presentation of the Muses is a corollary to its destabilization of tradition. In the proem's final stanza, Spenser suggests that his text will explain the enigma of the Muses' despair:

Vouchsafe ye then, whom onely it concernes,
To me those secret causes to display;
For none but you, but who of you it learnes
Can rightfully aread so dolefull lay. (ll. 49–52)

These lines might initially endorse Snare's reading of *The Teares* as a lament for a poetry of enlightened initiates – 'The "secret causes" of the Muses [sic] apparently can be known only to those whom the Muses instruct'.[37] But as he recognizes, line 52 contains 'a rather provocative ambiguity'.[38] I go further: all four lines are fraught with difficulty. In the first place, does the phrase 'whom onely it concernes' apply to the Muses ('ye') or the narrator ('To me')? 'Onely' should be glossed as 'specially' rather than 'uniquely':[39] since the phrase can apply grammatically either to the Muses or the narrator, the 'concern' cannot be unique. There is a further problem, as Snare's comment unconsciously indicates, in the relationship between the pronoun 'it'

36 *The Hous of Fame*, ll. 520–22. In Chaucer, *Works*, p. 287. Compare also Chaucer's other references to 'Yee sustren nyne ek, that by Elicone / In hil Pernaso listen for t'abide' in *Troilus and Criseyde* III.1809–10 and *Anelida and Arcite* ll. 16–17. For Chaucer, Helicon and Parnassus seem virtually interchangeable.

37 Snare, 'The Muses on Poetry', p. 36.

38 *Ibid.*

39 See *OED*, 3rd definition of the adverbial 'only'.

and 'those secret causes' in the following line. Does Spenser mean that the pronoun is synonymous with 'those secret causes'? If so, these lines must read: 'Condescend [you Muses], who those secret causes specially concern, to display those secret causes to me'. Such a construction is unnecessarily incoherent. The 'secret causes' must be causes of something, and this stanza should bear some relation to the proem's inversion of the Heliconian idyll. The pronoun in fact refers back to the previous couplet – 'Can griefe then enter into heavenly harts, / And pierce immortal breasts with mortall smarts?' (ll. 47–48) – in which case, 'it' denotes the 'griefe'. So in lines 48–49 the poet wishes 'to display' the 'secret causes' of the Muses' 'griefe'. The origins of the crisis *specially* concern the Muses, but must also concern the narrator and the reader.

Lines 51–52 present further problems which also reflect on the audience-reception of the Muses' laments. In Snare's view the sole ambiguity is the 'doleful lay' which he correctly identifies as both the Muses' laments and the poem as a whole.[40] He does not consider what activity is described by 'rightfully aread so dolefull lay', or who 'learnes' this skill from whom. In this context, 'aread' must mean 'interpret' or 'unriddle' rather than the misleading 'utter'.[41] As DeNeef has shown, Spenser uses 'read' and its cognates like 'aread' to describe a wide range of interpretative activities: DeNeef lists fifteen different usages of the verb in *The Faerie Queene* alone.[42] He argues that Spenser conceives of reading as 'an ethical action' in which the reader must respond imaginatively to the demands of the text in hand.[43] So the dedicatory sonnet of *Virgils Gnat* reveals that 'Too much reading, too much glossing upon the text, is as dangerous as no reading at all'.[44] DeNeef's Spenser is always conscious of the potential dubiety of reading. In both *The Teares'* proem and the *Virgils*

40 Snare, 'The Muses on Poetry' p. 36.

41 *OED* 3 (instead of 1). See also Oram's note in *YESP*, p. 271; and A. Leigh DeNeef, *Spenser and the Motives of Metaphor* (Durham, NC: Duke University Press, 1982), p. 154, for 'unriddle'.

42 DeNeef, *Spenser and the Motives of Metaphor*, p. 154.

43 *Ibid.*, p. 145.

44 *Ibid.*

Gnat sonnet, he tries to exercise some control over his readers: the '*Oedipus* unware' who can 'reade the secrete of this riddle rare' is requested to 'rest pleased with his owne insight'. Similarly, the 'dolefull lay' is an enigma which either the Muses 'or who of you it learnes' must 'rightfull aread', that is, 'properly interpret'. DeNeef's view of Spenserian reading offers a useful way into this difficult line. Though I accept that Spenser wishes to control the reception of his texts, he is also aware, as the *Virgils Gnat* sonnet demonstrates in miniature, that this desire is an authorial fantasy. What he cannot disclose about his relationship with Leicester can be 'easily knowen' through an allegorical reading of 'this Gnatts complaint'. On a larger scale, *The Teares* presents the cultural crisis as an upsurge of Ignorance which results in the collapse of 'ethical' reading. So while the narrator may want to ensure that we 'rightfully aread' the Muses' complaints, neither he nor the Muses can guarantee the 'rightfulness' of subsequent readings of *The Teares*.

The transmission and reception of meaning also lies at the heart of line 51: who is the object of the Muses' education? The immediate context of the proem indicates that the 'who' of line 51 should be the poet, whose 'dolefull lay' is about 'to display' 'those secret causes'. This formulation is close to Snare's idea that the Muses' 'instruction' is open only to a select few. Spenser's use of the verb 'learnes' works against this reading. 'To learn' is conceptually very different from 'to be instructed': 'who of you it learnes' suggests a critical search for the 'causes' of the Muses' 'griefe', rather than the passive reception of a quasi-religious mystery. 'Who of you it learnes' comprises both the poet – who is trying to 'display' or make manifest the 'secret' of the Muses' despair – and the reader, who 'learnes' about the crisis through reading *The Teares*. In a way that is basically in accord with DeNeef's conception of Spenserian reading, the narrator's request to the Muses indicates that the burden of 'rightfully aread[ing]' is shared by the Muses, the poet and the reader.

The sentence reads: 'Condescend to display to me [you Muses] the secret causes [of your grief], which concern you especially, since nobody except you, or whoever learns it from you, can properly interpret this/such a sad song'. This paraphrase shows that the narrator conceives of his text as a means of revealing these 'secret causes' rather than of keeping them hidden. The narrator's request to the Muses (the closest the proem comes to an invocation) also promises its readers that the 'dolefull lay' will explain why the Muses' position has altered so disastrously.

The Causes of the Crisis

As my contrast of Melpomene and Calliope reveals, the different Muses share analogous perceptions of the crisis: they despair and complain because human beings are abandoning poetry and the accumulated wisdom of its traditions. The Muses' despair is acute because, as the patrons of poetry, they cannot understand what motivates 'foolish men' to spurn it. In Melpomene's words:

> Whie then doo foolish men so much despize
> The precious store of this celestiall riches?
> Why doo they banish us, that patronize
> The name of learning? (ll. 145–48)

For Melpomene there is no rational answer to these questions. By 'despiz[ing]' poetry, 'men' are 'depriv'd of sense and minde' (ll. 156). As the gulf between rational Muses and their irrational audience widens, so their ability to communicate meaningfully with each other collapses. Within the framework of this pessimism, the Muses advance differing if related 'causes' of the crisis. The reader in turn can expect to construct some sort of answer to Melpomene's 'impossible' questions.

These explanations initially locate the crisis within existing social structures. So Calliope's complaint continues Verlame's concern with 'eternizing' and the corresponding anxiety that the nobility should patronize such poetry. Both Calliope and Clio reiterate this concern and lament that the nobility have become paradoxically 'Base minded', scorning learning as 'a base thing' (ll. 86–88). The pressure on poetry registered by the Muses is the result of the nobility's abandonment of their traditional patronage of learning.[45] The second and most important 'cause' of the crisis is shadowed by the monstrous figure of Ignorance. Initially, he represents the social opposite of nobility: Clio refers to 'they that dwell in lowly dust, / The sonnes of darknes and of ignoraunce' (ll. 67–68). Ignorance is subsequently developed into more than just a personification of the unlearned 'multitude' (l. 326). Particularly in the complaints of Euterpe and Terpsichore, he incarnates the 'hellish' physical and intellectual 'horrour' (l. 259) challenging the Muses' prestige.

> *(Euterpe)*
> He armd with blindnesse and with boldness stout,
> (For blind is bold) hath our fayre light defaced;
> And gathering unto him a ragged rout
> Of *Faunes* and *Satyres*, hath our dwellings raced
> And our chast bowers, in which all vertue rained,
> With brutishnesse and beastlie filth hath
>   stained. (ll. 265–70)

> *(Terpsichore)*
> So wee that earst in joyance did abound
> And in the bosome of all blis did sit,
> Like virgin Queenes with laurell garlands cround,
> For vertues meed and ornament of wit;
> Sith ignorance our kingdome did confound,
> Bee now become most wretched wightes on ground … (ll. 307–12)

45 Clio in particular laments the absence of fluid social mobility: 'It most behoves the honorable race / Of Mightie Peeres' – as the financially enabling class – 'true wisedome to sustaine' (ll. 79–80) through their patronage. In this view, there is a causal relationship between the inhibition of élite recruitment and the decay of poetry. In taking this position, Clio is in the mainstream of sixteenth-century political theory. Sir Thomas Smith, for example, in *De Republica Anglorum* (1583) concedes that 'as other common wealthes were faine to doe, so must all princes necessarilie followe, where vertue is to honour it'. Smith remains convinced that 'auncient race' is more likely to provide such virtue, but cannot escape the conclusion that some form of social mobility – or honouring of virtue – is a necessary part of a modern commonwealth. See Sir Thomas Smith, *De Republica Anglorum*, ed. Mary Dewer (Cambridge: Cambridge University Press, 1982), p. 71.

Euterpe describes the rise of Ignorance as a rape of Helicon, while Terpsichore sees it as a usurpation (ll. 337–38). Despite his different guises, Ignorance has a similar impact on each Muse. According to Euterpe, the Muses' pastoral 'dwellings' are 'stained' by 'brutishnesse and beastlie filth': the rise of Ignorance is a sexual defilement, assisted by the perennially concupiscent satyrs.[46] Ignorance's destruction of the Muses' cultural authority spoliates the pastoral Euterpe represents.

Similarly, Terpsichore describes the Muses' decline as a progress masterminded by Ignorance. Her complaint charts the Muses' tragic descent from the high point when their 'royall thrones ... lately stood / In th'hearts of men to rule them carefully' (ll. 313–14), to the nadir of their exile 'From our own native heritage' (l. 341). In this *Mirror for Magistrates*-style complaint, Ignorance plays the rôle of the usurper who supplants the 'queenly' Muses. Ignorance is not simply a 'base' opponent, but a knowing perverter of intellectual tradition. When Ignorance's protégés 'say their musicke matcheth *Phoebus* quill' (l. 330), they deliberately invert traditional critical discourse: the beauty of Apollo's writing is drowned out by 'fond newfangle-nesse' (l. 327). Ignorance's cultural 'toyes' (l. 325) usurp the Muses' poetic 'vertue' and 'wit' (l. 310).

Throughout the poem, Ignorance is a multifaceted 'cause' of the crisis: a symbol of barbarism for Thalia, the rapist of Helicon for Euterpe, 'the enemie' of theological 'grace' for Urania, and the over-turning of intellectual tradition for Terpsichore. He is a metamorphic embodiment of poetic disaster. The wounds he makes cannot readily be healed; Ignorance causes the crisis and leads the Muses collectively to despair. In Urania words, 'hell and darknesse and the grieslie grave / Is ignorance' (ll. 496–97): symbolically, Ignorance is the 'grave' of the poetic tradition; *The Teares* shows them entering his 'darknesse'.

Spenser's vision of the Muses' despair is then profoundly pes-simistic. This pessimism is a bold transformation of the conflicts between the Muses and Ignorance in Du Bellay's *La Musagnoeomachie* and Ronsard's *Ode à Michel de L'Hospital*. French panegyric becomes

46 Compare the rôle of satyrs in *The Faerie Queene*, I.VI and especially III.X. See also Hamilton's note in *FQ*, p. 87.

English complaint. It has long been recognized that these texts had an impact on passages of *The Teares*.[47] Their value for the present discussion is their embodiment of the Pléiade's initial poetic idealism, which powerfully counterpoints *The Teares*' pessimism. For Du Bellay and Ronsard, the Muses are efficacious, neo-classical guarantors of the Pléiade's project. More importantly, the French Ignorance is a 'Monstre hideux',[48] who can be defeated. *La Musagnoeomachie* recounts a mythic battle between Ignorance's 'furieuse armée' and the assembled forces of French culture:[49]

> Dieu en Cirene adoré,
> Ceint de branche verdissante,
> Marie un archet doré
> Avec la corde puissante
> De ma Lire menaçante.
> Sur les aeles de ton nom
> Guinde bien hault le renom
> De la guerre commencée
> Par moy l'Angevin Alcée,
> Suivant les scadrons divers,
> Qui l'Ignorance ont chassée
> Par la foudre de leurs vers.[50]

Du Bellay's message is clear and optimistic. His 'war of the Muses' unifies 'les scadrons divers' of neo-classical authority to administer 'la foudre' of true poetry against Ignorance. Here Du Bellay shows himself as the Angevine Alcaeus, whose war poetry successfully matches the divine patronage of Apollo and the Muses with 'la corde puissante / De ma Lire menaçante'. *La Musagnoeomachie* offers the

47 Renwick, *Complaints*, p. 211, uses both texts to parallel Euterpe's account of Ignorance; while Satterthwaite, *Ronsard and Du Belley*, pp. 66–92, compares these and related poems by Du Bellay and Ronsard with *The Teares*. He is more interested, however, in 'temperamental affinities' between the poets than how Spenser adapted his reading.

48 *La Musagnoeomachie* 78. In Joachim Du Bellay, *Oeuvres Poétiques*, 6 vols, ed. Henri Chamard (Paris: Société des Textes Français Modernes, 1907–31), Vol. V, p. 7.

49 *Ibid.*, Vol. V, pp. 8, 12.

50 *Ibid.*, V, p. 24.

prospect of a new age in which the morally destructive Ignorance is hounded out of French society. The authority of the Muses is vindicated by the rhetorical battle fought on their behalf by Du Bellay and his allies.

Despite its more complex myth of literary history,[51] the basic perspective of the *Ode à Michel de L'Hospital* on the conflict between Ignorance and the Muses is analogous to that of *La Musagnoeomachie*. Ronsard's theory of poetic inspiration[52] is linked to his own historical account of European literature as a fall from the ancient inspired poetry of 'les Poëtes sainctz' to post-Roman barbarity.[53] At this point in time, 'L'Ignorance arma / L'aveugle fureur des Princes, / Et leurs aveugles Provinces / Contre les Soeurs [i.e. the Muses] anima'.[54] The Muses return to heaven for the duration of the middle ages, to re-emerge under the enlightened protection of Michel de l'Hospital. Like *La Musagnoeomachie*, the Ode climaxes with the triumphant re-establishment of a pure poetry, sponsored by the Muses, in France. For Ronsard, Hospital initiates a return to the values of 'les Poëtes sainctz' in a modern setting. He has 'ramené dans l'univers / Le Choeur des Pierides Muses';[55] Ronsard's own poetic example (shown by his mastery of the Pindaric form) confirms the efficacy of this neoclassical aesthetic. As in Du Bellay, the one-sided war between Ignorance and the Muses in Ronsard supports his self-advertising confidence in the new age which, he believes, his poetry inaugurates.

It should be immediately clear that *The Teares* is a very different style of poem from either the *Ode* or *La Musagnoeomachie*. Spenser's Muses command greater attention within his text, and symbolize more diverse poetic and intellectual traditions than those of Du Bellay and Ronsard. The French Muses are images of the kind of poetry the Pléiade wants to believe it is writing: that is, one which follows in its practice the great tradition of the classical canon in the vernacular. By contrast, the English Muses contemplate the death of poetry as their constituency van-

---

51 Ronsard also outlines this in the *Abbregé de l'Art poëtique françois* (1565).
52 See pp. 144–45 above.
53 *Ode*, l. 418. In Ronsard, *II Odes, Hymns and Other Poems*, p. 44.
54 *Ibid.*, p. 49.
55 *Ibid.*

ishes. Yet Spenser's most profound innovation from these texts is his metamorphic presentation of Ignorance. For Ronsard and Du Bellay, Ignorance is connected with the artistic mistakes of the past rather than of the future; it is a monster defeated in the 1550s by the Pléiade's new poetry.[56] Spenser clearly knew both poems well enough to draw on them and to adapt their image of Ignorance to suit his own purposes. A defeated monster of the past re-emerges 'of *late* / Out of dredd darkness'[57] to become the devourer of the Muses' authority.

The parallel also focuses attention on the relentless circularity of the English poem. The *Ode* and *La Musagnoeomachie* recount the resolution of a conflict between the Pléiade and the medieval past. After their respective victories, the poets look forward to writing the *Franciade*, or to consolidating *L'Olive*. *The Teares* reaches no such positive conclusions because Ignorance is here a more universal anti-poetic principle than its French precursors. The procession of Muses ends where it began: with unlightened lament. *The Teares* runs into what seems to be a philosophical and artistic dead end.

A Dead End?

This dead end or aporia is worth looking at in detail. Along with Maclean, I argue that the complaints of Urania and Polyhymnia offer two possible ways out of it.[58] Through the final pair of Muses, Spenser asks whether a Christian or a humanist poetics will be able to lift this despair to resurrect traditional poetry.

The reader of *Complaints* would expect Urania's lament to embody a Christian aesthetic. As in 'L'Envoy' to *Ruines of Rome*, Spenser praises Du Bartas's 'heavenly Muse', whose divine poetry lifts its readers towards God. The sonnet's comparison of Du Bellay with Du Bar-

56 *Ibid.*, p. 261. Cave and Castor note that Ronsard's Ignorance 'may be taken as designating in a general sense the alleged barbarism of the Middle Ages', or the specific poetic school of the *grands rhétoriqueurs*, whose 'mistakes' the Pléiade sought to amend.

57 My italic.

58 Compare Maclean's article in *The Spenser Encyclopedia*, pp. 182–83.

tas as terrestrial and devotional poets bears witness to the Spenserian view that Uranian, or divine, poetry is the apogee of poetic kinds. In *The Teares*, Urania's complaint articulates a Christian view of human knowledge underpinned by a neo-Platonic cosmology. Knowledge of 'Natures cunning operation' is a moral prerequisite for the Christian which ultimately reveals 'what to man, and what to God wee owe' (ll. 501–04). Through a spiritually enlightened perception of the phenomenal world – rather than, as in *The Ruines of Time*, a vaunting ambition for immortality – human beings can 'mount aloft unto the skie, / And looke into the Christall firmament' (ll. 505–06). The goal of this intellectual ascent is a revelation of the Godhead:

> And there with humble mind and high insight,
> Th'eternall Makers majestie wee viewe,
> His love, his truth, his glorie, and his might,
> And mercie more than mortall men can vew.
> O soveraigne Lord, ô soveraigne happinesse
> To see thee, and thy mercie measurelesse ... (ll. 511–16)

Given the prestige accorded to this view elsewhere in *Complaints*, and its anticipation of the visionary 'Sabaoths sight' which ends *The Mutabilitie Cantos*, readers could expect Urania's ecstatic vision to counter the Muses' despair, and in some way unify the Muses' complaints. Her ideal is both doctrinally authoritative in its 'humble' revelation of 'The'eternall Makers majestie', and intellectually complex in its presentation of creation as a divinely ordained *'Hierarchie'* (l. 507). Moreover, it is a powerful demonstration of the literary resources of traditional poetry. Urania's stanza binds together a descriptive sentence in the quatrain (ll. 511–14) with an exclamation in the couplet (ll. 515–16) which dramatize the wonder which 'we' are able to 'viewe'. By the addition and subtraction of an 'i', the quatrain deftly registers the perceptual distance between 'what mortall men can *vew*' and the visionary's transcendent *'viewe'* of God's 'majestie'.[59] The solemn incantation of the couplet then gives utterance to the longing for such a transcendence.

Urania's poetic ideal is 'To make men heavenly wise, through hum-

---

59 My italics.

bled will' (l. 522). As a Christian Muse, her 'heavenlie discipline' is open to all who are prepared to humble their 'will'. Yet her complaint turns on her discovery that the 'love of blindnesse and of ignorance' has persuaded 'wretched men' 'To dwell in darkenesse without sovenance' (ll. 482–86).[60] Without such remembrance men consign themselves to 'hell' (l. 496) – the theological embodiment of this intellectual 'darknesse'. Urania decides that instead of facilitating human 'insight' of heaven, she should take refuge there from the 'loathsome den' of earth:

> How ever yet they mee despise and spight,
> I feede on sweete contentment of my thought,
> And please my selfe with mine owne selfe-delight,
> In contemplation of things heavenlie wrought:
> So loathing earth, I looke up to the sky,
> And being driven hence I thether fly. (ll. 523–28)

Urania's flight is the logical product of her poetics: in response to the crisis she enacts the visionary ascent 'aloft unto the skie' (l. 505). It symbolizes the limitations of the Muses' power. From heaven, Urania can 'behold the miserie of men', but she has no power to give them 'the blis that wisedom would them breed' since they have voluntarily confined themselves in their 'loathsome den, / Of ghostly darknes' (ll. 529–32). Urania is a Christian Muse not a redeemer; she cannot absolve men of the sin of wilful intellectual 'blindnesse'.

The image of Urania's flight is a piece of Spenserian myth-making, emphasizing the powerlessness of the Muses in the face of the crisis. As Renwick noted,[61] Urania's flight imitates that of Astraea – the 'last of the immortals' to abandon 'the blood-soaked earth' during Ovid's Iron Age.[62] It has been long recognized that Spenser was familiar with

60 Urania recapitulates Melpomene's Wisdom poetics when she laments the literal brutalization of men 'When th'heavenlie light of knowledge is put out, / And th'ornaments of wisdome are bereft' (ll. 488–89). The parallel images of Wisdom as a form of light and Ignorance or vice as a form of darkness or blindness derive directly from Biblical sources; compare Wisdom 7.29 and Renwick, *Complaints*, p. 215.

61 *Ibid.*, p. 216.

62 *Metamorphoses* I.149–50. In Ovid, *Metamorphoses*, (1916), Vol. I, pp. 12–13.

Comes's identification of Astraea as 'the embodiment of Justice', and the equation of the goddess with the 'virgo' who returns to the earth to bring about a new golden age in Virgil's fourth *Eclogue*.[63] As Yates comprehensively demonstrates, this myth played a vital part in the eulogy of Queen Elizabeth, and has a place in *The Faerie Queene*. It also occurs at the beginning of *Mother Hubberds Tale*, where the narrative frame describes a plague occurring in the same month 'in which the righteous Maide, / That for disdaine of sinfull worlds upbraide, / Fled back to heaven'.[64] Here the myth both signals the negative astronomical conjunction which 'powr'd on th'earth plague, pestilence, and death'[65] and the absence from the world of the guiding justice of 'the righteous Maide'. Without Astraea's stabilizing authority, the Fox and the Ape are able to impose themselves on the world unhindered.

But why does Spenser make Urania imitate Astraea in *The Teares*? To understand this, we should concentrate on Ovid's Iron Age rather than Yates's image of Elizabeth-Astraea.[66] According to *Metamorphoses* I, the Iron Age signals the outbreak of evil: 'Straightway all evil burst forth into this age of baser vein' in the forms of deceitfulness and violence.[67] Astraea, as the goddess of Justice, leaves the earth when men finally dispense with piety.[68] The literary motif of Urania's flight is directly modelled on that of Ovid's Astraea. Spenser is less interested in trying to amalgamate Urania and Astraea into a composite figure than in following the outline of Ovid's narrative, which uses Astraea's departure as a symbol of the moral degradation of the

63 For Comes, see *Var.* VIII, pp. 350. For the wider discussion of Astraea in Elizabethan England, see Frances A. Yates, *Astraea: The Imperial Theme in the Sixteenth Century* (London: Routledge and Kegan Paul, 1975; rpt. London: Pimlico, 1993), pp. 29–87.

64 *Mother Hubberds Tale*, ll. 1–3.

65 *Ibid.*, l. 8.

66 See the Appendix below for a detailed consideration of the possible connection between Urania's flight and Polyhymnia's panegyric of Elizabeth.

67 *Metamorphoses* I.128–29. In Ovid, *Metamorphoses* (1916), Vol. I, pp. 10–11.

68 *Ibid.* I paraphrase the start of line 149, 'victa iacet pietas', 'Piety lay vanquished'.

Iron Age. Urania's flight symbolizes the degradation of a world which has turned its back on poetry. This symbol also shows that Urania's Christian poetics provides only a contemplative solution to the Muses' aporia. Urania is rapt in solitary 'selfe-delight', but she, like Astraea, is unable to influence human behaviour 'on earth' (l. 483).

As Urania's flight is the Christian-Platonic way out of the dead end which confronts the Muses, so Polyhymnia's panegyric of Queen Elizabeth represents the humanist alternative. Polyhymnia's complaint represents a more complex humanist poetic than the 'eternizing' idealism of Calliope. It is constructed in three parts: lines 541–58, lamenting the shortcomings of current poetry; lines 559–70, outlining poetry's ancient status as vessel of 'The sacred lawes'; and lines 571–94, presenting Elizabeth as the sole survivor in the general collapse of poetic value. These parts are closely interconnected. The complaint against 'mard' poetry stresses the vital order which informs Polyhymnia's ideal. Poetry 'tie[s]' 'winged words' with 'sweet numbers and melodious measures' creating 'a tunefull Diapase of pleasures' (ll. 547–49). This notion of poetry as a musical harmony[69] is violently juxtaposed against the orderless 'Heapes of huge words uphoorded hideously' which have 'mard the goodly face of Poësie' (ll. 553, 557). Similarly, poetry derives its ancient authority from its association with ritual order:

> Whilom in ages past none might professe
> But Princes and high Priests that secret skill,
> The sacred lawes therein they wont expresse,
> And with deep Oracles their verses fill:
> Then was shee held in soveraigne dignitie,
> And made the noursling of Nobilitie. (ll. 559–64)

In this ideal past, the practice of poetry is restricted to 'Princes and high Priests', whose poetic texts implicitly 'expresse' social order through 'sacred lawes' and 'deep Oracles'. Poetry's 'soveraigne dignitie'

---

69 According to *OED*, 'Diapase' or 'diapason' is a 'consonance of the highest and lowest notes of the musical scale' (1); it possibly also conveys the idea of 'A rich outburst of sound' (4a). Compare *YESP*, p. 289, for Oram's note.

reflects the 'Nobilitie' of its erstwhile practitioners and its efficacy as a tool of government. Polyhymnia's complaint sees poetry and order as inseparable principles, visible both in the command of verbal technique and the imperial polities 'of Kesars and of Kings' (l. 570). As the 'Heapes of huge words' are a technical symptom of the decline in poetry's prestige, so the pollution of its once 'hidden mysterie' by 'the base vulgar' (ll. 567–68) is a social symptom. The absence of aristocratic patronage allows poetry to be 'prophaned' (l. 566), inverting proper order: its 'holie things' are trodden 'under foote' (l. 569). This complaint follows the same train of thought as those of Clio and Calliope. As poetry is neglected by the aristocracy, so its recovery (and the recovery of the order it embodies) becomes less feasible; in Clio's words, 'all that in this world is worthie hight / Shall die in darknesse' (ll. 105–06). Unlike Clio and Calliope, Polyhymnia discovers in the person of Queen Elizabeth an exception to the general rule that 'now nor Prince nor Priest doth [poetry] maintayne' (l. 565):

> One onelie lives, her ages ornament,
> And myrrour of her Makers majestie;
> That with rich bountie and deare cherishment,
> Supports the praise of noble Poësie:
> Ne onelie favours them which it professe,
> But is her selfe a peereles Poëtresse. (ll. 571–76)

Polyhymnia's praise of Elizabeth is specific: 'Divine *Elisa*' (l. 579) is the modern successor to the ancient 'Princes and high Priests', combining the rôles of patron and 'Poëtresse'. Polyhymnia offers a humanist idealization of an Elizabeth[70] whose support of poetry symbolizes her political prerogative. As the 'myrrour of her Makers majestie', she reflects divine authority in her person, and as 'a peereles Poëtresse' artistically imitates her divine maker.[71] Her representa-

---

70 Compare Oram's comment in *YESP*, p. 266: 'This is ... a picture of Elizabeth as her poets and learned men would have liked her to be, not as she was, and it attempts by mirroring her ideal self to persuade her to live up to it'.

71 Compare Sidney's conception of the 'poet-maker', and his traditional analogy of 'the heavenly Maker' and the poet as maker. In Sidney, *Miscellaneous Prose*, pp. 77–79.

tion of the divine 'majestie' is implicitly made possible by her own poetic skill. Polyhymnia intimates that Elizabeth's patronage provides a stable environment for poetry. In this guise, the Queen recalls Du Bellay's image of the French royal family leading the assault against Ignorance in *La Musagnoeomachie*: her 'royall P'laces / Be fild with praises of divinest wits' (ll. 580–81) as she makes a space for poetry at the heart of her kingdom. Like *The Ruines of Time*, this panegyric restates the reciprocal duties of poet and patron.

Even so, Spenser goes on to suggest that this ideal may be no more able to resist the crisis than Urania's:

> Some few beside, this sacred skill esteme,
> Admirers of her glorious excellence,
> Which being lightned with her beawties beme,
> Are thereby fild with happie influence:
> And lifted up above the worldes gaze,
> To sing with Angels her immortal praize.
>
> But all the rest as borne of salvage brood,
> And having beene with Acorns alwaies fed;
> Can no whit savour this celestiall food,
> But with base thoughts are into blindnesse led,
> And kept from looking on the lightsome day ... (ll. 583–93)

This conclusion paradoxically reveals the limitations of Elizabeth's 'happie influence'. In lines 583–88, she is presented as a source of intellectual enlightenment. The select 'few' who 'esteme' poetry and admire Elizabeth are 'lightened with her beawties beme' and 'lifted up above the worldes gaze'. The enlightening Queen is the antithesis of Ignorance, who earlier 'defaced' the Muses' 'fayre light' (ll. 265–66).[72] The panegyric implies that Elizabeth's patronage of 'divinest wits' (l. 581) will facilitate a revival of poetry: these poets 'her eternize with their heavenlie writs'. For Polyhymnia, the poetic élite find their ideal patron in Elizabeth.

---

72 Compare Oram's note in *YESP*, p. 290: 'Elizabeth is compared with the moon whose astral "influence" affects the characters and the lives of human beings'.

Yet lines 589–93 problematize the notion that Elizabeth could revive poetry. Her 'happie influence' is restricted to 'Some few'; the majority prefer 'Acorns' to 'this celestiall food'. Though it may be that, as Snare argues,[73] Spenser intends poetry to be restricted to a social and political élite, Polyhymnia implicitly presents the disparity between the 'few' who 'esteme' poetry and 'all the rest' who do not as a reason for complaint. When Terpsichore laments that the Muses' 'royall thrones ... lately stood / In th'hearts of men to rule them carefully' (ll. 313–14), she does not specify a class of 'men' because she means that poetry once ruled the entire human community. Polyhymnia's vision of the 'few' who love both poetry and Elizabeth is pregnant with a sense of a diminished present. Since the transcendence of Elizabeth's poet-admirers mirrors Urania's transcendence, it implies that the poetry of praise, like the poetry of contemplation, can only be understood or accepted 'above the worldes gaze' – above any human audience. Polyhymnia's final turn back towards despair is then inevitable. Though Elizabeth ideally represents one route out of the Muses' dead end, the prevailing 'blindnesse' of men will mean that it is not taken.

Both Urania and Polyhymnia offer partial solutions to the Muses' despair. The tension between these incomplete solutions reveals Spenser's central intellectual difficulty in trying to forge a new poetry of his own. A purely Christian poetry will eventually concentrate solely on the 'contemplation of things heavenlie wrought'. It will not be of much use in reconstructing the value of poetry 'on earth', because the mystic goal is its primary objective. Though Urania's transcendence exerts a powerful attraction for Spenser, in the context of *The Teares*, she cannot redeem the human community from the 'hell and darknes' of Ignorance. Similarly, the humanist poetics of Polyhymnia displays a strong sense of poetry's ongoing cultural and

---

73 Compare Fletcher's note on lines 565–70 in *Var.* VIII, p. 333. It is unquestionable that Muses like Polyhymnia and Thalia attack the presumption of 'the base vulgar': they should know their place, which is within the audience of traditional poetry. Spenser never suggests that it is essentially inappropriate for non-nobles to have access to poetry; rather texts like *The Teares* and *Mother Hubberds Tale* reveal an anxiety about how the 'multitude' will use and respond to poetry.

political value. Yet its idealized image of Elizabeth is not unequivocal. Though she may provide the basis for an innovative poetry of praise elsewhere in Spenser's oeuvre, here the 'eternized' patron and her 'Admirers' mirror only each other. The juxtaposition of Urania and Polyhymnia highlights the fact that Christian and humanist poetics are themselves diminished poetic alternatives, which by offering impossible hope, can only confirm the Muses' despair. For Spenser as a practising poet, neither of these traditional poetics is able to provide decisive support for the new poetry he wants to create.

It is for this reason that the poem's final stanza pessimistically anticipates the death of poetry. While the quatrain recapitulates the previous link-stanzas, the couplet emphatically and abruptly closes the Muses' procession:

> Eftsoones such store of teares shee forth did powre,
> As if shee all to water would haue gone;
> And all her sisters seeing her sad stowre,
> Did weep and waile and made exceeding mone,
> And all their learned instruments did breake:
> The rest vntold no liuing tongue can speake. (ll. 595–600)[74]

In breaking 'their learned instruments', the Muses parallel the gestures of Colin Clout in the 'Januarye' eclogue, and of Verlame at the beginning of *The Ruines of Time*.[75] It is an action which sums up the Muses' despair. Each complaint has shown that either through the encroachment of Ignorance or the idleness of the nobility, the Muses' poetry no longer exerts its rightful influence over its human audience. After their 'exceeding mone' there is nothing left for them to do but enact their frustration. By breaking their instruments, the Muses renounce their intellectual vocation. When the love-sick Colin Clout breaks his pipe because it 'pleasest not, where most I would',[76] he announces that his poetry cannot persuade Rosalind to love him; similarly, the Muses' poetry does not attract the 'salvage brood' (l. 589). To break one's 'learned instruments' is, for Spenser, to abandon

74 This stanza has been quoted from *Var.* VIII, p. 79.
75 See p. 106 above.
76 'Januarye', l. 68.

one's artistic calling. But what in Colin is merely frustrated pique, in the Muses is far more serious: it signals their abandonment both of poetry and the 'mortall mindes' who disdain it. It is not yet clear whether this move is temporary (as in the Muses' return to Olympus in Ronsard's *Ode*) or permanent.

Some clarification of this problem is afforded by the fascinating final line of *The Teares*. Most editions, with the exception of the *Variorum*, print the line as it appears in the 1591 Quarto, 'The rest vntold no louing tongue can speake'.[77] The 1611 Folio changes 'louing' to 'liuing'; subsequent editors have tended to prefer the Quarto reading on the general principle that it is the more authoritative text.[78] But in the words of the *Variorum* textual commentary, '"louing" makes un-Spenserian nonsense'.[79] This chapter has argued that *The Teares* is concerned with the survival and relevance of poetic traditions: in this light, 'liuing' makes much better sense, despite its late appearance in the Folio. The line powerfully suggests that the Muses have permanently abandoned the present age. No 'liuing tongue can speake' any further because the Muses have broken their 'learned instruments' so depriving humanity of the means of poetic expression. Poetry's 'liuing tongue' is silenced with the despairing closure of the Muses' complaints.[80]

The corrected final line indicates the character and concerns of *The Teares* as a whole. The text voices the Muses' despairing laments in the face of an apparently insoluble crisis. The final line, with its intimation of an unspoken or unspeakable enigma, reawakens Melpomene's baffled questions and the whole issue of the Muses' despair: why has poetry been rejected?; and from this: what does the Muses' despair mean within *Complaints*?

---

77 See *Var.* VIII, pp. 691–92, 712–13, for full textual discussion of *The Teares*.

78 See for example Renwick, *Complaints*, pp. 268–69.

79 *Var.* VIII, p. 713. The only defence that I can see for 'louing' is that it fits the poem's fictional scenario that the Muses' complaints are recorded by a sympathetic narrator: because he 'loves the Muses', he leaves 'The rest' of their predicament 'vntold'.

80 Maclean in *The Spenser Encyclopedia*, pp. 182–83, plausibly sees the Folio last line as 'a first expression of the poet's longing for' the 'Saboaths sight' at the close of *The Mutabilitie Cantos*.

The Muses answer Melpomene by repeatedly showing that the present age has repudiated traditional poetry. To borrow Terpsichore's metaphor, in the kingdom where Ignorance reigns, the poetry of the usurped Muses is 'ignorable'. More specifically, Spenser claims that the poetry of the Muses has lost its natural constituency in the nobility, and is ignored by the 'ugly Barbarisme' of 'the base vulgar'. The Muses lament the social and literary dilemma of a poet like Spenser who wants to write within the authority of tradition, but is aware that if he does so his poetry will fail to find a receptive and generous audience.

The Teares also shows that the decline of traditional poetry is partly a consequence of the incompatibilities between the Muses' different 'aesthetics'. Humanist and Christian Muses are equally unable to reassert their cultural pre-eminence: in the final analysis, both Urania and Polyhymnia retreat from the crisis. So while the Muses' laments may be said to continue the conflict in *The Ruines of Time* between humanist and Christian priorities, as a whole *The Teares* defuses this rivalry by revealing the inadequacy of both poetics. Since neither Urania nor Polyhymnia can dispel the crisis, neither a Christian nor a humanist poetics will alone be able to support Spenser's new poetry.

Yet *The Teares* is more than a register of failure. The 'conceit' of the Muses' despair enables Spenser to showcase his transformation of the complaint mode into a vehicle for the discussion of poetics. The laments of Melpomene and Terpsichore interpret the crisis by restoring the conventional moralistic trope of the tragic fall. In Spenser's innovative complaint, the survival of traditional poetry is compared to the survival of a rightful monarch. As with the other three of Spenser's major *Complaints*, his new poetry is brought into being through the critical reuse of traditional strategies – indeed, in this case, through the articulation of poetic failure itself. The paradox of *The Teares* is that it affirms the liveliness of poetry's 'tongue' through the utterance of its decline.

The Teares displays the tensions within poetry which have largely been effaced in the translations and, to an extent, in *The Ruines of Time*. Spenser now faces up to the possibility that 'goodly Poësie' may not civilize 'ugly Barbarisme': *The Teares* states the defeat of poetry in such a way as to make a new poetry possible. In so doing, it bridges the divide between *The Ruines of Time* and *Mother Hubberds Tale*.

While continuing the debate between humanism and Christianity, it anticipates the *Tale*'s radical problematizing of the notion of poetry as moral art. Through the fable of the Muses' despair, Spenser externalizes the difficulties which poetic tradition poses for him, and anticipates his transformation of that tradition in the *Tale* and *Muiopotmos*.

CHAPTER FIVE
Cracking the Nut?
Mother Hubberds Tale's Attack
on Traditional Notions of Poetic Value

As for Mother Hubberts tale,
Cracke the nut, and take the shale ...
Nicholas Breton, from 'An Epitaph upon Poet Spenser' (1600)[1]

Breton's couplet ambiguously aligns *Mother Hubberds Tale* in the mainstream of Western poetics by evoking what can be called the 'poem as nut' aesthetic. This tradition, which can be traced to Augustine, finds its classic expression in Fulgentius's commentary on *The Thebaid*.[2] Fulgentius states that 'poetic songs are seen to be comparable with nuts':[3] poetic fiction is like a nut, possessing an outer casing (the literal sense) and an inner 'kernel' (the mystical or allegorical sense). The reader must 'Cracke the nut' to obtain a 'kernel' of 'doctrine wyse'[4] contained *within* the fiction. While this formula had been used as a defence against the accusation that poetic fiction is mendacious and morally dubious,[5] by the sixteenth century it had become specifically associated with beast fable. Chaucer uses it in *The Nun's Priest's Tale* (ll. 3438–46); Henryson's *Fables* are prefaced with

1 Nicholas Breton, *Melancholike Humours*, ed. G. B. Harrison (London: Scholartis, 1929), p. 45. See also Harold Stein, *Studies in Spenser's Complaints* (New York: Oxford University Press, 1934), pp. 83–84.

2 For Fulgentius and Augustine, see Robert P. Miller (ed.), *Chaucer: Sources and Backgrounds* (New York: Oxford University Press, 1977), pp. 53–57.

3 *Ibid.*, p. 57.

4 Henryson, 'Prologue' to *The Fables*. In *The Poems*, ed. Denton Fox (Oxford: Clarendon, 1981; revised edn 1987), pp. 3–5.

5 See Miller, *Chaucer* pp. 53–57, see also Anthea Hume *Edmund Spenser: Protestant Poet* (Cambridge: Cambridge University Press, 1984), pp. 162–66, for a discussion of the poetics of 'secret wisdom', or hermeticism; and pp. 19–22 above.

a comprehensive restatement of the commonplace.[6] Breton's comment identifies the *Tale* as a beast fable that should be interpreted allegorically.

But what does Breton understand the poem's 'shale', or allegorical meaning, to be? The 'Epitaph' offers no further hints; the couplet shares the obscurity which characterizes the other contemporaneous allusions to the *Tale*'s suppression.[7] Like even the best reconstructions of the poem's history, Breton's comment is ambiguous and uncertain. His vocabulary does not help: 'shale' meaning kernel is awkward, and perhaps the result of straining for rhyme.[8] But the difficulty of the word alerts the reader to another facet of contemporary allusions – that the *Tale* was considered to be 'obscure even in the sixteenth cen-

---

6 See Henryson, 'Prologue' and p. 187.

7 The *Tale* was apparently 'called in' in the early 1590s, which implies that all unsold copies were collected and burnt. The poem's exclusion from the 1611 Folio edition of Spenser's works is widely interpreted as evidence that it was read as an attack on Burghley, and was consequently suppressed to avoid offending his son, Robert Cecil. For full details and quotation of the allusions, see Harold Stein, *Studies in Spenser's Complaints* pp. 79–86; Var. VIII, pp. 580–85, 685–86. Despite the obscurity of many of these allusions, it is clear that the poem enjoyed some notoriety. Josephine Waters Bennett's discovery of an account book from 1596 reveals that by this time the *Tale* was being sold separately from the rest of *Complaints* at a high price. From this evidence, she argues that 'the suppression was still in force but not effective in 1596'; see Josephine Waters Bennett 'A Bibliographical Note on *Mother Hubberds Tale*', *ELM*, 4 (1937), pp. 60–61.

8 *OED* gives a range of definitions for 'shale', most of which are the opposite of what Breton seems to mean, as in shale 2, 'A shell or outer covering of a nut, which encloses the kernel; also the pod of beans etc.'. Ironically, the dictionary also cites Lydgate's use of the word in formulating the 'poem as nut' aesthetic: 'The husk is falle, brokyn is the shale, / The noote kernel, Closyd in scripturys, … / Al openly shewith his sweetnesse'. From 'Letabundus', ll. 227–30, in *The Minor Poems*, ed. H. N. MacCracken (*EETS* Extra Series CVII. London: Oxford University Press, 1911), pp. 56–57. However, it would be perverse to read Breton's lines as meaning, 'As for *Mother Hubberds Tale*, break open the nut, discard the kernel and take away with you the cracked nut'. Though such a gloss is an intriguing possibility in the light of the *Tale*'s satirical import, this would necessitate a reading of Breton's poem which would make it a good deal more subtle and critically devious than this reader found it to be.

tury'.[9] For Spenser's contemporaries, a poem which attacked Burghley was necessarily dangerous; one way of discussing such a text is to pretend, like Nashe, to find it obscure. Such a procedure raises the interest of the reading public in a 'dangerous' text, while explicitly establishing the writer's innocence.[10] Yet aside from this satirical obscurity, the *Tale* remains complex and challenging. Breton's couplet raises the question of how – if at all – this 'nut' should be 'cracked'. In this chapter, hermeneutic nut cracking inevitably raises the larger issue of how Spenser incorporates *Complaints'* overarching concern with poetry into this satirical fable.

The previous chapter argues that *The Teares of the Muses* is a watershed in *Complaints'* 'poetics in practice'. Poetry, embodied by the conflicting Muses has been seen to be decisively ambiguous – riven with conceptual dissonances. This marks a shift from the translations discussed in the first part of the book, where the texts combine the humanist project of a vernacular, neo-classicizing poetry with more specifically English ideological and theological agendas. This process of amalgamating competing views of poetry finds its clearest expression in *The Ruines of Time*. In *The Teares*, poetry is presented as an ambiguous edifice which may not civilize an indifferent society. As the next of the major *Complaints* in my arrangement,[11] the fable narrative of *Mother Hubberds Tale* draws out the implications of this insight, questioning traditional notions of poetic meaning both in its content and its form. This chapter will present the *Tale* as a practical

9 Stein, *Studies in Spenser's Complaints*, pp. 82–84.

10 See *Var.* VIII, pp. 580–81, for the exchange between Harvey and Nashe. Compare Middleton's politic self-advertisement in *Father Hubberds Tale* (1604): 'Why I call these *Father Hubburd's Tales*, is not to have them called in again, as the Tale of *Mother Hubburd* ... for I entreat here neither of ragged bears, or apes, no, nor the lamentable downfall of the old wife's platters, – I deal with no such metal.' In *Var.* VIII pp. 580–81.

11 See pp. 31–34 above for discussion of my re-ordering the 1591 *Complaints* volume.

assay in a problematizing aesthetic, partly anticipated by the debates
of *The Teares* and *The Ruines of Time*.[12]

The Teares shows both that poetry is internally various and disso-
nant, and that seduced by the influence of 'ugly Barbarisme',
mankind has abandoned poetry. The implication of these revelations
is that poetry will not be able to perform the civilizing functions
ascribed to it by humanists like Sidney.[13] In its presentation of the Fox
and the Ape as amoral poets, the *Tale* heightens the sense of moral
crisis by suggesting that poetic skill is essentially ambiguous. This
position dissents from the claims of Ciceronian and humanist
rhetoric that a good speaker or poet must be a good man. If poets are
morally ambiguous, poems cannot teach in the straightforward way
envisaged by traditional didactic theories. The ambiguity of poetry in
The Teares (which arose both from the conflict between competing
'aesthetics' and the challenge to the prestige of traditional poetry)
becomes in the *Tale* a more fundamental uncertainty about poetic
facility. Are those endowed with poetic talent necessarily 'good'? –
and from this, is poetry necessarily educative? These questions
underpin the satirical narrative.

Mirroring this thematic argument, the chapter will show that the
form of the beast fable, and its reliance on the 'poem as nut' aesthetic,
is also problematized in the *Tale*. Where Aesopic beast fable employs
a didactic *moralitas* to expound the 'pretty allegories' of 'the formal
tales of beasts',[14] the *Tale* eschews any clear-cut moralization.

---

12 My reading of the *Tale* is analogous to the interpretations of Jonathan Crewe,
Hidden Designs: The Critical Profession and Renaissance Literature (New York and
London: Methuen, 1986), pp. 55–65, and Richard Rambuss, *Spenser's Secret Career*
(Cambridge: Cambridge University Press, 1993), pp. 81–92. Crewe suggests that
the poem explores the ambivalences of '"sympathetic' representation' – like me,
Crewe draws out the analogies between the Fox and the Ape's complaints and those
of unrewarded Elizabethan poets like Spenser; similarly, Rambuss argues that the
Tale is a deliberate violation of Spenser's elaborately constructed self-presentation as
a suitable repository of secrets through its satirical exposé of social corruption
through the poetic medium of complaint.

13 See pp. 16–23 above.

14 Sir Philip Sidney, *Miscellaneous Prose of Sir Philip Sidney*, ed. Katherine Dun-
can-Jones and Jan Van Dorsten (Oxford: Clarendon, 1973), p. 87.

Spenser's manipulation of the beast fable genre radically questions poetry's claims to be an educative art form. Against the prevailing intellectual orthodoxy (distilled in Sidney's *Defence*), the *Tale*'s form opens the prospect that if poetry teaches, it does not do so mechanistically. This chapter will present the text's interpenetration of form and content as symptomatic of its self-conscious questioning of the truisms of contemporary poetics.

I argue that the *Tale*'s deflection of the normative operation of medieval allegory constitutes a novel conception of poetry. This new poetry evokes the complexity of lived experience as opposed to the abstraction of moral goals. Like the narrator, the reader must come to terms with a complex world in which the Fox and the Ape are at liberty to defraud whoever they can. As Spenser questions his intellectual patrimony, he begins to evolve in practice a new mimetic poetry. This chapter and the next elucidate the implications of this evolution.

The form of *Mother Hubberds Tale*

In the wake of Greenlaw's imaginative reconstruction of the poem's compositional history and its relation to external events, the *Tale*'s textual condition has long been at the centre of critical debate. Greenlaw relates Spenser's admission (in the dedication to Lady Compton and Mounteagle) that the poem was 'long sithens composed in the raw conceipt of my youth' with its episodic nature and reads the text as an historical allegory of Protestant opposition to the Alençon marriage in 1579. Though Greenlaw's reading of the poem and Elizabethan history has been convincingly challenged,[15] his basic assumption that the *Tale* was 'almost certainly revised

---

15 Greenlaw's study was first published as 'Spenser and the Earl of Leicester', *PMLA*, 25 (1910), pp. 535–61; then reprinted as Chapter III of *Studies in Spenser's Historical Allegory* (Baltimore: Johns Hopkins University Press, 1932; rpt. London: Frank Cass, 1967), pp. 104–32. Stein, *Studies in Spenser's Complaints*, pp. 78–100, provides a sceptical critique of Greenlaw's ideas.

before publication'[16] has remained influential. Yet the dedication is the only external evidence that the poem is early work. As Bjorvand and Schell observe in an analogous context, such self-depreciation-cum-retraction has a conventional cast to it.[17] Re-read sceptically, the dedication seems more interested in offering a self-consciously modest critical account of the *Tale* than in revealing its manuscript history:

> ... these my idle labours; which having long sithens composed in the raw conceipt of my youth, I lately amongst other papers lighted upon, and was by others, which liked the same, mooved to set them foorth. Simple is the device, and the composition meane, yet carrieth some delight, even the rather because of the simplicitie and meannesse thus personated.

By characterizing the poem as juvenilia, Spenser links 'the raw conceipt' of his youth with the 'simplicitie and meannesse' of 'the device'. He presents a wholly conventional image of the headstrong young writer experimenting in a 'simple' comic mode. Critical naïvety is salvaged by the 'delight' of the poem's low comedy of 'simplicitie and meannesse thus personated'. Spenser's remarks simultaneously prepare the reader for a poem which lacks elevated critical aspirations, while promising the 'delight' of a crude 'device' which catches an entertainingly 'low' subject.

From this perspective, the 'biographical-literary myth'[18] acts as a cover for Spenser. By stating at the point of publication that the *Tale* is an old poem, he hopes to reduce its topicality and satiric potential; as a crude sample of his juvenilia, Spenser presents it as a curio which anonymous 'others' asked him to publish on literary grounds alone. Yet the poem is a sophisticated and mature performance in a low style. Its technical and intellectual sophistication makes a late dating for the *Tale* more plausible than Spenser's own account. Though we

16 Oram in *YESP*, p. 327.

17 See Bjorvand and Schell's discussion of the dedication to *Fowre Hymnes* (specifically its retraction of the eroticism of the first two *Hymnes*) in *YESP*, pp. 683–84.

18 *Ibid.*

can't be sure whether the poem was revised prior to publication, there are strong internal grounds for dating it in the late 1580s.

The point at issue is not whether Spenser was telling Lady Compton and Mounteagle the truth.[19] Rather, this approach demonstrates that the dedication is itself ambiguous: it does not supply clear evidence that the *Tale* is an early text. It rather seems to be a disingenuous cover for a poem Spenser knew was dangerous. Images of the text's supposedly chequered composition have distracted attention from its careful design, fostering the idea that it is as 'simple' – or indeed 'primitivistic'[20] – as the dedication claims.

While the *Tale* is a different sort of narrative from *Muiopotmos* or *Virgils Gnat*, it is no less subtly constructed. Its episodic form makes the poem less symmetrical than the other narrative *Complaints*. In *Muiopotmos* for example, Spenser builds a complex frame of balancing images because of the brevity of the poem's central dramatic action: the symmetrical structure provides a rhetorical framework through which the reader is challenged to interpret the justice of Clarion's fate. By contrast, the *Tale*'s frame identifies the narrative as 'a strange adventure' (l. 37) – first orally recited to the poem's ailing narrator as a 'meanes of gladsome solace' (l. 20) by the 'good old woman … Hight Mother *Hubberd*' (ll. 33–34). This impromptu tale is then not the same kind of narration as more witty and literate 'tales' like *Virgils Gnat* and *Muiopotmos*.[21] The narrator explicitly contrasts his writing of Mother Hubberd's tale with more elevated poetry: 'No Muses aide me needes heretoo to call; / Base

19 Or indeed whether the dedication of the *Fowre Hymnes* to the Countesses of Cumberland and Warwick represents an accurate picture of the composition of these poems.

20 S. K. Heninger, Jr, *Sidney and Spenser: The Poet as Maker* (University Park and London: Pennsylvania State University Press, 1989), p. 359.

21 *Ibid.* Heninger distinguishes between the *Tale* and texts like *Muiopotmos* and *The Shepheardes Calender* from the perspective that Spenser was a 'Uranian' poet whose texts are formally structured according to a neo-Platonic, numerological poetics. The *Tale* is eccentric because of its avoidance of any structure on the basis of 'significant numbers'. However, the claim that the rest of Spenser's work relies on such an aesthetic can reduce complex texts into tabular arrangements of line references. Numerology is suggestive, but cannot be the sole hermeneutic key for the interpretation of Spenser's poetics.

is the style, and matter meane withall' (ll. 43–44). This couplet replaces a formal invocation. As with the dedication, there is no compelling reason to take this authorial comment at face value.

Despite its stylistic 'baseness', the *Tale*'s four episodes are linked by the Fox and Ape's progressive climb through the class structure. In between the two extremes at either end of the narrative, the *Tale* presents the Fox and the Ape as 'self-fashioning' individualists who exploit the fragilities of each social estate. They progress from impersonating shepherds (ll. 25–339), then clerics (ll. 340–574), then courtiers (ll. 576–942), before their climactic masquerade as the Lion King and his chief minister (ll. 943–1384). Despite the wide range of narrative styles in the text (ranging from dramatic debate, discursive summary, expostulation to epic parody), the poem is unified by the simplicity of its narrative premises. Firstly, the rogues[22] are thoroughly self-interested: impersonation is their means to the end of gaining material advantage and power. Secondly, the society in which they operate reacts passively to their self-promotive efforts. Though the Fox and the Ape must be eventually 'smoked'[23] by each successive milieu for the narrative to progress, each unmasking has the unlikely corollary of allowing them to pose successfully in a higher social class. The text owes a clear structural debt to estate satire. But more than this, the episodes are connected by the rogues' growing ability to 'impersonate'[24] at higher levels in society: their 'adventure' sees the

22 I refer to the Fox and the Ape as 'rogues' or 'the protagonists' to indicate their essential ambiguity. A term like 'villains' or 'anti-heroes' would typecast them too readily and blur the connection between the *Tale* and other 1590s rogue narratives.

23 As Parolles 'was first smoked by the old Lord Lafew' in *All's Well That Ends Well* III.vi.82. The image is doubly appropriate since C. T. A. Onions, *A Shakespeare Glossary*, revised ed. by R. D. Eagleson (Oxford: Clarendon, 1986), p. 255, records its origin in the practice of unearthing a fox by fire.

24 *Mother Hubberds Tale*'s subtitle, *Prosopopoia*, means of course 'personification'. Kent Van den Berg extends the term further by making use of Puttenham's gloss of it as 'the counterfeit in personation'. He argues that the designation covers the fictional idea of animals 'standing for' people as well as the practice of the rogues and ultimately Mercury. See 'The Counterfeit in Personation: Spenser's *Prosopopoia*', in *The Author in his Work: Essays on a Problem in Criticism*, ed. Louis Martz and Aubrey Williams (New Haven: Yale University Press, 1978).

growth of their plausibility and audacity. The narrative is held together through its consistent focus on individualism and social mobility, sharply reflecting anxieties about the fluidity of social class in England. The self-interested individual with no stable social position is intimately connected with the problem of poetry.[25]

Summarizing the *Tale* raises the question of its genre, initially in terms of anthropomorphism and estate satire. In comparison with *The Ruines of Time* and *Muiopotmos*, the *Tale* seems to require little generic explanation. As Breton's comment illustrates, the poem has always been seen as a beast fable. Spenser's development of the traditional genre – layering it with contrasting literary modes – makes the *Tale* a complex concoction similar to the other *Complaints*. The *Tale* exploits, and eventually amends, the beast fable's normative expectations.

So what is the traditional form of the beast fable? By the sixteenth century, the two major forms of European fable literature had flowed together.[26] These were firstly the Aesopic fables originating from classical Greece; and secondly the twelfth-century French epic cycle, *Le Roman de Renart*. Aesopic fables combine brief, frequently anthropomorphic, narratives with a directive *moralitas*. These texts aim to impart practical wisdom; in basic form Aesopic fable has remained popular as children's literature.[27] The stories from the *Renart* cycle

25 A further indication of the poem's structural integrity is provided by Helen Cooper, *Pastoral: Mediaeval into Renaissance* (Totowa, NJ: Rowman and Littlefield, 1977), p. 161, who notes that 'the standard of judgement throughout the poem, is the welfare of sheep', arguing for the poem's status as a pastoral because the rôles adopted by the Fox and the Ape 'are all aspects of the single pastoral metaphor'. Such a reading may have problems combining the rôle of courtier with this pastoral metaphor, though the figure of 'The Shepheard of the Ocean' in *Colin Clouts Come Home Againe* is both a shepherd and a courtier. Cooper's comments provide a persuasive image of the *Tale* unified by a central metaphor, and help us to see the poem as a unified narration.

26 Compare William Caxton, *The History of Reynard the Fox*, ed. N. F. Blake (*EETS*, original series, no. 263. London, New York and Toronto: Oxford University Press, 1970), pp. xi–xii. Blake sees Reynardian fable as essentially a development on the Aesopic tradition. The point can be made, however, that the *Roman* itself constituted a fresh kind of anthropomorphic fiction, in which satirical and comic priorities temporarily supplanted the didactic aesthetic.

27 On classical Aesopic fable, see S. A. Handford (trans.), *Fables of Aesop* (Harmondsworth: Penguin, 1954), pp. xiii–xx.

were initially less didactic and more satirical.[28] But as the stories from the original cycle passed into other European cultures, they became assimilated into the moralistic aesthetic of traditional fable.

Henryson's *Fables* are a useful example of this process. Henryson draws on both Aesopic and Reynardian sources, yet neither the 'Prologue' nor the texts themselves advertise their divergent origins.[29] All fables derive from the poet's mythical 'maister Esope'.[30] And for Henryson, they are all appropriate vehicles for moral instruction. As the 'Prologue' outlines, the 'feinʒeit fabils of ald poetre' are valuable because they can 'repreif' their audience of their 'misleuing ... be figure of ane vther thing'. It becomes the task of the adept, nut-cracking audience to extract 'ane morall sweit sentence / Oute of the subtell dyte of poetry'.[31] Beast fable here exists to serve up the instructive *moralitas* with which Henryson closes his tales.

Though the original *Roman* is a kind of beast fable in which satirical entertainment displaces conventional moralism,[32] Spenser and his contemporaries would probably only have had access to the Reynard cycle through later texts like Henryson's which have already grafted Aesopic moralism on to the original stories.[33] The beast fable literature available to Spenser was strongly didactic.

28 On the Reynard tradition, see Patricia Terry (trans.), *Renard the Fox* (Berkeley, Los Angeles and Oxford: University of California Press, rpt. 1992), pp. 3–23; and Blake in Caxton, *The History of Reynard the Fox*, pp. xi–xxi.

29 Fox traces at least half the collection to 'the very common collection of Aesopic fables, in rhetorical Latin elegiacs, ascribed to Gualterus Anglicus'. The remaining fables go 'back directly or indirectly to the *Roman de Renart*'. In Henryson, *The Poems*, pp. 187, 200.

30 *Ibid.*, p. 56.

31 *Ibid.*, pp. 3–5. Fox believes that Henryson's argument that 'Esope ... Be figure wrait his buke, for he nocht wald / Tak the disdane off hie nor low estate' means that 'the external finery of the work will please the unlearned, and the hidden truths the learned' (p. 189). Though Henryson's text is not unambiguous, this would be a logical and conventional development of the 'poem as nut' motif.

32 See Terry, *Renard the Fox*, p. 3.

33 Compare Caxton's preamble to his text, in which he stresses its utility: 'for them that vnderstandeth it / it shall be ryght Ioyous playsant and proffitable'. In Caxton, *The History of Reynard the Fox*, p. 6.

The crucial point about Henrysonian fable – and most medieval fables beyond the *Roman* – is that the morally authenticating *moralitas* is not just a didactic tool, but ultimately an agent of control which limits poetic performance. One of Henryson's finest fables, 'The Sheep and the Dog', is ostensibly an attack on legal corruption.[34] Unusually, the *moralitas* breaks the conventional mould by adding the victimized sheep's complaint against 'this cursit consistorie'[35] to its more predictable social allegory of the fable's chief characters. But in the final stanza, the sheep – now voicing Henryson's concluding moral comment – glosses injustice as God's punishment to mortals 'for our grit offence' of original sin. He sends 'troubill and plagis soir' to force sinful humanity to amendment. In such a world, 'We pure pepill as now may do no moir / Bot pray to the' – the sheep is left with only the pious hope of 'gude rest' in heaven.[36] This is a conventional point of closure. By recalling 'our grit offence' and looking forwards to the hope of salvation, the sheep's complaint is framed by a quietism that dilutes the earlier denunciation of legal abuses. Henryson implicitly contrasts divine equity with the fallen justice of humanity; this pious ending makes the allegory less politically incisive and returns the reader's attention to the start of the *moralitas*, where 'tirrane men' are warned of the punishments waiting for them after death.[37] Such admonition in turn fits in with the *Fables'* overall aim of reproving the reader 'of thi misleuing'. Specific abuses of power highlighted in 'The Sheep and the Dog' are drawn back into the overarching context of traditional piety. The fable is determined by what Henryson deems his characters 'might signify';[38] what Henryson himself can say is limited by the controlling presence of the *moralitas*.

The nearest Spenser comes to Henrysonian fable is in the 'Februarie' and 'Maye' eclogues from *The Shepheardes Calender*, in which Thenot and Piers use stylized fables from the Aesopic tradition to try and enforce their side of a debate. While authorial sympathy with the different speakers rightly remains a contentious issue throughout the

34 See Fox's notes in Henryson. *The Poems*, pp. 207–12.
35 *Ibid.*, pp. 51–54.
36 *Ibid.*, p. 54.
37 *Ibid.*, p. 51.
38 *Ibid.*, p. 52.

Calendar, it is clear that in using fable as a debating tool, Spenser was alive to the possibility of writing a traditional fiction that broke with the medieval conception of allegory. In each case, the fable-teller's *moralitas* is either interrupted for being 'little worth', or ignored by an impervious listener.[39] In these eclogues, the admonitory fable is shown as a supple kind of poetic narration, but its attendant moral is not necessarily either heeded or rehearsed. The *Tale's* ambiguity is partly foreshadowed in these texts.

The *Tale's* form shows that there is no necessary correlation between fable and moralism. Most noticeably, Spenser abandons the device of a separate *moralitas*. Its disappearance means that the poem's satirical elements are not softened, as in 'The Sheep and the Dog', by a normative moral context. Because the *Tale* lacks a Henrysonian *moralitas*, its presentation of social corruption can be taken as a forthright political attack on bad government. This was, after all, the way in which contemporary readers saw the poem's attacks on Burghley.[40]

Alongside Spenser's incorporation of particularized social satire into the *Tale*, his usage of estate satire also deflates that genre's didactic expectations. Though capable of being deployed neutrally,[41] estate satire was predominantly a hortatory mode, as in Gower's 'Prologus'

---

39 'Februarie', l. 240. Hume, *Edmund Spenser*, pp. 15–28, argues that in the case of 'Maye' modern critics' perception of the 'poise' between Piers and Palinode misses the point and that authorial sympathy is firmly with Piers. Her reading suggests that the 'Maye' fable must be read in line with the 'poem as nut' aesthetic; nevertheless, the 'conflictus' form of these eclogues still leaves interpretation 'open'. Cooper, *Pastoral*, p. 157, notes that in the 'Februarie' fable 'allegory is a secondary consideration ... it works first of all poetically, on the first, the narrative, level of meaning, and it acts metaphorically as an illustration of the themes of time, authority, age and winter'. Cooper describes a metaphorical referral rather than a one-to-one allegory; this is a useful benchmark for the *Tale*.

40 Compare the comment of the Catholic writer of *A Declaration of the True Causes of the Great Troubles* (1592) in *Var.* VIII, p. 581: 'yf any will undertake to justfie [Burghley's] actions in his course of government, let him know, that there is sufficient matter of reply reserved for him, which is not extracted out of *Mother Hubberds* tale, of the false fox and his crooked cubbes ...' The last comment seems a clear allusion to the Fox's nepotism in office in lines 1151–58.

41 See Chaucer's *General Prologue* to *The Canterbury Tales*, and Derek Pearsall, *The Life of Geoffrey Chaucer: A Critical Biography* (Oxford: Blackwell, 1992), pp. 249–50.

to *Confessio Amantis*, which sees 'divisioun' as the cause of the general 'confusioun' which afflicts the three estates.[42] Gascoigne's *The Steele Glas* (1576) is a sixteenth-century example – a metrified expostulation to the various classes to recognize their communal responsibilities; Gascoigne informs the aristocracy, 'You were not borne, al onely for your selues: / Your countrie claymes, some part of al your paines'.[43] This 'satire' is a call to the various classes to amend their behaviour: by telling them what they are not doing, or doing wrong, Gascoigne holds up an improving template of social conduct. In contrast, the *Tale* uses estate satire predominantly as a tool for sequencing the narrative. But the Fox and the Ape's 'strange adventure' wittily reverses the usual progression downwards from the aristocracy to the commons. In traditional estate satire, the downward movement seems indicative of the basically reverential assumption that – whatever else is wrong with human society – the hierarchy is fixed. Spenser's adaptation indicates the opposite. The estates have become fluid; the chancing individualist can exploit this new openness to progress upwards through the classes. It is as if Chaucer described the Cook becoming a knight, or even a king.

The satirical elements in the *Tale* pressurize the moralizing traditions of the fable genre. Yet this should not disguise the fact that the text is imbued with moral judgements. These vary from ironic criticism of the Fox and the Ape, to wholesale interventions in which the narrator asserts the values they have muddied. Yet this critical commentary intensifies satire rather than adding moralism. In the description of the Fox as chief minister, Spenser uses a variant on 'The Sheep and the Dog' fable to illustrate the corruption of the Fox's government. This is rounded off with the comment, 'so everie one was used, / That to give largely to the boxe refused' (ll. 1223–24). As in later satire, this assessment combines implicit outrage at bribery with an amused understanding of the mechanics of corrupt gover-

42 'Prologus' to *Confessio Amantis*, ll. 851–52. In John Gower, *The English Works*, 2 vols, ed. G. C. Macaulay (Oxford: Clarendon, 1901), Vol. I, p. 28.

43 George Gascoigne, *The Complete Works*, 2 vols, ed. J. W. Cunliffe (Cambridge: Cambridge University Press, 1907–10), Vol. II, p. 154.

nance. Such criticism is evidently based on ethical values, but the text makes no suggestion about how these abuses could be amended.

The narrator's interventions reflect his anxiety with the story he retells, incidentally raising the question of how the *Tale* uses the complaint mode. It could be argued that the *Tale's* jettisoning of the *moralitas* and its revelation of the ambiguity of poetry and poetic talent, makes it a quasi-carnivalistic fable, aiming to subvert all received ideas and authority. Such a reading is undermined by Spenser's pervasive use of the complaint mode. Complaint articulates the social and literary anxieties which the fable raises for the narrator: the rogues' social ascent makes the existing hierarchy and conventional literary values questionable. In the third episode, the narrator feels constrained to intervene as he becomes aware of the fable's failure to correspond, when 'write[n] in termes' (l. 41), with his memory of it as a recreative fiction. Where traditional fable fleshes out the writer's didactic preconceptions, the *Tale* shows the narrator's disturbed response to the oral tale he rewrites. Its inversion of normative values provokes complaint, rather than celebration.

Through the motif of malcontent, as exhibited by the rogues, the Priest, the Mule, and indeed the narrator's own famous complaint of the 'pitifull' condition of the 'Suter' to Court (ll. 891–916), Spenser uses complaint to explore wider social tensions.[44] Though the Fox and the Ape's impostures allow them to infiltrate 'the system', their condition as outcasts remains constant. The malcontented complaint is both a fiction they use to dupe the unwary,[45] and a reflection of a basic tension within society. As social outcasts, the rogues have no 'hope' of the 'due remedie' (l. 57) which they feel they deserve; their complaints point to a sense of the imperfection of existing social structures. Spenser's deployment of complaint throughout the *Tale* means that it cannot simply be a rejection of all received ideas: the narrator and his characters complain because they are profoundly anxious about the world they inhabit and its unstable values.

44 See below, pp. 185–93.
45 See lines 227–96, and pp. 187–89 below.

What are the implications of the *Tale*'s generic form? As the original *Roman de Renart* shows, a fable without explicit moralization was a possibility which had been exploited by earlier satirists. But the *Tale* goes beyond abandonment of the *moralitas*. Its combination of fable with social satire and the self-conscious complaints of its literate narrator make its form into a miniature of Spenser's poetic dilemma. A conventional reading of the *Tale* would ally its appropriation of traditional forms with Spenser's procedure in texts like *Virgils Gnat* and *Ruines of Rome*, where he handled his intellectual patrimony reverentially, while making it articulate his own concerns. Structured as an inverse estate satire, the *Tale* should express outrage at contemporary social disintegrations and confirm conservative expectations. However, the text's heterodox synthesis of genres shows Spenser's awareness that the didacticism of the past is no longer available: the present is always changing. The complaining narrator dramatizes Spenser's uneasy sense of the drift within traditional forms; his narrative can no longer authenticate the received allegorical poetics.

Finally, as in *The Ruines of Time*, analysis of the *Tale*'s generic form reveals a self-conscious interpenetration of form and content. By refusing to operate within the hermeneutic parameters of the 'poem as nut' aesthetic, the *Tale* exploits the philosophical tensions within traditional poetics. If traditional forms lose their didactic justification, the value of poetry itself becomes ambiguous. This is a major shock, since the Fulgentian tradition reflected a deeply entrenched desire both in readers and writers to guarantee for art some kind of moral basis. We feel better about our enjoyment of something if we believe it is doing us some good.[46] By showing that this proposition is intellectually flawed, the form of the *Tale* supports its problematic content.

---

46 Compare Kenneth John Atchity, 'Spenser's *Mother Hubberds Tale*: Three Themes of Order', *PQ*, 52 (1973), pp. 161–72. Atchity claims that the *Tale* is a literary tonic which 'makes us feel better'.

Amoral Poets in Amoral Texts: Reading
Mother Hubberds Tale

The form of the *Tale* indicates Spenser's continuing ambivalence about poetic meaning in *Complaints*. We must now ask how the fable narrative fits in with the volume's overarching, self-conscious concern with poetry. At first sight, it may seem that the *Tale* has little direct connection with the ostensible concerns of either the translations or the major *Complaints*. Certainly, the *Tale* introduces a new generic note to the volume. Yet as we have seen, the novelty of the fable belies the generic connections between the *Tale* and surrounding texts. I argue that the poem's satirical narrative is based on the notion that the Fox and the Ape are amoral poets. From this premise, I see the poem disclosing Spenser's perception that poetic talent includes no predisposition towards virtue. In this way, the text articulates the *Complaints* volume's growing uncertainty about the art of poetry. *The Teares* shows poetry to be ambiguous; the *Tale* consolidates this discovery by intimating that poets and the texts they produce may be amoral. As such, this comic poem does not just voice theoretical issues in practice, but constitutes a form of fictional representation which is not controlled by conventional didactic imperatives. As in *The Teares* (where a new poetry is made from the failure of traditional poetry) Spenser's recognition of the amorality of poetry opens the prospect of a new, more nuanced, formulation of the relationship between poetry and morality. Where Henryson authenticates his *Fables* through the device of the *moralitas*, Spenser offers an amoralistic fable which is ultimately self-authenticating. Fiction has become independent.

This section will establish from a close reading of the first episode that the Fox and the Ape are characterized as amoral poets. It will then analyse the breakdown in the narrator's confidence in Mother Hubberd's tale through the third episode and the finale. This will reveal that the Fox and the Ape are amoral poets in what has become an amoral text.

'Craftie and unhappie witted': The Fox and the Ape as Amoral Poets

I have described the *Tale* as a picaresque adventure.[47] The rogue became a fashionable literary figure during the 1580s and 1590s. As a text which explores the varied social activities of its morally dubious protagonists, the *Tale's* publication in 1591 is in tune with the growing literary interest in the rogue. But where it differs from texts like *The Unfortunate Traveller* (1594) and *The Jew of Malta* (c.1588–92) is in its identification of its rogues as *poetic* impostors:

> Whilome (said she) before the world was civill,
> The Foxe and th'Ape disliking of their evill
> And hard estate, determined to seeke
> Their fortunes farre abroad, lyeke with his lyeke:
> For both were craftie and unhappie witted;
> Two fellowes might no where be better fitted. (ll. 45–50)

The tale begins with a densely ironic depiction of the rogues' 'estate'. 'Craftie and unhappie witted' highlights their destructive potential, combining an idea of the rogues' intellectual capacity with the forcefully ambiguous 'unhappie', here suggesting their avowed volition towards 'unhap' – to bad or evil fortune.[48] 'Wit' is a key term in the *Tale*.[49] As in line 790, where the Courtier 'enrich[es] the storehouse of his powerfull wit' through political activity, here it primarily conveys an idea of intellectual and poetic performance. To be 'wittie' is to possess an ambiguous control over language; the predominant sense of the rogues being 'unhappie witted' is that they have active verbal intelligence which is at the service of their 'craft'. Sidney

---

47 The term 'picaresque' derives from the Spanish word 'picarón' meaning 'rogue'; as a literary term 'picaresque' then designates sixteenth-century Spanish rogue fiction. See *OED*, 'picaresque'. I use the word for its general applicability to the *Tale*, rather than to suggest a direct influence on Spenser.

48 Compare *Muiopotmos*, ll. 233–34, and see my comment on this oxymoron in Chapter 6 below, pp. 237–39.

49 Elsewhere, the noun designates idle courtiers, and also those 'noble wits' who are misled by the Ape's poetry; see lines 158, 416, 549, 709, 821, 830.

repeatedly uses the term in the *Defence* in drawing an analogy between the human creativity of poetry and God 'the heavenly Maker'. Poetry is 'the highest point of man's wit', which links human makers to their divine originator.[50] By applying the adjective 'witted' to the Fox and the Ape, Spenser indicates their association with poets from the outset. By qualifying 'witted' with 'unhappie', he immediately emphasizes the fundamental ambiguity of the rogues' talents.

This compact phrase is succeeded by the ironic poise of line 50, in which 'fitted' stands as an index of the Fox and the Ape's ambiguity. The reader must supply the question 'fitted to what?', since the next line provides no answer. Oram suggests that 'fitted' is an ironic version of 'found', giving the sense, 'Two better fellows might not be found anywhere'.[51] In the light of the previous line, we could also suggest that 'Two fellowes might no where be better fitted anywhere or nowhere'; their potential is ambiguous. This couplet is not a moral yardstick by which to judge the Fox and the Ape, but an ironic intimation of their abilities: 'Two fellowes might no where be better fitted' *because* they are 'craftie and unhappie witted'.

This early formulation of the protagonists as potential poets is pivotal to the rest of the poem. At the root of the rogues' characterization as poets is a questioning of the humanist contention that poetic ability is supported by moral intelligence – a view which Sidney echoes in his designation of poetry as 'the highest point of man's wit'. This view derives from Quintillian's argument that there is a vital interdependence between eloquence and morality: 'I am not merely saying that the orator ought to be a good man: I say that he will not even become an orator unless he *is* a good man'.[52] Since the precedent of classical rhetoric was powerful during the sixteenth century, Quintillian's views registered on its didactic poetics. Jonson's *Discoveries* state: 'Cicero said much when he said, *dicere recte nemo potest, nisi qui prudentur intelligit*'.[53] For Jonson, the association between virtue and

50 Sidney, *Miscellaneous Prose*, pp. 78–79.

51 *YESP*, p. 337.

52 Quintillian, *Institutio Oratoria*, 12.1. In *Ancient Literary Criticism: The Principal Texts in New Translations*, ed. D. A. Russell and M. Winterbottom (Oxford: Oxford University Press, 1972), p. 417. See also Cicero, *On the Orator*, I.30–32.

eloquence is so powerful that he considers poor speakers to be virtu-
ally mad: 'Neither can his mind be thought to be in tune, whose
words do jar … Negligent speech doth not only discredit the person
of the speaker, but it discrediteth the opinion of his reason and judge-
ment.'[54] It is precisely this fundamentalizing connection between elo-
quence and virtue that the *Tale* challenges. Or, to invert Jonson's
psychological idealism, Spenser suggests that a plausible speaker may
yet be amoral and without orthodox 'reason and judgement'.

The Fox's first speech stresses his ambiguous artistic ability. Using
the conventions of the complaint form that the reader of *Complaints*
is by now accustomed to,[55] the Fox artfully deploys his 'sense of
injured merit' to appeal to the Ape:

> Thus manie yeares I now have spent and worne
> In meane regard, and basest fortunes scorne,
> Dooing my Countrey service as I might,
> No lesse I dare saie than the prowdest wight;
> And still I hoped to be up advaunced,
> For my good parts; but still it hath mischaunced. (ll. 59–64)

The Fox's complaint is a familiar theme effectively presented. He has
done his 'Country service' without reward; he endures the sight of
'losels lifted up on high, where I did looke' (l. 67). Combining dra-
matic complaint and lively proverbial expression (l. 68), the speech
constructs the Fox's self-image as a victim of 'basest fortunes scorne'
who will take action to remedy this 'meane regard'. Since the text has
already given an ironic depiction of the Fox and the Ape's abilities, it
is difficult to see this speech as anything other than a 'craftie' con-
trivance, artfully manipulating the complaint mode.

---

53 *Discoveries*, ll. 2643–45. In Ben Jonson, *The Complete Poems*, ed. George Parfitt
(Harmondsworth: Penguin, 1975), p. 438. Parfitt translates the Cicero as 'No one can
be a good speaker who is not a sound thinker', and notes Jonson's reliance on John
Hoskyn's *Directions for Speech and Style* 'in reading *recte* for Cicero's "bene"', p. 600.

54 *Ibid.*

55 The Fox's complaint that his good deeds have not been rewarded parallels the
sense of outrage displayed by Verlame, the Gnat and the Muses, though unlike these
complainants, the Fox's complaints are fictional.

The succeeding exchange shows the imitative and extemporizing components of the rogues' verbal craft. The Ape's first words ape the Fox's: 'For I likewise have wasted much good time, / Still wayting to preferment up to clime' (ll. 75–76); he reproduces accurately the previous speech's malcontented content and its formal pattern of lament. The rhetorical furnishings of these opening complaints alert the reader to their origins in 'craft' rather than reality;[56] the Fox and the Ape are imposing their perspective onto the social world of the text to give their departure a stronger motivation than mere resentment at an 'evill / And hard estate' (ll. 46–47).

This passage conveys an impression of the rogues as masters of verbal contrivance – as self-interested worldly poets, using the complaint mode to 'colour' their actions positively. These complaints bear more than a passing resemblance to Nashe's grumbles in *Piers Penniless* (1592). This affinity reveals the nexus of associations between poverty, malcontent and poetic facility at work in the *Tale*:

> … all in vain I sat up late and rose early, contended with the cold and conversed with scarcity; for all my labours turned to loss, my vulgar Muse was despised and neglected, my pains not regarded, and I myself, in the prime of my best wit, laid open to poverty … I grew to consider how many base men, that wanted those parts which I had, enjoyed content at will and had wealth at command.[57]

Like the Fox, Piers implies that having worked hard for no reward he must turn his attentions elsewhere to survive. The Fox and the Ape 'determine' to explore the 'wide' world where 'good may gotten be' (l. 101),[58] while Piers composes 'His Supplication to the Devil' in the hopes of better reward from that quarter. This parallel helps to show the subversive potential in the Fox and the Ape's dialogue. By decid-

56 Harry Berger, Jr, 'The Prospect of the Imagination: Spenser and the Limits of Poetry', *SEL*, 1 (1961), pp. 104–05, accepts too readily the authenticity of the rogues' complaints.

57 Thomas Nashe, *The Unfortunate Traveller and Other Works*, ed. J. B. Steane (Harmondsworth: Penguin, 1972), pp. 52–53.

58 This line has been quoted from *Var.* VIII, p. 109, because *YESP* misprints it.

ing to pool their resources since 'two is better than one head' (l. 182) and seek their fortunes abroad, the Fox and the Ape become images of social 'malcontent'[59] whose 'craft' endangers society. This first exchange reveals the rogues as embodiments of social and poetic dysfunction. Like Clio's complaint in *The Teares*, both Spenser and Nashe indicate the potentially disastrous consequences for Elizabethan society if the 'craftie' and learned are not advanced socially, or at least controlled, by the governing class. Effectively unlicensed, they may go to the Devil, or use their skills for their own advantage. When the Fox says 'I meane to turne the next leafe of the booke' (l. 68), he is not just making use of a current proverb,[60] but also giving a threatening statement of intent: he will use his wit in the social arena to advance his own interests. The 'next leafe' of the Fox's 'booke' conveys an idea both of his own self-fashioned 'fortune', and the poetic text which is 'fashioned' from their exploits. Already the Fox notes his authorial rôle in the narrative in anticipation of his final 'uncasing'.

Malcontents are necessarily dangerous. As the Fox puts it, 'Hard is our hap, if we (emongst so manie) / Light not on some that may our state amend' (ll. 170–71). His project will test the social system's capacity to protect itself from 'Machevill's' 'climbing followers'.[61] The Ape's imitation of a discharged soldier illustrates the Fox's power to

59 Harvey's criticism of the *Tale* in *Fovre Letters* (1592) is pertinent here. Harvey asserted that 'Mother Hubbard, in heat of choller, forgetting the pure sanguine of her sweete Feary Queene, wilfully ouer-shott her malcontented selfe'. This fits in with his general argument against Greene and Nashe that 'Inuectiues by fauour haue bene too bolde'. However, as Nashe's reply in *Strange Newes* (1593) makes clear, Harvey makes no distinction between fictional malcontent and the thing itself. Harvey correctly uses the term for the *Tale* and *Piers Penniless*, but fails to appreciate that a writer can use such basic materials without becoming a dangerous subversive. Nashe and Spenser may be subversive writers, but their subversive point is more nuanced than the objections made by Harvey to their published works of 1591–92. See *Var.* VIII, pp. 580–81; Gabriel Harvey, *Fovre Letters*, ed. G. B. Harrison (Elizabethan and Jacobean Quartos. Edinburgh: Edinburgh University Press, 1967), p. 15; and Thomas Nashe, *Strange Newes* (Facsimile edn, London and Menston: The Scholar Press, 1969), sigs. E 2–3, H 3.

60 See *Var.* VIII, p. 351.

61 Christopher Marlowe, 'The Prologue' to *The Jew Of Malta*, ed. T. W. Craik (The New Mermaids. London: Ernest Benn, 1966), p. 9.

shape reality through a fiction. In adopting the garb of a soldier, the Ape enters into the Fox's poetic game. Imposture, or what might be called non-textual imitation of reality, is the rogues' methodology:

> Be you the Souldier, for you likest are
> For manly semblance, and small skill in warre:
> I will but wayte on you, and as occasion
> Falls out, my selfe fit for the same will
>   fashion. (ll. 199–202)

The Fox's words have the impact of an artistic fiat: 'Be you the Souldier' he instructs, and immediately the text describes the Ape 'clad Souldierlike' (ll. 204–18). The Fox creates the illusion by the force of his intelligence; the connections between the Ape's appearance and a soldier's are then 'bodied forth' in the text. The Fox's poetic talent prepares the ground for the theatre of the Ape acting the soldier.

In the poem's first incident, the Fox manifests himself as a self-conscious self-fashioner. As Greenblatt has shown, in sixteenth-century English 'fashion' was a remarkably flexible verb, which denoted meanings as diverse as 'to fashion oneself, change the appearance one presents to the world', and to 'compose a poem'.[62] In the *Tale*, 'to fashion' is decidedly the verb of the individualist. As in line 167, the Fox's use of the word here suggests his view of himself as a plastic he can mould to whatever specifications he wishes. In effect he announces that he is his own text. Similarly, he emphasizes the Ape's 'manly semblance' and his ability to utilize his body as a means to an end. This fashioning will then have an impact on the world analogous to that of a literary text on its readers; it will 'fashion' its percipients – in this case those the Fox and the Ape chance to meet – to accept the rogues' disguise as real.[63]

62 Stephen Greenblatt, *Renaissance Self-Fashioning from More to Shakespeare* (Chicago and London: Chicago University Press, 1980), pp. 2–3. Crewe, *Hidden Designs*, p. 60, also links this passage to the notion of 'self-fashioning'.

63 In the 'Letter to Ralegh', Spenser uses 'fashion' both to describe the didactic purpose of *The Faerie Queene*, and his task as its writer; in *FQ*, pp. 737–38; see also pp. 22–23 above.

Once the Ape has been 'fashioned' as a soldier, he is in a position to exploit the 'simple husbandman'. The poem dramatizes the rogues' mobile fraud in action:

> This yron world (that same he weeping sayes)
> Brings downe the stowtest hearts to lowest state:
> For miserie doth bravest mindes abate,
> And make them seeke for that they wont to scorne,
> Of fortune and of hope at once forlorne.
> The honest man, that heard him thus complaine,
> Was griev'd, as he had felt part of his paine ... (ll. 254–60)

Through the performance of his rôle, the Ape convinces the husbandman of the veracity of his woes. The husbandman responds to the Ape 'as he had felt part of his paine'. The Ape's performance taps into what the husbandman believes to be a shared experience of hardship. Though the reader's awareness that the Ape's improvisation is bogus undercuts this empathy, the ambiguity of line 260 indicates the complex implications of the Ape's impersonation. Though 'he' refers primarily to the husbandman, it also suggests the Ape's enthusiastic involvement in his rôle: 'he' (the Ape) 'had felt part of his paine', or was vitally immersed in the complaint he counterfeits. As Spenser depicts fraud in action, he shows the complex ambiguity of the performer's relationship to the thing he copies. The Ape cannot but feel 'part of his paine'.

The rogues' decimation of the flock of 'fleecie sheepe' (l. 289) puts this rôle-play into perspective. The reader sees the successful working of the Fox and the Ape's disguises and the confirmation of the danger implicit in the earlier exchanges. Through their self-fashioning, they obtain a position from which they can abuse the pastoral trust they have been given. The narrative leaves the reader in no doubt of the resonance of their 'false treason and vile theeverie' (l. 315):

> For not a lambe of all their flockes supply
> Had they to shew: but ever as they bred,
> They slue them, and upon their fleshes fed:
> For that disguised Dog lov'd blood to spill,
> And drew the wicked Shepheard to his will.

So twixt them both they not a lambkin left,
And when lambes fail'd, the old sheepes lives they
    reft … (ll. 316–22)

At this point at least, the narrator has a grip on the rogues' identities: 'that disguis'd Dog' retains his taste for blood, while the 'wicked Shepheard' is a creature of the Fox's 'will'. Yet the narrator's commentary cannot alter the fact that the impostors have successfully assaulted the pastoral environment. Spenser captures the horror of these events with a few deft touches: simple syntactic connectives lead the reader through the abuse of the shepherd's rôle in a procession of almost banal di- and monosyllables in lines 317–18. Line 318 in particular conveys a sense of the narrator's moral revulsion, heightened by the slight ambiguity of the personal pronouns, as though the Fox and the Ape were cannibalizing their own 'fleshes'. Cannibalism is metaphorically what they have achieved, since to abuse the rôle of the shepherd is to transgress a basic taboo of agrarian-pastoral society. More generally, the Fox and the Ape's behaviour compromises the theistic image of benevolent hierarchy embodied in Psalm 23 and the parable of the Good Shepherd.[64]

As bad shepherds, the Fox and the Ape's behaviour supports their characterization as amoral poets. By implication, they neglect the responsible relationship of the shepherd/poet to his sheep, which is at the heart of *The Shepheardes Calender* and the pastoral tradition. The linguistic and imitative tools of the poet have assisted their entry into the pastoral world; once within that world, the rogues take advantage of their position to indulge their appetites. In butchering their flock, the Fox and the Ape display a knowing contempt for the communitarian images of pastoral poetry and the redemptive theology underlying Psalm 23. The symbol of the lamb as a token of primary trust has been reduced to a food value, grist to the individualist's mill. The first episode's climax displays the Fox and the Ape as skilled impostors, whose artistic gifts (suasive oratory, imitation, impersonation) equip them to defraud guileless innocents like the husbandman. Poetic talent is ambiguous; the itinerant minstrel

---

64 See Cooper, *Pastoral*, pp. 95, 205.

of the medieval tradition has become a sixteenth-century coney-catcher living on his mercurial wits.[65]

The first episode shows the Fox and the Ape as amoral poets, who have let loose their talents onto the social world for material advantage. In the remainder of the first half of the poem, the rogues' 'fashioning' as poets is a satirically useful counter for the narrative through which it can explore the corruption of both the Church and the Court. Having established that the rogues can utilize their poetic skills at will, Spenser begins these episodes with the Priest and the Mule's satiric monologues. Through these figures, Spenser expatiates on the corruption of the Church (ll. 415–540) and the Court (ll. 607–52). In the first half of the poem, the Fox and the Ape's amoral artistry enables them to exploit the institutional corruption of English society. The conceit is satirically valid so long as their impersonations are controlled by normative values which can be easily identified through ironic counterpoint. The Priest's advice on 'How to obtain a Beneficiall' is described as 'holesome counsell' (ll. 486; 553) – a pun which indicates both its value for the individualists, and its moral 'holes'. During the course of the third episode, this satirical mode of narration begins to collapse; gradually the text is forced to recognize its own amorality.

The Crisis

If the *Tale* had consisted of only the first two episodes, the adventures of its amoral protagonists would have been reconcilable with the 'poem as nut' aesthetic. But their continued progression into the upper echelons of society poses the narrator a fundamental problem:

65 See Robert Greene, *A Notable Discovery of Coosnage*, etc., ed. G. B. Harrison (Elizabethan and Jacobean Quartos. Edinburgh: Edinburgh University Press, 1966). Greene's tracts are among the classics of 1590s rogue literature. They parallel the *Tale* inasmuch as there is a central ambiguity in Greene's approach to the 'coney-catchers'. On the one hand, Greene wishes to appear as a serious moralist who is making 'notable discoveries' of underworld fraud; but on the other, as a professional writer, Greene needs his 'coosinors' as the scandalous hard copy which will attract readers.

how should he interpret the success of his fictional creations? A con-
ventional answer would be that Spenser alters his characterization
according to the satirical point he is trying to score.[66] Such an argu-
ment is not altogether satisfying. Since the *Tale* is unified by the idea
of the Fox and the Ape's upward mobility, the poem cannot be bro-
ken into discrete units of satirical meaning. Satirical referents do not
determine the course of the narrative; rather they emerge as a result
of the progress of the adventure. The narrator's intervention in the
third episode highlights his troubled awareness of the Fox and the
Ape's ambiguity. Here it becomes clear that the rogues' operations
cannot be restricted to small-scale coney-catching, or evaluated con-
ventionally. Though their behaviour is reprehensible, the narrator
becomes aware as his tale continues that its fictional energy derives
from the self-interest of his amoral protagonists. Since the narrator
recognizes that they are effectively the makers of 'his' fiction, his nar-
rative is forced to describe their work with grudging admiration:

> ... the fond Ape himselfe uprearing hy
> Upon his tiptoes, stalketh stately by,
> As if he were some great *Magnifico*,
> And boldlie doth amongst the boldest go.
> And his man Reynold with fine counterfesaunce
> Supports his credite and his countenaunce.
> Then gan the Courtiers gaze on everie side,
> And stare on him, with big lookes basen wide,
> Wondring what mister wight he was, and whence ...
> (ll.663–71)

66 Berger, 'The Prospect of Imagination', pp. 104–05, sees the Fox and the Ape
as having 'no reality, no interior form at all ... Their emptiness, the source of pain,
makes them parasites on the reality of others ...' This reading ignores i) the fact that
'protean figures' or not the Fox and the Ape are more 'real' in the poem than the ideal
Courtier; ii) that the contrast between the ideal Courtier and the Fox and the Ape
derives from the *narrator's* realization that they are not being effectively countered by
the society they inhabit; and iii) that the poem is a good deal lighter in tone than
Berger would admit: the rogues make effective comedy because of the reader's aware-
ness of their imposture. However, Berger's assessment that 'to impersonate, is the
condition of [the Fox and the Ape's] survival' is valid.

This is brilliantly effective poetry partly because Spenser is describing a glamorous fiction in the making; to render such an incident the narrative must convey something of the Ape's 'newfanglenesse' (l. 675) and consequent glamour. The Ape's entrance to Court is an exciting moment as readers and courtiers participate in 'star[ing]' at the Ape as a walking fiction encrusted with fashionable 'accoustrements', behaving 'altogether ... *Alla Turchesa*' (ll. 672–77). The fact that the Ape is an impostor does not substantially deflect the narrative's fascination with the fiction he makes. This is the heart of the narrator's dilemma: the Ape is such an accomplished fraud that the truth lying behind his appearance may not emerge. The Ape therefore becomes much more than a satirical cypher. Because of the apparent difficulty of dislodging 'his credite and his countenaunce', he is a threat to the narrator's confidence in received definitions of good and evil. By making him visually impressive, the narrator is partly forced to collude with the Ape's delusive appearance. Though his pretensions are undercut by his needing to 'uprear' himself 'Upon his tiptoes', the effect of his entrance to the Court is determined by 'his lookes loftie, as if he aspyr'd / To dignitie, and sdeign'd the low degree' (ll. 678–79). The Ape's fiction begins to impose its values onto the surface of the *Tale* itself.

The power of the Ape's imitative skills is felt in the presentation of his thefts and his growing influence at the Court. His skill in 'legier demaine' (l. 701) is abetted by a corresponding confidence that he can 'laugh ... out' any accusations (l. 703). The Ape defends his fiction through derision: he 'scoffe[s]' his accusers 'out with mockerie, / For he therein had great felicitie' (l. 705–06). Though the text makes it clear that this 'mockerie' is a sneering, unselective sarcasm, the Ape's 'felicitie ... therein' discommodes the narrator:

> So whilst that other like vaine wits he pleased,
> And made to laugh, his heart was greatly eased.
> But the right gentle minde would bite his lip,
> To heare the Javell so good men to nip:
> For though the vulgar yeeld an open eare,
> And common Courtiers love to gybe and fleare
> At everie thing, which they heare spoken ill,

And the best speaches with ill meaning spill;
Yet the brave Courtier ...
Doth loath such base condition, to backbite
Anies good name for envie or despite ... (ll. 709–17; 719–20)

In this extract, it can be seen that the outline of the ideal Courtier, which breaks the *Tale*'s primary mode of narration, is occasioned by the narrator's disgust at the Ape's 'mockerie'. While we may infer that the narrator believes there is a difference between sarcasm and satire, he concedes that scoffing is a kind of skill – and this is why the Ape's powers alarm him. 'Backbiting' is related to the satirist's mode of attack on his adversaries.[67] The Ape's proficient 'mockerie' demonstrates that the tools employed in satire can be used negatively; indeed it can become a form of self-aggrandizing creativity, as displayed when the Ape 'with sharp quips joy'd others to deface, / Thinking that their disgracing did him grace' (ll. 707–08). For the first time in the poem, the rogues' poetic abilities are directed towards a recognizably literary activity: the Ape uses satire to bolster his position at Court at the expense of 'the right gentle minde'. The narrator rightly feels that his own rôle as the writer of the tale is under pressure from rogues' amoral poetry.

It is crucial to the narrative's ambivalence that the Ape's poetry provoke the narrator's description of 'the brave Courtier'. At Court, the Ape is licensed to 'play the Poet' (l. 810). This formulation serves to remind us that the Ape is only a 'play ... Poet' and not the real thing. The narrator wants to view the Ape's literary excursion as a manifest sham. Yet the manner in which his text distinguishes between the ideal Courtier's poetry and the Ape's suggests a certain desperation on his part: that for him, as for us, the humanistic conception of the art is being squeezed by the more cynical approach of the Ape:

---

67 This is especially true of the predominantly medieval mode of satirical 'flytings', as in *The Flyting of Dunbar and Kennedie* in *The Poems of William Dunbar*, ed. W. Mackay Mackenzie (Edinburgh: The Porpoise Press, 1932), pp. 5–20; or the later *Flyting Betwixt Montgomerie and Polwart*. One may think of the quarrel between Nashe and Harvey as a late example of 'flyting', albeit a slightly one-sided contest.

His Minde [the Courtier] unto the Muses he withdrawes;
Sweete Ladie Muses, Ladies of delight,
Delights of life, and ornaments of light:
With whom he close confers with wise discourse,
Of Natures workes, of heavens continuall course,
Of forreine lands of people different,
Of kingdomes change, of divers government,
Of dreadfull battailes of renowmed Knights;
With which he kindleth his ambitious sprights
To like desire and praise of noble fame,
The onely upshot whereto he doth ayme ... (ll. 760–70)

   [the Ape] could fine loving verses frame,
And play the Poet oft. But ah, for shame
Let not sweete Poets praise, whose onely pride
Is vertue to advaunce, and vice deride,
Be with the worke of losels wit defamed,
Ne let such verses Poetrie be named:
Yet he the name on him would rashly take,
Maugre the sacred Muses, and it make
A servant to the vile affection
Of such, as he depended most upon,
And with the sugrie sweete thereof allure
Chast Ladies eares to fantasies impure. (ll.809–20)

The Courtier's interest in poetry accords with his humanist function as the intellectually able and disinterested adviser to the Prince: poetry enriches his mind and strengthens his 'ambitious sprights'. The passage has the force of a declamatory blueprint, setting down in the style of Castiglione the intellectual accomplishments desirable in a courtier.[68] For the narrator, poetry is an ideal civilizing practice, as Spenser himself claims in the 'Letter to Ralegh'.[69]

   Yet this blueprint is wrenched from the narrator by the Ape's 'mockerie': it is a self-conscious complaint, through which the narra-

68 Renwick, *Complaints*, pp. 239–42, parallels the episode at Court with extensive quotations from Hoby's translation of Castiglione.

69 See pp. 22–23 above.

tor hopes to reassert the aesthetic values which the Ape's practice demeans. The idealism of the first extract is highlighted by the tone and vocabulary of the second. For the Ape, poetry is an adjunct to his other 'thriftles games' (ll. 800–08); specifically, it is a part of his rôle as a courtly bawd (ll. 808–10). The narrator feels he must reaffirm the ideal purpose and function of poetry. In line 810, the median caesura combines with the abrupt closure of a sentence in mid-line (unusual for the *Tale*'s heroic couplets) to mark the narrator's intervention. He defends his ideal of 'Poets praise' against 'the worke of losels wit', but he cannot deny that the Ape's work is skilful, intelligent, and indeed 'witty'. The Ape's use of poetry appals the narrator; however, he cannot dismiss him as stupid or artless. The cry 'Ne let such verses Poetrie be named' is a plea rather than an instruction: the narrator knows that the ability to frame 'fine loving verses' is a part of his characters' fashioning. The Ape remains an impostor because he 'takes the name' of poet in defiance of 'the sacred Muses'.

The unsettling quality of the Ape's poetry is illustrated by comparing this passage with Jonson's suggestively titled epigram, 'On Poet-Ape'.[70] Poet-Ape is a plagiarist who grows from acquiring 'the reversion of old plays' to a position where he can buy off all available texts: 'now grown / To a little wealth ... He takes up all, makes each man's wit his own.'[71] Plagiarism has serious consequences for other writers' posthumous fame: 'after-times / May judge it to be his, as well as ours'.[72] The literary thief may persuade 'after-times' that his 'frippery of wit' was behind the works of finer writers. Though Jonson recognizes the subversive potential of such theft, the epigram is framed by his patrician disdain for 'Poor Poet-Ape'; his thefts have become 'so bold ... As we, the robbed, leave rage, and pity it'.[73] This

---

70 Ben Jonson, *The Complete Poems*, ed. George Parfitt (Harmondsworth: Penquin, 1975), p. 51. The *Epigrams* were first published in Jonson's *Works* of 1616, though many were almost certainly written earlier. See also Rosalind Miles, *Ben Jonson: His Life and Work* (London and New York: Routledge and Kegan Paul, 1986), p. 173.

71 Jonson, *The Complete Poems* p. 51.

72 *Ibid.*

73 *Ibid.*

'pity' derives from Jonson's sureness that the difference between his work and the Poet-Ape's is absolute; the final couplet admonishes the thief, 'Fool, as if half-eyes will not know a fleece / From locks of wool, or shreds from the whole piece!'[74] Spenser's 'Poet-Ape' is not such a self-evidently bad poet. He unnerves the narrator precisely because his imposture cannot be written off with Jonsonian hauteur; the Ape's poetry is effective in its dubious 'allure'.

This effectiveness is apparent in the narrator's vocabulary. He uses the adjective 'sweete' to describe the Muses (l. 761) and 'Poets praise' (l. 811); but the noun also occurs in his depiction of the Ape's verse as 'the sugrie sweete' (l. 819). In the first two instances, the adjective conveys ideas of poetry's benignity and harmony;[75] suggesting the narrator's ideal of what 'proper' poetry should be.[76] This recalls the ancient defence of poetry as a characteristically 'sweet' form of education. Inverting the 'poem as nut' formula, this topos views a given poem's fictional casing as an attractive confection, which beguiles readers into also accepting its bitter doctrinal centre. For Lucretius, poetry resembles medicinal 'rank wormwood', which doctors disguise with 'the sweet yellow fluid of honey' to delude sick children.[77] Sidney describes the didactic message of poetry as 'a medicine of cherries'.[78] The Ape adopts and distorts even this quality of sweetness through his verse. By being 'sugrie sweete', his poetry is at once mildly tautologous and doubly 'alluring', almost as if the Ape had noted the narrator's repetition of 'sweete' and wilfully incorporated an aspect of the word into his own work. In his hands, the 'sweetness'

74 *Ibid.*

75 Compare *OED* 6, 'Having an agreeable or benign quality, influence, operation or effect'.

76 Compare Thalia's evocation of 'that same gentle Spirit, from whose pen / Large streames of honnie and sweete Nectar flowe', in *The Teares*, ll. 217–18. Sweetness is synonymic with poetic beauty.

77 Lucretius, *De Rerum Natura*, trans. W. H. D. Rouse (Loeb Classical Library. Cambridge, Mass. and London: Harvard University Press and Heinemann, 1924; revised edn 1975/1982), I.936–50, pp. 78–79.

78 Sidney, *Miscellaneous Prose*, pp. 91–92. See also his *An Apology for Poetry*, ed. Geoffrey Shepherd (London: Thomas Nelson, 1965; rpt. Old and Middle English Texts. Manchester: Manchester University Press, 1973), p. 182.

of poetry is overdone: it is symptomatic of his amoral duplicity and his distortion of what should be a didactic art form. The narrative's ambiguity about the Fox and the Ape's poetic skills is now revealed as an ambiguity about poetry. The reader only has the narrator's assertion that there is a perceptible difference between the work of 'sweete poets' and 'the sugrie sweete' produced by the Ape. The two kinds of poetry taste the same.

The Resolution

After three episodes, the *Tale* is in philosophical crisis. In the course of its account of the Fox and the Ape's 'strange adventure', the narrative has been forced to acknowledge that their abilities are virtually indistinguishable from those of a 'right poet'. The Ape's deployment of satirical 'mockerie' questions the narrator's use of deflationary irony, while his amorally successful verse undermines the basis of the narrator's aesthetics. Allied to these problems is the complete breakdown of what Oram calls 'the system': the norms of behaviour and law. Oram claims that the final episode differs from the others because in the previous episodes, 'the system worked': the Fox and the Ape 'were exposed by their own greed', whereas in the final episode a *deus ex machina* is needed to restore order.[79] It seems to me that Oram gives 'the system' too much credit by undervaluing the relative insignificance of the Fox and the Ape's exposures in comparison with the scale of their impostures. In the Court episode for instance, Spenser handles the discovery of the Fox's 'craftie feates' (l. 920) of extortion and fraud very briefly. Since Elizabethan society viewed crimes of financial double-dealing like coining as a form of treason,[80] there is a sly humour in the account of this 'punishment':

79 Oram in *YESP*, p. 332.
80 See for example Charles Nicholl, *The Reckoning: The Murder of Christopher Marlowe* (London: Jonathan Cape, 1992), p. 238. Nicholl rightly connects coining with pro-Catholic sedition, but usefully insists on the gravity of crimes of financial imposture in Elizabethan England.

But yet this Foxe could not so closely hide
His craftie feates, but that they were descride
At length, by such as sate in iustice seate,
Who for the same him fowlie did entreate;
And hauing worthily him punished,
Out of the Court for euer banished. (ll. 919–24)[81]

This dénouement follows the brilliant account of the Fox's 'coosinage
and cleanly knaverie' (l. 857) in support of the Ape's magnificent
appearance at Court. The Fox commits a range of crimes from
impersonation (l. 861) to fraud and obtaining money under false
pretences. Yet his punishment is no more specific than being 'fowlie
… entreate[d]' and being 'Out of the Court for euer banished'.[82]
Compare this 'iustice' with that which determines the fate of Munera
in *The Faerie Queene* V.II. Munera's golden hands and silver feet are
'Chopt off, and nayld on high' by Talus to illustrate to the populace
the ideal punishment for the 'vnrighteous', who sell 'iustice'
(V.II.26).[83] She is then flung 'Ouer the Castle wall' to drown 'in the
durty mud' (V.II.27).[84] This instant and brutal 'iustice' represents the
ideal means of cleansing away the sins embodied in Munera; the vio-
lence of the imagery fits the iniquity she represents as a Lady Meed
figure thriving on theft, extortion and bribery. Talus is an inflexible
law enforcement figure; when he begins his assault on Munera
'Withouten pitty of her goodly hew', Artegall significantly feels a
twinge – '*Artegall* him selfe her seamlesse plight did rew' (V.II.25).[85]
But the narrative insists that Talus's response is the correct one, mea-

---

81 In this case, I have preferred to quote from *Var.* VIII, p. 129, since its preser-
vation of the original orthography more graphically demonstrates the parallel
between 'iustice' and 'Iustice'.

82 I accept that rustication from court was a serious punishment to hard-up
Elizabethan courtiers, as a poem like Ralegh's *The 21st: and last booke of the Ocean to
Scinthia* demonstrates. However, the Fox's dismissal is hardly as emotive an event as
Ralegh's rustication; moreover, as the rest of the *Tale* reveals, it does not in any way
hinder the Fox's subsequent career.

83 *FQ*, p. 538.

84 *Ibid.*, p. 539.

85 *Ibid.*, p. 538.

suring up to a true standard 'Of Iustice': 'Yet for no pitty would [Artegall] change the course / Of Iustice, which in Talus hand did lye' (V.II.26).[86] The just hand of Talus chops off the golden and corrupt hands of Munera in his rôle as the embodiment of enacted Justice. This must remain unmoved by either Munera's bribes or her agony.

The 'uncivil' world of the *Tale* is very different. With Munera in mind, the lines on the unmasking of the Fox bring out the corruption and/or laxity of 'such as sate in iustice seat'.[87] Far from illustrating the system's ability to detect and punish impostors, these lines suggest the incompetence of the judicial system, and that it too is a good target for satire. This impression is confirmed by the fact that the narrator's malcontent complaint of the 'Suters state' immediately precedes the rogues' rustication. As the narrator bitterly puts it, 'Whoever leaves sweete home ... And will to Court for shadowes vaine to seeke, / Or hope to gaine, himselfe will a dawe trie' (ll. 909, 912–13). This image of Court hardly encourages the reader's confidence in its ability to dispense justice; it provokes satirical complaint.

A further point against Oram's view is the narrative's structural use of estate satire. Over the first three impersonations, a pattern emerges whereby each unmasking results in promotion – there are reasons to believe that even after the final episode their career may not have reached its apex. This pattern is more than just a means of carrying the narrative forward. The rogues are effective impersonators; the social hierarchy permits their self-fashioning penetration of the different estates, and is undermined by them. The poem is dominated by gullible husbandmen and somnolent monarchs, powerless to prevent or detect the rogues' impostures. This narrative pattern also comically reverses the Boethian image of the wheel of Fortune: far from being cast down by 'froward fortune' (l. 66), the rogues are repeatedly thrust back up even when they have apparently fallen off the wheel.

---

86 *Ibid.*

87 The 'iustice' of the *Tale* is always in the lower case (compare the 'judgement' of line 1376), whereas Book V explores the philosophical absolute of 'Iustice'. Hence in V.II.26, Talus embodies 'the [absolute] course / Of Iustice', whereas Munera sold a compromised – and therefore uncapitalized – 'iustice'.

So the final episode begins as Spenser has shown that normative moral referents of society – which should ensure the moral accountability of poetic texts – have been weakened by the corruption of 'the system'. The Court episode reveals that amoral skill can achieve actual power. Hence the defence of a humanistic poetics falls to the narrator alone. He can do little more than assert the value of his values; he cannot demonstrate from the tale he tells that they are valuable. The Fox and the Ape encounter the sleeping lion at a point in the poem where their agile individualism has eroded the narrator's confidence either in society or in poetry. The system has failed: the reader is given tangible proof of its failure in the figure of the sleeping Lion.

The crown-stealing incident distils much of the text's philosophical problem. On the one hand, we are offered a comic deflation of the Fox's argument in tempting the Ape to steal the Lion's 'royall signes' (l. 1016). Yet however bogus this argument may be, the rogues achieve their aim of gaining sovereign power. The comedy of the crown-stealing incident becomes a part of the poem's wider self-consciousness. The narrator comments that 'it good sport had been him [the Ape] to have eyde' in the nervous act of theft (l. 1013). By making the reader conscious of an almost balletic visual joke in the Ape's movements,[88] the narrator aestheticizes the serious issue of the usurpation. The reader attends to the Ape's nervousness at the expense of the gravity of the theft. This comic irony is then itself embroiled in the questions the poem asks about poetic fiction: how can the Fox and the Ape's impostures be described without there being some element of humour and delight in their craftiness? The poet's tools of comedy and ironic representation deflate but do not defeat the Fox and the Ape.

Once the rogues have reached agreement about 'Whether of them should be the Lord of Lords' (l. 1020), Spenser shows them again using their creative powers to make others swallow their scenario. But here the impostors' power becomes absolute. This success is the climax of the narrator's philosophical dilemma, and he cannot resolve it with the resources so far at his disposal. In the first three episodes, the Fox and the Ape's abuses were limited to the rôles they adopted –

88 See line 1012, 'Now went, now stept, now crept, now backward drew'.

killing sheep, defrauding parishioners and exploiting poor suitors. Once they have 'become' King and chief minister, their potential to create havoc is unlimited. And again, the text makes it clear that the Fox and the Ape owe their eminence to their linguistic skills:

> The subtile Foxe so well his message sayd,
> That the proud beasts him readily obayd:
> Whereby the Ape in wondrous stomack woxe,
> Strongly encorag'd by the crafty Foxe;
> That King indeed himselfe he shortly thought,
> And all the Beasts him feared as they ought … (ll. 1101–06)

The Fox's suasive speech convinces the 'proud' Tiger and Boar to 'obay' him; this leads the Ape to begin to believe that he really is the King. The narrative procedure of the *Tale* is seen in miniature in these lines: the Fox persuades his interlocutors that the Ape is the Lion, which has the effect of confirming the Ape in the reality of the part he plays. Their virtuosity has guided the Fox and the Ape to such a point that they are able to feel thoroughly at home in the riskiest of all their impersonations. Spenser caps the Ape's conviction/delusion with the superb doubleness of line 1106: 'ought' the beasts to fear this 'mock-King' (l. 1091) or the reality he counterfeits? The almost clichéd gesture of obedience has become in Spenser's hands an illustration of the ambiguity of the 'mock-King' and his authority. The beasts 'ought' to fear the Ape, not because he is their rightful ruler, but because of the danger he embodies.

The Ape's assumption of power is at once the summit of the rogues' self-fashioning imposture and Spenser's final demonstration of the collapse of 'the system'. By showing the facility with which the Fox and the Ape can 'tyrannize at will' (l. 1127) he displays the effectiveness of their fictional projection of themselves onto society, and that society's corresponding inability to contain their 'climbing' impersonations. Moreover, the usurpation dramatizes the narrator's earlier anxieties. Once the Ape occupies 'the Regall throne' (l. 1111) the narrator's problem becomes even more acute. How can the narrative wrest power from the Fox and the Ape? And even more importantly, can it offer a convincing reassertion of social and intellectual coherence?

Rescue of a sort comes with the intervention of Mercury. But this rescue is also the *Tale's* crowning irony. Having delineated the Fox's stranglehold on the means of power (ll. 1137–1224), Spenser's corrupt kingdom of the beasts seems unchangeable. Once the impostors have imposed their fictions on the seat of government, fiction begins to replace the truth. The introduction of Jove and Mercury is a means of rectifying the chaos. Their presence seems to reveal that there is a further level of authority prepared to restore order in the name of Jove's responsibility for 'The care of Kings' (l. 1225). Yet the gods bear a disquieting resemblance to the poem's other absent and permissive authority figures: the husbandman, the 'Ordinarie' (l. 562) and the Lion. Jove's first inclination is to destroy the 'usurping Ape' (l. 1233) with thunderbolts and drive him 'downe to hell, his dewest meed' (ll. 1236–37); yet the pervadingly comic tone of the poem would be at odds with such violence.

> But him avizing, he that dreadfull deed
> Forebore, and rather chose with scornfull shame
> Him to avenge, and blot his brutish name
> Unto the world, that never after anie
> Should of his race be voyd of infamie ... (ll. 1238–42)

Jove's resolution seems strong enough, though Mercury's intervention does not unequivocally carry it out: the disjunction between the rogues' final punishment and Jove's 'avizing' returns attention to this passage. What is Spenser up to? Formally, the Jove material parodies the epic topos of the *deus ex machina*. Spenser draws on Virgil's account of Jove's message to Aeneas (again using the agency of Mercury) in *Aeneid* IV, and Ovid's conception of the gods' ambiguous involvement in human affairs in the *Metamorphoses*. In the *Tale*, Jove wants to punish the Fox and the Ape in a way which exceeds their status. As animal impostors their 'names' are already 'brutish' and cannot logically be blotted any further. Jove's response is symptomatic of the growing erosion of textual authority in the unfolding narrative. The comic illogic of his reaction to the rogues contrasts with the narrator's clearer judgement of them in the first half of the poem.[89] The

89 Compare lines 314–20.

more successful the rogues are, the less the written text of the *Tale* is able to enforce an authoritative judgement on them.

The amorality of the denouement is embodied in the figure of Mercury. As in *The Ruines of Time*, ll. 666–72, Spenser amalgamates different aspects of the god's conventional identity to suit his own particular purposes. In *The Ruines of Time*, Mercury appears both as the 'shepherd' of Sidney's ashes to heaven and as a divine type of Sidney's poetic ability.[90] In the *Tale*, Mercury's primary identity is that of amoral fixer and thief, armed with an impressive paraphernalia of magical devices: the caduceus and, in this case, 'his dreadfull hat' l. (1279).[91] Spenser's text combines parody of Virgil[92] with the god's wider profile (deriving from the Homeric Hymn to Hermes and Ovid) as both a poet and a thief.[93] For the reader of the *Tale*, it is no surprize that Mercury the thief should coexist with Mercury the poet:

> Tho on his head his dreadfull hat he dight,
> Which maketh him invisible in sight …
> Through power of that, his cunning theeveries
> He wonts to worke, that none the same espies;
> And through the power of that, he putteth on
> What shape he list in apparition. (ll. 1279–80; 1287–90)

These lines deftly indicate Mercury's kinship with the Fox and the Ape. His magic hat assists his 'cunning theeveries'; as the narrative has shown, the mortal rogues use poetic guile for analogous ends. As a divine thief, Mercury looks suspiciously like the rogues' mythic rôle

90 See pp. 130–31 above.

91 W. L. Renwick (ed.), *Complaints* (London: The Scholartis Press, 1928), p. 244, disputes Spenser's scholarship as to the original owner of the hat, and misses the point that the passage deliberately plays with mythic and poetic sources.

92 Spenser's description of the caduceus (ll. 1291–99) expands *Aeneid* IV.241–44.

93 See the Homeric Hymn's description of Hermes's creation of the lyre (ll. 25–61) alongside his equal delight in the 'sheer trickery' witnessed in his theft of Apollo's cattle (l. 64ff.). In Hesiod, *Hesiod; The Homeric Hymns and Homerica*, The Loeb Classical Library, ed. and trans. Hugh G. Evelyn-White (Cambridge, Mass. and London: Harvard University Press and Heinemann, 1914), pp. 365–69. Compare also *Metamorphoses* II.685ff. for Ovid's version of the cattle-stealing incident.

model.[94] His magical invisibility counterpoises the rogues' use of disguise; like the god, they wish to be thieves whose thefts go unnoticed. Further, Mercury's divinity endows him with the ultimate power to fashion himself to 'What shape he list in apparition'. The rogues' flexibility is also an attribute of Mercury. By emphasizing that the god of eloquence is also a self-fashioning thief,[95] Spenser brings back to the surface of the poem the earlier tension between the ideal Courtier and the Ape.

For the *Tale* as a whole, Spenser's description of this *deus ex machina* problematizes the close of the poem even before the Lion King's authority is restored. Since Mercury is the rogues' divine counterpart, he cannot credibly represent any unambiguous form of moral authority. Far from being reinstated by Mercury's intervention, the narrator's humanist values are, if anything, further diminished.

The entrance of the amoral Mercury acts as a prompt for the comic finale, and as a thematic indication that the poem lacks a determining moralistic structure. This combination of comedy and textual amorality in turn demonstrates the kind of satiric fiction Spenser makes possible in the *Tale*.

This mimetic satire can be seen in the parodic comedy of the closing lines. This passage brilliantly recalls the elaborate trial scenes from the *Renart* cycle, originating with 'Le Jugement de Renart'. In these texts, Reynard persistently avoids the punishment he deserves

94 Compare Autolycus in *The Winter's Tale*: 'My father named me Autolycus; who, being as I am, littered under Mercury, was likewise a snapper-up of unconsidered trifles' (IV.iii.24–26). Autolycus is associated directly with poetry (of a kind) through the ballads he sings and sells.

95 The caduceus (ll. 1291–99) is an analogous symbol of Mercury's poetic powers. As in Ovid's account of Argus's murder (*Metamorphoses* I.671–721), the caduceus had been associated both with Mercury's rôle as the 'summoner' of the dead (compare *Aeneid* IV.241–44) and as an amoral poet. In the context of *The Faerie Queene* Book IV, Fowler argues that the caduceus is a 'primary attribute' of Mercury's 'character as a god of concord'. Though the *Tale* is a very different Spenserian text from Book IV, the symbolic association between the caduceus and concord – as a form of enforced divine harmonization – is present in both texts. See Alistair Fowler, *Spenser and the Numbers of Time* (London: Toutledge and Kegan Paul, 1964), p. 157.

through both his quick thinking and the lion king Noble's chronic inability to see through Reynard's lies.[96] Reynard's trial is a travesty of justice, through which the writers attack the nepotistic links between monarchy and all-powerful nobility in medieval Europe. In the Tale, Spenser radically compresses the narrative of the Renart cycle to create a comic denouement which incidentally reveals that, like the Blatant Beast, the Fox and the Ape will get 'into the world at liberty againe':[97]

> Yet him [the Ape] at last the Lyon spide, and caught,
> And forth with shame unto his judgement brought.
> Then all the beasts he causd' assembled bee,
> To heare their doome, and sad ensample see:
> The Foxe, first Author of that treacherie,
> He did uncase, and then away let flie.
> But th'Apes long taile (which then he had) he quight
> Cut off, and both eares pared of their hight;
> Since which, all Apes but halfe their eares have left,
> And of their tailes are utterlie bereft. (ll. 1375–84)

This passage immediately follows the famously comic description of the Ape, pursued by the Lion, 'flying … From rowme to rowme, from beame to beame' (ll. 1372–73). This image seems to indicate that at last, divinely ordained authority will force the impostors to resume their proper shapes and stations: the Ape must submit 'unto his judgement'. The next couplet announces bluntly that the beasts are assembled 'To heare their doome, and sad ensample see'. This ponderous line suggests the rogues will be sentenced without trial and publicly punished, in the manner of Renart's inconclusive execution.[98] Any process of law is either compressed out of the narrative or deemed unnecessary in the case of such evident malefactors.

---

96 See Terry, *Renard the Fox*, pp. 94–140. See also Caxton's *History of Reynard the Fox*, the first half of which closely follows the outline of the 'Jugement' narrative.
97 VI.XII.38, in *FQ*, p. 708.
98 See Terry, *Renard the Fox*, pp. 132–34.

Yet comically, Spenser opts out of the conclusion offered by this 'sad ensample' formula. In reminding the reader that the Fox is the 'first Author of that treacherie' he recalls to the surface of the text the fact that the Fox's work throughout the poem has been in part poetic, or authorial – as the fashioner of the 'strange adventure'. The rogues have a pivotal rôle in the fictional making of the poem even at the moment when they appear to be on the point of being decisively unmasked. Ascription of authorial responsibility to the Fox stands alongside his 'uncase[ing]'. This implies that he is stripped of his current disguise as chief minister: such a punishment is substantially no different from the treatment he received earlier from 'such as sate in iustice seate'. So the Fox's release is an indictment of the Lion's reinstated government, and a wider recognition that the individualist principle embodied by the Fox cannot be stifled. It also provides a comic ending for the poem, in which its chief impersonator is at liberty to pursue his career beyond the textual ken of the reader.

As Oram notes, the Ape's punishment will make him 'harder to unmask because he will resemble all the more closely the human beings he imitates'.[99] Further to this I would note Spenser's use of another obvious pun in line 1384 on 'tailes'. The rogues' ability to escape from their previous fictions is the leitmotif of the *Tale*. As superior coney-catchers and amoral poets, they show an unerring ability to shed their previous tales/tailes. Like Greene's pamphlets, the poem attempts to pin down the impostors and identify their various 'tailes'. But as a complex work of art, in its closing lines the poem intimates the impossibility of 'either confound[ing], or convert[ing] such base Cooseners'.[100] The Fox and the Ape return to the same 'wide world' at the end of the tale that they started from. The reader can be relatively sure that they will not be settling quietly into 'sweete home' and 'meane estate' (l. 909) with equanimity.

The trial scene's ambiguity also indicates Spenser's self-conscious awareness that the rogues, as self-conscious fictional characters, cannot simply be tidied away. Since the Fox and the Ape embody the disruptive idea that poetic talent is amoral, Spenser avoids the easy

99 *YESP*, p. 332.
100 Greene, *The Second Part of Conny-Catching*, p. 10.

option of suggesting that such amorality can be controlled through punishment. However desirable, the force of law cannot execute the principle, or indeed the talent, of the amoral individualist.

In his brief envoy, the narrator blames Mother Hubberd's 'bad … tongue' for the rhetorical lapses that have crept into his text of 'her discourse' (ll. 1385–88). This comment indicates that he is unable to follow the *Tale's* radical problematizing of traditional poetics. In the place where Henryson would have inserted an allegorical *moralitas*, Spenser shows instead his narrator's intellectual exhaustion after rewriting the oral tale; these lines convey his disgust both at Mother Hubberd and his own 'weake … remembrance'. The narrator registers the amoral energies of the text he has written; yet he is unable – as the spokesman for an inflexible humanist poetics – to salvage any comfort from his work. In the light of the narrator's failure, what conclusions – if not moral instructions – should be drawn from the *Tale*?

The premise underlying this reading is that the *Tale* explores, through the Fox and the Ape's 'adventure', the dubiety of poetic talent. The amorality of poets leads the text both formally and thematically to concede the amorality of poetic texts. Since the contemporary 'defence of poetry' against puritanical objections to stage plays and fiction depended heavily on the idea that poetry was the ideal form of moral instruction,[101] Spenser's practical questioning of the nexus between morality and poetry is radical. The *Tale* does not simply advocate an amoral poetics. Through its use of the complaint mode, it suggests that traditional poetry and traditional notions of social hierarchy must change if they are to survive. The narrator, like the Muses, cannot preserve the value of traditional poetry. But he, like they, can at the least provide an innovative complaint which records these poetic and social anxieties. Through such complaints, Spenser creates a new poetry.

The *Tale's* problematizing of literary didacticism goes beyond the drama of the narrator's 'aporia'. The poem is a more comprehensive satire than its immediate literary forebears, since it is no longer tied either to a rigid allegorical aesthetic or to the hierarchical assump-

101 See pp. 15–23 above.

tions of conventional estate satire. Spenser's account of the rogues' adventure illustrates the pervasive complacency of the different estates, and suggests that society has become fluid, whether the élite sanctions this development or not. The Fox and the Ape, who in late medieval poetry would have symbolized the private vices of individual types, are here the enablers of a complex satirical complaint.

By undermining literary didacticism, the *Tale* raises the philosophical question of how fiction can refer, or work allegorically. I have argued that the *Tale* eschews traditional didacticism. But this does not mean that Spenser consequently discards the poetry of metaphorical referral; clearly, *The Faerie Queene*'s 'darke conceit' reflects his wider artistic commitment to an allegorical poetics throughout the 1580s and 1590s. The *Tale* nonetheless exhibits Spenser's awareness that the principles of allegorical referral are no longer as straightforward as they were for a writer like Henryson, or even Gascoigne. Because the social world in which poetry operates has changed, poetry too must adopt new strategies if it is to capture the complexity of lived experience. In the world of the *Tale*, everything is suddenly up for grabs: the individualist can use his poetic talents amorally. One 'lesson' that can be drawn from the poem is that the social world is ambiguous and dangerous; it does not necessarily embody the ideal justice of earlier philosophical and poetic speculation.

This is one kind of response to the perception that traditional didacticism is no longer a valid poetic method. Yet the *Tale*'s problematizing of didacticism anticipates the Ovidian environment of *Muiopotmos*, in which Spenser again confronts the problem of how poetry is to refer and make sense of the puzzling amorality of the outside world. The Fox and the Ape's answer – that the amoral world should be embraced by the amoral individualist – is one which Spenser cannot fully accept, yet he records it through complaint. In delineating poetic amorality in action, the *Tale* constitutes a radical departure in *Complaints*' 'poetics in practice'. Developing from the exploration of the conceptual dissonances in traditional poetry in *The Ruines of Time* and *The Teares*, the *Tale* both in form and content erodes conventional notions of the value of poetry. Its central conclusion is that poetry itself is amoral. As the self-conscious 'new Poet',

Spenser redefines poetry in an unsettled present by writing a 'new complaint', which lacks the moral reassurance of traditional complaint. The *Tale*, like *Muiopotmos*, shows Spenser in the act of re-evaluating the intellectual patrimony he accepted more unequivocally in *Virgils Gnat* and *Ruines of Rome*. And in the figure of the anxious narrator, Spenser brilliantly objectifies the anxieties and frustrations of the humanist poet who is only too aware of the fragility of his conceptual inheritance.

CHAPTER SIX

'Excellent device and wondrous slight':
Muiopotmos and *Complaints'* Poetics

> Such beauty, set beside
> so brief a season,
> suggests to our stunned reason
> this bleak surmise:
> the world was made to hold
> no end or *telos*,
> and if – as some would tell us –
> there is a goal,
> it's not ourselves.
> No butterfly collector
> can trap light or detect where
> the darkness dwells.
>
> *Joseph Brodsky*, 'The Butterfly'

A poem about tapestries is necessarily ecphrastic.[1] I begin with an ecphrasis – a mode which for Spenser invariably entails reflection on the nature of artifice.

At the climax of *The Faerie Queene* II, Guyon and the Palmer discover the enchantress Acrasia with her current lover. This voyeuristic moment enables Spenser to present her both as a delusive artist and as a work of art:

> Vpon a bed of roses she was layd,
> As faint through heat, or dight to pleasant sin,
> And was arayd, or rather disarayd,
> All in a vele of silke and siluer thin,
> That hid no whit her alabaster skin,

---

1 On ecphrasis, see pp. 241–42 below.

213

> But rather shewd more white, if more might bee:
> More subtile web *Arachne* cannot spin,
> Nor the fine nets, which oft we wouen see
> Of scorched deaw, do not in th'aire more lightly flee.[2]

Acrasia is an erotically provoking self-fashioner. Spenser focuses on her 'vele' as a key part of her sexual armoury, which as Bender notes 'almost becomes a part of [her] body.'[3] In comparing the 'vele' with Arachne's 'subtile web', Spenser heightens the reader's sense of the danger underlying Acrasia's attractiveness; like the spider's web, her artifice is designed to entangle and destroy her prey. Yet the web – like the veil – remains 'subtile' – an artful construction, ambiguous because of its skilful manufacture. In evoking Arachne at the moment before Acrasia is herself caught in the Palmer's 'subtile net',[4] Spenser signals the fundamental ambiguity of artifice. Acrasia's veil is an erotic enchantment which is being used perversely; the Palmer's 'net' shares the veil's subtlety, but has a corrective and restraining function:

> that same net so cunningly was wound,
> That neither guile, nor force might it distraine.[5]

Dundas compares this net with Vulcan's;[6] equally it is an immediate counterpoint to Arachne's web. For Spenser, Arachne embodies a basic tension within human art: it is skilful, yet also amoral. The morality of its usage cannot be guaranteed. As in part Spenser's retelling of Arachne's story, *Muiopotmos* is itself a fine reflection on the 'excellent device and wondrous slight' essential to both tapestry and poetry.

---

2 II.12.77, *FQ,* p. 296.

3 John B. Bender, *Spenser and Literary Pictorialism* (Princeton: Princeton University Press, 1972), p. 43. See also Judith Dundas, *The Spider and the Bee: The Artistry of Spenser's Faerie Queene* (Urbana and Chicago: University of Illinois Press, 1985), pp. 183–84, who notes 'The net and web comparisons ... add ... a moral caution against the trap Acrasia has set, but they also confirm the artistic beauty of her raiment'.

4 II.12.81, *FQ, loc. cit.*

5 II.12.82, *FQ,* p. 297.

6 Dundas, *The Spider and the Bee,* p. 6. Compare *Muiopotmos,* ll. 369–74.

In the second part of this book I have argued that the 'poetics in practice' embodied by the major *Complaints* is a cumulative development from *The Ruines of Time*'s 'broken verse' to a new kind of mimetic fiction exhibited in *Mother Hubberds Tale*, and now *Muiopotmos*. The first pair of major texts enact the tension in Spenser's thought between Christian and Classical poetics. These poems are clearly self-conscious complaints with an explicit concern with the status and meaning of poetry. With the second pair, it may seem that Spenser has moved away from his concern with poetry to the less explicitly self-conscious world of beast-fable. Yet as the previous chapter has shown, Spenserian narrative gives expression to aesthetic and social anxieties through complaint. Through these two narratives, Spenser articulates his sense that traditional didacticism can no longer be meaningful; the poems constitute a novel approach to fictional mimesis. In this writing, Spenser presents the mortal condition radically, replacing traditional moral imperatives with his insight into the complexity of the contingent. As we have seen, the *Tale* explores the failure of social structures to respond to the threat posed by the poetic individualist. *Muiopotmos* focuses on the questionable justice of mortal fate and the ambiguity of artistic images. It is utterly appropriate that the culmination of the poetics of Spenser's *Complaints* should be such a 'curious networke' of competing genres, interpretations and images.

Recent criticism has questioned the old idea that *Muiopotmos* must

---

7 *Muiopotmos* criticism essentially falls into two camps. On one side, there are the allegorizers like Brice Harris, 'The Butterfly in *Muiopotmos*,' *JEGP*, 43 (1944), pp. 102–16, Don C. Allen, *Image and Meaning: Metamorphic Traditions in Renaissance Poetry* (Baltimore: Johns Hopkins University Press, 1960), pp. 20–41, and R. A. Brinkley, 'Spenser's *Muiopotmos* and the Politics of Metamorphosis,' *ELH*, 48 (1981), pp. 668–76. They argue that the poem is allegorical, as in Allen's seminal reading of Clarion as the Platonic psyche. On the other side, there are the anti-allegorizers: Judith Anderson, '"Nat worth a boterflye": *Muiopotmos* and the *Nun's Priest's Tale*,' *JMRS*, 1 (1971), pp. 89–106, Judith Dundas, '*Muiopotmos*: A World of Art,' *YES*, 5 (1975), pp. 30–38, and Andrew D. Weiner, 'Spenser's *Muiopotmos* and the Fates of Butterflies and Men,' *JEGP*, 84 (1985), pp. 203–20. The latter group stress the entomological aspects of the text and claim, with varying degrees of enthusiasm, that it is unnecessary to read Clarion and Aragnoll as anything other than a butterfly and a spider.

be allegorical.[7] In the two most notable dissensions from traditional criticism, Dundas and Weiner argue that it is a mistake to read too much into the story of a butterfly's death. Dundas sees the poem as a self-contained 'world of art',[8] which is primarily concerned with beauty; Weiner sees the narrator as a deranged psychotic imposing an inappropriate human allegory onto natural events which are without moral implication. Despite their welcome abandonment of historical allegories, these readings misrepresent the full complexity of the poem, ignoring its place in Spenser's poetics.

Like the *Tale*, *Muiopotmos* is a Spenserian modification of beast-fable; it relays a 'significant' narrative which exceeds its apparent external stimuli: its central incident means more than a spider killing of an butterfly. Rather than constituting an historical allegory, the poem's significance is connected with Spenser's overarching concern in *Complaints* with poetry. Like the other major texts, *Muipotmos*'s deployment of the complaint mode signals its preoccupation with art. Where in *The Ruines of Time* Verlame's complaint for mortal transience leads to the consideration of poetic 'eternizing', in *Muiopotmos*, the complaint for the inequity of the mortal condition raises questions about the morality and meaning of art. In the tapestry competition, Spenser juxtaposes the moral art of Pallas with the immoral art of Arachne. Pallas wins the competition, but the view of the gods' government embodied in her tapestry is undermined by the wider story of *Muiopotmos*; equally, she wins not because of her didactic fable, but through the perfect butterfly in the margin of her composition. This chapter will read *Muiopotmos* as an elaborate illustration of the ambiguities that surround art. A work of art needs both 'excellent device' and, more ominously, 'wondrous slight' to reflect a world which is itself ambiguously ordered.

---

8 See Dundas '*Muiopotmos*: A World of Art' p. 33, where she argues that *Muiopotmos* is a text in which 'Spenser has made beauty the touchstone of value'. This 'aesthetic' viewpoint leads to the downplaying of any allegorical referral in the text. Though Dundas offers a good critique of traditional allegorical approaches (see also Weiner's essay) her view of the text simply as an aesthetic bauble diminishes its disquieting qualities, and indeed the ontological questions which Clarion's fate explicitly raises.

Even among the major *Complaints*, *Muiopotmos* is a self-conscious enigma, whose singularity derives from both its parodic tone and its symmetrical structure. This structure has only rarely been the focus of previous criticism.[9] Spenser constructs a simple narrative in a shifting rhetorical mode. This enables him to establish tensions between the narration and the moralizing commentary in their interpretation of the central image of Clarion's fate. The text imitates a spider's web; its meanings are produced through interplay between its constituent parts. I approach *Muiopotmos*'s interpretative cruxes through analysis of the poem's structure and genre. Once we understand how the web has been made, we may then – unlike Clarion – unravel its wider implications. Despite its enigmas, *Muiopotmos* fits into *Complaints*' poetics as both an illusive piece of self-reflexive 'slight', and as a series of questioning polarities about art and its relation to the mortal environment.

Symmetrical Structure

Muiopotmos is constructed on a principle of elaborate symmetry. I identify four main sections which balance and mirror each other in format and tone. The first section is a contradictory mock-epic *propositio* and *invocatio* (ll. 1–16).[10] The second section presents the butterfly Clarion, includes an inset tale explaining why butterflies have beautiful wings, and then describes Clarion's flight through a pastoral environment (ll. 17–208). The third section is a moralizing, yet contradictory, hinge between the two main portions of narrative (ll. 209–40). Finally, the fourth section presents the spider Aragnoll, followed by an inset tale explaining why he hates butterflies, concluding with Clarion's death (ll. 241–440).

9 The only recent analysis of *Muiopotmos*'s structure is F. E. Court's 'The Theme and Structure of Spenser's *Muiopotmos*', *SEL*, 10 (1970), pp. 1–15. Court divides the poem into twelve sections of varying shapes and sizes and does not fully address the poem's symmetrical structure.

10 Compare W. L. Renwick (ed.), *Complaints* (London: The Scholartis Press, 1928), p. 251.

This formal symmetry repays closer scrutiny. The two chiefly narrative sections both sandwich Ovidian 'aetion' tales[11] between the narration of the poem's central action. These sections mirror each other in moving from narrative to inset and back again to narrative. The narrative units are in turn ambiguously framed by the two discursive sections. Neither of these provides an authoritative statement of intent or generic signal, therefore no moralization can be taken as definitive or authorially sanctioned.[12]

On a miniature scale, this form resembles the structured interweaving of narrative, comment and symbolic allegory in *The Faerie Queene*'s books. Canto 10 of Book I is an allegorical preparation of the Red Cross Knight for the theological burden of confronting the Old Dragon. The contemplative canto in 'The House of Holiness' is sandwiched between the narrative incidents in the Cave of Despair (I.IX) and the battle with the Dragon (I.XI), which mark respectively the lowest and highest points in Red Cross's career as the Knight of Holiness. To bridge these two incidents, Spenser plunges Red Cross into a process of self-scrutiny and allegorical reformation. To defeat the Dragon, Red Cross must be schooled in the virtue of holiness. Similarly, *Muiopotmos*'s Ovidian insets provide contextualized explanations of Clarion's wings and Aragnoll's grudge, and are crucial to the text's wider meanings. The inset tale on Arachne poses vital questions about mimetic art and 'forejudgement', while the Astery tale opens the debate about the gods' justice. These insets reveal the operation of an analogous structural and symbolic form to that of *The Faerie Queene* books. Interpretative weight falls on these artfully marked out digressions from the central narrative.

As well as its overarching contrasts between Clarion/Aragnoll, Astery/Arachne, Clarion/Astery and Aragnoll/Arachne, the poem is shaped by a series of metaphorical and stylistic parallels. As Clarion's wings are favourably compared with Cupid's, so Aragnoll's web is preferred to Vulcan's net (ll. 97–104; 361–68). These bal-

---

11 See p. 223 below.

12 The poem's overall symmetrical pattern can be notated as: authorial address (lines 1–16 and 209–40)/narrative/digression/narrative (lines 17–208 and 241–440).

anced mock-epic similes reinforce the paradoxical similarity of the protagonists implicit in the description of them as 'two mightie ones' (l. 3). The similes heighten the reader's awareness of the text's symmetrical presentation of Clarion (ll. 17–208) and Aragnoll (ll. 241–440). Most importantly, both images reveal the text's consistent preference for the works of mortals over those of the gods. Further balanced images include the catalogue of herbs and flowers, which is opposed to the image of Aragnoll in his den. This parallel is important since the beneficial natural garden Clarion 'pastures' on is juxtaposed with Aragnoll – the embodiment of a malevolent artifice paradoxically occupying the same pastoral environment as the herbs and flowers. Art and Nature are ambiguously linked by symmetrical pairing. Finally, *Muiopotmos* begins and ends with parodic adaptations of Virgil, while the body of the text imitates and transforms Ovid.[13]

This symmetrical structure is the formal basis of *Muiopotmos*: the poem is like a diptych, hinged on the parallels between its discrete sections – or wings – of narrative and comment. As such, though the poem remains elusive, its parallels can help to orient the reader. The preference for Clarion's wings and Aragnoll's web over their divine counterparts has a cumulative impact suggestively in tension with the outcome of the tapestry competition. Though these parallels do not give a single 'answer' to *Muiopotmos*, they crucially alert the reader to its elaborate construction.

A Curious Generic Network

Allied to this formal symmetry, *Muiopotmos* is a patchwork of generic signals and parodic devices, which are frequently in tension with each

---

13 R. A. Brinkley, 'Spencer's *Muiopotmos* and the Politics of Metamorphosis', p. 672, argues that Arachne is an Ovidian poet while Pallas is a 'Vergillian/Augustan artist'. This reading is related to the idea that *Muiopotmos* comments on the Elizabethan political scene through a re-reading of Ovid and Virgil.

other.[14] So the narrative climax is initiated through a simile from tra-
ditional beast-fable (ll. 401–08); the narrator then invokes the 'Trag-
ick Muse' to help him 'to devise / Notes sad enough, t'expresse this
bitter throwe' (ll. 409–16). The fable image accords with Clarion's
physical status as a butterfly and sets in train moralistic expectations
about his death: as a lamb slaughtered by 'a wily Foxe', he may be
guilty of false security like the 'Kiddie' of the 'Maye' eclogue, or
indeed the shepherd of *Virgils Gnat.* But the invocation of
Melpomene contradicts this impression. It implies that Clarion is a
noble figure whose death has drastic implications for the human
community; as the text puts it, 'the drerie stownd is now arrived, /
That of all happines hath us deprived' (ll. 415–16) Only the death of
a tragic hero – or his parodic simulacrum – can have such an impact.
This crux reveals many of the tensions within *Muiopotmos.* The
reader must decide whether it is simply a parody of elevated genres,
or whether it has stronger connections with beast-fable and the com-
plaint mode, both of which have featured prominently in the for-
mulation of *Complaints'* poetics.

Parody in *Muiopotmos* is specialized; Spenser is not interested in
mock-heroic as a literary joke or as topical allegory. It coexists with
more important literary modes. These modes – including fable and
complaint – raise the question of how *Muiopotmos* functions sym-
bolically, and how it relates to the other *Complaints* as a miniature
poetics. Despite the beguiling presence of parody, we must be pre-
pared to read beyond the burlesque veneer.

In the first stanza, the narrator proposes the subject as an epic con-
flict in the manner of Virgil; he 'sing[s] of deadly dolorous debate, /
Stir'd up through wrathfull *Nemesis* despight' (ll. 1–2). But the sec-
ond stanza concentrates on the 'tragicall effect' of this 'debate' and

---

14 The best recent discussion of genre and *Muiopotmos* is in S. K. Heninger, Jr,
Sidney and Spenser: The Poet as Maker (University Park and London: Pennsylvania
State University, 1989), pp. 362–77. He sees essentially the same genres at work in
the poem as I do, but argues that the poem is at root Spenser's one successful essay
in Sidneyan mimesis, linking the poem with Sidney's definition of poetry as 'a speak-
ing picture'. My reading will tend to reverse this emphasis by suggesting that the
mimesis of *Muiopotmos* is distinctly un-Sidneyan: art has lost its didactic function.

invokes Melpomene's help in the delineation of Clarion's tragic fall
(ll. 9–16). The narrator is now less interested in 'open warre' than in
a metaphysical process. According to this invocation, the poem's real
subject is Clarion's 'declyne', and the 'rancour' which contributes to
the manufacture of tragic events. Yet the first two stanzas are not alto-
gether irreconcilable. Rhetorically, the distinction between the two
stanzas remains: the first proposes the poem's subject through epic
formulae, the second invokes the Muse of Tragedy. However, the first
stanza does not overtly contradict the tragic invocation of the second,
since it evokes '*deadly dolorous* debate' and '*mortall* fight'.[15] These epi-
thets are suggestive of both epic and tragedy. In classical criticism,
epic is usually described as the progenitor of tragedy: the different
genres share identical subject matter.[16] The verbal congruence
between these stanzas indicates that the apparently conflicting modes
of tragedy and epic may be drawn together in the ensuing text. As
Bond notes, the second stanza ends with a question directly imitated
from the start of the *Aeneid*.[17] Yet the major obstacle to this reading
is that the heroes 'Drawne into armes, and proofe of mortall fight' (l.
4) are no more majestic than a butterfly and a spider.

After the grandiose terminology of the first section, the third
stanza administers a comic jolt: 'Of all the race of silver-winged Flies
/ Which doo possesse the Empire of the Aire ... Was none more
favourable, nor more faire ... Then *Clarion*' (ll. 17–22). Despite the

15 My italics.

16 Heninger, *Sidney and Spenser*, pp. 362–77, explains the poem in terms of a
dualistic opposition between the premises of tragedy and epic. But the proposition
that tragedy and epic are thematic opposites is difficult to substantiate. Plato com-
ments in *The Republic* that Homer is 'the original master and guide of all the great
tragic poets'. In Plato, *The Republic*, trans. Desmond Lee (Harmondsworth: Pen-
guin, 1974), p. 422. In the *Poetics*, Aristotle shares this view and further notes that
'Epic differs from tragedy in the length of its plot and in its metre', which is essen-
tially a stylistic distinction. For Aristotle, see D. A. Russell and M. Winterbottom,
(eds), *Ancient Literary Criticism: The Principal Texts in New Translations* (Oxford:
Oxford University Press, 1972), pp. 95, 124. See also C. W. Macleod's reading of
'The *Iliad* as a tragic poem' in his edition of *Iliad* Book XXIV (Cambridge: Cam-
bridge University Press, 1982), pp. 1–8.

friction between epic and tragedy, the text has so far maintained that it is concerned with 'two mightie ones of great estate'. This claim must be re-evaluated once we discover that Clarion is a butterfly. The logical conclusion this stanza suggests to the contradictions of the first section (and of the poem as a whole) is that *Muiopotmos* is a parody of epic and tragedy. At one level, this is undoubtedly the case. This evidence has provided critics with the stimulus for the view that the poem is an historical allegory of various incidents in contemporary politics. If *Muiopotmos* is mock-heroic, the argument runs, Spenser must have had specific targets in mind who he wanted to parody. But unlike later mock-heroic satire, *Muiopotmos* contains no unequivocal topical referent to locate the literary joke in the external world.[18] Parody in *Muiopotmos* would seem to be an end in itself.

A purely parodic text exists chiefly as a literary joke, like Chaucer's *Sir Thopas*.[19] There are elements of this kind of writing in *Muiopotmos*: Spenser juxtaposes the rhetorical inflation of epic against the miniature 'debate' which he actually describes. But if *Muiopotmos* is read solely as a demonstration of literary humour and panache, its pertinence to *Complaints'* poetics can be overlooked. I suggest that its parodic elements are indicative of its concern with artistry. Where pure parody is a form of intellectual display, in this case parody stresses the literary liaisons between *Muiopotmos* and those texts

---

18 Court, 'The Theme and Structure of Spenser's *Muiopotmos*', traces the colourful critical career *Muiopotmos* has enjoyed as an historical allegory, though without any convincing historical moorings. Even Harold Stein, *Studies in Spenser's Complaints* (New York: Oxford University Press, 1934), p. 105, writing at the height of the enthusiasm for historical allegory as the hermeneutic arbiter of Spenserian texts, concedes that 'there seems to be no theory sufficiently substantiated to warrant any further assumptions about the poem other than that it may be allegorical and is delightful'. See Brice Harris, 'The Butterfly in *Muiopotmos*', for a more ambitious assay at historical allegory.

19 *Sir Thopas* has itself been read as an historical allegory; see Robinson's notes in Geoffrey Chaucer, *The Works*, ed. F. N. Robinson (London: Oxford University Press, 1957), pp. 736–37. More recently, however, J. A. Burrow has argued that the text 'is essentially a literary burlesque'. See his 'Chaucer's *Sir Thopas* and *La Prise Nuevile*', in *English Satire and the Satiric Tradition*, ed. Claude Rawson (Oxford: Blackwell, 1984), p. 55.

Spenser wishes to evoke. By making parodic contact with Virgil, Ovid, beast-fable and even contemporary herbalists,[20] Spenser draws attention to the textual network in which his poem is enmeshed. Appropriately for a poem which is concerned with the ambiguity of artifice, these parodic elements indicate that *Muiopotmos* exists through the referred context of those texts it imitates and parodies. To understand its network of allusion, the reader must appreciate what genres it appropriates.

Muiopotmos is frequently seen as an Ovidian narrative – or 'epyllion' – in the style of *Hero and Leander* and *Venus and Adonis*. This fashionable 1590s form exploits the erotic content and rhetorical variety of the *Metamorphoses* to explore sexuality in the novel form of a small epic.[21] Imitating the *Metamorphoses* both in heterodox narrative content and style, these poems range in tone from parody of epic and tragedy to a miniaturist delicacy which pays precise attention to detail, as in Marlowe's description of Hero's 'Buskins'.[22] Spenser's text has clear connections with this kind of writing. It includes two inset tales (one of which is directly imitated from *Metamorphoses* VI) which are, like their Ovidian prototypes, 'aetion' narratives.[23] Such stories explain the mythic causes of given phenomena, following Callimachus's *Aetia* (or *Causes*), itself one of Ovid's sources. The Astery and Arachne insets explain respectively why butterflies have beautiful wings, and why Aragnoll hates butterflies. Though *Muiopotmos* is not predominantly concerned with the erotic, Arachne's tapestry depicts Jove's abduction of Europa, tangentially aligning the text with the sexual agendas of Ovid's Elizabethan successors. *Muiopotmos's*

20 See Bond's notes in *YESP*, pp. 420–21.

21 For fuller discussions of the so-called 'epyllion', see Clark Hulse, *Metamorphic Verse: The Elizabethan Minor Epic* (Princeton: Princeton University Press, 1981); Roe in William Shakespeare, *The Poems*, ed. John Roe (Cambridge: Cambridge University Press, 1992), pp. 15–21.

22 *Hero and Leander*, ll. 31–36, in Christopher Marlowe, *The Complete Poems and Translations*, ed. Stephen Orgel (Harmondsworth: Penguin, 1971), p. 18. See also Shakespeare's description of Adonis's horse in *Venus and Adonis*, ll. 289–218, in Shakespeare, *The Poems*, pp. 95–96.

23 See E. J. Kenny's Introduction to A. D. Melville's translation of Ovid's *Metamorphoses* (Oxford and New York: Oxford University Press, 1987), pp. xxi–xxiv.

pervasive use of ecphrasis, and its consequent concern with the relationship between Art and Nature, is also apparent in the Ovidian texts.[24]

Despite its widespread comparison with these poems,[25] *Muiopotmos* is not a straightforward erotic narrative. Unlike Shakespeare and Marlowe, Spenser's usage of Ovid is problematic. The influence of Ovid jostles that of Virgil. The poem's final image is the unmetamorphosized body of Clarion dying like Virgil's Turnus. Though some critics view this simply as parodic – an 'artificial epic conclusion'[26] – the tone of this passage is elusive. For me it is indicative of the harsh, un-Ovidian theology at work in *Muiopotmos*, which excludes the possibility of regenerative metamorphosis.[27] *Muiopotmos* is also a miniature about insects and arachnids: though Ovidian narratives use parodic techniques, they rarely venture into a realm as specialized as that of Clarion and Aragnoll.

Muiopotmos's generic web must therefore include beast – or indeed insect – fable. As we have seen, the *Tale* is a self-conscious modification of the didactic expectations of traditional fable. Yet through the narrator, Spenser still articulates a traditional conception of fable's lowly place in the neo-classical hierarchy of literary kinds:

> No Muses aide me needes heretoo to call;
> Base is the style, and matter meane withall.[28]

The 'style' is 'base' *because* the 'matter' is 'meane' – of low literary and social status. Since his tale is both conceptually 'meane', and told in a 'Base' way, literary decorum dictates that the narrator should not invoke the 'aide' of any Muse. The 'lowness' of the beast-fable genre

24 Compare Shakespeare, *The Poems* pp. 95–96, and *The Rape of Lucrece*, ll. 1366–1575, pp. 208–16.

25 Compare Hulse, *Metamorphic Verse*.

26 Judith Dundas, '*Muiopotmos*: A World of Art', p. 37.

27 Compare the close of *Venus and Adonis*, where the dead Adonis is transformed into 'A purple flower', ll. 1165–88, in Shakespeare, *The Poems*, pp. 137–38.

28 *Mother Hubberds Tale*, ll. 43–44.

precludes the need of a neo-classical agent of inspiration.[29] Though the narrator's view is problematized by the parodic appearance of Jove and Mercury, this distinction between fable and the 'elevated' genres is traditional. Sidney sees Aesop as the type of the poet as 'the right popular philosopher':[30] fables are poetic food for the masses which needn't be rhetorically elevated to have an educative function.

Muiopotmos is a quintessentially neo-classical text: it invokes Melpomene, imitates Ovid, parodies Virgil and includes elaborate ecphrases. Since fable is a 'low' literary style, this poem is not a traditional fable. Yet neither is the *Tale*. As a working classification of *Muiopotmos*, beast-fable has certain advantages. Firstly, it allies *Muiopotmos* directly with the *Tale* as a text which modifies the fable tradition for its own purposes. The *Tale* problematizes the medieval assumption that fable can be allegorized didactically, *Muiopotmos* similarly shows the failure of didactic art to educate its percipients. In each case, Spenser uses a beast-fable to explore the limits of the didactic aesthetic. Secondly, the presence of fable allows the text's usage of the complaint mode to be read seriously rather than as an example of further parody. This is important, since it is through complaint that *Muiopotmos* – like the *Tale* – highlights the link between its narrative and its concern with poetics. *Muiopotmos*'s inset tales assert the power of the gods, while the narrator's complaints question divine equity. The complaint mode signals the problems in the gods' artistically reinforced hegemony.

To argue that *Muiopotmos* is a fable is to maintain that the story of Clarion and Aragnoll is a symbolic, or 'significant', narrative. As with the *Tale*, the story of the butterfly and the spider is anthropomorphic;

---

29 Compare Sidney's 'Lamon's Tale', which begins with a similar disclaimer: 'A shepherd's tale no height of style desires / To raise in words what in effect is low ... I then, whose burdened breast but thus aspires / Of shepherds two the silly case to show / Need not the stately Muses' help invoke.' In *Sir Philip Sidney* ed. Katherine Duncan-Jones (The Oxford Authors. Oxford and New York: Oxford University Press, 1989), p. 139. See also Helen Cooper, *Pastoral: Mediaeval into Renaissance* (Totowa, NJ: Rowman and Littlefield, 1977), p. 147.

30 Sir Philip Sidney, *Miscellaneous Prose of Sir Philip Sidney*, ed. Katherine Duncan-Jones and Jan Van Dorsten (Oxford: Clarendon, 1973), p. 87.

the protagonists are presented in terms of 'mortall' psychology. This is a 'significant' narrative not in the sense that it contains an on-going allegorical *significatio* – in the manner of a text like *The Pilgrim's Progress* – but because it is susceptible to the complex readings Spenser subjects it to. The 'fly-fate' of the title carries wide significance. This goes against the approaches of Weiner and Dundas, who argue that Clarion and Aragnoll are no more than an insect and an arachnid. In this view, there is a gulf between this ontological 'fact' and the text's implication that Clarion is capable of moral choice.[31] These critics are reacting against the traditional allegorical reading of *Muiopotmos*, typified by Allen's argument that the poem allegorizes the soul's fall into the world of the senses.[32] Weiner is probably right to be unconvinced by this reading since it depends on the dubious hypothesis of a link between butterflies and the Platonic idea of the soul in Spenser's text; questioning Allen should not however lead to the conclusion that Clarion and Aragnoll cannot 'stand for' rational beings. Rather, abandoning Allen's neo-Platonic allegory should encourage the adoption of a more nuanced attitude towards the poem's symbolic narration.

I suggest the most rewarding approach to *Muiopotmos* is one related to Alpers's reading of *The Faerie Queene*. Despite the vast difference in scale between the two texts, this comparison is justified both because the miniature was probably written while Spenser was preparing the first instalment of the epic for publication,[33] and because of their analogous narrative forms. Alpers argues that *The Faerie Queene* is not a restricted or iconographic allegory, in which described detail corresponds to a specific allegorical referent. He sees

31 See Andrew D. Weiner, 'Spenser's *Muiopotmos* and the Fates of Butterflies and Men', pp. 216–17; Judith Anderson, '"Nat worth a buterflye": p. 97; and Dundas, '*Muiopotmos*: A World of Art'.

32 See Don C. Allen, *Image and Meaning: Metamorphic Traditions in Renaissance Poetry*, pp. 20–41.

33 See *Var.* VIII, pp. 598–99, for critical conjecture about dating. While there is no conclusive proof, I incline on stylistic grounds towards a date in the late 1580s to early 1590s.

Spenser manipulating literary tradition to reveal 'the truths inherent in the traditions and conventions of poetry'.[34] Spenser's use of allegorical techniques is subordinate to his 'rhetorical mode' of addressing the reader while recycling conventional poetic vocabulary to delineate the psychological bases of human experience.[35] For Alpers, those readings which equate poetic images simplistically with allegorical referents dilute the full implications of *The Faerie Queene's* 'darke conceit'. *Muiopotmos* is also an example of this distinctively Spenserian mode of narration. The poem conveys more than its surface appears to, yet is impoverished by readings which seek to impose on it a single allegorical key.

Alpers's view has further implications for the reading of *Muiopotmos*. It accommodates the innovatory character of Spenser's usage of 'the traditions and conventions of poetry' throughout his oeuvre. Here Spenser exploits the fable tradition because of the symbolism inherent in fable narratives. The story of the butterfly and the spider is told as a symbolic enigma which the text may elucidate. Like the Fox and the Ape, Clarion and Aragnoll are described as rational creatures: Aragnoll bears a familial grudge against butterflies; Clarion is the 'careles' object of Muscaroll's paternal anxiety. Spenser's 'own kind of poetic narration'[36] is an idiosyncratic adaptation of the fable genre which continues the generic synthesis of the *Tale*.

Alpers's attention to the 'rhetorical mode' of *The Faerie Queene* helps to explain why *Muiopotmos* mixes so many different genres. As the epic's conventional diction signals Spenser's complex utilization of poetic tradition, so the miniature's blend of genres is a strategy through which Spenser explores the philosophical and critical assumptions within those traditional genres. The symbolic and exemplary attributes of fable allow Spenser to use Clarion's fate as an archetype through which to question the equity of the gods. The fable genre, as in Henryson, habitually voices social and philosophi-

---

34 Paul Alpers, *The Poetry of The Faerie Queene* (Princeton: Princeton University Press, 1967), p. 330.

35 *Ibid.*, pp. 3–35, 311–12.

36 *Ibid.*, pp. 174, 234.

cal quietism;[37] *Muiopotmos* turns this on its head by making the justice of Clarion's death its key problem. These questions are in turn raised by the incorporation of the complaint mode into the text. This juxtaposition of different modes heightens the poem's central enigma, expressed through Spenser's artful and innovatory manipulation of traditional genres. *Muiopotmos* is a symbolic and syncretic narration.

As such, it furthers the *Complaints* volume's innovatory usage of the complaint mode itself. The close connection between fable and complaint allows passages which are usually read as straightforward parody, like the tragic invocations, to be seen as potentially serious inquiries about cosmic justice. The complaint mode is Spenser's most immediate method of raising uncomfortable questions. Lines 209–40 constitute a complex reordering of a conventional disquisition on Fortune, directed towards inquiring 'Who then can save, what [the heavens] dispose to spill?' This passage resembles the aporetic complaints of the *Tale's* narrator, which highlight the disintegration of his normative values. Here the narrator's complaint offers contradictory explanations of Clarion's behaviour. The text seems to adopt a moralistic stance (ll. 217–20), but then addresses the gods' rôle in the manufacture of mortal fate. Such a complaint is the antithesis of the quietism counselled in the *Mirror for Magistrates*; *Muiopotmos's* narrator is prepared to contemplate the possibility that the gods' government of the cosmos is unjust.

As in all the major *Complaints*, the complaint mode is an integral part of Spenser's self-conscious poetics. Though this complaint is not explicitly concerned with literary issues, *Muiopotmos's* questioning of the gods' hegemony reflects on Venus and Pallas's deployment of art to assert their authority.

Briefly then, *Muiopotmos* makes generic contact with epic and tragedy through parody, the 1590s Ovidian narratives, beast-fable and the complaint mode. As in *The Ruines of Time*, its mixture of competing genres reveals the text's self-consciousness. Like *The Ruines of Time* and the *Tale*, form and content interpenetrate: the

37 See pp. 178–81 above.

symmetrical structure and generic mélange repeatedly reflect back
on the text's artful construction, as the text itself ponders other
artistic images. Despite the strangeness of the blend, the symbolic
quality of the fable genre has a determining impact on how the
poem is read. Spenser does not construct this elaborate fable sim-
ply in order to over-complicate the emblem of a butterfly in a spi-
der's web, but to get at the more significant artistic and theological
issues underlying the protagonists' conflict. As in the *Tale*, Spenser's
use of the fable genre is in tension with its traditional critical pro-
file. This tension is wholly appropriate for a poem concerned with
the ambiguity of artifice.

'A goodly worke': *Muiopotmos* on Poetry and Theology

My task is to elucidate the implications of *Muiopotmos*'s symbolism
to its interrelated concerns with justice and artistry. I argue that
Muiopotmos questions neo-classical theology, and specifically the
rôle the gods play in determining the fate of mortal beings. Inter-
secting with this theological debate, the poem's concern with the
ambiguity of artistry – witnessed both in the work of the gods and
the mortal protagonists – is a further development of the major
Complaints' self-conscious poetics. *Muiopotmos* follows the *Tale* not
just as a novel fable, but in its innovative recognition of the failure
of even divine didacticism. In Spenser's poetics, Art exhibits a 'won-
drous slight' which is no longer unambiguously at the service of
external moralism.

The figure of Clarion embodies both mortal fate and artificial self-
presentation. He is described not as an actual 'Flie' but as an epic
hero:

> Upon his head his glistering Burganet,
> The which was wrought with wonderous device,
> And curiously engraven, he did set ...
>
> Therein two deadly weapons fixt he bore,
> Strongly outlaunced towards either side,

> Like two sharpe speares, his enemies to gore:
> Like as a warlike Brigandine, applyde
> To fight, layes forth her threatfull pikes afore,
> The engines which in them sad death doo hyde:
> So did this flie outstretch his fearefull hornes,
> Yet so as him their terrour more adornes. (ll. 73–75; 81–88)

Clarion's antennae are transformed into 'weapons' firstly on the basis of a visual resemblance between butterflies' antennae and 'two sharpe speares', and secondly through parody of the Homeric trope of the hero arming himself for battle.[38] Yet the relation between metaphors and referents is problematic.[39] Since this parodic arming is also a description of a butterfly's body, to what anatomical feature can Clarion's 'glistering Burganet' be linked? Like the rest of his armour, it is not a natural part of his body. 'Wrought by wondrous device' it's an artificial accoutrement attached to the body of the Fly, who therefore becomes a work of art rather than an artfully described butterfly. Homeric parody allows Spenser to 're-embody' the butterfly in the terms of epic poetry. From parodic resemblance, the text ecphrastically reorders Clarion's butterfly-shape as an art-work.

At the climax of this mock-heroic arming, Clarion's wings are seen as 'Painted with thousand colours, passing farre / All Painters skill' (ll. 90–91). He 'dights' his wings in the manner of a soldier; they are artificial wonders, 'Painted' additions to the fly, desirable as art objects independent of their owner. In their elaboration, the wings resemble the ecphrastic shields of Achilles and Aeneas.[40] Yet they lack the shields' usefulness as armour; the wings' material beauty seems to be an end in itself:

---

38 See *The Iliad* XI.15–46 for the arming of Agammemnon.

39 See Anderson, '"Nat worth a buterflye"', pp. 94–95, who compares this passage with *The Nun's Priest's Tale* and usefully notes that 'We are more aware of Clarion as an object or as a vehicle of meaning than is the case with Chauntecleer'. See also Bender, *Spenser and Literary Pictorialism*, p. 163, who observes – rather uncomfortably – 'As a description, the comparison in series of these attributes with similar mythological objects remains fairly abstract, but the parts of the butterfly do come to the mind's eye'.

40 See *The Iliad* XVIII.408–678; *The Aeneid* VIII.625–731.

Full manie a Ladie faire, in Court full oft
Beholding them, him secretly envide,
And wisht that two such fannes, so silken soft,
And golden faire, her Love would her provide;
Or that when them the gorgeous Flie had doft,
Some one that would with grace be gratifide,
From him would steal them privily away,
And bring to her so precious a pray. (ll. 105–12)

As 'fannes', Clarion's wings appear thoroughly artificial. Spenser
describes the wings in seductively material terms – 'so silken soft, /
And golden faire'. These parallel adjectival phrases are not parallel in
meaning: 'silken soft' implies its grammatical reverse – 'soft silk' – or
'soft as silk'. The fabric of the wings is palpably 'soft' and 'silken'; the
two terms almost coalesce into a sensualized compound noun.
'Golden faire' is more abstract and more visual. The wings are 'faire',
that is beautiful and unblemished;[41] and 'golden', which suggests
both their beauty and their potential value. This implies that the
attractive wings would be attainable at a price; as the rest of the
stanza makes clear, they could conceivably be stolen on behalf of the
ambiguously 'faire' Court ladies. This description establishes that
the butterfly's wings are both works of art and potential commodi-
ties. Already Spenser begins to problematize the distinction between
Art and Nature. Clarion's wings are works of art which he himself
uses as opulent clothes (l. 91). Yet this stanza draws an implicit con-
trast between the innate fairness of the wings and the possibly cos-
metic beauty of the Court ladies. The wings embody the tension
throughout the arming of Clarion between the metaphorical
description of a 'real' butterfly and the ecphrastic rendering of a
work of art. This concentrated stanza insists both on the wings' arti-
ficiality and their residual, natural perfection. Their material
fragility shadows the ultimate fragility of their owner, either as a
naïve work of art or as a mortal butterfly.

---

41 Compare. *OED* 3: 'Free from blemish or disfigurement ... Free from moral
stain'.

The reader's difficulties equating the Herculean Clarion (ll. 70–72) with his butterfly anatomy are more than incidental to the parody. Clarion both is and isn't a butterfly: his anatomy is artificial – strapped on like the armour of a hero – yet is dangerously valuable because of its glamorous appearance. Clarion's arming raises the question of how these appendages perform in battle. That they offer no defence against Aragnoll's web suggests a more fundamental artificiality in Clarion. It could be argued that because the terms of his description are transparently hyperbolical, he is no more than an opportunity for poetic ornamentation which Spenser exploits. Yet artifice implies a covering which disguises something within, like Clarion's 'hairie hide of some wilde beast' which 'Made all that him so horrible did see, / Think him *Alcides* with the Lyons skin' (ll. 66, 70–71). At one level a butterfly cannot be anything like Hercules, yet Clarion's 'ornament' (l. 68) persuades viewers 'that him so horrible did see' to 'Think' of him in this way. Clarion's ornament is both the 'hide' in which he hides and the poetic covering which equates him rhetorically with epic heroes. Spenser's text clearly implies that there is something underneath these laboriously adopted coverings.

But what? Clarion's ontological status is, in this passage at least, enigmatic. His armour – and its ultimate ineffectiveness – suggests that Clarion is symbolically a naïve work of decorative art. His superfluous opulence is paralleled by the purposive, satanic, artifice of Aragnoll. Spenser is careful to disguise precisely what Clarion symbolizes. The reader is delighted by what seems to be simultaneously an ecphrastic rendering of a work of art and a continued parodic metaphor that describes a real butterfly. The tension in the description of Clarion is a valuable intimation of his function throughout the text: he is both a reflection on the nature of artifice and a mortal being.

While the Astery inset supplements the image of Clarion's wings, it constitutes an important change of tone as Spenser freights Clarion's story with theological concerns. The tale is the first instance of the unfair punishment of a mortal by the gods. Astery's transformation generates a tension between the gods' justice and the actual deserts of their mortal vassals:

Eftsoones that Damzel by her heavenly might,
She turn'd into a winged Butterflie,
In the wide aire to make her wandring flight;
And all those flowres, with which so plenteouslie
Her lap she filled had, that bred her spight,
She placed in her winges, for memorie
Of her pretended crime, though crime none were:
Since which that flie them in her wings doth
    beare. (ll. 137–44)

Though Astery's metamorphosis explains why butterflies have beautiful wings, the beauty of the insect should not obscure the severity of her punishment. Venus gives 'hastie credit to th'accuser' (l.135), punishing Astery 'Eftsoones' for the 'secret aide' her enemies said she received from Cupid in gathering flowers. So Venus acts without full consideration of Astery's guilt; her jealousy of Cupid and Psyche makes her take pre-emptive action against the innocent nymph. The flowers Venus puts into Astery's wings supposedly symbolize her error – 'for *memorie* / Of her pretended crime'.[42] While having flowers 'placed in her wings' is hardly as severe a punishment as wearing a scarlet letter, Venus's judicial intention is analogous to Hawthorne's: the criminal bears a monitory symbol of her crime. Yet as Astery's crime was 'pretended', so being 'turn'd' into a butterfly is something of a 'pretended' punishment. The beauty of the butterfly's wings becomes a paradoxical emblem of Astery's still 'unstained hewe' (l. 120). The Astery tale is a paradox which generates contrasts elsewhere in the poem. Astery's unmerited punishment gives butterflies beautiful wings; in *Muiopotmos* beauty is dangerous: the beautiful Clarion is susceptible to Aragnoll's envy, and is in danger of false security and the wrath of the gods. Similarly, Venus functions as a paradigm of the gods' behaviour towards mortals. Astery's fate is mirrored by Arachne's (and Europa's) while Clarion is the text's central victim of divine displeasure. The tale of Astery invites the reader to scrutinize the behaviour of the gods and ask whether the demonstrable unfairness of Astery's fate makes Clarion's correspondingly

42 My italic.

unjust. Early in the poem, it establishes the tensions within the gods' governance of mortal affairs, also drawing attention to the ambivalent quality of Clarion's beautiful inheritance from Astery. It displays Astery as the art-work created by Venus's 'heavenly might'; as both mortal and artifice, the butterfly embodies the gods' inequity and their amoral artistry.

Clarion's flight through 'the gay gardins' is a key ambiguity, offering two contradictory natural and artificial readings of his behaviour. The first (anticipating the readings of Weiner and Dundas) stresses the naturalness of butterflies 'Feeding … bounteouslie' (l. 151) on the natural world – Clarion blamelessly explores the gardens to find nourishment. The second views Clarion as an over-curious 'glutton' (l. 179) responsible for the spoliation of 'the pleasures of that Paradise' (l. 186). These readings symbolize the debate embodied in Clarion between Art and Nature. The pastoral adapts the popular topos of the creative contention between Art and Nature in a highly idiosyncratic way.[43] So Sidney claims that Art excels Nature because it depicts a 'golden' world superior to the fallen world of Nature.[44] Similarly, in the ecphrastic description of Lucrece's 'piece / Of skilful painting', Shakespeare comments 'A thousand lamentable objects there, / In scorn of nature, art gave liveless life'.[45] For both Sidney and Shakespeare, Art's triumph over Nature results from their concern with Art or poetry rather than Nature; the topos offers a brilliant hyperbole through which the writer expresses the power of Art. But in *Muiopotmos*, as the arming sequence demonstrates, Spenser is concerned to present Clarion as an anomalous blend of the natural and the artificial. The gardens epitomize Clarion's own ambiguity:

43 See Roe's discussion of the topos in *Venus and Adonis* in Shakespeare, *The Poems*), pp. 3–5. See also Dundas, *The Spider and the Bee*, Chapter 2, '"So Lively and So Like": The Pursuit of Illusion', pp. 34–67, for a full discussion of Spenser's reaction to the *paragone* of Art and Nature.

44 Sidney, *Miscellaneous Prose*, p. 78.

45 *The Rape of Lucrece*, ll. 1366–74; in Shakespeare, *The Poems*, p. 208.

There lavish Nature in her best attire,
Powres forth sweete odors, and alluring sights;
And Arte with her contending, doth aspire
T'excell the naturall, with made delights:
And all that faire or pleasant may be found,
In riotesse excesse doth there abound. (ll. 163–68)

This stanza is remarkable because it elides the differences between
Art and Nature in a way Sidney and Shakespeare do not. Since Art's
profile in the poem is already ambiguous, the faintly judgemental
description of Art's emulous attempt 'T'excell the naturall, with
made delights' is unsurprising. The text exemplifies precisely this
aspiration in its description of a butterfly as a work of art. What is
more surprising is the description of Nature in cognate terms. If Art's
'made delights' are dubious because of their manufacture, then
Nature's 'alluring sights' – the originals of Art's copies – are them-
selves not without danger. The 'riotesse excesse' pervading the garden
seems to be the result of a creative amalgam between Art and Nature.
This metaphoric marriage of Art and Nature is vital to *Muiopotmos*,
since it reveals that the ambiguity of artifice is paralleled by the ambi-
guity of the natural world. Like the world of art, which contains both
Clarion's wings and Aragnoll's web, the natural order is both 'good or
ill' (ll. 201–02), beneficial *and* noxious. The ambivalence of Nature
prepares the reader for the dénouement in which Clarion, the naïve
work of Art, will be killed by Aragnoll, the satanic artificer, at the
behest of the gods. The created world contains both 'The wholsome
Saulge' (l. 187) and Aragnoll who is 'The shame of', and a part of,
'Nature' (l. 245). Clarion is a microcosm of the contention, symbol-
ically revealing the ambiguities of both Art and Nature. Art is fragile
and cosmetic, while Nature is unpredictable and unsafe.

During the first narrative section (ll. 17–208), the text's focal con-
cern is Clarion's ambiguous ontology. This debate provides the initial
stimulus for the narrator's central complaint (ll. 209–40) which jux-
taposes a celebration of Clarion's hedonism with a lamenting analy-
sis of his fate. The 'natural' view of Clarion initially sees him as the
rightful 'Lord of all the workes of Nature', naturally entitled 'To take
what ever thing doth please the eie' (ll. 211–14). This optimism pro-

vokes an immediate reassessment, stressing in traditional terms the
transience of all creatures. The debate about Clarion's enigmatic sta-
tus is shelved as the narrator insists on his essential frailty as a 'vassal'
of the gods' will (l. 231). Neither Nature nor Art can fully conceal
Clarion's fragility.

The narrator's central complaint articulates a creaturely anxiety
about the position of mortal beings in a determined cosmos:

> And whatso heavens in their secret doome
> Ordained have, how can fraile fleshly wight
> Forecast, but it must needs to issue come?
> The sea, the aire, the fire, the day, the night,
> And th'armies of their creatures all and some
> Do serve to them, and with importune might
> Warre against us the vassals of their will.
> Who then can save, what they dispose
>   to spill? (ll. 225–32)

This stanza formulates a dualistic divide between degraded mortals –
'fraile fleshly wight[s]' – and the 'secret doome' of the 'heavens'. We
cannot 'Forecast' this 'secret doome'; what the gods will 'must needs
to issue come' irrespective of our finite projections. The natural
world here images the gods' 'Warre' against mortal beings; 'The sea,
the aire, the fire, the day, the night', are terrifying manifestations of
an inscrutable cosmos. This anxious view of creation resembles that
of Calvin, for whom 'the integrity of the universe and the survival of
mankind were … directly and constantly dependent on God's mys-
terious will'.[46] Natural phenomena like storms intimate the fragile
bases of terrestrial order: 'when the sun and moon rise up, they can
destroy the whole earth'.[47] The difference between Spenser and
Calvin is that Calvin's chaotic nature is held together by the Christ-
ian 'God's mysterious will'; in *Muiopotmos*, this deity is absent from
the tyrannical 'heavens'. This stanza concludes that whoever the gods

46 William J. Bouwsma, *John Calvin: A Sixteenth Century Portrait* (New York
and Oxford: Oxford University Press, 1988), pp. 33–34.
   47 *Ibid.*

'dispose to spill' cannot be saved. This grim assessment reflects on the fates of Astery and Arachne, who are decisively transformed by their contact with Venus and Pallas. Yet since the 'least mishap the most blisse alter may' (l. 220), mortal life is a treacherous battleground in which 'thousand perills lie in close awayte / About us daylie, to worke our decay' (ll. 221–22). Such an insight could easily shade into conventional quietism: since there can be no 'assurance'[48] of mortal happiness, the best option for Clarion, as for Churchyard's Mistress Shore, maybe to 'Defye this world, and all his wanton wayes'.[49]

But the complaint goes on to suggest that the gods' government is not only inscrutable, but also unjust. As in the tale of Astery, mortals can be the unwitting victims of a god's credulous jealousy. The announcement of Clarion's fate also develops the poem's case against the gods:

> Not thou, O *Clarion*, though fairest thou
> Of all thy kinde, unhappie happie Flie,
> Whose cruell fate is woven even now
> Of *Joves* owne hand, to worke thy miserie:
> Ne may thee helpe the manie hartie vow,
> Which thy olde Sire with sacred pietie
> Hath powred forth for thee, and th'altars sprent:
> Nought may thee save from heavens avengement. (ll. 233–40)

At one level, this stanza contrasts metaphorically the 'cruell fate' of a mortal being with its innate desire for continuance. This view would

---

48 The narrator's question, 'who can him assure of happie day; / Sith morning faire may bring fowle evening late' (ll. 218–19), may glance at the theological concept of assurance which held that 'the godly consideration of Predestination, and our Election in Christ is full of sweet, pleasant, and unspeakable comfort to godly persons ... because it doth greatly establish and confirm their faith of eternal Salvation to be enjoyed through Christ'; Article XVII, 'Of Predestination and Election', from the Thirty-Nine Articles of Religion (1571); in *The Book of Common Prayer*, p. 697. Appropriately for the pagan context of *Muiopotmos*, it is precisely such an 'assurance' which the narrator lacks. Compare Weiner, 'Spenser's *Muiopotmos*', and Alan Sinfield, *Literature in Protestant England, 1560–1660* (London: Croom Helm, 1983).

49 *Shores Wife* in Lily B. Campbell (ed.), *The Mirror for Magistrates* (Cambridge: Cambridge University Press, 1938; rpt. 1960), p. 386.

read the phrase 'Whose cruell fate is woven even now / Of *Joves* owne hand' as a hyperbolic periphrasis for Jupiter's planetary operation as a negative influence on fate.[50] Such a reading is surely erroneous. Since Jove's involvement in Clarion's fate parallels Venus's punishment of Astery, and prefigures his 'Imperiall' appearance in Pallas's tapestry (ll. 308–12), it's unlikely that this Jove is just an astrological symbol. Jove is the active 'weaver' of Clarion's fate – a further demonstration of the gods' ambiguous use of artifice.[51] This formulation deftly combines both the cruelty of the gods' governance and its artistic design.

Clarion's fate is 'heavens avengement'; yet there is no explanation of how he has offended the gods. At this crucial moment, the reader is left unsure how to interpret the narrator's commentary. The poem's other victims of divine displeasure offer illuminating counterpoints. Arachne's hubris causes her transformation; Astery's punishment is undeserved. Clarion's fate bisects these extremes: though he has done little to merit his death, like the shepherd in *Virgils Gnat*, he may be culpably naïve. He becomes enmeshed in the graphic oxymoron: an 'unhappie happie Flie'.[52] He is 'unhappie' in his bad fortune, which will result in his death. 'Unhappie' also means 'unfortunately happening' – Clarion's death is not just bad luck, it is an evil occurrence, an un-hap brought about by the gods' arbitrary malevolence. Conversely, Clarion remains 'happie' in his birth and his beauty. His existence remains a fortunate gift, a good hap he enjoys. The oxymoron highlights the typological similarity of Clarion and the epic heroes his story parodies. Like Achilles, he has the 'unhappie happie' fate of dying a young death. He does not 'declyne' into old age and its atten-

50 See De Lacy's view, summarized in *Var.* VIII, p. 400, that 'Jove is here the planet rather than the god … for the god himself was subject to fate, and in astrology Jupiter "in certain positions and certain mundane houses … is powerful for evil."'

51 Spenser only uses the verb 'woven' in this case as a metaphor for Jove's manufacture of Clarion's fate. See below, p. 248, for the verbs used in the tapestry competition.

52 Heninger, *Sidney and Spenser*, p. 376, also draws attention to the importance of this epithet.

dant anxieties, imaged in the helpless figure of his own 'olde Sire'. Instead he leaves his body, Turnus-style, as an aesthetisized 'spectacle of care'. His fate may be 'cruell' and subject to tragic treatment, but Clarion gains significance through literary analogy. 'Unhappie happie' both coheres and contradicts: like his flight through the gardens, it constitutes a drastic interpretative crux. Both adjectives are equally true and untrue, since the reader cannot be sure whether Clarion has decisively contributed to his 'hap' or not. The words of the poem hold this problem in a taut suspension; Clarion remains enigmatic.

The central complaint is then not just a hinge between the presentation of Clarion and that of Aragnoll; it focuses attention on the question of the equity of Clarion's fate. Though this is foreshadowed in the Astery inset, the initial description of Clarion presents him chiefly as an amalgam of artifice and instinct. The narrator's complaint maintains Clarion's ambiguous status, but stresses that he is a mortal rather than a god, whose tenure in the gardens is necessarily transitory. By the opening of the second major section of narrative, Clarion's embodiment of the contention between Art and Nature is sharpened by the recognition of his impending doom. As the complaint points out, 'except a God, or God him guide' (l. 223) nobody – however blessed with the 'lavish' gifts of Art and Nature – can escape this 'sad hap and howre unfortunate' (l. 421).

The second narrative 'wing' of *Muiopotmos* presents Aragnoll as the symbolic opposite of Clarion. Where Clarion is a naïve, mortal work of art, Aragnoll is a malevolent artificer; where Clarion is the object of the gods' wrath, Aragnoll is the agent through which their 'avengement' is enacted:

> It fortuned (as heavens had behight)
> That in this gardin, where yong *Clarion*
> Was wont to solace him, a wicked wight
> The foe of faire things, th'author of confusion,
> The shame of Nature, the bondslave of spight,
> Had lately built his hatefull mansion,
> And lurking closely, in awayte now lay,
> How he might anie in his trap betray. (ll. 241–48)

Aragnoll's rôle as the divinely appointed avenger is immediately apparent. The 'fortune' which generates Clarion's 'cruell fate' also orders ('behight') that Aragnoll should be 'lurking closely, in awayte' for this 'hap'. But Aragnoll also embodies an active evil; as 'The foe of faire things' he parallels Clarion's beauty; as 'th'author of confusion' and 'bondslave of spight', he is a satanic figure. Aragnoll is the innately 'wicked' instrument of the gods' will. The questions raised by the narrator's complaint about the gods' equity become acute, since the divine will is expressed through an evil creature. In brief, the gods' employment of Aragnoll questions the purpose of evil and the suffering it creates. How can just gods tolerate evil and mortal suffering? Augustinian Christianity negotiates this problem by arguing that as God shows 'His benevolence in *creating* good Natures, He shows his Justice in *exploiting* evil wills'.[53] Milton uses this argument to explain why God tolerates Satan's 'dark designs'; in a Christian teleology, Satan's 'malice served but to bring forth / Infinite goodness, grace and mercy shown / On man by him seduced'.[54] God exploits Satan's 'malice' to save man. *Muiopotmos* lacks any such redemptive paradox. Aragnoll is here simply the means by which the gods' mysterious revenge is executed. The alignment of evil and the gods' will is unequivocal. This stanza carries the anxieties of the central complaint into the body of the narrative by indicating that the neo-classical gods cannot be reconciled with the redemptive and sacramental God of Christianity. The gods' 'cruelty' is as innate as Aragnoll's 'olde / Enfestred grudge' (ll. 353–54) against butterflies.

Aragnoll also embodies the ambiguity of art. He is the 'hatefull' 'author' not just of 'confusion', but also of his ominous 'mansion' and 'trap'. The text progresses from Clarion's naïve decoration to a series of skilful, amoral weavers. Jove's 'cruel hand' begins an artistic design which is completed by Aragnoll's 'cursed cobweb'.

The Arachne inset unites the divergent strands of theological necessity, mortal presumption, and the ambiguity of artifice to offer

53 C. S. Lewis, *A Preface to Paradise Lost* (London: Oxford University Press, 1942), p. 67. Lewis is paraphrasing Augustine's *City of God* XI, 17.

54 *Paradise Lost* I.209–20.

a resolution in Pallas's tapestry. This constitutes a successful marriage between didacticism and decoration. Yet even after Pallas's totalizing artifice, Clarion's fate remains a potent anomaly. Pallas's precedent does not give her – or the didactic aesthetic she symbolizes – ultimate control of *Muiopotmos*.

The inset is a subtle adaptation of its Ovidian source.[55] In the *Metamorphoses*, the competition between Pallas and Arachne is part of a group of tales concerned with contests between gods and mortals, in which the gods invariably defeat their presumptuous opponents.[56] So Golding viewed the tale as an illustration of the moral 'that folk should not contend / Against their betters, nor persist in error to the end'.[57] As Spenser would have been aware, this reading oversimplifies Ovid's text.[58] Since the Arachne story follows the singing contest between the Muses and Pierides, Ovid establishes a liaison between poetry and tapestry as related mimetic art forms. Spenser adapts Ovid by using visually and poetically metaphorical verbs to describe the process of weaving: Arachne 'figur'd' and 'pictur'd', whereas Pallas 'made'.[59] The different verbs are suggestive of the different aesthetics underlying the tapestries. Even in Ovid, the Arachne story is a debate about aesthetics.

55 See *Var.* VIII, pp. 400–01, for Reed Smith's summary of the differences between Ovid and Spenser's versions.

56 From V.294 to VI.400, Ovid narrates a series of such contests and divine revenges, including the stories of Niobe and Marysas.

57 Arthur Golding, *Shakespeare's Ovid: Golding's Translation of the Metamorphoses*, ed. W. H. D. Rouse (London: Centaur, 1961); 'The Epistle', ll. 121–22, p. 3. Golding's version of the Arachne story is also conveniently reprinted in *The Penguin Book of Renaissance Verse 1509–1659*, ed. David Norbrook and H. R. Woudhuysen (Harmondsworth: Allen Lane, The Penguin Press, 1992), pp. 671–76.

58 Compare Jonathan Bate, *Shakespeare and Ovid* (Oxford: Clarendon, 1993), p. 31: 'Golding's Epistle probably constituted Shakespeare's only sustained direct confrontation with the moralizing tradition – that is, if he bothered to read it and did not skip straight to the English text ... [*Metamorphoses*] had an energetic life as a linguistic resource that could not be contained by the work of moralization'.

59 Compare lines 277, 289, 305, 329. Golding, following Ovid, uses visual metaphors interchangeably ('painted', 'picturde' and 'portray') for both tapestries; see Norbrook and Woudhuysen (eds), *The Penguin Book of Renaissance Verse* pp. 671–76.

This debate takes place in Ovid and Spenser's ecphrases. Paraphrasing Bender, ecphrasis is the literary description of real or imagined works of visual art.[60] Though Baxandall has linked early humanist ecphrasis with the development of a sophisticated critical appreciation of actual works of art,[61] the tapestries of Ovid and Spenser evoke changing, quasi-cinematographic images in narrative sequence rather than the static 'frames' of a genuine *historia*. Spenser's Europa is visualized simultaneously looking at the land, calling 'her play-fellowes aide', holding up the hem of her dress, and travelling further out into the sea (ll. 281–88). Description of an imaginary tapestry gives way to the telling of a tale. The most celebrated instance of this kind of ecphrasis in classical poetry is Virgil's description of the pictures of the Trojan War in the Temple of Juno in *Aeneid* I; Shakespeare's evocation of Lucrece's 'piece / Of skilful painting' imitates this original. Such ecphrasis offers a symbolic image which reflects on the narrative it emerges from.[62] Similarly, both Ovid and Spenser's descriptions of the tapestries embody the conflict between the goddess and the girl through two opposing visions of the relationship between the gods and mortals. Spenser self-consciously modifies Ovid by presenting Pallas's tapestry as a humanist didactic text, which is in turn undermined by the wider context of *Muiopotmos*. Ecphrasis is the means through which Spenser introduces poetic concerns to the surface of his text.

Though Spenser's version is a recognizable imitation of the Ovidian original, it constitutes a more schematic encounter between the human and the divine. Spenser's Pallas comes 'down to prove the truth' (l. 267) that she is the better weaver without the elaborate contextualization employed by Ovid; all the reader is told about Arachne is that she has 'rashly dar'd / The Goddesse selfe to chalenge to the field' (ll. 269–70). Pallas and Arachne are divine and human oppo-

60 Bender, *Spenser and Literary Pictorialism*, p. 51n. See also pp. 162–67, where *Muiopotmos* is interpreted as an extended ecphrasis.

61 Michael Baxandall, *Giotto and the Orators: Humanist Observers of Painting in Italy and the Discovery of Pictorial Composition* (Oxford: Clarendon, 1971), pp. 85–87, 90–96.

62 Compare Roe's note in Shakespeare, *The Poems*, pp. 284–85.

sites; the result of their competition will have a bearing on *Muiopot-mos's* wider exploration of the relation between gods and mortals. This symbolic depiction of the encounter contrasts strongly with that of Ovid, who stresses the comic similarity between Pallas and Arachne, their equality in talent, temper and vanity. Spenser simply notes the enormous rashness of Arachne's challenge: she is a 'pre-sumptuous Damzel' up against the power of 'The Goddesse selfe'.

Unlike their Ovidian counterparts, Spenser's tapestries are not artistically equal because of this ontological gulf between their weavers. In *Muiopotmos*, Arachne's tapestry is a superbly realized image of Europa and the Bull (ll. 277–96). Spenser retains one image from the mélange of divine rapes depicted by Ovid's Arachne and her implicit concern with 'the lewdnesse of the Gods'.[63] The narrator's framing comment ambiguously reworks Ovid's tribute to the aes-thetic perfection of Arachne's work:

> ultima pars telae, tenui circumdata limbo,
> nexilibus flores hederis habet intertextos.
>
> Non illud Pallas, non illud carpere Livor
> possit opus: doluit successu flava virago
> et rupit pictas, caelestia crimina, ... [64]

> And round about, her worke she did empale
> With a faire border wrought of sundrie flowres,
> Enwoven with an Yvie winding trayle:

63 Golding in Norbrook and Woudhuysen, *The Penguin Book of Renaissance Verse*, p. 675.

64 Ovid, *Metamorphoses*, The Loeb Classical Library, 2 vols, ed. and trans. F. J. Miller (Cambridge, Mass. and London: Harvard University Press, 1916), Vol. I, pp. 296–97. Miller's translation: 'The edge of the web with its narrow border is filled with flowers and clinging ivy intertwined. Not Pallas, nor Envy himself, could find a flaw in that work. The golden haired goddess was indignant at her success, and rent the embroidered web with its heavenly crimes.' Golding's version makes a more causal link between Arachne's subject matter and Pallas's vandalism: 'Who there-upon did rende the cloth in pieces every whit, / Bicause the lewdnesse of the Gods was blased so in it'; in Norbrook and Woudhuysen, *The Penguin Book of Renaissance Verse*, p. 675.

A goodly worke, full fit for Kingly bowres,
Such as Dame *Pallas*, such as Envie pale,
That al good things with venemous tooth devowres,
Could not accuse. Then gan the Goddese bright
Her selfe likewise unto her worke to dight. (ll. 297–304)

Ovid signals Pallas's realization that she has not won the competition. Since no technical flaw can be found in Arachne's work, Pallas resorts to violence to humble her opponent. In *Muiopotmos* the narrator's comment effects the transition from Arachne's tapestry to Pallas's; since this is the half-way point in the competition, the comment has different implications from Ovid's.

Spenser deviates from Ovid in stressing the tapestry's function as erotica. Line 300, 'A goodly worke, full fit for Kingly bowres', indicates its skilful manufacture and its potential as a decoration for a regal boudoir.[65] 'Full fit for kingly bowres', Arachne's work is defined as a fashionable hanging of the same genre as the 'costly clothes of *Arras* and of *Toure*' which decorate the erotically charged dwellings of Malacasta and Busirane in *The Faerie Queene* Book III.[66] This is an important parallel, since in both these passages, Spenser's delight in artifice coexists with an underlying awareness of the moral limitations of art; as Dundas observes, 'The art object may be fully appropriate to the lustful setting but it also partakes of the same sin'.[67] By indicating that Arachne's tapestry deserves a 'lustful setting', Spenser highlights the moral ambivalence of erotic art in a way which Ovid does not.

Spenser also inserts an original line into a passage which is otherwise straight translation, further altering the character of the comment. Spenser concurs with Ovid that Arachne's tapestry was 'A goodly worke', and that neither 'Dame *Pallas*' nor 'Envie pale' could

65 Compare *OED* 'bower' 2a and b, 'An inner apartment … a bedroom … A boudoir'. The Bower of Bliss combines these meanings with *OED* 3, 'A shady recess, arbour'.

66 III.I.34ff and III.XI.28ff; in *FQ*, pp. 311, 406.

67 Dundas, *The Spider and the Bee*, p. 53.

find fault with it. Line 302 heightens the description of Envy by noting, almost gratuitously, that it 'al good things with venemous tooth devowres'. This powerful statement of Envy's universal malignity overturns the explicit sense of the sentence. The implication is that, as 'A *goodly* worke', the tapestry will ultimately serve Envy's appetite for 'all good things'.[68] The narrator's praise of Arachne's tapestry reveals its vulnerability as a piece of decorative opulence. As such, the tapestry recalls Clarion's status as a similarly fragile artifice. Just as Spenser seems closest to Ovid, he introduces a trope from the complaint tradition which allows him to highlight the paradoxical flimsiness of human artifice. This miniature complaint against Envy anticipates the close of *The Faerie Queene* Book VI, where Spenser laments that even his 'homely verse' cannot 'Hope to escape' the Blatant Beast's 'venemous despite' (VI.XII.41).[69] Art – however 'homely' or 'fit for kingly bowres' – is not immune to Envy's 'venemous tooth'. This point has a pivotal bearing on *Complaints'* poetics. After Verlame's naïve confidence in poetry's power to 'eternize', the major *Complaints* have consistently stressed the limitations of art's preservative and educative qualities. Like the *Tale*, *Muiopotmos* illustrates the difference between art's idealized powers and its actual limitations.

Pallas's tapestry is a thematic response to the moral failings which she sees in Arachne's work and a corrective exemplum of her moralistic aesthetic. As in the *Metamorphoses*, Pallas's image 'of the old debate, / Which she with *Neptune* did for *Athens* trie' (ll. 305–06) lacks visual detail in comparison with Arachne's; it is a dry, ponderous theme described in cold, non-figurative language:

> Twelve Gods doo sit around in royall state,
> And Jove in midst with awfull Majestie,
> To judge the strife betweene them stirred late:
> Each of the Gods by his like visnomie
> Eathe to be knowen; but Jove above them all,
> By his great lookes and power Imperiall. (ll. 307–12)

---

68 My italics.
69 *FQ*, p. 709.

Pallas's Jove is clearly not the 'true Bull' which is 'so lively seene' in Arachne's work (ll. 279–80). But this is the purpose of her tapestry. Since Arachne's tapestry is a sensualized erotic image with an ambiguous function, Pallas eschews pure decoration. She portrays the gods through their 'like visnomie' rather than in the transmuted form of a bull. Pallas's work attempts the harder artistic feat of depicting Jove's 'great lookes and power Imperiall' as they actually are. Like Milton's God, such an image of 'awfull Majestie' does not readily lend itself to the sensual detail of Europa's 'daintie feete, and garments gathered neare' (l. 284).[70] Because of its grandiose subject, Pallas's tapestry exceeds Arachne's erotic image both as a portrayal of an epic incident and a symbolic icon of the gods as embodiments of equity. Spenser's description indicates the seriousness of the issues at stake in 'the olde debate':

> Before them stands the God of Seas in place,
> Clayming that sea-coast Citie as his right,
> And strikes the rockes with his three-forked mace;
> Whenceforth issues a warlike steed in sight,
> The signe by which he chalengeth the place,
> That all the Gods, which saw his wondrous might
> Did surely deeme the victorie his due:
> But seldome seene, forejudgement proveth true. (ll. 313–20)

The 'debate' is an inset miniature of the tapestry competition. The gods produce contrasting 'signes' – the horse and the 'fruitfull Olyve tree' (l. 326) – to assert their respective 'rights' to Athens. As the first god to produce his 'signe', Neptune parallels Arachne in producing an image so powerful that 'all the Gods ... Did surely deeme the victorie his due'. Arachne's tapestry also appears to be a sure winner. But this stanza articulates a cautionary moral against such 'forejudgement'. As such, Pallas's work engages directly with the issues at stake in her competition with Arachne and in the wider narrative of Clarion's fate. By

70 Compare Bender, *Spenser and Literary Pictorialism*, pp. 166–67, who reads the competition solely on decorative criteria and articulates the reader's aesthetic hunch that Arachne should win. Hence his comment that Pallas's tapestry 'is a fairly dull picture' avoids any consideration of the symbolic values it contains.

dramatizing the moment at which the gods believe Neptune must 'surely' win, Pallas draws attention to the gulf between expectation and what actually happens. Pallas's quasi-moralistic attack on 'fore-judgement' reflects both on Arachne's presumption and Clarion's false security. While Muscaroll 'forered',[71] or predicted, that Clarion 'would sure prove such an one, / As should be worthie of his fathers throne' (ll. 29–32), Pallas points out that such predictions are almost fore-doomed to disappointment. Pallas's tapestry embodies a didactic warning to Arachne, Clarion, and the reader against 'forejudgement'.

While Ovid makes it clear that Pallas won the contest for Athens, Spenser carefully avoids concluding the story. Instead, he artfully juxta-poses Neptune's 'signe' with Pallas's 'fruitfull Olyve tree' and the admiration which this causes. Though the reader can assume that Pallas won, since her tapestry is triumphantly framed 'with a wreathe of Olyves hoarie' (l. 328), her tapestry avoids 'forejudgement' by keeping the result of 'the olde debate' notionally (and wittily) in the balance. Pallas creates a didactic text which playfully adheres to its own prescriptions.

This tapestry is not just a didactic fable. Pallas clinches victory through her perfect mimesis of a butterfly, uniting didacticism with a decorative opulence which exceeds even Arachne's:

> Emongst those leaves she made a Butterflie,
> With excellent device and wondrous slight,
> Fluttring among the Olives wantonly,
> That seem'd to live, so like it was in sight:
> The velvet nap which on his wings doth lie,
> The silken downe which on his back is dight,
> His broad outstretched hornes, his hayrie thies,
> His glorious colours, and his glistering eies.

---

71 I take this word to be the past participle of 'foreread', meaning to 'signify beforehand' or 'predict'; in context this would mean Clarion's youth foretold to Muscaroll that his son would be a worthy heir to him. Morris's gloss of 'foretold', in *The Works of Edmund Spenser* (The Glove Edition. London: Macmillan, 1869; 1897), p. 720, is therefore to be preferred to Smith and De Selincourt's 'betokened' in *The Poetical Works of Edmund Spenser* (London: Oxford University Press and Humphrey Milford, 1932), p. 686.

> Which when *Arachne* saw, as overlaid,
> And mastered with workmanship so rare,
> She stood astonied long, ne ought gainesaid,
> And with fast fixed eyes on her did stare,
> And by her silence, signe of one dismaid,
> The victorie did yeeld her as her share:
> Yet did she inly fret, and felly burne,
> And all her blood to poysonous rancor turne. (ll. 329–44)

In Ovid, Pallas sidesteps objective judgement of the tapestries through her tantrum: she reacts angrily to Arachne's representation of the gods as sexual criminals, and settles the contest through violence. Spenser rewrites this part of the story. Through her marginal butterfly Pallas demonstrates an artifice superior to Arachne's 'goodly worke': Pallas has 'made a Butterflie', a mimetic image that 'seem'd to live' even more than Arachne's 'true sea, and true Bull' (l. 280). She has beaten Arachne at her own decorative game. This is Arachne's reading of Pallas's tapestry: she focuses on the butterfly, which convinces her that she has been 'mastered with workmanship so rare'. Through her astonished silence she becomes a 'signe' of acknowledged defeat.

The different weavers' different aesthetics are shown in the verbs that describe the artistic process. Arachne's verbs, 'figur'd' and 'pictur'd', suggest a decorative pictorialism which can represent three-dimensional objects and narrative scenes with ingenuity. These verbs also metaphorically describe the process of poetic composition, as in Spenser's use of portraiture as a metaphor for his poetic task in the proem to *The Faerie Queene* III.[72] But here these verbs render the figurative decoration which is the cornerstone of Arachne's aesthetic. Pallas's main verb is the unequivocally poetic 'made'. Sidney uses the Greek derivation of 'poet' as 'maker' to highlight Art's supremacy over Nature, and to establish the crucial humanist correlation between the mortal poet and 'the heavenly Maker of that maker'. A 'maker' is for Sidney a moral artist, whose mimesis has 'this end, to

72 *FQ*, pp. 304–05.

teach and delight'.[73] As the work of a divine 'maker' then, Pallas's tapestry embodies this didactic aesthetic.[74]

Yet Arachne's response to Pallas's tapestry is vitally incomplete. The ecphrasis of Arachne's tapestry stresses its decorative opulence. Such perfection, 'workmanship so rare', is exactly what Arachne sees in Pallas's butterfly: a mimetic beauty which she cannot equal. Her recognition of this produces her inward agitation and transforms into a spider. While Spenser does not make the cause of her metamorphosis explicit, lines 343–44 imply that she is tormented by 'Envy pale'; her 'rancor' is awakened by the 'workmanship' displayed in Pallas's 'excellent device'. Arachne's response is triggered by a detail in the margin of Pallas's work, rather than by its didactic totality. Though Spenser acknowledges the importance of this border by according it a self-contained stanza, as a border it remains a decorative adjunct to Pallas's central design. Arachne misses Pallas's didactic point.

The tapestry competition is then a contest between two different aesthetics. Arachne's tapestry is a decorative image with an erotic and controversial subtext. Spenser dilutes the controversial side of her work by focusing on one divine rape, rather than the eighteen depicted by Ovid's Arachne.[75] Her once-comprehensive indictment of the gods' relations with mortals is transformed into a mildly salacious image. Arachne's tapestry maintains *Muiopotmos*'s wider concern with divine justice in the context of an art-work whose primary purpose is as a decorative ornament. By contrast, Pallas incorporates decoration in the same frame as a complex symbolic 'storie'. Like Arachne's, her tapestry contains a mythical narrative and a perfect representation of the phenomenal world; it also includes a warning against 'forejudgement' and a hierarchical image of the gods in council. This conveys an idea of the gods' fundamental equity: they 'sit around in royall state ... To judge the strife' between Pallas and Neptune. For the artist-goddess, these images embody divine justice and

73 Sidney, *Miscellaneous Prose*, pp. 77–80.
74 See pp. 18–22 above.
75 See Ovid, *Metamorphoses* (1916), Vol. I, pp. 294–97.

rectitude. In its totality therefore, Pallas's tapestry is a humanist text which 'makes' a convincing representation, both in its detail and symbolism, of the world as the justly-ordered province of just gods.

Pallas's tapestry contrasts with the wider narrative which sees the 'fate' ordained by the gods as arbitrary and cruel. Though her tapestry is a Sidneyan 'speaking picture',[76] the tension between Pallas's view of fate and that of the main narrative cannot be ignored.

The Arachne inset is a crux which juxtaposes the certainty of Pallas's theology and aesthetics with the uncertainty generated by the central complaint and Clarion's death. The reader must decide whether the gods are benevolent arbiters of fate, or cruel masters at war with 'fraile fleshly wight[s]'. The brilliance of *Muiopotmos* is that it raises these theological issues in tandem with poetics and the ambiguity of artifice. Pallas's use of didactic art to support the concept of divine equity may imply the existence of a causal nexus between her divine skill and the moral she embroiders. Her art reproduces the correct view of divine governance. But equally, Spenser's characterization of Pallas's skill as 'excellent device and wondrous slight' may suggest that her victory is another instance of the gods' unfair power over mortals. In which case, its moral would ironically mirror the injustice of Clarion's death.

At one level, Pallas provides a coherent, god-oriented view of fate. 'Forejudgment' or any kind of 'Forecast' is unwise; Pallas may imply that fate is outside the gods' control. She also displays the gods as an imposing hierarchy, centred on Jove's 'awful Majestie' and supreme 'power Imperiall'. Jove is the heart of Pallas's tapestry; he dominates his daughter's world-view. The butterfly's placement in the margin of the tapestry indicates the subordinate status of the phenomenal world: the butterfly is a symbolic 'vassal' of the gods' 'will'. By incorporating this image within her border, Pallas suggests that there is a rightful place for such 'vassals' in the Jove-governed universe. The butterfly symbolizes the gods' control of mortal fate, and their authority to define what place each mortal should occupy and in art

76 Sidney, *Miscellaneous Prose*, p. 80; compare Heninger, *Sidney and Spenser*, pp. 362–77, and note 14 above.

what subjects should be depicted. Butterflies are properly marginal to the great debates of the gods.

This pious view of fate is not supported by the rest of *Muiopotmos*. As the central complaint articulates, Jove 'weaves' Clarion's 'cruell fate' through the agency of Aragnoll. This powerfully suggests the malignity of fate manufactured by the gods. Pallas's qualification of the gods' foreknowledge (ll. 318–20) creates a tension within her theology: either they have an absolute authority over mortal life or they do not. Pallas's equivocation reveals the weak link in her argument. If 'all the Gods', and specifically the otherwise all-powerful Jove, are ignorant of the result of the 'debate' for Athens, then their control of fate is conditional, as in Homer's theology. But if Jove does have absolute foreknowledge, Pallas's equivocation paradoxically implies that the narrator's complaint is correct and that her tapestry is theologically mendacious. Her 'slight' would denote not just her mimetic skill, but also the deception she 'makes'. Despite its aesthetic, Pallas's tapestry does not convey a Christian idea of fate. Jove fails to shadow the Christian God because both Pallas and the narrator agree that his government rests solely on ambiguous power; if he controls fate, he does so arbitrarily and without the Christian God's redemptive teleology; if fate is external to him, his power cannot be compared with 'Th'eternall Makers majestie'.[77] The neo-classical gods' authority is constructed on a shifting metaphorical ground: Jove may have 'great lookes and power Imperiall' to Pallas, but the Ovidian corpus of stories equally reveals him as a bull. The brilliance of Pallas's tapestry does not give it the final authority of philosophical coherence. While the Arachne inset explains why Aragnoll hates butterflies, the artistic competition does not unequivocally sanction one theology or aesthetic.

So Clarion's death remains unaltered by Pallas's intervention and returns to the theological rumination of the central complaint. The balanced image of Aragnoll's net reiterates the narrator's preference (first shown in the comparison of Clarion's wings with Cupid's) for mortal rather than divine artifice. Not only is Aragnoll's 'curious

77 *The Teares of the Muses*, l. 512.

networke' a finer piece of cunning than Vulcan's net; this allusion comically undermines Pallas's image of divine dignity:

> Ne doo I thinke, that that same subtil gin,
> The which the *Lemnian* God framde craftilie,
> *Mars* sleeping with his wife to compasse in,
> That all the Gods with common mockerie
> Might laugh at them, and scorne their shamefull sin,
> Was like to this. (ll. 369–74)

Plato would have censored Homer's version of this story from his republic precisely because its image of the gods was 'hardly suitable to encourage the young to self-control'.[78] To convey the skilful artifice of Aragnoll's web, Spenser chooses a scandalous image which had constituted a key example in Plato's case against poets. With a single stroke, Spenser symbolizes the ambiguity of mortal artifice – Aragnoll's web is not 'like to this', it is finer – and the moral ambiguity of the neo-classical pantheon. The gods' final appearance in *Muiopotmos* is as divine adolescents, indulging in 'common mockerie' of their colleagues, not as sage governors.

The object of these gods' revenge is conversely shown as a type of false security, lacking 'Suspition of friend, nor feare of foe' (l.377). The mode of Clarion's death suggests that he errs in his interpretation of the world. He believes that he can walk 'at will … In the pride of his freedom principall' (ll. 379–80) in his father's kingdom. Fortified by the central complaint, the reader knows better. Clarion is punished because his assumptions about the nature of his world are incorrect; like Arachne he is guilty of presumption, or like Astery of insouciance. Yet the text remains unspecific about whether Clarion's death is the result of 'cruell Fate, / Or wicked Fortune' (ll. 417–18). A certain hermeneutic balance is maintained throughout, rendering arguments about Clarion's responsibility otiose. Nevertheless, the narrative establishes that his death is produced by the gods. While the idealized mimetic butterfly can flutter 'among the Olives wantonly', Clarion the symbolic butterfly suffers a tragic fate on Jove's artistic

---

78 Plato, *The Republic*, pp. 145–46.

whim. Through his naïvety he never recognizes that the artifice he delights in is crucially ambiguous. Spenser, on the other hand, does. Like Brodsky, the contemplation of a butterfly 'suggests to our stunned reason / this bleak surmise: / the world was made to hold / no end or *Telos*'.

Muiopotmos is a fitting finale to *Complaints*'s 'poetics in practice'. In just over four hundred lines, it illustrates the ambiguity both of artifice and of the mortal world. It confirms Spenser's growing scepticism in the major *Complaints* about traditional poetics; with the *Tale* it offers an innovative mimesis no longer motivated by moral precepts.

As I noted at the outset, Spenser's use of ecphrasis and parody means that the text is consistently concerned with artifice. The narrative encompasses the mortal works of Clarion, Aragnoll and Arachne, alongside the divine 'slight' of Venus, Jove and Pallas. Their contrasting art-works develop Spenser's perception, first realized in the Fox and the Ape, that artistic talent contains no innate predisposition towards virtue. Aragnoll shows that a satanic 'author of confusion' can also create the 'finely sponne ... subtil gin' (ll. 360, 369). Alongside the *Tale*, *Muiopotmos* suggests that the self-serving artist – whether mortal or divine – can create works whose appearance is no different from those of a Sidneyan 'right Poet'. Moreover, in Pallas's tapestry, Spenser raises the question of whether didactic art is actually effective. *Muiopotmos*'s ecphrases conventionally highlight the beauty of Clarion's wings and Europa's feet, but they also indicate that art is neither durable nor necessarily understood by its audience. The poem reveals the limitations of both decorative and didactic poetries.

This concern with art coexists with a complex theological agenda. As we have seen, the gods' government is presented as an artistically reinforced hegemony, manifested in their arbitrary impulses. The narrator's central complaint displays a terrifying image of the created world enslaved to the 'cruell' designs of 'the heavens' and Jove. Against this background, Clarion's fate becomes a symbolic instance of the mortal condition. Though Spenser carefully differentiates *Muiopotmos*'s pantheon from the Christian God, Clarion's artistic murder articulates a quasi-Calvinist anxiety about the place of the individual in a determined cosmos. Through the classical gods, Spenser explores the idea of divine inequity and formulates his own artistic strategy for coping with the ambiguity of things 'Betwixt the centred earth, and azure skies' (l. 19).

Muiopotmos problematizes both literary didacticism and the gods' governance to form a new kind of fiction. This is not driven by a didactic 'fore-conceit', but depends on Spenser's perception of the complexity of lived experience. The poem constitutes a realistic mimesis, which reverses Sidney's idea that a 'golden' didactic Art can improve on the 'brazen' world of Nature. The contention between Art and Nature is here unresolved because Spenser realizes that both are more complex than they seem in conventional critical discourse. Since Spenser's Art is not determined by didacticism, his poem tries to reflect the full complexity of a disturbing Nature, which will not necessarily yield a definable moral. Through its symbolic narrative, *Muiopotmos* offers an image of the natural world as simultaneously beautifully created yet essentially hazardous. The new mimesis is one in which the conventional descriptions of Art and Nature fruitfully coalesce.

The second part of this book has observed the process by which Spenser's received conceptions of poetry become problematic in practice. This is witnessed in the tension between Christian and Classical poetics, then in the questioning of literary didacticism. The major *Complaints* embody a new poetics, which redefines what it is possible for poetry to express. Through the outward conservatism of the complaint mode, Spenser forces his poetic vocabulary to articulate new-found anxieties about the world he inhabits and the poetics he has inherited. The narrator's central complaint of *Muiopotmos* is a superb miniature of this process. Through the rhetorical tropes of conventional quietism, Spenser negotiates a course which allows him to question the philosophical basis of the gods' hegemony and conventional complaint poetry. Innovative complaint articulates the complexities of the mortal condition, and constructs a mimesis no longer tied to moralistic imperatives. This is the self-conscious discovery of the *Complaints* volume; it anticipates the increasing scepticism of the 1596 instalment of *The Faerie Queene*.

CHAPTER SEVEN
The New Poetry beyond the *Complaints*

In the dedicatory sonnet to *The Choice of Valentines*, Nashe dismissively notes that 'Complaints and praises everyone can write', though not everyone can write 'of love's pleasures'.[1] He presents his erotic poem, probably composed in 1592,[2] as something daringly new in comparison with the drab traditionality of 'pangs in stately rhymes'.[3] Nashe's cocksure claim to novelty provides a useful starting point as I conclude this study. Though he alludes to traditional complaint, his remark invites consideration of the new poetry beyond the *Complaints* volume. Now I want to ask what are the further implications of the innovatory poetic Spenser proposes in the major *Complaints*. Inevitably, this inquiry will repudiate the suggestion that Spenser's poems are work that 'everyone can write'. The transformation of traditional forms and the rethinking of poetry's relation to the external world in the *Complaints* illuminate the poetic novelty of two supreme examples of 'the new poetry': *The Faerie Queene* and *Shakespeare's Sonnets*.

Conclusions

I have argued that Spenser's relationship to tradition is more complex than is usually thought. This complexity is exhibited in two related areas. Spenser's manipulation of the complaint mode displays a critical and innovative response to that traditional form. As a consequence of this self-consciousness, Spenser makes the *Complaints* into

1 Thomas Nashe, *The Unfortunate Traveller and Other Works*, ed. J. B. Steane (Harmondsworth: Penguin, 1972), p. 458.
2 See Charles Nicholl, *A Cup of News: The Life of Thomas Nashe* (London: Routledge and Kegan Paul, 1984), p. 90.
3 Nashe, *The Unfortunate Traveller* p. 458.

practical explorations of traditional poetics. In the translations, he adopts classic complaint texts to voice his own intellectual and personal agendas. These poems are exercises within the warrant of the complaint tradition: *Virgils Gnat* translates *Culex* and uses the 'Gnatts complaint' as a suasive oration through which Spenser can petition his own patron. Similarly, *Ruines of Rome* self-consciously anglicizes Du Bellay's innovative lament over Rome. In each text, Spenser showcases his ability to write effective traditional complaint and incorporate the result within his own developing oeuvre.

In the major poems the complaint mode is progressively transferred from traditional topics towards a new poetics. *The Teares of the Muses* and *Mother Hubberds Tale*, for instance, use complaint to voice the collapse of the authority of traditional poetics and of the poet's didactic rôle. The major *Complaints* show Spenser transforming traditional complaint from stylized lament into a complex, self-reflexive meditation on the lament form.

Spenser's new poetic is then an attempt to redefine the value of poetry and its capacity to reflect external reality. This attempt is driven by his dilemma as a poet who instinctively wants to write under the authority of tradition, but is hampered by his realization that traditional poetics have become outmoded. So I present the major poems as a development from the conflictual poetics of *The Ruines of Time* and *The Teares of the Muses* to the radical beast fable narratives of *Mother Hubberds Tale* and *Muiopotmos* to suggest that poetry is an ambiguous art of reflection. This, in brief, is Spenser's 'innovative mimesis'. In traditional theories of mimesis, the poet's representation rests on a didactic preconception of a moral which is keyed into an essentially morally ordered world. By his demonstration of the failure of these strategies in *Mother Hubberds Tale* and *Muiopotmos* Spenser suggests that the relationship between poetry and the world is more problematic than traditional aesthetics recognized. His 'innovative mimesis' is one which acknowledges the complexities of Art and Nature – like the hybrid Clarion, who is neither a natural butterfly nor a parodic text, but a complex amalgam of the two.

So in its exploration of Spenser's tense response to the literary tradition, this study prompts a revision of the received view of his relationship with the past. Spenser is conventionally characterized as a nostalgic writer who longs to return to an idealized golden age.[4] My reading of the major *Complaints* makes this view untenable. Spenser certainly recognizes the value of the past, as in the mythologized figure of Sidney in *The Ruines of Time*, who represents a fading human and poetic nobility. But he also realizes that former prestige is not sufficient to reinvigorate an ailing poetic tradition. As 'the new Poet', Spenser renovates old forms and re-establishes the precarious value of poetry, while recognizing its theological and conceptual deficiencies as a part of the complexities of fallen nature. And it is precisely this reformed understanding of original sin which differentiates Spenser's amoral poetics from the cognate discoveries of Chaucer and Langland.[5] The novelty of Spenser's 'new poetry' derives from the complex relationship between the historical moment which destabilizes traditional Christianity, and Spenser's individual preoccupation with the problems and ambiguities of metaphorical referral.[6] Read in this way, *Complaints* reveal that Spenser indeed merits his original accolade of 'the new Poet'.

Implications

If this study helps to revise literary-historical understanding of Spenser, it also prompts new ways of regarding the Elizabethan poetic Renaissance, and invites a more directly historicized reading of the *Complaints* themselves.

Such a reading sees the volume both as a reflection of social change and an embodiment of conceptual change during the period of its composition. Spenser's intellectual predicament (as revealed in the major poems) reflects the difficulties of allegiance within sixteenth-century society whether to traditional or to novel modes of belief. Collinson

---

4 See pp. 11–13 above.

5 See pp. 12–13 above.

6 Compare Jonathan Bate, *The Genius of Shakespeare* (London: Picador, 1997). Bate accounts for Shakespeare's 'peculiarity' as a confluence of both historical moment and individual talent; see especially pp. 328–40.

reveals that the Elizabethan Reformation was an attritional struggle between the Church of England and the forces of radical reform.[7] Though the *Complaints* have little to say about such disputes as the vestments controversy,[8] their formal predicament, caught between old and new forms, is symptomatic of the years of their composition.

On a deeper level the *Complaints'* new poetic can be seen to distil the conceptual changes which occurred during the sixteenth century. This new poetic illustrates the complexity of the world which poetry represents. Over the sequence of poems, Spenser moves away from traditional didacticism towards a new relativism. This change has important implications. A didactic view of art promotes the idea that moral values are absolute truths common to artist and audience alike. So Lydgate's 'An Holy Meditation' reiterates the traditional Christian idea that salvation can be ensured if his reader is prepared to 'make confessyōn / Of þy trespas': 'If þou do þus þane shal þy soule weende / To heavens blisse which ha þe noon eende'.[9] In this view, human behaviour can be ameliorated through didactic expostulation: the reader learns something morally beneficial from the experience of the writer.

This kind of moralization is alien to Spenser's poetry because his concepts of salvation and original sin are characteristic of Reformed or Translated rather than Traditional Christianity.[10] Lydgate believes that although human beings are fallen, the imperfections of their lives can be amended through confession; the *Complaints* suggest that this solution is ultimately facile. As in *The Faerie Queene* I, Spenser describes original sin in essentially Calvinist terms as a universal predicate of human existence.[11] This new emphasis on fallen

7 Collinson (1967; 1990), pp. 29–44.

8 But compare *Mother Hubberds Tale*, ll. 459–74.

9 Lydgate *The Minor Poems*, ed. H. N. MacCracken (*EETS* Extra Series CVII. London: Oxford University Press, 1911), p. 48. Lydgate is a useful example, not because he is a better poet than Chaucer or Langland, but because he remained influential throughout the fifteenth and sixteenth centuries. Though a follower of Chaucer, Lydgate has no time for the amoral poetic of his master.

10 John Bossy, *Christianity in the West 1400–1700* (Oxford: Oxford University Press, 1985), see pp. 3–5, 35–42, 91–97 for the contrast between traditional and reformed Christian theories of salvation and sin.

11 William J. Bouwsma, *John Calvin: A Sixteenth Century Portrait* (New York

nature, as Spenser demonstrates in *Mother Hubberds Tale* and *Muiopotmos*, creates problems for traditional didactic poetry. If mortality is fundamentally sinful, the poet can no longer offer traditional moral counsel. Experience, as Clarion discovers, is not a question of 'right' or 'wrong' conduct, but is a complex negotiation of a dangerous world. The relativism of the *Complaints'* new poetic is paradoxically a testament to the power of the new theology of the Church Militant, which insists that God's design for the world and the individual is ultimately inscrutable.

So understanding Spenser's dilemma in the *Complaints* emphasizes a key point: that the new poetry of the 1580s and 1590s is an encounter between traditional and innovatory literary ideas. The phrase 'the new poetry' specifically describes the process by which traditional forms are self-consciously renovated by poets like Spenser and Shakespeare.[12] In the rest of this chapter, I suggest that 'the new poetry' creatively transforms its traditional inheritance.

The encounter between tradition and novelty is immediately apparent in *The Faerie Queene*, which Spenser's contemporaries recognized as a triumph of new poetry,[13] but whose chivalric setting later readers have seen as the expression of a nostalgia for an idealized medieval past.[14] The *Complaints'* treatment of the complaint mode anticipates *The Faerie Queene's* treatment of medieval allegory: in both, a traditional literary form is critically assimilated into an innovatory poetic vocabulary. As the major *Complaints* exploit the mode to problematize the art of poetry, so *The Faerie Queene* exploits the symbolic expectations of medieval allegory to develop an experiential poetic narration. Through chivalric quest, Spenser explores the complex psychology which underlies religious and moral choices.

Indeed, the vantage point provided by *Complaints* offers a new insight into *The Faerie Queene's* location in 'Fairyland'. Most critics have broadly followed John Hughes's assessment that 'it is plain that

12 See pp. 10–11 above.

13 See for example the Commendatory Verses to *The Faerie Queene*, and the panegyrics to Spenser in Nashe's *Pierce Penniless* (1592) and Hall's *Virgidemiarum* I.iv (1598).

14 See pp. 11–13 above.

by the literal sense of Fairyland [Spenser] only designed an utopia, an imaginary place'.[15] Such a utopia is the perfect setting for an epic of chivalric romance. In recent years the Fairyland conceit has come under greater scrutiny in terms of the theological profile of the 'elfin race',[16] and of the relationship between ideality and reality that it presents.[17] The question that most directly touches on the novelty of *The Faerie Queene* is that of whether Fairyland is a representation of an ideal world which never existed, or a fictionalized reflection of a given reality. At first sight, Fairyland appears as a nostalgic idealization of the antique world. DeNeef argues that the elves are 'mythic figure[s] of the human imagination' which Spenser brings into contact with 'real', or quasi-historical, figures like Arthur and Redcross.[18] Fairyland then functions as the location in which Spenser enacts a Sidneyan mimesis by bringing his poem's idealized mythic 'fore-conceit' in contact with historical fact. Yet this view diminishes interaction between the text and the external world. DeNeef's Guyon battles with ideal rather than actual opponents, like the Acrasia he describes as 'a faerie fantasy'.[19]

My reading of the major *Complaints* suggests that the Fairyland conceit can be understood as a device through which Spenser brings to consciousness the complex relation between poetic mimesis and the external world. *Mother Hubberds Tale* and *Muiopotmos* show that poetry is not necessarily a vehicle for Sidneyan mimesis. He also demonstrates through satire and theological meditation that poetry can, and possibly should, reflect the real rather than the ideal. So what does it mean to call Fairyland 'an imaginary place'? The Proem to Book II provides some answers. In this teasing address to the

---

15 John Hughes (ed.), *The Works of Mr. Edmund Spenser* (1715), in *Edmund Spenser: A Critical Anthology*, ed. Paul J. Alpers (Harmondsworth: Penguin, 1969), p. 93.

16 See Anthea Hume, *Edmund Spenser: Protestant Poet* (Cambridge: Cambridge University Press, 1984), pp. 145–61, for a summary of this controversy.

17 See A. Leigh DeNeef, *Spenser and the Motives of Metaphor* (Durham, NC: Duke University Press, 1982), pp. 102–10.

18 *Ibid.*, p. 106.

19 *Ibid.*, p. 107.

Queen and the reader, Spenser admits that 'all this famous antique history / Of some th'aboundance of an idle braine / Will iudged be' since nobody knows 'Where is that happy land of Faery'.[20] He then urges the reader to reflect that 'dayly … Many great Regions are discouered, / Which to late age were neuer mentioned'.[21] The discovery of Peru and Virginia should warn the reader that 'later times things more vnknowne shall show' – we should be prepared for 'other worldes' to appear in the Moon and 'euery other starre vnseene'.[22] This elegant and witty Proem culminates with a final joke which provides the literalist reader with more explicit directions for Fairyland:

> Of Faerie lond if yet he more inquire,
>> By certaine signes here set in sundry place
>> He may it find; ne let him then admire,
>> But yield his sence to be too blunt and bace,
>> That no'te without an hound fine footing trace.
>> And thou, O fairest Princesse vnder sky,
>> In this faire mirrhour maist behold thy face,
>> And thine owne realmes in lond of Faery,
> And in this antique Image thy great auncestry.[23]

For DeNeef this stanza 'adopts a disturbing perspective' by apparently separating the poet as the source of power and knowledge from the ignorant reader of this 'riddle'.[24] DeNeef reads *The Faerie Queene* as an enactment of Sidney's theory of mimesis, conceiving of the poet and reader as engaged in a shared project of didactic self-enrichment. Read in this way, the simultaneously 'blunt' and cajoling tone of the stanza's first five lines is certainly 'disturbing'. Yet following the comic tone of the Proem's previous three stanzas, these lines can be read as the culmination of Spenser's joke. If you want to know more about Fairyland, you can find it through 'certaine signes here set in sundry place'. The still puzzled reader must 'yield his sence to be too blunt

20 *FQ*, p. 169; Book II Proem 1.
21 *Ibid.*; Book II Proem 2.
22 *Ibid.*; Book II Proem 3.
23 *Ibid.*; Book II Proem 4.
24 DeNeef, *Spenser and the Motives of Metaphor*, p. 104.

and bace' because he is unable to follow a 'fine footing', or faint trail, 'without an hound'. This kind of reader can't follow his nose. The reader's nose, or critical 'sence', should lead him to the 'certaine signes' of the stanza's last four lines, which signal that the poem is a 'faire mirrhour' to the Queene in which she may see her 'owne realmes in lond of Faery'.

At one level, the Fairyland conceit represents England and English history. By producing this serious claim out of the jokey tone of his previous advice, Spenser shows that the conceit serves two related purposes. Fairyland is what he claims it is not: a 'painted forgery',[25] or a fictional landscape. Poetry, as the Ape and Arachne demonstrate, is ambiguous precisely because of its capacity to fictionalize. This Proem shows Spenser's sophisticated appreciation of the licence such power affords him. As well as mirroring the Queen's glory, he is able in the same text to represent (if he pleases) 'th'aboundance of an idle braine'. The Proem equally shows that the Fairyland conceit is an attempt to represent 'matter of iust memory',[26] albeit by 'couert' rather than direct means.[27] Fairyland is both fictional and historical. I suggest that it may be possible to approach it through the major *Complaints*' meditations on poetry's relation to the external world. As we have seen, Spenser becomes progressively more aware of the problematic nature of poetic mimesis and the inadequacy of conventional theoretical negotiations of this problem. Hence it could be argued that Fairyland is a self-conscious means of acknowledging tensions he had also explored in these shorter poems. Spenser's Fairyland is not the folkloric hinterland of medieval romances like *Sir Orfeo* but a self-consciously formulated mental terrain.[28] The literary past is absorbed and transformed by 'the new Poet'.

25 *FQ*, p. 169; Book II Proem 1.
26 *Ibid.*
27 *FQ*, p. 170; Book II Proem 5.
28 Compare with Paul Alpers, *The Poetry of The Faerie Queene* (Princeton: Princeton University Press, 1967), p. 37, who states that *The Faerie Queene*'s stanzas do not 'imitate or create a reality external to the speaker'. Alpers argues that the epic is an address from the poet to the reader which 'derive[s] from narrative materials'.

As a glimpse of the possibilities of 'the new poetics' in reading *The Faerie Queene*, we can compare the self-reflexive inconclusiveness of the major *Complaints* with the narrative inconclusiveness typical of *The Faerie Queene* as a whole, here exemplified by Book I. The major *Complaints* avoid definitive closures of narrative and argument. The beast protagonists live on to posture another day; even Clarion's identity remains unfixed at his death. Similarly, in *The Teares of the Muses*, the ultimate fate of the Muses remains 'vntold', while only the mythologized figure of Sidney allows a resolution to the tension between poetic eternizing and Christian transcendence in *The Ruines of Time*. Spenser's avoidance of closure is characteristic of his developing resistance to the moralism of traditional poetry. He accepts that lived experience is more complex than the learned experience promoted by traditional moralism.

Consider a few of the many inconclusive narratives in Book I. The stories of Fradubio (II), Sansioy (V), Satyrane (VI) as well as the Redcross Knight himself are left in the balance; even Duessa is allowed to escape from her unmasking to reappear in different guises in subsequent episodes. These loose ends are not the product of carelessness; rather, they express the view that post-lapsarian experience is provisional. Spenser adheres to the Reformed notion of original sin as a basic condition of living; according to the Thirty-Nine Articles, 'Birth-sin' is 'the fault and corruption of the Nature of every man, that naturally is ingendered of the offspring of *Adam*; whereby man is very far gone from original righteousness, and is of his own nature inclined to evil'.[29] As Bossy has shown, during the sixteenth century, this conception of original sin effectively erased the traditional notion that through confession and repentance, Christians could make satisfactory amends for their sins.[30] This doctrine has profound implications for the writing of poetry. If human life is predicated on a sin which can only be cleansed by an inscrutable divine grace, then traditional didactic and narrative strategies become meaningless. Lydgate's received wisdom will not help the sixteenth-century Chris-

29 Article IX; *The Book of Common Prayer*, p. 696.
30 Bossy, *Christianity in the West*, p. 92.

tian, whose spiritual experience begins with the apprehension of ineradicable sin: grace is no longer available through confession. The traditional capacity of poetry to moralize, and even tell a story to its end, is compromised by the Reformed understanding of original sin.

The Faerie Queene I is Spenser's attempt to write a religious and patriotic poem which both avoids the pitfalls of traditional aesthetics and reflects the complexity of the experiential world. Spenser repeatedly highlights the new religious and poetic values which find expression in narrative provisionality. So in the Fradubio episode, the crux comes when Redcross asks the 'Wretched man, wretched tree' (I.II.33) how long he has to remain 'in this misformed house':

> We may not chaunge ... this euill plight,
> Till we be bathed in a liuing well;
> That is the terme proscribed by the spell.
> O how, said he, mote I that well out find,
> That may restore you to your wonted well?
> Time and suffised fates to former kynd
> Shall vs restore, none else from hence may vs
> vnbynd. (I.II.43)[31]

This dialogue is alive with the philosophical and narrative innovations of Spenser's poetics. Fradubio tells Redcross that he can only be released from bondage through 'a liuing well'; as Hamilton notes, this image 'refers to the biblical well of life' and to 'that liuing well' which subsequently refreshes the Knight himself in his fight with the dragon.[32] At this stage in the book, Redcross responds in accordance with the traditional quest motif of chivalric romance and asks how he can find the well.[33] The reply deftly betrays Spenser's modification of the chivalric literary landscape: only progressive 'chaunge' through 'Time and suffised fates to former kynd' has the power to 'vnbynd' Fradubio and Fraelissa. Redcross assumes conventionally that his rôle is to 'restore' Fradubio's 'wonted well'; he is reminded of human dependence on 'Time' as the unveiler of God's design. Since Redcross

31 *FQ*, pp. 51–54.
32 *Ibid.*, p. 54.
33 *Ibid.*

cannot 'restore' Fradubio through a decisive chivalric deed, Spenser cannot predict at the moment of narration Fradubio's ultimate fate.

The motif of provisionality is most apparent in the treatment of Redcross's quest, and especially in the second half of the book, where he progresses from degradation and despair to a recovery of faith and grace in preparation for his encounter with the Dragon. Though the poem narrates his defeat of the Dragon, it also makes clear that it is no more than a stage in the continued moral-spiritual struggle for 'right'. In the 'House of Holinesse', his vision of 'The new *Hierusalem*' makes him long for his final pilgrimage instead of returning 'Backe to the world, whose ioyes so fruitlesse are'.[34] His guide, 'heavenly Contemplation', paradoxically insists that his business with the world remains unfinished: 'ne maist thou yit / Forgo that royall maides bequeathed care'.[35] Similarly, though Book I concludes with the betrothal of Redcross and Una, it defers their marriage by remembering the Knight's promise to return 'Vnto his Farie Queene'.[36] As Hume comments, 'Because there is no attaining perfection in this life, no book of the poems ends with uncomplicated repose'.[37]

So Redcross's completion of his primary quest is provisional. In his symbolic rôles as Saint George and Everyman, the Knight's adventures reflect the new sense of the complexity of mortal life. His spiritual journey can unobtrusively become an embodiment of the experience of English Protestants during the 1580s and 1590s. God's design is beyond temporal scrutiny: the victories achieved by Redcross and the English state cannot close the story. In the opening and closing stanzas of Canto XII, Spenser uses conventional 'nautical metaphors' to describe his poetic task.[38] But although 'his feeble' poetic 'barke a while may stay' at the end of the book, even this tra-

34 *Ibid.*, pp. 138–42; I.X.57, 63.

35 *Ibid.*; I.X.46, 63.

36 *Ibid.*, p. 162; I.XII.41.

37 Hume, *Edmund Spenser*, p. 106.

38 See Ernest R. Curtius, *European Literature and the Latin Middle Ages*, trans. Willard R. Trask (Bollingen Series XXVI. Princeton: Princeton University Press, 1953; new edn 1990), pp. 128–30.

ditional topos is pregnant with process: after running repairs, Spenser's ship must sail 'againe abroad / On the long voyage whereto she is bent'.[39] His new poetry constitutes a 'long voyage' towards its appropriately 'vnperfite' vision of 'that Saboaths sight' at the close of *The Mutabilitie Cantos*.[40] The process of writing poetry mirrors the process of witnessing protestant life, whose goal can only be reached 'at that same time when no more Change shall be'.[41]

Approaching *The Faerie Queene* through the *Complaints*, the reader becomes receptive to a new poetry fashioned from the transformation of traditional materials. Book I adapts motifs like the chivalric quest to create Spenser's 'own kind of poetic narration'.[42] Yet this transformation of literary tradition is not restricted to Spenser – it's evident in a range of late 1580s and 1590s texts. But my final example of this trend reworks a Renaissance rather than a medieval genre. *Shakespeare's Sonnets*[43] (1609) radically modify the form of the amatory sonnet sequence, displaying in a different context the complexity of experience which a genuinely new poetry discovers in its subject matter.

First anglicized by Sidney's *Astrophil and Stella* (written *c*.1581–82), the sonnet sequence was the most modish poetic form of the 1580s and 1590s; its popularity is shown by the numerous Petrarchan sonnets written in English at this time.[44] As texts like Shakespeare's Sonnet 130 and Hall's *Virgidemiarum* I.vii (1598) demonstrate, the popularity of the form quickly gave way to repetitive banality. Hall mocks the archetypal rejected poet-lover who

39 *FQ*, pp. 155, 162; I.XII.1, 42.

40 *Ibid.*, p. 735; VII.VIII.2.

41 *Ibid.*

42 Alpers, *The Poetry of The Faerie Queene*, p. 174.

43 See Katherine Duncan-Jones (ed.), *Shakesepeare's Sonnets* (The Arden Shakespeare. Walton on Thames: Thomas Nelson, 1997), pp. 85–88, for an argument for the reinstatement of the 1609 Quarto's title as the title of the sequence.

44 The most celebrated sequences after Sidney's are Daniel's *Delia* (1592), Barnes's *Parthenophil and Parthenophe* (1593), Drayton's *Idea* (1594), and of course Spenser's *Amoretti* (1595) – but there were many others. See Maurice Evans (ed.), *Elizabethan Sonnets* (London, Melbourne and Toronto: Dent. Everyman's Library, 1977).

'poures ... forth in patched *Sonettings* / His loue, his lust, and loath-some flatterings: / As tho the staring world hangd on his sleeue'.[45] By the late 1590s, the rhetorical gestures and amatory strategy of the sonnet sequence had become predictable. It is this form of 'loath-some', and derivative, 'flatterings' which Shakespeare recasts. Where traditional sonnet sequences rely on the basic conceit of the 'loue-sicke Poet' petitioning his single 'disdainfull dame, / With publique plaints of his conceiued flame',[46] Shakespeare's presents a triadic rela-tionship between a poet, a young man and his mistress as a narrative enactment of the poet's fluctuating emotions. At a stroke, Shake-speare gives the notion of the sonnet *sequence* an internal logic (arguably lost in English after *Astrophil and Stella*) by turning the group of poems into a closet drama between conflicting characters and values. Here the form explores the experience, rather than the lit-erary conventions, of love.

Shakespeare's modifications of the traditional sonnet sequence are well-known. The object of the poet's idealized love is a young man. The poet finds in this 'man right fair' the beauty, inspiration and commitment (in spite of the 'canker' of his faults) which a conven-tional sonneteer discovers in a young woman.[47] In conflict with this positive love is the negative love the poet experiences with the Dark Lady. She is not the heavenly and unattainable ideal of conventional sonnets but a hellish sexual partner, literally and metaphorically 'a woman coloured ill'.[48]

What is slightly less familiar is the extent to which the sequence turns on Shakespeare's re-evocation of the traditional dichotomy between the body and the soul in Sonnet 146, the climactic after-word to the main drama. The conflict between the poet's 'Poor soul' and his 'sinful earth' is a metaphoric resolution of the wider conflict

45 *The Poems of Joseph Hall, Bishop and Exeter and Norwich*, ed. Arnold Daven-port (1949; rpt. Liverpool: Liverpool University Press, 1969), p. 18.

46 *Ibid.*

47 William Shakespeare, *The Sonnets and A Lovers Complaint*, ed. John Kerrigan (Harmondsworth: Viking Penguin, 1986), pp. 148, 124; Sonnets 144 and 95.

48 *Ibid.*, p. 148, Sonnet 144.

in the sequence between his 'Two loves'.[49] At first, it seems that Shakespeare's thinking is in tune with the tradition embodied by Lydgate: the soul is imprisoned in the body and kept from its spiritual goal; as Lydgate's soul quaintly puts it to his body, ' þy foule delyte and þyne Iniquytee / Of vertous study offten destourbeþe me'.[50] Yet there is a crucial difference. Lydgate's 'An Holy Meditation' restates of conventional wisdom: he has not experienced the sensuality his soul accuses his body of cherishing, he merely invokes the traditional dichotomies as a spur to 'vertuous study'. But Sonnet 146 is the exhausted product of the entire sequence, emerging directly from the poet's unstinting dramatization of his 'Two loves ... of comfort and despair'.[51] In its closing formulation of the body/soul dichotomy, the sonnet beautifully communicates the poet's sense of the accumulated waste of his different loves:

> Then, soul, live thou upon thy servant's loss,
> And let that pine to aggravate thy store;
> Buy terms divine in selling hours of dross;
> Within be fed, without be rich no more:
>   So shalt thou feed on Death, that feeds on men,
>   And Death once dead there's no more dying then.[52]

The poet's address to his soul claims that the negative experience of his loves can be turned to spiritual advantage: the soul can 'live ... upon' the body's amatory 'loss' through exchanging the starvation of the body for 'terms divine', or 'godly stretches of time'.[53] The emotional and erotic deprivation of the body enriches the soul 'Within'; the dissolution of time will generate eternity. Like Spenser in *The Teares of the Muses*, Shakespeare makes a statement of defeat into an announcement of victory. Indeed, the sonnet mirrors in miniature the process I have observed in all the major *Complaints*, where a new poetry is salvaged from the wreckage of traditional poetics. The soul's transcendence

---

49 *Ibid.*

50 Lydgate, *The Minor Poems*, p. 44.

51 Shakespeare, *The Sonnets and A Lovers Complaint*, p. 148; Sonnet 144.

52 *Ibid.*, p. 149.

53 *Ibid.*, p. 379 (Kerrigan's paraphrase).

paradoxically provides the poet with a novel resolution to the tensions between his two loves which he has found no conventional poetic means of effecting: *Shakespeare's Sonnets* do not close like *Astrophil and Stella* with the gradual fading of the relationship between the lovers, or like the *Amoretti* with their marriage day in the *Epithalamion*. The poet's desire for transcendence is a product of his experience rather than, as in Lydgate, a condition of his dogma. The couplet of this sonnet contrasts powerfully with Donne's 'Death be not proud'. Donne asserts his faith in the face of passing time and the imminence of death culminating like Shakespeare with the idea that eventually death itself 'shalt die'.[54] But Shakespeare's formulation, despite its scriptural echoes,[55] is also in the context of the final Dark Lady Sonnets a punningly appropriate repudiation of sex: the death of 'dying' is both the end of time, and an end to the 'waste of shame' of orgasms.[56]

Like Spenser, Shakespeare creates a new poetry which is powerfully original because of his critical engagement with the literary tradition. After such an engagement, they can return to familiar images like the soul's transcendence of the body or Saint George killing the Dragon. In each case, the new text is not a dogmatic reassertion of traditional wisdom, but an attempt to embody in poetry the complexity of lived experience. This poetry has lasted because, like the experience of the narrator of *Mother Hubberds Tale*, its 'gladsome', if ambiguous, 'solace' has become a part of the experience of its subsequent readers.[57]

---

54 John Donne, *The Complete English Poems*, ed. C. A. Patrides (Everyman's Library. London and Melbourne: Dent, 1985), p. 441.

55 See Kerrigan's notes in Shakespeare, *The Sonnets and A Lovers Complaint*, p. 379.

56 *Ibid.*, p. 141; Sonnet 129. As another example of the widespread pun on 'dying', 'death' etc., compare *The Choice of Valentines*: 'Together let our equal motions stir / Together let us live and die, my dear'. In Nashe, *The Unfortunate Traveller*, p. 464.

57 *Mother Hubberds Tale*, l. 20. I have borrowed the idea of poetry becoming a part of the reader's experience from an evocative paragraph by Raymond Carver: 'V. S. Pritchett's definition of a short story is "something glimpsed from the corner of the eye, in passing". First the glimpse. Then the glimpse given life, turned into something that will illuminate the moment and just maybe lock it indelibly into the reader's consciousness. Make it a part of the reader's own experience, as Hemingway so nicely puts it. Forever, the writer hopes. Forever.' In *No Heroics, Please: Uncollected Writings*, ed. William L. Stull (London: Harvill, 1991), p. 127.

APPENDIX

Urania-Astraea and *'Divine Elisa'*
in *The Teares of the Muses* (11.527–88)

Spenser possibly intended Urania's flight in *The Teares of the Muses* (ll. 527–32) to foreshadow Polyhymnia's panegyric of Elizabeth (ll. 571–88).[1] As Yates argues, Astraea became a symbol for the Queen, especially in her Virgilian incarnation as the inaugurator of a new golden age.[2] The Elizabethan settlement is imaged in the idea of Astraea's descent back into the world in the person of Elizabeth. So Peele's *Descensus Astraeae* (1591) presents 'this gentle nymph *Astraea* faire' as a goddess inimical to 'cruel warres', but now miraculously 'Shadowing the person of a peerlesse Queene'.[3] The Elizabeth-Astraea formula became a powerful myth at the service of the Elizabethan state. But it is one which (Yates notwithstanding) Spenser seems reticent of using explicitly.[4] Though Astraea is Artegall's tutor in Justice in *The Faerie Queene* V.I, in his depiction of Mercilla – the

1 See Chapter 4 above, pp. 159–61.

2 Frances A. Yates, *Astraea: The Imperial Theme in the Sixteenth Century* (London: Routledge and Kegan Paul, 1975; rpt. London: Pimlico, 1993), pp. 29–87.

3 George Peele, *Selection*, ed. Sally Purcell (Oxford: Fyfield Books, 1972), pp. 71–72. see also Yates, *Astraea*, pp. 60–61.

4 *Ibid.*, pp. 69–74. Yates argues that Astraea underlies the various images of Elizabeth in *The Faerie Queene*: Gloriana, Belphoebe, Mercilla, Una. While this may be true on a general level, Yates's analysis is undermined by her rather monolithic conception of the poem as the *Aeneid* of 'the Elizabethan golden age', and her assumption that 'Here, if anywhere, we should expect to find Astraea enshrined'. Yet despite Yates's ingenious associations of Astraea with Mercilla and Ariadne, the fact remains that none of these potential 'enshrinings' deliver a clear instance of Spenser praising Elizabeth under the shadow of Astraea.

allegorical symbol of Elizabeth as a just monarch – Spenser makes no unequivocal allusion to the Astraea material.[5]

Even though Polyhymnia's praise of Elizabeth gives an opportunity to present her as both the redescended Astraea and true patron of poetry, I believe that Spenser does not take it. If he had incorporated an unequivocal image of Elizabeth as Astraea/Urania in Polyhymnia's complaint, this figure could dispense both ideal justice and artistic patronage befitting 'this golden age' she presides over, and eradicate the mortal sin which Urania believes has precipitated the crisis.[6] Polyhymnia's panegyric (ll. 571–82) does at first seem to recall Urania's vocabulary. The phrase 'Makers majestie' reduplicates line 512, which is at the heart of Urania's vision; yet in this case it is a simple compliment rather than the visionary goal of human knowledge. Similarly, in calling Elizabeth 'The true *Pandora* of all heavenly graces', Spenser evokes another common epideictic trope.[7] Peele provides an inclusive mythic blazon of the Queen when he calls her 'Our faire *Astraea*, our *Pandora* faire, / Our faire Eliza, or *Zabeta* faire'.[8] But in the context of *The Teares*, Pandora is not Astraea. The compliment is a straightforward allusion to the etymology of the name 'Pandora' and serves to illustrate Polyhymnia's praise of the Queen as a patron. Elizabeth is the giver of 'all gifts' to the 'divinest wits' of Polyhymnia's élite group of court poets. Though the identification of the Queen with Pandora constitutes an analogous form of myth-making to the Astraea symbol, it does not connect Elizabeth with Urania or Astraea.

We may speculate why Spenser avoided this syncretic flattery. The obvious answer is that, as is argued above, the Queen's 'happie influence' is necessarily restricted. Spenser does not want to suggest that

5 Alistair Fowler, *Spenser and the Numbers of Time* (London: Routledge and Kegan Paul, 1964), p. 197, sees the image of Arthur and Artegall flanking Mercilla's throne (V.IX.37) as an icon of Virgo balanced by the knights' contrasting virtues. This would be the closest Spenser comes to authorizing this panegyric tradition.

6 From Peele's *Anglorum Feriae* (1595) in David Norbrook and H. R. Woudhuysen (eds), *The Penguin Book of Renaissance Verse 1509–1659* (Harmondsworth: Allen Lane, The Penguin Press, 1992), pp. 121–22.

7 Compare Yates, *Astraea*, p. 29.

8 Peele, *Selection* pp. 71–72.

she can actually dispel the crisis – she is an isolated source of intellectual enlightenment to 'Some few'. The syncretic figure I am describing would have too much power, and could indeed be seen as blasphemous. (Though such considerations do not seem to have worried Peele.) Furthermore, as I argue above, Spenser carefully does not amalgamate Urania and Astraea: Urania's flight imitates Astraea's in Ovid. An amalgamation of the Muse with the goddess (and then the Queen) would create an unwieldy hybrid, who would no longer be a Muse. The imitation of Ovid suggests the gravity of the cultural crisis (things have become so bad that Urania is now behaving like Astraea) but does not create a saviour figure.

BIBLIOGRAPHY

Primary Texts

1 Spenser

Spenser, Edmund. *The Works of Edmund Spenser.* Ed. R. Morris. The Globe Edition. London: Macmillan, 1869, corrected ed. 1897.

— *Complaints.* Ed. W. R. Renwick. London: Scholartis, 1928.

— *Daphnaïda* and Other Poems. Ed. W. R. Renwick. London: Scholartis, 1929.

— *The Poetical Works of Edmund Spenser.* Ed. J. C. Smith and E. de Selincourt. London: Oxford University Press and Humphrey Milford, 1932.

— *The Works of Edmund Spenser:* A Variorum Edition. 10 vols. Ed. E. A. Greenlaw *et al.* Baltimore and London: Johns Hopkins University Press and Oxford University Press, 1932–49.

— *The Faerie Queene.* Longmans Annotated English Poets. Ed. A. C. Hamilton. London: Longmans, 1977.

— *The Yale Edition of the Shorter Poems of Edmund Spenser.* Ed. William A. Oram *et al.* New Haven and London: Yale University Press, 1989.

2 Others

Bennett, J. A. W. and G. V. Smithers, eds. *Early Middle English Verse and Prose.* Oxford: Clarendon, 2nd edn., 1968.

Bible. The Geneva Bible. Geneva, 1560. Facsimile edn. Ed. Lloyd E. Barry. Madison: University of Wisconsin Press, 1969.

Boccaccio, Giovanni. *Genealogie: Paris 1531.* Rpt of the 1531 edn published by P. Le Noir. Ed. Stephen Orgel. New York and London: Garland, 1976.

The Book of Common Prayer. Oxford: Oxford University Press no date.

Breton, Nicholas. *Melancholike Humours.* Ed. G. B. Harrison. London: Scholartis, 1929.

Brooks-Davies, Douglas, ed. *Silver Poets of the Sixteenth Century.* Everyman's Library. London and Vermont: Dent and Charles E. Tuttle, new edn, 1992.

Browne, William. *Poems of William Browne of Tavistock.* 2 vols. Ed. Gordon Goodwin. The Muses' Library. London: George Routledge, no date.

Bullough, Geoffrey, ed. *Narrative and Dramatic Sources of Shakespeare,* III. London and New York: Routledge and Kegan Paul and Columbia University Press, 1975.

Campbell, Lily B., ed. *The Mirror for Magistrates.* Cambridge: Cambridge University Press, 1938; rpt. 1960.

Castiglione, Baldasare. *The Courtier.* 1561. Trans. Sir Thomas Hoby. Everyman's Library. London: Dent, 1928.

Caxton, William. *The History of Reynard the Fox.* Ed. N. F. Blake. *EETS,* original series, no. 263. London, New York and Toronto: Oxford University Press, 1970.

Chaucer, Geoffrey. *The Works.* Ed. F. N. Robinson. London: Oxford University Press, 1957.

Cicero. *On the Good Life.* Trans. Michael Grant. Harmondsworth: Penguin, 1971.

Davies, Sir John. *The Poems.* Ed. Robert Krueger and Ruby Nemser. Oxford: Clarendon, 1975.

Davies, R. T., ed. *Medieval English Lyrics: A Critical Anthology.* London: Faber and Faber, 1963; new edn, 1966.

Donne, John. *The Complete English Poems.* Ed. C. A. Patrides. Everyman's Library. London and Melbourne: Dent, 1985.

Dryden, John. *Sylvae* (1685). Scolar Press Facsimile. London and Menston: The Scolar Press, 1973.

Du Bellay, Joachim. *Oeuvres Poétiques.* 6 vols. Ed. Henri Chamard. Paris: Société des Textes Français Modernes, 1907–31.

— *Poems.* Ed. H. W. Lawton. Blackwell's French Texts. Oxford: Blackwell, 1961.

— *Les Regrets, Les Antiquités de Rome et La Défense et Illustration de la Langue française.* Édition établie par S. De Sacy. Paris: Gallimard, 1967.

Evans, Maurice, ed. *Elizabethan Sonnets.* Everyman's Library. London and Melbourne: Dent, 1977.

Evelyn-White, Hugh G., ed. *Hesiod, The Homeric Hymns and Homerica.* The Loeb Classical Library. Cambridge, Mass., and London: Harvard University Press and Heinemann, 1914.

Gascoigne, George. *The Complete Works.* 2 vols. Ed. J. W. Cunliffe. Cambridge: Cambridge University Press, 1907–10.

Golding, Arthur. *Shakespeare's Ovid: Golding's Translation of the Metamorphoses.* 1567. Ed. W. H. D. Rouse. London: Centaur, 1961.

Gower, John. *The English Works*. 2 vols. Ed. G. C. Macaulay. Oxford: Clarendon, 1901.

Greene, Robert. *A Notable Discovery of Coosnage (1591); The Second Part of Conny-Catching* (1592). Elizabethan and Jacobean Quartos. Ed. G. B. Harrison. Edinburgh: Edinburgh University Press, 1966.

Hall, Joseph. *The Poems*. Ed. Arnold Davenport. First edn, 1949; rpt. Liverpool: Liverpool University Press, 1969.

Handford, S. A., trans. *Fables of Aesop*. Harmondsworth, Penguin, 1954.

Harington, Sir John. *The Sixth Book of Virgil's Aeneid Translated and Commented on by Sir John Harington (1604)*. Ed. Simon Cauchi. Oxford: Clarendon, 1991.

Harvey, Gabriel. Fovre Letters. Elizabethan and Jacobean Quartos. Ed. G. B. Harrison. Edinburgh: Edinburgh University Press, 1967.

Henryson, Robert. *The Poems*. Ed. Denton Fox. Oxford: Clarendon, 1981; revised edn, 1987.

Hesiod. *Hesiod; The Homeric Hymns and Homerica*. The Loeb Classical Library. Ed. and trans. Hugh G. Evelyn White. Cambridge, Mass. and London: Harvard University Press and Heinemann, 1914.

Hoccleve, Thomas. *Selections from Hoccleve*. Ed. M. C. Seymour. Oxford: Clarendon, 1981.

Homer. *Iliad* XXIV. Ed. C. W. Macleod. Cambridge: Cambridge University Press, 1982.

Horace. *Odes*. Trans. James Michie. London: Rupert Hart-Davis, 1966.

Jonson, Ben. *The Complete Poems*. Ed. George Parfitt. Harmondsworth: Penguin, 1975.

Kerrigan, John, ed. *Motives of Woe: Shakespeare and 'Female Complaint'*. A Critical Anthology. Oxford: Clarendon, 1991.

Livy. *The Early History of Rome: Books I–V of The History of Rome from its Foundation*. Trans. Aubrey de Sélincourt. Harmondsworth: Penguin, 1960; revised edn, 1971.

Lodge, Anthony and Kenneth Varty, eds. *The Earliest Branches of the 'Roman de Renart'*. New Alyth, Perthshire: Lochee Publications, 1989.

Lucretius. *De Rerum Natura*. The Loeb Classical Library. Ed. W. H. D. Rouse. Cambridge, Mass. and London: Harvard University Press and Heinemann, 1924; revised edn, 1975.

Lydgate, John. *The Minor Poems*. Ed. H. N. MacCracken. *EETS* Extra series CVII. London: Oxford University Press, 1911.

Marlowe, Christopher. *The Jew of Malta*. Ed. T. W. Craik. London: Ernest Benn, The New Mermaids, 1966.

— *The Complete Poems and Translations*. Ed. Stephen Orgel. Harmondsworth: Penguin, 1971.

Milton, John. *Paradise Lost*. Ed. Alastair Fowler. Longmans Annotated English Poets. London and New York: Longmans, 1968; revised edn, 1971.

Mulcaster, Richard. *The First Part of the Elementary (1582)*. Scolar Press Facsimile. Menston: The Scolar Press, 1970.

Nashe, Thomas. *Works*. 5 vols. Ed. Ronald B. McKerrow. 1903; rpt. Oxford: Blackwell, 1958.

— *Strange Newes*. Facsimile edn. London and Menston: The Scholar Press, 1969.

— *The Unfortunate Traveller and Other Works*. Ed. J. B. Steane. Harmondsworth: Penguin, 1972.

Norbrook, David and H. R. Woudhuysen, eds. *The Penguin Book of Renaissance Verse 1509–1659*. Harmondsworth: Allen Lane, The Penguin Press, 1992.

Ovid. *Metamorphoses*. The Loeb Classical Library. 2 vols. Ed. Frank Justus Miller. Cambridge, Mass. and London: Harvard University Press and Heinemann, 1916.

— *Metamorphoses*. Trans. A. D. Melville. Oxford and New York: Oxford University Press, 1987.

Peele, George. *Selection*. Ed. Sally Purcell. Oxford: Fyfield Books, 1972.

Petrarch, Francesco. *Lord Morley's 'Tryumphes of Fraunces Petrarcke': The First English Translation of the 'Trionfi'*. Ed. D. D. Carnicelli. Cambridge, Mass.: Harvard University Press, 1971.

— *Petrarch's Lyric Poems: The 'Rime Sparse' and Other Lyrics*. Ed. Robert M. Durling. Cambridge, Mass. and London: Harvard University Press, 1976.

Plato. *The Collected Dialogues*. Ed. Edith Hamilton and Huntingdon Cairns. Bollingen Series, 71. Princeton: Princeton University Press, 1961.

— *The Republic*. Trans. Desmond Lee. Harmondsworth: Penguin, 1974.

Ronsard, Pierre de. *L'Art Poétique: Cinq Prefaces*. Cambridge: Cambridge University Press, 1930.

— *Poésies Choisies*. Ed. Pierre de Nolhac. Paris: Garnier, 1959.

— *Poèmes*. Ed. André Barbier. Oxford: Blackwell, 1962.

— *II Odes, Hymns and Other Poems*. Ed. Grahame Castor and Terence Cave. Manchester: Manchester University Press, 1977.

Russell, D. A. and M. Winterbottom, eds. *Ancient Literary Criticism: The Principal Texts in New Translations*. Oxford: Oxford University Press,

1972.

Scaliger, Julius Caesar. *Select Translations from Scaliger's Poetics*. Trans. F. M. Padelford. Yale Studies in English. New York: Henry Holt, 1905.

Shakespeare, William. *The Sonnets and A Lovers Complaint*. Ed. John Kerrigan. Harmondsworth: Viking Penguin, 1986.

— *The Poems*. Ed. John Roe. Cambridge: Cambridge University Press, 1992.

— *Shakespeare's Sonnets*. Ed. Katherine Duncan-Jones. The Arden Shakespeare. Walton on Thames: Thomas Nelson, 1997.

Sidney, Mary, Countess of Pembroke. *The Triumph of Death and Other Unpublished and Uncollected Poems*. Ed. G. F. Waller. Salzburg Studies in English Literature. Salzburg: Universität Salzburg, 1977.

Sidney, Sir Philip. *An Apology for Poetry*. Ed. Geoffrey Shepherd. London: Thomas Nelson, 1965; rpt., Old and Middle English Texts. Manchester: Manchester University Press, 1973.

— *Miscellaneous Prose of Sir Philip Sidney*. Ed. Katherine Duncan-Jones and Jan Van Dorsten. Oxford: Clarendon, 1973.

— *Sir Philip Sidney*. Ed. Katherine Duncan-Jones. The Oxford Authors. Oxford and New York: Oxford University Press, 1989.

— and The Countess of Pembroke. *The Psalms of Sir Philip Sidney and the Countess of Pembroke*. Ed. J. C. A. Rathmell. New York: New York University Press, 1963.

Smith, G. Gregory, ed. *Elizabethan Critical Essays*. Oxford: Oxford University Press, 1904.

Smith, Sir Thomas. *De Republica Anglorum*. Ed. Mary Dewar. Cambridge: Cambridge University Press, 1982.

Stow, John. *The Survey of London*. Ed. H. B. Wheatley. Everyman's Library. London and Melbourne: Dent, 1912; revised edn, 1987.

Terry, Patricia, trans. *Renard the Fox*. Rpt. Berkeley, Los Angeles and Oxford: University of California Press, 1992.

Tottel's Miscellany. Ed. Edward Arber. English Reprints. London: Constable, 1921.

Villon, François. *Œuvres*. Texte et traduction présentés par André Lanly. Paris: Librairie Honoré Champion, 1992.

Virgil. *Works*. The Loeb Classical Library. 2 vols. Ed. H. Rushton Fairclough. Cambridge, Mass. and London: Harvard University Press and Heinemann, 1918; revised edn, 1934.

— *Aeneid VI*. Ed. Sir Frank Fletcher. Oxford: Clarendon, 1941.

— *The Aeneid*. Trans. C. Day Lewis. Oxford: Oxford University Press,

1956; rpt., 1986.
— *The Eclogues*. Trans. Guy Lee. Harmondsworth: Penguin, 1984.
— *The Works of Virgil*. Trans. John Dryden. London and New York: Frederick Warne, no date.

Secondary Texts

Adler, Doris. 'Imaginary Toads in Real Gardens.' *ELR*, 11 (1981), 235–60.
Allen, Don C. *Image and Meaning: Metamorphic Traditions in Renaissance Poetry*. Baltimore: Johns Hopkins University Press, 1960.
Alpers, Paul. *The Poetry of The Faerie Queene*. Princeton: Princeton University Press, 1967.
— ed. *Edmund Spenser: A Critical Anthology*. Penguin Critical Anthologies. Harmondsworth: Penguin, 1969.
Anderson, Judith. '"Nat worth a boterflye": *Muiopotmos* and the *Nun's Priest's Tale*.' *JMRS*, 1 (1971), 89–106.
Atchity, K. J. 'Spenser's *Mother Hubberds Tale*: Three Themes of Order.' *PQ*, 52 (1973), 171–62.
Attridge, Derek. *Well-Weighed Syllables: Elizabethan Verse in Classical Metrics*. Cambridge: Cambridge University Press, 1974.
Auden, W. H. *The Dyer's Hand*. London: Faber and Faber, 1963.
Auerbach, Erich. *Mimesis: The Representation of Reality in Western Literature*. Trans. Willard R. Trask. Princeton: Princeton University Press, 1953.
Bate, Jonathan. *Shakespeare and Ovid*. Oxford: Clarendon, 1993.
— *The Genius of Shakespeare*. London: Picador, 1997.
Bawcutt, Priscilla. *Gavin Douglas: A Critical Study*. Edinburgh: Edinburgh University Press, 1976.
Baxandall, Michael. *Giotto and the Orators: Humanist Observers of Painting in Italy and the Discovery of Pictorial Composition 1350–1450*. Oxford-Warburg Studies. Oxford: Oxford University Press, 1971.
Bellenger, Yvonne. *Du Bellay, ses Regrets qu'il fit dans Rome: Étude et Documentation*. Paris: A.-G. Nizet, 1975.
Bender, John B. *Spenser and Literary Pictorialism*. Princeton: Princeton University Press, 1972.
Bennett, J. A. W. *The Oxford History of English Literature Volume II: Middle English Literature*. Ed. Douglas Gray. Oxford: Clarendon, 1986.
Bennett, Josephine Waters. 'A Bibliographical Note on *Mother Hubberds*

Tale.' ELH, 4 (1937), 60–61.

— 'Spenser's Muse.' *JEGP*, 31 (1932), 200–19.

— *The Evolution of The Faerie Queene.* Chicago: Chicago University Press, 1942.

Berger, Harry Jr, 'The Prospect of Imagination: Spenser and the Limits of Poetry.' *SEL*, 1 (1961), 93–120.

Bernard, John D. *Ceremonies of Innocence: Pastoralism in the Poetry of Edmund Spenser.* Cambridge: Cambridge University Press, 1989.

Binns, J. W. 'Alberico Gentili in Defence of Poetry and Acting.' *Sren*, 19 (1972), 224–72.

— *Intellectual Culture in Elizabethan and Jacobean England: The Latin Writings of the Age.* Leeds: Francis Cairns, 1990.

Bjorvand, Einar. 'Spenser's Defence of Poetry: Some Structural Aspects of the *Fowre Hymnes.*' In *Fair Forms: Essays in English Literature from Spenser to Jane Austen.* Ed. Maren-Sofie Røstvig. Cambridge: D. S. Brewer, 1975.

Booth, Stephen. *An Essay on Shakespeare's Sonnets.* New Haven and London: Yale University Press, 1969.

Bossy, John. *Christianity in the West 1400–1700.* Oxford: Oxford University Press, 1985.

Bouwsma, William J. *John Calvin: A Sixteenth Century Portrait.* New York and Oxford: Oxford University Press, 1988.

Bradbrook, M. C. 'No Room at the Top: Spenser's Pursuit of Fame.' In *Elizabethan Poetry.* Ed. J. R. Brown and Bernard Harris. Stratford-Upon-Avon Studies 2. London: Edmund Arnold, 1960.

Brink, Jean R. 'Who Fashioned Edmund Spenser?: The Textual History of *Complaints.*' SP, 88 (1991), 153–68.

Brinkley, R. A. 'Spenser's *Muiopotmos* and the Politics of Metamorphosis.' *ELH*, 48 (1981), 668–76.

Brown, Richard Danson. 'A "goodlie bridge" between the Old and the New: Spenser's Transformation of Complaint in *The Ruines of Time.*' *Renaissance Forum*, 2.1 (1997), web location: http://hull.ac.uk/english/renforum/v2no1/ brown.htm.

— 'Forming the "First Garland of Free Poësie": Spenser's Dialogue with Du Bellay in *Ruines of Rome.*' Forthcoming in *Translation and Literature*, 1998.

— '"A talkatiue wench (whose words a world hath delighted in)": Mistress Shore and Elizabethan Complaint.' *RES*, 49, 1998 395–415.

Burrow, J. A. 'Chaucer's *Sir Thopas and La Prise Nuevile.*' In *English Satire and the Satiric Tradition.* Ed. Claude Rawson. Oxford: Blackwell, 1984.

Buxton, John. *Sir Philip Sidney and the English Renaissance.* London: Macmillan, third edn, 1987.

Cain, Thomas H. 'Spenser and the Renaissance Orpheus.' *UTQ,* 41 (1971), 24–47.

— *Praise in 'The Faerie Queene'.* Lincoln and London: University of Nebraska Press, 1978.

Cartmell, Deborah. '"Beside the shore of siluer streaming *Thamesis*": Spenser's *Ruines of Time.' SSt,* 6 (1985), 77–82.

— *Edmund Spenser and the Literary Uses of Architecture in the English Renaissance.* Unpublished DPhil thesis. University of York, 1986/87.

Castor, Grahame. *Pléiade Poetics: A Study in Sixteenth-Century Thought and Terminology.* Cambridge: Cambridge University Press, 1964.

Cave, Terence. *The Cornucopian Text: Problems of Writing in the French Renaissance.* Oxford: Clarendon, 1979.

Cheney, Donald. 'Spenser's Birthday and Related Fictions.' *SSt,* 4 (1983), 3–31.

Cheney, Patrick. *Spenser's Famous Flight: A Renaissance Idea of a Literary Career.* Toronto: University of Toronto Press, 1993.

Collinson, Patrick. *The Elizabethan Puritan Movement.* London: Jonathan Cape, 1967; rpt. Oxford: Clarendon, 1990.

Cooper, Helen. *Pastoral: Mediaeval into Renaissance.* Totowa, NJ: Rowman and Littlefield, 1977.

Court, Franklin E. 'The Theme and Structure of Spenser's *Muiopotmos.' SEL,* 10 (1970), 1–15.

Crewe, Jonathan. *Hidden Designs: The Critical Profession and Renaissance Literature.* New York and London: Methuen, 1986.

Cummings, R. M., ed. *Spenser: The Critical Heritage.* London: Routledge and Kegan Paul, 1971.

Curtius, Ernst R. *European Literature and the Latin Middle Ages.* Trans. Willard R. Trask. Bollingen Series XXVI. Princeton: Princeton University Press, 1953; new edn, 1990.

Danby, John F. *Poets on Fortune's Hill: Studies in Sidney, Shakespeare, Beaumont and Fletcher.* London: Faber and Faber, 1952.

Dasenbrook, Reed Way. 'The Petrarchan Context of Spenser's *Amoretti.'* PMLA, 100 (1985), 38–50.

Davis, Norman, Douglas Gray, Patricia Ingham and Anne Wallace Haddrill, eds. *A Chaucer Glossary.* Oxford: Clarendon, 1979.

DeNeef, A. Leigh. '"The Ruines of Time": Spenser's Apology for Poetry.' *SP,* 76 (1979), 262–71.

— *Spenser and the Motives of Metaphor*. Durham, NC: Duke University Press, 1982.

Duncan-Jones, Katherine. *Sir Philip Sidney: Courtier Poet*. London: Hamish Hamilton, 1991.

Dundas, Judith. '*Muiopotmos*: A World of Art.' YES, 5 (1975), 30–38.

— *The Spider and the Bee: The Artistry of Spenser's Faerie Queene*. Urbana and Chicago: University of Illinois Press, 1985.

Dunlop, Alexander. 'The Drama of *Amoretti*.' SSt, 1 (1980), 107–20.

Edmond, Mary. *Hilliard and Oliver: The Lives and Works of Two Great Miniaturists*. London: Robert Hale, 1983.

Elcock, W. D. 'English Indifference to Du Bellay's *Regrets*.' MLR, 46 (1951), 175–84.

Ellrodt, Robert. *Neoplatonism in the Poetry of Spenser*. Travaux de Humanisme et Renaissance, 35. Geneva: Droz, 1960.

Emerson, O. F. 'Spenser's *Virgils Gnat*.' JEGP, 17 (1918), 94–118.

Ferguson, Margaret W. '"The Afflatus of Ruin": Meditations on Rome by Du Bellay, Spenser, and Stevens.' In *Roman Images*. Selected Papers from the English Institute. New Series, No. 8. Ed. Annabel Patterson. Baltimore: Johns Hopkins University Press, 1982.

Fichter, Andrew. '"And nought of *Rome* in *Rome* perceiu'st at all".' SSt, 2 (1981), 183–92.

Foster, Leonard. *The Icy Fire: Five Studies in European Petrarchism*. Cambridge: Cambridge University Press, 1969.

Fowler, Alistair. *Spenser and the Numbers of Time*. London: Routledge and Kegan Paul, 1964.

Fraser, Russell. *The War Against Poetry*. Princeton: Princeton University Press, 1970.

Friedman, John Block. *Orpheus in the Middle Ages*. Cambridge, Mass.: Harvard University Press, 1970.

Gadoffre, Gilbert. *Du Bellay et le Sacre*. Paris: Gallimard, 1978.

Gordon, Alex L. *Ronsard et la Rhétorique*. Travaux de Humanisme et Renaissance. Geneva: Droz, 1970.

Grant, Patrick. *Images and Ideas in Literature of the English Renaissance*. Amherst: University of Massachusetts Press, 1979.

Greenblatt, Stephen. *Renaissance Self-Fashioning from More to Shakespeare*. Chicago and London: Chicago University Press, 1980.

Greene, Thomas M. *The Light in Troy: Imitation and Discovery in Renaissance Poetry*. New Haven: Yale University Press, 1982.

Greenlaw, Edwin A. *Studies in Spenser's Historical Allegory*. Baltimore: Johns

Hopkins University Press, 1932; rpt., London: Frank Cass, 1967.

Hamilton, A. C. *et al. The Spenser Encyclopedia.* Toronto, Buffalo and London: University of Toronto Press and Routledge, 1990.

Hannay, Margaret P., ed. *Silent But for the Word: Tudor Women as Patrons, Translators and Writers of Religious Works.* Kent, Ohio: Kent State University Press, 1985.

— *Philip's Phoenix: Mary Sidney, Countess of Pembroke.* New York and Oxford: Oxford University Press, 1990.

Hardison, O. B., Jr. *The Enduring Monument: A Study of the Idea of Praise in Renaissance Literary Theory and Practice.* Chapel Hill: University of North Carolina Press, 1962; rpt., Westport, Connecticut: Greenwood Press, Publishers, 1973.

— 'Amoretti and the Dolce Stil Novo.' *ELR,* 2 (1972), 208–16.

Harris, Brice. 'The Butterfly in *Muiopotmos.*' *JEGP,* 43 (1944), 302–16.

Harris, Duncan and Nancy L. Steffen. 'The Other Side of the Garden: An Interpretive Comparison of Chaucer's *Book of the Duchess* and Spenser's *Daphnaïda.*' *JMRS,* 8 (1978), 17–36.

Helgerson, Richard. *Self-Crowned Laureates: Spenser, Jonson, Milton, and the Literary System.* Berkeley: University of California Press, 1983.

— *Forms of Nationhood: The Elizabethan Writing of England.* Chicago: University of Chicago Press, 1992.

Heninger, S. K., Jr. *Sidney and Spenser: The Poet as Maker.* University Park and London: Pennsylvania State University Press, 1989.

Herendeen, W. H. 'Spenserian Specifics: Spenser's Appropriation of a Renaissance Topos.' *M & H,* ns 10 (1981), 159–88.

Hieatt, A. Kent. 'The Genesis of Shakespeare's *Sonnets:* Spenser's *Ruines of Rome: by Bellay.*' *PMLA,* 98 (1983), 800–14.

Hill, Christopher. *The English Bible and the Seventeenth-Century Revolution.* Harmondsworth: Allen Lane, 1993.

Honigmann, E. A. J. *Shakespeare: The 'Lost Years'.* Manchester: Manchester University Press, 1985.

Hough, Graham. *A Preface to The Faerie Queene.* London: Duckworth, 1962.

Hulse, Clark. *Metamorphic Verse: The Elizabethan Minor Epic.* Princeton: Princeton University Press, 1981.

Hume, Anthea. *Edmund Spenser: Protestant Poet.* Cambridge: Cambridge University Press, 1984.

Jackson Knight, W. F. *Roman Virgil.* Revised edn, Harmondsworth: Penguin, 1966.

Janzen, J. Gerald. *Job*. Interpretation: A Bible Commentary for Teaching and Preaching. Atlanta: John Know Press, 1985.

Judson, Alexander C. *The Life of Edmund Spenser*. Baltimore and London: Johns Hopkins University Press, 1945.

Keller, Joseph. 'The Triumph of Vice: A Formal Approach to the Medieval Complaint against the Times.' *AnM*, 10 (1969), 120–37.

King, John N. *Spenser's Poetry and the Reformation Tradition*. Princeton: Princeton University Press, 1990.

Kristeller, Paul Oskar. *Renaissance Thought: The Classic, Scholastic and Humanistic Strains*. Revised and enlarged edn of 'The Classics of Renaissance Thought'. New York: Harper, 1961.

Lascelles, Mary. 'The Rider on the Winged Horse' (1959). In *Notions and Facts: Collected Criticism and Research*. Oxford: Clarendon, 1972.

Lewis, C. S. *The Allegory of Love: A Study in Medieval Tradition*. Oxford and New York: Oxford University Press, 1936.

— *A Preface to Paradise Lost*. London: Oxford University Press, 1942.

— *Spenser's Images of Life*. Ed. Alastair Fowler. Cambridge: Cambridge University Press, 1967.

Lotspeich, H. G. 'Spenser's *Virgils Gnat* and its Latin Original.' *ELH*, 2 (1935), 235–41.

Maclean, Hugh. '"Restlesse anguish and unquiet paine": Spenser and the Complaint, 1579–1590.' In *The Practical Vision: Essays in English Literature in Honour of Flora Roy*. Ed. Jane Campbell and James Doyle. Waterloo, Can.: Wilfred Laurier University Press, 1978.

MacLure, Millar. 'Spenser and the Ruins of Time.' In *A Theatre for Spenserians*. Ed Judith M. Kennedy and James A. Reither. Toronto: University of Toronto Press, 1973.

McNeir, Waldo and Foster Provost. *Edmund Spenser: An Annotated Bibliography 1937–1972*. Pittsburgh: Duquesne University Press, 1975.

Manley, Lawrence. *Convention: 1500–1750*. Cambridge, Mass. and London: Harvard University Press, 1980.

— 'Spenser and the City: The Minor Poems.' *MLQ*, 43 (1982), 203–27

Martines, Lauro. *Society and History in English Renaissance Verse*. Oxford: Blackwell, 1985.

Miles, Rosalind. *Ben Jonson: His Life and Work*. London and New York: Routledge and Kegan Paul, 1986.

Miller, David L. 'Spenser's Vocation, Spenser's Career.' *ELH*, 50 (1983), 197–231.

Miller, Robert, ed. *Chaucer: Sources and Backgrounds*. New York: Oxford

University Press, 1977.

Miskimin, Alice S. *The Renaissance Chaucer*. New Haven: Yale University Press, 1975.

Mounts, Charles. 'Spenser and the Countess of Leicester.' *ELH*, 19 (1952), 191–202.

Nelson, William. *The Poetry of Edmund Spenser: A Study*. New York: Columbia University Press, 1963.

Nicholl, Charles. *A Cup of News: The Life of Thomas Nashe*. London: Routledge and Kegan Paul, 1984.

— *The Reckoning: The Murder of Christopher Marlowe*. London: Jonathan Cape, 1992.

Onions, C. T. *A Shakespeare Glossary*. Enlarged and revised by R. D. Eagleson. Oxford: Clarendon, 1986

Oram, William A. '*Daphnaïda* and Spenser's Later Poetry.' *SSt*, 2 (1981), 141–58.

Orwen, William R. 'Spenser and the Serpent of Division.' *SP*, 38 (1941), 198–210.

Osgood, Charles Grosvenor, ed. *A Concordance to the Poems of Edmund Spenser*. The Carnegie Institution of Washington, 1915; rpt. Gloucester, Mass.: Peter Smith, 1963.

Paster, Gail Kern. *The Idea of the City in the Age of Shakespeare*. Athens: University of Georgia Press, 1985.

Pearsall, Derek. *The Life of Geoffrey Chaucer: A Critical Biography*. Oxford: Basil Blackwell, 1992.

Peter, John. *Complaint and Satire in Early English Literature*. Oxford: Clarendon, 1956.

Prescott, Anne Lake. *French Poets and the English Renaissance: Studies in Fame and Transformation*. New Haven: Yale University Press, 1978.

— 'Response to Deborah Cartmell, Volume VI.' *SSt*, 7 (1986), 289–94.

Rambuss, Richard. *Spenser's Secret Career*. Cambridge: Cambridge University Press, 1993

Rasmussen, Carl J. '"How Weak Be the Passions of Woefulness": Spenser's *Ruines of Time*.' *SSt*, 4 (1981), 159–81.

— '"Quietnes of Minde": *A Theatre for Worldlings*.' *SSt*, 1 (1980), 3–27.

Rebhorn, Wayne A. 'Du Bellay's Imperial Mistress: *Les Antiquitez de Rome* as Petrarchist Sonnet Sequence.' *RenQ*, 33 (1980), 609–22.

Renwick, W. L. 'The Critical Origins of Spenser's Diction.' *MLR*, 17 (1922), 1–16.

— (ed.), *Complaints* (London: The Scholartis Press, 1928.

Ringler, William. 'Spenser and Thomas Watson.' *MLN*, 69 (1954), 484–87.

Rosenberg, Eleanor. *Leicester, Patron of Letters*. New York: Columbia University Press, 1955.

Satterthwaite, Alfred W. *Spenser, Ronsard and Du Bellay: A Renaissance Comparison*. Princeton: Princeton University Press, 1960.

Sinfield, Alan. *Literature in Protestant England, 1560–1660*. London: Croom Helm, 1983.

Smith, A. J. 'Theory and Practice in Renaissance Poetry: Two Kinds of Imitation.' *BJRL*, 47 (1964), 212–43.

— *The Metaphysics of Love: Studies in Renaissance Love Poetry from Dante to Milton*. Cambridge: Cambridge University Press, 1985.

Smith, Hallet. *Elizabethan Poetry: A Study in Conventions, Meaning and Expression*. Cambridge, Mass.: Harvard University Press, 1952

— 'The Use of Convention in Spenser's Minor Poems.' In *Form and Convention in the Poetry of Edmund Spenser*. Ed. William Nelson. New York: Columbia University Press, 1961.

Snare, Gerald. 'The Muses on Poetry: Spenser's *The Teares of the Muses*.' *Tulane University Studies in English*, 17 (1969), 31–52.

Stapleton, M. J. 'Spenser, the *Antiquitez de Rome*, and the Development of the English Sonnet Form.' *CLS*, 27 (1990), 259–74.

Stein, Harold. *Studies in Spenser's Complaints*. New York: Oxford University Press, 1934.

Stern, Virginia F. *Gabriel Harvey: His Life, Marginalia, and Library*. Oxford: Clarendon, 1979.

Strong, Roy. *The Cult of Elizabeth: Elizabethan Portraiture and Pageantry*. London: Thames and Hudson, 1977.

Tillyard, E. M. W. *Shakespeare's History Plays*. London: Chatto and Windus, 1944; rpt. Harmondsworth: Penguin, 1962.

Tuve, Rosamund. *Spenser, Herbert, Milton*. Ed. Thomas P. Roche, Jr. Princeton: Princeton University Press, 1970.

Van den Berg, Kent. 'The Counterfeit in Personation: Spenser's *Prosopopoia*.' In *The Author in his Work: Essays on a Problem in Criticism*. Ed. Louis Martz and Aubrey Williams. New Haven: Yale University Press, 1978.

Van Dorsten, J. A. 'Literary Patronage in Elizabethan England: The Early Phase.' In *Patronage in the Renaissance*. Ed. Guy F. Lytle and Stephen Orgel. Princeton: Princeton University Press, 1981.

— 'How Not To Open the Sidneian Text.' *Sidney Newsletter*, 2.2 (1982), 4–7.

Waldman, Milton. *Elizabeth and Leicester*. London: Collins; rpt. The Reprint Society, 1946.

Weiner, Andrew D. 'Spenser's *Muiopotmos* and the Fates of Butterflies and Men.' *JEGP*, 84 (1985), 203–20.

Wells, Margaret Brady. 'Du Bellay's Sonnet Sequence *Songe*.' *FS*, 26 (1972), 1–8.

Williams, James G. 'Proverbs and Ecclesiastes.' In *The Literary Guide to the Bible*. Ed. Robert Alter and Frank Kermode. London: Fontana, 1987.

Wilson, Rawdon. 'Images and "Allegoremes" of Time in the Poetry of Spenser.' *ELR*, 4 (1974), 56–82.

Winn, James Anderson. *John Dryden and his World*. New Haven and London: Yale University Press, 1987.

Yates, Frances A. *Astraea: The Imperial Theme in the Sixteenth Century*. London: Routledge and Kegan Paul, 1975; rpt., London: Pimlico, 1993.

INDEX

Aesop, 172, 177–8, 225
Allen, Don C., 64–5, 226
Alpers, Paul, 226–7
Amphion, 16, 78, 87, 111–12, 118
Ariosto, Ludovico, 21, 56, 68
 Orlando Furioso, 21
Aristotle, 15, 17, 138
Astraea, 159–61, 271–3
Augustine of Hippo, 20–1, 82,
 169, 240
 City of God, 82
Augustus, Emperor, 42

Bartas, Guillame Salluste Du ,
 79–83, 157–8
 Uranie, 81
Basil the Great, 21
Baxandall, Michael, 242
Bellay, Joachim Du, viii, 63–95
 passim, 105–6, 132, 144,
 154–7, 163, 256
 Les Antiquités de Rome, 63–95
 passim, 101, 103, 105–6, 132
 *La Défense et Illustration de la
 Langue Française*, 65–71, 84,
 86
 La Musagnoeomachie, 144,
 154–7, 163
 L'Olive, 157
 Poemata, 70
 Les Regrets, 70, 90
 'Songe', 33, 74, 94, 105–6, 125
Bembo, Pietro, 40
Bender, John B., 12, 214, 242

Bersuire, Pierre, 119, 129
 Reductorium Morale, 119
Bjorvand, Einar, 174
Boccaccio, Giovanni, 128–30
Bond, Ronald, 6, 24, 221
Breton, Nicholas, 169–71, 177
 'An Epitaph upon Poet Spenser',
 169
Brink, Jean R., 5–6
Brodsky, Joseph, 213, 253
Browne, William, 61–2
 Britannia's Pastorals, 61–2
Byrd, William, 99
 *Psalms, Sonnets, and Songs of
 Sadness and Piety*, 99

Cain, Thomas H., 117
Calimachus, 223
 Aetia, 223
Calvin, John, 236
Camden, William, 103, 106,
 111–13
 Britannia, 106, 111–12
Camoens, Luis de, 56
Castiglione, Baldassare, 197
Cauchi, Simon, 57
Cecil, William, Lord Burghley, 4,
 123–4, 171, 180
Ceres, 43–4
Chaucer, Geoffrey, 9–10, 13, 56,
 104, 141, 148–9, 169, 181,
 222, 257
 Book of the Duchess, 104, 108
 Hous of Fame, 104, 107–8, 148

Nun's Priest's Tale, 9, 169
  Sir Thopas, 222
Churchyard, Thomas, 54, 108,
  237
  Shores Wife, 108–9, 237
Cicero, 186
Cocke, H., 3
Collinson, Patrick, 257–8
Comes, Natalis, 160
Curtius, E. R., 24

Daniel, Book of, 104, 107
Daniel, Samuel, 27
  Complaint of Rosamund, 27
Dante Alighieri, 74
  Divina Commedia, 104
  La Vita Nuova, 74
DeNeef, A. Leigh, 150–1,
  260–1
De Selincourt, E., 11
Dolce, Lodovico, 57
Donne, John, 25, 123
Douglas, Gavin, 45–6, 51
  Eneados, 45–6
Dryden, John, 46
  Sylvae, 46–7
Dudley, Robert, Earl of Leicester,
  32, 46–67 *passim,* 99–137
  passim, 151
Dudley Sidney, Marie, 115
Dumaeus, 41, 45, 55
Dundas, Judith, 214, 216, 226,
  234, 244

E. K., 13, 85
Elizabeth I, Queen of England,
  61–2, 160–5, 271–3
Emerson, O. F., 45
Eurydice, 119

Ezekiel, Book of, 104

Friedman, John Block, 119
Fulgentius, 169

Gascoigne, George, 57, 181, 211
  Steele Glas, 181
Gentili, Alberico, 16
Golding, Arthur, 241
Gower, John, 180
  Confessio Amantis, 181
Greenblatt, Stephen, 190
Greene, Robert, 209
Greene, Thomas M., 66, 71–8
Greenlaw, Edwin, 173
Grimald, Nicholas, 136
  'The Muses', 136

Hall, Joseph, 25, 266–5
  Virgidemiarum, 266
Harington, Sir John, 19–22, 52,
  57–9
  *Orlando Furioso in English
  Heroical Verse,* 21, 57
  *The Sixth Book of Virgil's
  "Aeneid" Translated and
  Commented on by Sir John
  Harington,* 19–22, 52,
  57–9
Harvey, Gabriel, 56, 101, 136
  *Smithus, vel Musarum
  Lachrymae,* 136
Hawthorne, Nathaniel, 233
Henri II, King of France, 78
Henryson, Robert, 10, 169,
  178–80, 184, 210–11, 227
  Fables, 169, 178–9, 184
  'The Sheep and the Dog',
  179–81

Hesiod, 147
  Theogony, 147
Homer, 118, 138, 230, 251–2
Horace, 16, 23, 72, 112, 117
  Ars Poetica, 16, 117
  'Exegi monumentum' (*Odes*
    III.30), 112
Howard, Henry, Earl of Surrey, 26,
  56
Hughes, John, 259

Ignorance, 80, 133–67 *passim*

Jesus Christ, 114–19
Job, Book of, 140
Jonson, Ben, 186–7, 198–9
  Discoveries, 186
  'On Poet Ape', 198–9
Judson, Alexander, 11, 61

King, Edward, 99

Langland, William, 9, 257
  Piers Plowman, 104
Linus, 118
Lisle, William, 41
Lotspeich, H. G., 45
Lucretius, 199
Lydgate, John, 258, 263, 268
  'An Holy Meditation', 258

Maclean, Hugh, 30, 157
Maclure, Millar, 11
Marlowe, Christopher, 223–4
  Hero and Leander, 223
  The Jew of Malta, 185
Marston, John, 25
Menni, Vincentio, 57
Mercury, 130–1, 205–7

Milton, John, 99, 240, 246
  Lycidas, 99
Mirror for Magistrates, 26–7, 53–4,
  60, 108–9, 131, 154, 228
Lord Morley, 104
Mulcaster, Richard, 69
  The First Part of the Elementry,
  69

Nashe, Thomas, 171, 185, 255
  The Choice of Valentines, 255
  Piers Penniless, 185
  The Unfortunate Traveller, 185
Noot, Jan van der, 28–9
  Theatre for Worldlings, 28–9, 51,
  74, 90

Orwin, William R., x, 186, 200,
  202, 209
Sir Orfeo, 262
Orpheus, 16, 47, 78, 87, 115,
  117–19, 128–31
Ovid, 43, 159–60, 205, 218–19,
  223–54 *passim,* 273
  Metamorphoses, 43, 119, 147,
  160, 205, 223–54 *passim*

Paul, Saint, 9
Peele, George, 271–3
  Descensus Astraeae, 271
Peter, Saint, 114
Peter, John, 25
Petrarch, Francesco, 74, 104–5,
  137–8
  Rime Sparse, 74
  Trionfi, 104–5, 137
Plato, 138, 252
Pléiade, 13, 155–7
Ponsonby, William, 3–8, 103

Prescott, Anne Lake, 65–6, 68

Quintillian, 186

Rambuss, Richard, 6
Le Roman de Renart, 177–9, 183,
    207–8
Renwick, W. R., 83, 86, 100–2,
    105, 107, 126, 136, 159
Revelation, Book of, 104, 129
Ronsard, Pierre de, 70, 144–5,
    154–7, 166
    Franciade, 157
    'Ode à Michel de l'Hospital',
        144, 154–7

Scaliger, Julius Caesar, 8, 16
    Poetices libri septem, 16
Schell, Richard, 120, 174
Shakespeare, William, 11, 81, 224,
    234–5, 242
    The Rape of Lucrece, 27–8, 234,
        242
    Sonnets, 11, 81, 255–69 *passim*
    Venus and Adonis, 223
Shepherd, Geoffrey, 16, 26
Sidney, Mary, Countess of
    Pembroke, 32, 99, 104–5,
    113
Sidney, Sir Philip, 15–23, 26, 57,
    69, 81, 99–132 *passim,* 135,
    138, 141, 172–3, 185–6, 225,
    234–5, 248, 250, 253–4,
    260–1, 263, 266–7
    Astrophil and Stella, 266–7,
        269
    Defence of Poetry, 16–23, 173,
        185–6
Smith, Hallett, 11, 27

Snare, Gerald, 143–4, 149–50
Song of Songs, 129
Spencer, Alice, Lady Strange, 32
Spencer, Anne, Lady Compton and
    Mounteagle, 32, 173–5
Spencer, Elizabeth, Lady Carey, 32
Spenser, Edmund (works other
    than the *Complaints*),
    Amoretti, 269
    Daphnaïda, 1, 4–5, 104
    Epithalamion, 145–7, 269
    The Faerie Queene, x, 2–34
        passim, 60, 82, 85, 88, 92, 94,
        124, 126, 131, 158, 201, 211,
        213–4, 218, 226–7, 244–5,
        248, 254, 255–69 *passim*
    The Shepheardes Calender, 13,
        30, 34, 85, 165, 179, 192,
        220
Stanyhurst, Richard, 56
Stein, Harold, 3–7
Stow, John, 12
    The Survey of London, 12
Suetonius 41

Tasso, Torquato, 56
Thirty-Nine Articles of Religion,
    10, 122–3, 163
Tottel's Miscellany, 136

Virgil, 20, 40–61 *passim,* 72, 75–8,
    87, 160, 205, 219, 223–5,
    242
    Aeneid, 20, 41, 45–6, 75–7,
        205–6, 221, 242
    Eclogues, 41, 160
    'Virgil' (the pseudo-Virgilian
        author of *Culex*), 42–61
        passim, 94, 132

Culex, viii, 39–63 *passim*, 94, 132, 256

Walsingham, Sir Fracis, 123
Webbe, William, 16
  Discourse of English Poetrie, 16

Weiner, Andrew, 216, 226, 234
Williams, James G., 140
Wisdom, 139–42
Wyatt, Sir Thomas, 26, 56

Yates, Frances A. 160, 271–3